The Making *of an*
American
T H I N K I N G C L A S S

The Making *of an*
American
T H I N K I N G   C L A S S

Intellectuals and Intelligentsia
in Puritan Massachusetts

D A R R E N   S T A L O F F

New York   Oxford
OXFORD UNIVERSITY PRESS
1998

Oxford University Press

Oxford   New York

Athens   Auckland   Bangkok   Bogota   Bombay   Buenos Aires
Calcutta   Cape Town   Dar es Salaam   Delhi   Florence   Hong Kong
Istanbul   Karachi   Kuala Lumpur   Madras   Madrid   Melbourne
Mexico City   Nairobi   Paris   Singapore   Taipei   Tokyo   Toronto   Warsaw

and associated companies in
Berlin   Ibadan

Copyright © 1998 by Darren Staloff

Published by Oxford University Press, Inc.
198 Madison Avenue, New York, New York 10016

Library of Congress Cataloging-in-Publication Data
Staloff, Darren, 1961–
The making of an American thinking class : intellectuals and
intelligentsia in Puritan Massachusetts / Darren Staloff.
p.   cm.
Includes bibliographical references and index.
ISBN 0-19-511352-7
1. Puritans—Massachusetts—Intellectual life.   2. Elite (Social
sciences)—Massachusetts—History—17th century.   3. Massachusetts—
Intellectual life—17th century.   4. Massachusetts—Politics and
government—To 1775.   I. Title.
F67.S8   1998
974.4'02—dc21   96-53600

1 3 5 7 9 8 6 4 2

Printed in the United States of America
on acid-free paper

For T

All the towers of ivory are crumbling
And the swallows have sharpened their beaks
This is the time of our great undoing
This is the time that I'll come running
Straight to you

Nick Cave, "Straight to You"

ACKNOWLEDGMENTS

Acknowledgments are the most misunderstood pages in scholarly works. Conventionally, they are interpreted as a gesture of humility whereby the author graciously acknowledges the intellectual debts that have been incurred in the process of writing the work (as if publicly owning up to one's debts somehow helps to discharge them!). In fact, however, acknowledging debts is a way of bragging about one's intellectual creditworthiness in the eyes of various intellectual luminaries and authorities, especially when the work in question is a first book culled from a doctoral dissertation and the author has no collateral in the form of prior publications. Such is my own case, for I am convinced that nothing I could write could reflect as well on my abilities as the remarkable assemblage of scholars and institutions that found me creditworthy.

This book originated as a doctoral dissertation at Columbia University. There I was fortunate to find an adviser and mentor of the very first order in Alden Vaughan. Demanding but fair, Alden gave generously of his time and energy, both in discussing my ideas and in carefully critiquing and revising the manuscript. Alternating praise and criticism, Alden always pushed me to think and write clearly and, most important of all, always had enough faith in the project to give me more than enough rope to hang myself. I will be forever grateful for his continued encouragement, advice, and friendship.

Although I could not ask for a better mentor, I was blessed with a second, equally expert one. Richard Bushman arrived at Columbia after I had begun working on the dissertation, and he quickly assumed the role of an unofficial second adviser. He, too, has been a constant and willing source of sagacious counsel and friendly encouragement. An insightful and open-minded critic, Richard always insisted that I strive for greater analytic precision and clarity and that I have the courage of my convictions. Whatever cohesion and coherence my interpretation has are largely the result of the incredible critical synergy of these two master pedagogues. I am also grateful to Randall Balmer for his encouragement and criticism and to Andrew Delbanco for his well-considered warnings.

Two other scholars at Columbia greatly influenced my thinking as a historian and served as mentors, even if their role in this particular manuscript is less central. Eric Foner helped me formulate my thinking about the relations between culture, society, and politics, as well as realize the synthetic possibilities of the narrative form. One of the best teachers I have ever met, Eric offered valuable criticisms of my manuscript and patiently endured my bald and often sophomoric questions in his office. James Shenton first convinced me to consider becoming a historian, and in many ways his influence on my thinking has been the most profound, if subtle. From him I have learned to look for the strange and perverse in history and to always expect to find both terrifying sublimity and pathetic comedy. Without the friendship and support of these two scholars I most certainly would not have become a historian.

Several of my fellow graduate students at Columbia offered sufficient interest and criticism in my work to qualify as co-conspirators. Peter Field and John Recchiuti read, or had read to them, every page of every draft that I composed. Both share my interest in the history of an American thinking class, and while their work differs from mine in some of its theoretical and analytic frame, I have greatly benefited from their insights, suggestions, corrections, and warm friendship. Michael Sugrue has had as great an impact on my thinking about history as any single person. He is a generous friend and a remarkable intellect, and it will come as no surprise to those who know him that the first fumblings toward the project that ultimately has become this book came from his lips during one of our many conversations. I will always cherish those conversations and his disdain for anything but my very best work.

From Columbia I went as a postdoctoral fellow to the Institute of Early American History and Culture, a sort of finishing school for young colonial historians. There I continued to run up debts, not the least of which were institutional, as the financial support of the institute and a National Endowment for the Humanities Scholarship allowed me to complete the research I needed to extend the scope and breadth of my argument.

Personal debts there were also considerable. Michael McGiffert's advice and support, not to mention his considerable knowledge of Puritan divinity, proved a great boon. George Healey, Ronald Hoffman, Fredericka Teute, and John Selby all combined the roles of helpful critic and host with aplomb. Chandos Brown, Robert Gross, and Philip Gura all offered insights and suggestions that measurably impacted the final form of this book. An especially large debt is owed to three colleagues and close friends I made in Williamsburg. Kathleen Brown and Jon Sensbach helped create a critical and supportive environment, and each offered thoughtful advice and support when I proffered my text on them. Their fellowship made the experience extremely pleasant as well as profitable. David Ammerman arrived at the institute during the second year of my postdoctoral fellowship and, in his inimitable and irascible manner, quickly endeared himself to me. He patiently read and criticized the entire manuscript. One of the most demanding and hard-nosed critics I have ever encountered, David provided insights that were always right on target, and my book has benefited immensely from his critical acumen. He, too, has challenged me to have the courage of my conviction, and for that and his friendship I will always be profoundly indebted.

From the City College of New York I have received much-appreciated support for my work. The deans of humanities have been openhanded with both research funds and course release in the form of an Eisner fellowship. My colleagues in the Department of History have likewise been supportive. In particular, the chairmen, James Watts and Frank Grande, have tried to accommodate my research and writing needs despite a shortage of resources. Judith Stein and Robert Twombly have offered encouragement and valuable advice at various stages of the publication process. My greatest debt at City College, however, is to Louis Masur. It is rare to find a person who is as valued a critic as a friend, and I am thus fortunate to be a colleague of Lou's. His support and help in navigating this manuscript through the straits of publication have been monumental, as he all too well knows. Despite our friendship, I am sure he will never let me live it down.

Finally, I must thank my family, whose support and encouragement were instrumental to the completion of this manuscript. From my father's gentle reminder, "So, when is it going to be done?," to my mother's equally gentle rejoinder, "Enough already, Charlie; it'll be done when it's done," they gave me just the right combination of prompting and backing. My greatest debt, of course, is to my wife. Tatiana is, without exception, my toughest and most demanding critic. Her judgment is unerring and all the more forceful for its predictable forms. "Too many words" was a common, if crushing, observation, as well as the ubiquitous "is all this stuff necessary?" Most pointed and most useful, however, was the occasional "why should anyone care about this?," which forced me, as it should any historian, to recognize the difference between the interest in the interpretation of the past that most people share and the antiquarian curiosity that is unique to trained "professionals." To the extent that this work does generate genuine interest, it is the result of Tatiana's relentless criticism.

North Brunswick, New Jersey   D. M. S.
April 1997

CONTENTS

Appendix A

Appendix B
Toward a Postrevisionist Interpretation of Puritanism:

INTRODUCTION

Introductions, I am told, ought to serve as invitations, enticing the reader to peruse the text and engage with the argument of the author. When such a book is yet another study of New England Puritanism, perhaps an apology might be more in order. Few topics in early American history have been so thoroughly chronicled, analyzed, and painstakingly dissected. From spiritual sensibility to social structure and from demographics to divinity, the religious "precisionarians" that settled Massachusetts have received coverage far in excess of their numerical significance in seventeenth-century British America. No one appreciates more than I the trepidation with which a general student of American (or even colonial) history takes in hand the umpteenth tome promising to revolutionize our understanding of the famed New England Way. The least I can do is offer an explanation of how this book came to be written and why it is worth reading.

Like so many other studies of the New England Puritans, this book originated in a critical confrontation with the work of Perry Miller. My colleagues in graduate school had warned me about Miller. He was a notorious idealist and the progenitor of a tradition of unabashedly elitist intellectual history. More ominously, his work had a beguiling effect that sent otherwise healthy-minded young people scurrying into the archives to study the minutiae of a curmudgeony folk whose idea of a good read was Michael Wigglesworth's morbid poem, "The Day of Doom." As an aspiring student of antebellum southern history, I felt fairly confident in my immunity to such contagion. I was wrong.

I found Miller both utterly persuasive and profoundly disturbing. Elegant and urbane, Miller's works successfully explained the history of Puritan Massachusetts by evoking a "New England Mind" culled from a narrow range of remarkably abstruse and knotty theological treatises. Although subsequent scholarship has refuted many of the details (and even some of the essentials) of Miller's vision, his basic strategy of explicating the behavior of the Bay Puritans in terms of their theological beliefs and carefully formulated doctrines has been more than vindicated by its dominant role in the literature of Puritan studies. As a social historian with pronounced naturalistic inclinations, I was deeply troubled by this whole idealist mode of explanation. Yet there was no denying its success. I became obsessed with trying to explain why this strategy was so fruitful in interpreting the saga of New England Puritanism. In general terms, I found myself raising the old Cartesian question of interaction to the historical plane, namely, how did the ethereal elements of the world of ideas and mentalities actually impact the material world of historical events? More specifically, what were the social and political features of early Massachusetts history that gave technical theological doctrines such powerful causal efficacy?

The most plausible answer to my question came from David Hall's and Michael Walzer's studies of the Puritan ministry. Sophisticated theological doctrines shaped the history of Massachusetts because the educated divines who studied and formulated these doctrines had a preponderant influence over the colony's social and political life. This answer raised even more questions. How could an educated elite of ministers (and magistrates, as I learned from Timothy Breen) hold such dominant power in a fledgling colonial settlement? Granted the deference normally accorded a university degree, these educated leaders lacked the large-scale property interests normally associated with a ruling stratum. What were the institutional arrangements and practices that facilitated this remarkable empowerment? Finally, why did this elite choose to use their power to impose an order on Massachusetts derived from academic theology? What did it mean that the Bay Colony was patterned after a high cultural theory?

I sought the answers to these questions in the sociology of intellectuals. Two works in particular—Alvin Gouldner's three-volume *Dark Side of the Dialectic* and George Konrad and Ivan Szelenyi's *The Intellectuals on the Road to Class Power*—confirmed my most unsettling hunches. Professional intellectuals and intelligentsia comprised a collective interest. They were the great unexamined class in modern political history, whose will to power occasionally took the form of revolutionary ideological politics. I had a greater appreciation for Michael Walzer's claim that the Puritan divines were the precursors of the Jacobins and Bolsheviks. This realization undermined my whole conception of the class struggles that underlay modern ideological politics. It also failed to explain the different role and status of the Puritan educated elite in Massachusetts and England. Although the clergy was undoubtedly a critical element in the English Puritan movement, I remained convinced with Christopher Hill that its ultimate result was a bourgeois revolution that, in the last instance, served the interests of the landed gentry and urban merchants. Why did the Puritan intellectuals emerge as the dominant political group in Massachusetts while their colleagues in England were reduced to the status of ideological cheerleaders?

As I pored over the primary documents, gradually an answer began to emerge. Massachusetts differed from England in two vital respects. First, unlike their English counterparts, the Bay Puritans were not a small minority ruling over a divided society, much of which was ideologically disaffected. By excluding the ungodly, the founders of early Massachusetts were spared the necessity of either purging or accommodating such elements. Second, the thinking class that contributed to the colony's settlement and foundation was an extremely cohesive and class-conscious group. They constructed the institutions of church and state to facilitate the transformation of their high cultural and theoretical expertise into social and political power. They did this by creating a new form of political authority that I have called cultural domination. They legitimated their power by claiming to be the authentic bearers of the Puritan cultural and religious tradition. Through them, they insisted, the established Christian wisdom of the ages would exercise its sway over the New World Bible commonwealth. While the Puritan thinking class in England may have helped initiate the tradition of radical ideological politics, their colleagues in the Bay created a stable revolutionary regime. Puritan Massachusetts was a seventeenth-century one-party state.

By the time I had reached these conclusions, my focus had shifted considerably. Although I had a renewed respect for the Puritans and their Promethean role in the emergence of modern revolutionary politics, I was equally concerned with formulating a general approach to a social history of intellectuals. I saw the history of the Puritan intellectuals and intelligentsia as part of a larger sociopolitical story of the thinking class in America and the modern West. In hands more able than mine, this story might contribute to a larger understanding of the impact of intellectuals throughout the course of world history. I will be more than satisfied if this work provokes some small interest in the history of a class that is every bit as old as civilized history itself. If, in addition, it inspires a new sense of wonder and appreciation for the religious fanatics that tried to build a new Zion on the rocky shores of New England, so much the better.

All writers are the prisoners of language. Words are the tools we use to express our beliefs and views. In the course of telling my story, I have felt compelled at several points to attribute novel meanings to old and familiar phrases. In other cases, I have introduced neologisms of my own. Throughout, I have endeavored to keep such locutions from intruding any more than absolutely necessary in the flow of the story. After getting their feet wet in the prologue, the vast bulk of readers should be able to dive right into the narrative and navigate through what I hope is a fairly gripping story. For those of a more precisionarian bent—and what serious student of the Puritans is not?—I have included in Appendix A a brief glossary of key terms not explicated in the text itself. For such scholars, I have also included in Appendix B a brief historiographic essay situating my interpretation within the current literature on transatlantic Puritanism.

The Making *of an*
American
THINKING CLASS

And they assembled themselves together against Moses and Aaron, and said unto them, "Ye take too much upon you, seeing all the congregation are holy, every one of them, and the LORD is among them: wherefore then lift up yourselves above the congregation of the LORD?"

Numbers 16:3, King James Version

Marxist outlaws have not surrendered the dialectic, but continue to probe and wander its dark side. Only those who can move without joining packaged tours of the world can afford such a journey.

Alvin Gouldner, The Dialectic of Ideology and Technology (*1976*)

PROLOGUE

The Struggle for the Company

Accrding to Samuel Eliot Morison, the 120 patentees of the Dorchester Company of Adventurers, the first organized effort to colonize Massachusetts Bay, represented a fair sample of the leading elements of the Puritan movement in southwestern England.[1] Among them were landed gentry, who probably exerted the political influence necessary to procure the patent; merchant adventurers, who no doubt supplied the bulk of the £3,000 of initial joint stock; and, of course, representatives of the thinking class. This heterogenous membership was reflected in the range of purposes the colony was intended to serve. A permanent base for the Newfoundland and New England fishing industry, a bulwark against French (and therefore Roman Catholic) expansion, and a trading and evangelical outpost to the natives, Massachusetts was least of all intended as the site of a Bible commonwealth or Puritan republic.[2] Nonetheless, when John Winthrop reached the shores of Massachusetts Bay in the summer of 1630, he came with the avowed purpose of erecting just such a Puritan "city upon a hill."

The transformation of the projected colony from a source of mercantile profit to a holy commonwealth was the result of a dramatic shift of power within the Massachusetts colonization movement. In the late summer of 1629, a group of well-organized East Anglian Puritan intelligentsia, with the aid of ministerial intellectuals and a handful of sympathetic merchants, seized control of the Massachusetts Bay Company. This power grab was perhaps the single most important event in the political history of Puritan Massachusetts. Having gained control of the mechanisms of government, the Puritan thinking class was able to retain its political dominance until the loss of the charter over half a century later.

While Winthrop and his fellow "cadres" from the East Anglian intelligentsia gained control of the venture in late 1629, several members of the Puritan thinking class had been involved in the various attempts to colonize Massachusetts Bay since the Dorchester Company of Adventurers was organized in 1623. Two in particular, John Humfrey and John White, played a central role in the colonization of Massachusetts Bay over the next decade. John White, rector of the Church of the Holy

Trinity in Dorchester and a figure of imposing presence within that community, gave religious sanction to the undertakers and attempted to draw potential investors.[3] A member of White's church, John Humfrey was a graduate of Trinity College, Cambridge. A son-in-law of the earl of Lincoln, Humfrey had served as treasurer of the Dorchester Company of Adventurers (he was later elected deputy governor and assistant).[4] Like most of the intelligentsia who subsequently dominated the magistracy of the Bay Colony, Humfrey applied his high cultural training in the form of legal and administrative expertise.

After the Dorchester Company of Adventurers proved to be a failure in 1626 (primarily the result of bad luck and a lack of capital), a core of the original adventurers, including Humfrey and led by White, attempted to reorganize the company and persevere in the venture.[5] Accordingly, on March 19, 1628, six patentees were granted a patent from the Council for New England. From its very inception, the New England Company for a Plantation in Massachusetts Bay faced two significant problems. The patent, having been acquired under somewhat questionable circumstances, gave the adventurers a dangerously weak claim to the area within its patent relative to other claimants.[6] More threatening was the continuing shortage of venture capital among the West Countrymen, the very deficiency that had helped to undermine the Dorchester Company of Adventurers.

What is most striking about the way these problems were solved is the pivotal role played by White and Humfrey. They functioned as the company's liaisons to the larger Puritan movement and seem to have been singularly effective at "networking." Not long after the patent had been procured, John White traveled to London to attract that city's Puritan grand bourgeoisie to the worthy cause of colonization in New England.[7] Evidently Reverend White was both well connected and quite persuasive, for he quickly brought into the venture some of the largest investors in the mercantile community. Matthew Craddock, a major investor in the East India Company; Sir Richard Saltonstall, master of the Worshipful Company of Skinners and heir to the mayor of London; John Venn, warden of the Merchant Taylor's Company; and the Vassall brothers were the most prominent members of this group.[8] Closely associated with them was another John White, a lawyer from the capital, who was to become one of the most important players in the dramatic events of the next year.

With this one deal, John White of Dorchester solved both of the immediate problems facing the company. Not only did the London merchants supply the much-needed capital (roughly £3,000), but they were also instrumental in procuring the royal charter that gave the Governor and Company of the Massachusetts Bay in New England (as it was now called) clear title to the land between the Charles and Merrimack rivers.[9] Probably written by John White of London, the charter was in many ways similar to other colonial charters of the period, authorizing a corporation of merchant adventurers "for the planting, ruling, ordering and governing of New-England in America."[10] The charter was granted on March 4, 1629, and, as is well known, the seat of government was left unspecified, an omission that newly elected governor Matthew Craddock was soon to exploit.

Meanwhile, John Humfrey had been active. No doubt working through his father-in-law, the earl of Lincoln, Humfrey seems to have interested many members of the East Anglian Puritan community in the venture as early as the spring of 1628, possibly even late 1627 (before the Plymouth Council patent had been procured!).[11] The leading figures of this group were William Pynchon, "squire of Springfield in Essex" and a graduate of Hart Hall, Oxford; the young Isaac Johnson, another son-in-law of the earl of Lincoln and a graduate of Emmanuel College, Cambridge; and Richard Bellingham, who, as Cotton Mather put it, "was bred a lawyer."[12] Others somewhat less involved at this point but clearly interested were Captain Thomas Dudley, steward to the earl of Lincoln, and John Winthrop, Jr., a recent graduate of Trinity College, Dublin. Not long after this initial wave of interest, Dudley's son-in-law Simon Bradstreet, a graduate of Emmanuel College, Cambridge, and the elder John Winthrop, of Trinity College, Cambridge, and the Inns of Court, became active on behalf of the project. The most striking thing about this group was the preponderance of thinking-class membership, although many were also landholding members of the lesser gentry.

During the year 1628 this group established contact with the other parties involved in the venture, as Dudley recalled a few years later to the countess of Lincoln. "After some deliberation we imparted our reasons, by letters and messages, to some in London and the west country; where it was likewise deliberately thought upon, and at length with often negotiation so ripened . . . we procured a patent from his Majesty."[13] While Dudley was probably inflating the importance of the East Anglian group at this juncture, the three principal leaders listed above—Pynchon, Johnson, and Bellingham—were all included among the patentees in the royal charter. A minority faction among the West Country and London investors, this group expressed no intention on or before March 4, 1629, of seizing control of the corporation and its assets and transplanting themselves with the charter to the proposed colony. Yet this is precisely what they did, and within one year's span at that.[14]

The motivations behind this decision are not difficult to surmise. The rise of the Arminian movement within the Church of England and its purported program of smashing Puritan dissent, coupled with the defeat of the Protestant forces at La Rochelle, were widely perceived as portents of imminent doom. John Winthrop expressed this perception and the reaction of the East Anglian group in a letter to his wife, written just eleven days after the royal charter was granted: "[M]y dear wife, I am verily persuaded, God will bringe some heavye Affliction upon this land, and that speedylye. . . . If the Lord seeth it wilbe good for us, he will provide a shelter and a hiding place for us."[15] Particularly hard hit by Arminian repression were dissenting members of the thinking class. Attorneys like Winthrop lost their positions at court, ministers like Thomas Hooker (and eventually even John White) were silenced and otherwise deprived of their benefices, lectureships were eliminated, and the universities were purged under the watchful eye of episcopal visitations. Indeed, the condition of the universities was listed among the "Reasons to be Considered" for emigration written in the early summer or late spring of 1629: "The Fountaines of Learning and Religion are soe corrupted as (besides the unsupportable charge of there education) most children (even the best witts and of faierest hopes) are perverted, corrupted, and utterlie overthrowne by the multitude of evill examples and the licentious government of those seminaries."[16]

The active involvement of John Winthrop in the early summer of 1629 seems to have emboldened the other planters (as they soon were to be called in contradistinction to the others in the corporation, the adventurers) in their resolves. Dudley later recalled that in addition to the overblown accounts of New England, it was Winthrop's "coming into us" that led them to "come to such a resolution."[17] This resolution found formal expression in an agreement dated August 26, 1629, pledging that the dozen undersigned men would "so really endeavour the execution of this worke, as by God's assistance we will be ready in our persons, and with such of our severall families as are to go with us. . . . Provided always, that before the last of September next the whole government together with the patent for the said plantation be first by an order of court legally transferred and established to remain with us."[18] The agreement, which was reached, characteristically, in the halls of Cambridge, was signed by Isaac Johnson, Thomas Dudley, John Winthrop, William Pynchon, John Humfrey, and two of the London patentees, Richard Saltonstall and William Vassall, among others. While many of them were significant shareholders, they by no means represented a majority interest in the venture. And yet they had two important allies among the merchant adventurers in Matthew Craddock and John White of London.

In the spring and summer of 1629 London was still the center of official activities of the Massachusetts Bay Company, and the West Country and London merchants were the dominant element within that body. Even before receiving the royal charter, the West Countrymen had dispatched a military man from among themselves, Captain John Endecott of Dorset, with fifty planters to take command of the colony and give it the military discipline that had held Virginia together under Captain John Smith.[19] Endecott's selection as chief magistrate in the colony was confirmed by the newly organized company, and to further bolster the cohesion of the fragile settlement, three ministers were procured (who were to be included within the colonial council of assistants) and dispatched by the company.[20]

The exact arrangements surrounding the employment and "calling" of these first ministers are part of a story we shall turn to before long; at this point, what is significant was the way in which they were recruited. On March 23, Increase Nowell (the future ruling elder of the church of Boston and a leading magistrate of the colony) gave "intimation" to the General Court of the company that based on letters he had received from Isaac Johnson, "one Mr. Higgeson, of Lester, an able minister, proffers to goe to our plantation." John Humfrey was dispatched to "deal with him."[21] Nor was it simply coincidence that Johnson learned of Higginson's interest, for a letter from him to Winthrop's son-in-law, Emmanuel Downing, suggests that he and Winthrop, somewhat presumptuously, had taken it upon themselves to recruit and screen potential divines.[22] That the governor of the company, Craddock, was "in on" the machinations of the planters as early as April 1629 is uncertain but likely. He surely was sympathetically informed, if not in outright cahoots, by midsummer, as his actions in the following months were to demonstrate.

Things were going pretty smoothly for the merchant adventurers of the Massachusetts Bay Company when, at a General Court held on July 27 at Thomas Goffe's house, Craddock dropped the bombshell. The records of the Company of the Massachusetts Bay reveal that the governor waited until the very end of the session, when all other business had been transacted, before he "read certaine propositions conceived by himself, viz, that for the advancement of the plantation, the inducing and encouraging persons of worth and qualitie transplant themselves and famylyes thether, and for other weighty reasons therin contained, to transferr the government of the plantation to those that shall inhabit there."[23] The faces of the merchant freemen must have registered shock and disbelief as Craddock blandly proposed turning control over their rather substantial investment to a group of people with little or no interest in turning a profit for the adventurers. Needless to say, the proposal "occasioned some debate." Craddock skillfully ended the meeting, enjoining the participants "seriously to consider hereof, and to sett downe their particular reasons in wryting pro and contra, and to produce the same at the next Generall Court."[24] In so doing, he switched the field of debate from the ground of material interest to the domain of cultural virtuosity. In short, he tried to settle an institutional struggle between distinct interests with an essay contest.

The gambit succeeded. On August 29, three days after the signing of the Cambridge Agreement and after just one day of debate, the company agreed to send the government and charter with the planters to the new colony. Negotiations between the planters and adventurers must have occupied the next four or five weeks, because it was not until October 15 that the General Court returned to the exact relations between these groups and their respective obligations. On that date it was agreed "[t]hat the charge of the ministers now there, or that shall hereafter goe to resyde there, as also the charge of building convenyent churches, and all other publique works upon the plantation, bee in like manner indifferently borne, the one halfe by the Companyes joynt stock for the terme of 7 yeares, and the other halfe by the planters."[25]

This concession on the part of the merchants may have been offered as a token of good faith for the upcoming bargaining. If so, it was promptly ignored by the planters and their allies, Matthew Craddock and the two John Whites. On October 20, Governor Craddock informed the General Court that the "espetiall occasion" of their meeting was to elect a new government of assistants, "the government being to bee transferred into New England, according to the former order."[26] Before he could proceed with the election, the issues of the control of the joint stock and the disposition of the company's debt were raised. It was announced that certain articles of agreement had been reached the day before at the deputy governor's house between some of the planters and adventurers.[27] These agreements, which seem to have amounted to the forming of five standing committees (each comprised of one planter and one adventurer) to reach some sort of final agreement, were ratified by the General Court. Given equal representation with the merchants on the committees, the planter intelligentsia would strive to avoid the sort of unfavorable relationship with the merchant adventurers that had undermined the initial settlement of Virginia.

Just in case such a propitious "meeting of the minds" was unobtainable, the following fascinating provision was enacted by the court: "[I]n case the said committee, or the greater nomber of them, should differ in any one or more particulers, and not agree thereon, there was chosen for umpiers, Mr. Whyte, the councellor, Mr. Whyte, of Dorchester, and Mr. Davenport [later patriarch of New Haven], to whom the desition and determination of all such differences is referred."[28] Here is the first instance of the tactic John Winthrop employed with such stunning effect for the rest of his political career: when faced with a struggle against substantial rival interests, invoke the legitimating judgment of the ministry! As members of the thinking class,

Winthrop and his planter/soon-to-be-magistrate allies counted on the incipient class consciousness of their clerical brethren. Such class consciousness was probably further fostered by the debates between the merchant and planter committeemen, which could only serve to dramatize to the clerics that they shared with these planter intelligentsia a common high cultural tradition. As the late Alvin Gouldner might have put it, in contradistinction to the merchants, they shared a culture of critical discourse.

Before moving on to the election of the new government, Craddock took the time to ensure that in the future such outbursts would not disturb his well-orchestrated plans. Henceforth, freemen who wished to "propound such things as they conceive benefitiall for the business" might "present their opinions in wryting, but not to debate with them for interrupting their proceedings."[29] Having carried the motion, Craddock at last proceeded to the election of John Winthrop as governor and of John Humfrey as his deputy.

While the committees debated, the financial future of the company hung fire for the next month. Winthrop was apparently fairly confident of the outcome, for in October he wrote to his wife that they had "now agreed with the merchants, and staye only to settle our affairs."[30] On November 25, he convened the next session of the General Court and "made relation" of the fruits of the committee work: "That Notwithstanding there had bin all good concordencie and faire proceedings between them: yett . . . they could not bring the same to a wished effect, but only had reduced it to certaine propositions to bee represented to the consideration of the Company."[31] The propositions addressed the "inevitable necessitie" of raising more money, but "by reason of the small appearance" of the freemen, deliberation was postponed until the next Monday, when the entire company would be "summoned by ticketts to bee present." Before ending the meeting, White, in what appears to have been a prearranged gambit, moved to pack the upcoming General Court:

> Lastly, upon the motion of Mr. Whyte, to the end that this business might bee proceeded in with the first intention, which was chiefly the glory of God, and to that purpose that their meetings might be sanctyfied by the prayers of some faithfull ministers resident heere in London, whose advice would bee likewise requisite upon many occasion, the Court thought fitt to admit into the freedome of this Company Mr. John Archer and Mr. Phillip Nye, ministers heere in London, who . . . kindly accepted thereof: Also Mr. Whyte did recommend unto them Mr. Nathaniell Ward [later of Ipswich], of Standon.[32]

When the General Court reconvened on the last day of November, Winthrop moved that the "adventurers would bee pleased to double their adventures." The motion was promptly voted down. It was then agreed that ten people, five planters and five adventurers, be appointed undertakers of the joint stock for seven years and that several monopolistic privileges be "appropriated to the joynt stock" for that term. Finally a committee of four (including Reverend White, Increase Nowell, and Thomas Goffe) was appointed to "value the joynt stock" and report on their audit the next day.[33]

On December 1, Governor Winthrop opened the meeting with a few choice words: "Before I acquaint you with the occasion of this meeting, I must crave your patience, to prepare you."[34] The order of business was the "disengaging and orderinge the joint stock," and the proposal was that the stock be divided into an unencumbered plant-ing stock and a trading stock, each to be supervised by five undertakers. What fol-lowed was a classic Winthrop speech. After a few Old Testament allusions, Winthrop raised the objection that must have been most prominent in the minds of the adven-turers: "[W]hy should we forebeare our monye so longe etc.?" Winthrop answered this objection with a forceful argument that must have made the merchants squirm under the watchful gaze of the assembled clerics:

> Answer I: you have given it to God, and made such a protestation, as if Godes glorye and the wellfare of the plantation should require it, you would nott onely lende it, but lose it [there is, of course, no record of such a protestation]. . . .
> Consider the difficulty of plantations, when God himself would transplant Israel into Canaan, he was forced to feed them and clothe them by miracle. . . .
> [Y]ou are the foundations and beginninge of this work:
> you are as the family out of which it is derived, a father of a family will not send forth a Childe without a blessing and portion.

Having gained the initiative, Winthrop moved on to the hard sell:

> Consider your reputation, the eyes of all the godly are upon you, what can you doe more honorable for this Cytye, and the Gospell which you profess: then to denye your owne profitt, that we may saye Londoners can be willing to lose that the Gospell etc. . . .
> [N]ot to presume to muche upon your patience, this is the some of my mind, it is agreed by the Committee that the joint stock shalbe turned over to us charged with the engagementes, we to give you suche securyty as we are able (for I knowe you will not putt us to impossibilitys) for repayment of the perticular adventures at the end of 7 yeares.

The speech had its desired effect. The merchant adventurers sheepishly acceded to the planters' demands. Given the depleted nature of the extant stock, it was agreed that all outstanding shares would be devalued by two-thirds, and the adventurers were promised compensation in the form of New England land (a promise that seems to have come to naught). To promote future investment, it was resolved that hence-forth joint stock would be purchased from any three of the adventurer undertakers "that they shall beare noe part in the former."[35] Many of the adventurers, who upon this resolution doubled their subscription, took it to mean that they were purchasing unencumbered stock that was to be used for trading purposes. They would soon learn otherwise.

At the next and final meeting of the General Court in England, Winthrop asked the freemen to ratify the resolutions of the last court. When informed that all of the stock was to be devalued by two-thirds and not just the original subscription, "some ex-ception was taken by those who had doubled their adventures, conceiving them-selves to bee wronged in having their sommes drawne downe to soe lowe a rate as 1/3 part; alleadginge that the second part was paid in upon a proposition of trade."[36] Mr. Vassall, who henceforth was among the foremost enemies of the Massachusetts regime, stated that they "were content to give the first £50 to the plantation, soe as their other £50 might goe on wholly in this new stock." Winthrop forcefully re-sponded that "the undertakers would not continue their said undertaking but upon the same conditions," which they claimed had been reached at the last General Court.

A vote was held, and "by erection of hands" the planters carried the day. Having secured control of the government of the company and its assets, Winthrop closed the court on this magnanimous note: "And the matter in difference with them who had doubled their adventures being noe more to each of them than between £50 and £33 6s. 8d., was by mutuall consent referred to three ministers heere present, Mr. Davenport, Mr. Nye, and Mr. Archer, who are to reconcile the same between them."[37] What these men of God could have offered to the aggrieved merchants other than the promises for the hereafter associated with a scheme of works righteousness is unclear.

What had begun as a modest fishing venture and had blossomed into a mercantile colonization effort was now transformed into a Bible commonwealth led by the seventeenth-century equivalent of the ancient Hebrew judges, the Puritan intelligentsia. This transformation had required the aid and support of ministerial intellectuals, in addition to a handful of merchant allies. The future success of this Bible commonwealth would depend on the close cooperation and contact of these two strata of the thinking class. The search for an effective polity that would institutionalize the relation and rule of these two strata was the fundamental challenge facing the thinking class of Massachusetts in the years ahead.

I

THE CREATION OF THE
NEW ENGLAND WAY

Cultural Authority and the
Puritan Thinking Class

Few radical movements have enjoyed the auspicious conditions of the Puritan founders of Massachusetts. Far from the metropolitan authorities, the leaders of the settlement were able to inscribe their ideal holy commonwealth on the tabula rasa of the wilderness free from outside interference. Few issues, if any, so absorbed the attention of the colony's leaders as the foundation and support of the polity structure of Massachusetts. The resulting political and ecclesiastic system proved remarkably stable and enduring. Established largely by fiat and precedent in the very first years, the New England Way served as the institutional skeleton of the Bay social body until the loss of the charter and the onset of the Andros regime in the 1680s.

Despite their unquestioned importance, however, the interlocking institutions of church and state in Puritan Massachusetts defy simple analysis. Were the Bay churches the independent and lay-controlled congregations of a sect or part of an establishment dominated by the ministry? Was the General Court of Massachusetts a representative republic of the saints or, in Thomas Jefferson Wertenbaker's phrase, a Puritan oligarchy? Was the relation of church and state Erastian, as Ronald D. Cohen has claimed, or was it, as John Cotton argued, "the best form of Government in a Christian-Commonwealth," namely "theocratie"?[1] The obvious answer to each of these questions is both in one sense and neither in another. And while this answer bears some semblance of truth in registering the complexity of the Bay polity scheme, it utterly fails to offer the analytic clarity and coherence that are necessary for thorough historical understanding.

This confusion about early Massachusetts polity forms is certainly not the result of either a lack of information or a failure of perspicacity on the part of historians. Rather, it is the result of the shifting frame of reference, or larger historical context, in which these institutions are seen. On the one hand, the Massachusetts government is seen as one of several English colonial political establishments of the time. On the other hand, the Bay churches are viewed in the context of the larger drift toward sectarianism among the seventeenth-century vanguard of the Reformation in England known as Puritans. Certainly, on the surface of things, Massachusetts was both a colony and Puritan. Nonetheless, the failure of these contexts to mesh into a coherent whole suggest that greater depths need to be plumbed to grasp the nature of the New England Way.

Only when placed in the context of modern ideological politics does this unprecedented institutional arrangement take on a recognizable form. As Michael Walzer has pointed out, Puritanism was the first radical "sectarian" political movement.[2] Seventeenth-century Massachusetts, then, was an ideal Anglican-free environment where certain fundamental tendencies within the Puritan movement were able to develop unimpeded by the English political and ecclesiastic powers.[3] The principal fruit of this development was a peculiar, if precedential, system of political authority. Designed and staffed by a class-conscious and dissident educated elite, the institutions of church and state in Puritan Massachusetts comprised nothing less than one of the first stable revolutionary regimes in modern Western political history. The story of this political establishment and its evolution, as well as the role of the orthodox thinking class within it, begins with the founding of the first official ecclesiastic institution of Puritan Massachusetts, the precedent-creating church of Salem.

Gathered in the summer of 1629, the church of Salem at first sight seems the very exemplification of the kind of lay control Max Weber associated with sectarian congregationalism.[4] On August 6, the church was established through the mutual covenanting of thirty congregants after a day of prayer and fasting. The congregation then elected officers, both lay and clerical, by ballot. To conclude the day's events, the congregation wielded the ultimate symbolic power in subjecting their pastor and teacher to lay ordination.[5] The venerable Samuel Eliot Morison ascribed this flurry of lay activity to "the 'free aire of a new world' liberating repressed desires and energies. . . . One aspect of puritanism was the revolt of the laity from priestly control; desire for self-expression, to have a share in running the Church."[6] Looks, however, can be deceiving, for upon closer inspection several factors mitigate against this picture of a lay-controlled democratic congregationalism. To begin with, this great lay empowerment seems to have been imposed from above. The impetus behind the gathering of this church, as well as its organizational structure, came from the two ministers, Francis Higginson (the author of the covenant) and Samuel Skelton.[7] Both ministers were within their rights in imposing a church structure of their own choosing, for they had been jointly empowered by the company in London to arrange ecclesiastic matters in any fashion they found satisfactory: "For the mannor of their exercising their ministrie, and teaching both our own people and the Indians, wee leave that to themselves, hoping they will make Gods word the rule of [their actions], and mutually agree in the discharge of their duties."[8]

Equally curious is the fact that Samuel Skelton and Francis Higginson, while called by the congregation of Salem, were employed by the company. They had both signed rather handsome three-year contracts back on April 8, including £10 for books, £20 per year (£30 for Higginson, presumably due to his large family), £10 for traveling provisions, all "necessaries of diet, housing, firewood" as required on a regular basis, and 100 acres of land at the end of the term.[9] While subject to the symbolic power of lay ordination, the actual power of the purse lay in hands other than those of the congregants.

Even more troubling for the Morison interpretation than the establishment of the clerics was the nature of the government that established them. The most powerful legal authority in the colony at the time was the governing council, presided over by Captain Endecott. The company had dispatched seven of the purported twelve counselors, who, upon arrival and in cooperation with Endecott, were to choose an additional three counselors and extend to the "old planters" the privilege of choosing "2 of the discreetest and juditiall men from amongst themselves to bee of the government."[10] There is no evidence that these eight men ever extended this privilege, nor that they ever chose three colleagues. Indeed, two of the counselors were soon arrested and sent back to England, leaving only five counselors. The three most prominent counselors, at least in the letter from the company to Endecott of April 17, were "the three ministers, namely, Mr. Francis Higgenson, Mr. Samuell Skelton, and Mr. Francis Bright."[11] They were the very government of the colony!

Not only did the ministers hold significant political power, but they also were more than willing to use it. Thus, when their fellow counselors John and Samuel Browne (one a lawyer, the other a merchant, and both original patentees of the company) objected to the use of separatist forms and withdrew to form their own congregation, they were promptly purged from the government and shipped back to England.[12] While this action embarrassed and angered the company, the ministers had been authorized to organize church matters. Indeed, they had been told to "suppress" any disputes over church matters "and bee carefull to maintaine peace and unitie."[13] This they had certainly done, and vigorously.

What exactly happened in Salem on August 6? What was the meaning or point of "electing" established ministers or covenanting according to a pattern imposed and enforced from above? As the works of George Selement and Harry Stout suggest, the rituals of election and covenant were used to legitimate the cultural authority of the ministerial intellectuals.[14] The foundation of this cultural authority was built on the bedrock of Puritan biblicism.[15] By establishing a divinely authorized text containing the sum of human wisdom as the infallible guide to all problems, the Puritan ministers empowered themselves as the carefully trained interpreters of that text. "Every man was encouraged to read his Bible with his own eyes," Larzer Ziff informs us, "but he was equally required then to bring his understanding into line with the judgments of the ministry as they were expounded from the pulpit."[16] Although the Bible contained all relevant human knowledge, only those skilled in the ancient tongues and the various hermeneutical techniques in fashion at the time could see through to the deep structure of its meaning.[17] By paying homage to an ancient, largely mythic text, the Puritan ministers ensured the political importance of their literary critical skills. In so doing, they created a completely new form of political authority—in the Weberian sense of legitimate power—which I have called cultural domination.

Cultural domination, as here conceived, requires four formal supports. First of all, like charismatic authority, it requires recognition in the form of ritual election or some similar mechanism of consent like oath swearing or covenant signing.[18] Fealty is sworn to the "correct" cultural formation, in this case Puritan biblicism, and the officeholder is empowered only as the specially trained bearer and interpreter of that cultural tradition.[19] The "laity" generally conceive of this high cultural training—

whether centered around biblicism or some other intellectually legitimating principle like reason or rationality—as being endowed with an automatic efficacy that need simply be applied to any problem to generate a univocal solution.[20] The biblical truth is eternal and immutable, claimed Thomas Hooker, "but the alteration grows, according to mens apprehensions, to whom it is more or lesse discovered, according to God's most just judgement, and their own deservings."[21] Such belief gives rise to the second formal requirement, that officially authorized bearers of the cultural tradition must always agree in their public formulations or at least not disagree. If this condition is violated, the laity may come to see the cultural tradition as an amorphous collection of expressions or principles manipulated by "mandarins" for their own aggrandizement.[22] The third requirement is that all public expressions of the culturally dominant must be socially privileged. The greatest deference and ritual respect available must be bestowed on these public acts, including forced attendance, titulary homage, and silent obedience. Finally, to ensure the stability of the entire system, unauthorized cultural expressions must be carefully monitored and severely suppressed when they contradict or threaten to "desacralize" the authorized formulas.

In the framework of cultural domination, the events of August 6 take on a discernible pattern. The election and ordination of Skelton and Higginson legitimated them, at least in the eyes of the congregants, as the authentic bearers and interpreters of the cultural tradition of Puritan biblicism. The formal subscription to the church covenant served to authorize that cultural tradition as the binding principle of the religious community. Indeed, the first clause of Mather's copy of the Salem covenant specifically cites Puritan biblical exegesis as the binding principle of the community: "We Covenant with our Lord, and one with another; and we do bind ourselves in the presence of God, to walk together in all his ways, *according as he is pleased to reveal himself unto us in his blessed word of truth* [italics mine]."[23] Joining the church of Salem required a forthright and public ecclesiastic submission to the "revealed" precepts contained in the sacred texts. This ritual fulfilled the first requirement of cultural domination.

The second formal requirement, consensus among officially authorized bearers of the culture, had been achieved some months before, as reflected in the instructions sent to Endecott in the early spring: "Wee have, in the former part of our letter, certyfyed yow of the good hope wee have of the love and unanimous agreement of our ministers, they having declared themselves to us to bee of one judgement."[24] It was more than mere "good hope" on the part of the company that produced "unanimous agreement," however. Upon learning that Ralph Smith (a minister whose passage to Massachusetts had been granted) had a "difference of judgement in some things from our ministers," the company wrote to Endecott and ordered "that unless hee wilbe conformable to our government, yow suffer him not to remaine within the limitts of [our] graunt."[25] Nor were such principles of consensus solely the concern of the company's officers in England. It was after his arrival in Salem that Mr. Bright, the third potential minister and a conforming Anglican, was induced to remove to Charlestown and then return to England within the year because he could not agree with the ecclesiastic views of his colleagues.[26]

In accord with the third requirement of cultural domination, the Puritan divines were afforded the utmost attention and honor in their public declamations. Once ordained, the godly minister "may then look at himself as called by the Holy Ghost to exercise his talents in that office," explained John Cotton, "and the people may and ought to receive him, as sent of God to them."[27] In keeping with the "special dutyes of People to their ministers," Reverend John Fiske instructed the lay brethren that they were bound to "esteem & reverence them [the clergy] to hear them gladly, to hold fast their good-doctrine in faith & obedience; and withal to maintain their estates with honourable Provision."[28] The covenant specifically obliged the congregant to privilege the speech acts of the ministers above all others: "We will not in the congregation be forward either to show our own gifts and parts in speaking or scrupling, . . . but attend an orderly call thereunto, knowing how much the Lord may be dishonoured, and his gospel, and the profession of it, slighted by our distempers and weaknesses in public."[29] In practical terms, such an "orderly call" required far more than a silent and respectful auditory. Thomas Hooker claimed that the congregation was obliged to meekly submit to the will of their clerical officers in almost every aspect of church business: "[T]he Officer may by a superior united right, call them [the congregation] together, they cannot refuse. He may injoine them to hear, they may not withdraw. He may injoin them silence, if they shall speak disorderly or impertinently, he may dissolve the congregation, and they must give way while he delivers the mind of Christ out of the Gospel, and acts all the affairs of his Kingdome, according to his rule." Constrained by the need to find biblical warrant for his actions, the Puritan congregational minister nonetheless enjoyed impressive powers over his congregation as a result of the deference due him. "As it suits with his mind," Hooker concluded, "he is thus above the whole Church."[30]

The suppression of dissident religious formulations, the fourth requirement of cultural domination, was achieved with the aforementioned arrest and banishment of the Browne brothers. Such suppression was not left to the discretionary whims of the government, however, for it was enjoined by the church covenant as a religious obligation. Nathaniel Morton reported that a special clause was inserted into the covenant "about the Duty and Power of the Magistrate in Matters of Religion" precisely because the elders "foresaw that this Wilderness might be looked upon as a place of Liberty, and therefore might in time be troubled with erroneous spirits."[31] Hardly a place for religious liberty, the church of Salem was a carefully ordered institution whose regulations were both exacting and precise. Finally, to remove any doubt as to who would arbitrate these regulations, the covenant bound the congregants to civil and ecclesiastic obedience: "We do hereby promise to carry ourselves in all lawful obedience to those that are over us, in Church or Commonwealth [being the very same persons in this case], knowing how well-pleasing it will be to the Lord, that they should have encouragement in their places, by our not grieving their spirits through our irregularities."[32] Hierarchical in structure and ritual, the ecclesiastic component of the New England Way had been created in its most essential features. As Thomas Lechford noted, the same pattern enacted at Salem was to occur as a matter of course in the subsequent gatherings of the Bay churches.[33]

The church of Salem institutionalized a system of cultural domination by the ministerial intellectuals, not a "dictatorship of the thinking class." In fact, the congregants of the church of Salem enjoyed far more ecclesiastic power than their Puritan brethren in the English parishes. Only in Massachusetts was lay consent required to create a church, and nowhere in England were official elections held to "call" a cleric to office. This apparent contradiction between lay empowerment and clerical cultural domination is resolved by the Weberian distinction between power and authority. Power is simply the ability to effect a result. Authority, or legitimate domination, is a particular type of power that has achieved sanction in the eyes of those subject to it. As the degree of consent or legitimation offered increases, so does the amount of authority conferred.

It was precisely because the ministers sought authority rather than mere power that they adopted the covenant and election rituals of congregationalism. Empowered by the company to impose any ecclesiastic system they desired, they chose to confer the power of consent on the covenanting laity so that it might be returned to them in the form of cultural domination. Granted that their election was a foregone conclusion and that the power of the laity was largely spent once the church was gathered, it is nonetheless remarkable that the ministers empowered the "brethren" with a right of consent that might, in principle at least, be withheld. The decision appears less courageous considering that prior to Cotton's arrival in 1633 the principal indice of membership in the godly laity was attendance upon the sermons of Puritan divines coupled with a reasonable facility with the doctrines and principles contained therein.[34] The preaching of the Puritan ministry thus served to create a distinct "speech community" whose members were distinguished by their relative facility with that particular cultural tradition or sociolect. William Hunt has described this phenomenon in poststructural terms: "The communion of Saints was established by a shared semiotic competence, analogous to the linguistic competence that unites speakers of a common language." Whether described in a poststructural or sociological idiom, however, the point is the same. Both the status of the saint and that of the godly divine were "reciprocally authenticating."[35]

The remarkable authority enjoyed by the Bay clergy was a result of the importance attributed to lay consent. Only the brethren had the "liberty to choose their own officers," and this liberty, according to John Cotton at least, "ariseth to a power in them."[36] Yet despite such power, "all authority (properly so called) is in the hands of the Elders," noted John Allin and Thomas Shepard, "and the liberty of the people is to bee carryed in a way of Subjection, and obedience to them in the Lord."[37] This was because the purpose of this liberty or power was to confer authority upon those ministerial intellectuals whose preaching satisfied spiritual needs. Prior to their gathering in a congregation, Thomas Hooker claimed, the saints held all "power dispersed among themselves," but once they submitted to the church covenant "they voluntarily consent to unite this their power, and to devolve it upon one, to whom they will submit."[38] Here lay the key to Richard Mather's claim that the church government of the Bay congregations was "that kinde of Government, which the Philosophers that write of the best Common wealths affirme to be the best," namely, a classical mixed polity: "For in respect of Christ the head it is a Monarchy, and in respect of the Ancients and Pastors that Governe in Common, and with like Authority among themselves, it is an Aristocracy, or rule of the best men; and in respect that the people are not secluded, but have their interest in church matters it is a Democracy or popular state."[39] Far from inconsistent, the cultural domination of the ministerial intellectuals was predicated on the power of consent among an informed and culturally virtuous laity and would have been inconceivable without it.

The system of cultural domination was, in part at least, a result of certain dynamics within the English Puritan movement. Initially, Puritanism was a protest by "vanguard intellectuals." After the failure of the Elizabethan "classical" movement, the godly divines were pushed into the underground role of dissident nonconformists. The critical challenge facing the ministerial intellectuals, then, was to adopt organizational measures likely to induce the participation of followers.[40] As the disfavor and repression of the state continued—and in some cases intensified—the clerics were forced to offer their lay followers the only tangible reward they had: power within the movement.[41] This was the cause of the signal importance attached to lay consent by the Puritan ministerial intellectuals in Stuart England and Massachusetts.

Shortly after the church of Salem was gathered, Captain Endecott applied the rituals of cultural domination to the state. After consulting with the governing council—which included ministers Skelton and Higginson—Endecott summoned the settlers to a meeting in Salem. There he requested their consent and subscription to the principle "that in all cases, as well Ecclesiasticall, as Politicall, wee should follow the rule of Gods word." Yet this was hardly the democratic town meeting of New England lore, for as Endecott made painfully clear, failure to subscribe would result in immediate banishment from the colony.[42] Nor was political biblicism a severe constraint on the discretionary judgment of the governors, for the Scriptures detailed a broad range of political arrangements and a careful reading of the text could give warrant to a variety of policies and practices. According to Bozeman, the consequence of such biblicist politics was that "a sizable field opened within which magisterial—and clerical—interpretation was required."[43] It was precisely this realization that led one of the settlers, Thomas Morton, to propose the following clause in amendment: "So as nothing be done contrary, or repugnant to the Laws of the Kingdome of England." Without this clause, Morton feared that any subscription to the principle

> would proove a very mouse trap to catch some body by his own consent, (which the rest nothing suspected) *for the construction of the worde would be made by them of the Separation, to serve their owne turnes* [italics mine]: and if any man should, in such a case be accused of a crime (though in it selfe it were petty) they might set it on the tenter hookes of their imaginary gifts, and stretch it, to make it seeme capitall.[44]

When this proposal was rejected out of hand, Morton, alone among the settlers in his resolve, refused to consent to this principle. In short order he was arrested and transported to England in bolts. The thinking-class leadership of the colony knew what they were about, and they knew what was required to safeguard their newly created cultural domination. The basic lineaments of the New England Way had been established.

This system of cultural domination was the institutional precedent that Winthrop and his colleagues in the government inherited in the summer of 1630, a precedent that informed and underlay subsequent political and ecclesiastic polity development for the next thirty years. Significant innovations ensued in the years to come,

but the fundamental goal of all of the changes was the continued cultural domination of the Massachusetts thinking class. Indeed, the political history of Massachusetts in the pre-Restoration period can be reduced to two basic themes—the struggle
of various classes and groups against this domination and the struggle within the
thinking class for power and mastery.[45] The existence of divisions within the thinking class, or the limits of thinking-class consciousness, made possible the various
(largely unsuccessful) challenges to the political and cultural authority of the intellectuals and intelligentsia. Paradoxically, these lay challenges united members of the
thinking class and fostered their sense of solidarity and class consciousness.

Although the takeover of the Massachusetts Bay Company by Winthrop and his
clique of East Anglian planters ensured the continued cultural domination of the ministers, the arrival of the Winthrop fleet in the summer of 1630 brought to an abrupt
end the clerics' direct control of the colony's government. The initiatives of the future magistrates of the Bay Colony had, several months before their departure,
shifted the balance of political power within the thinking class from the ministerial
intellectuals to the professional intelligentsia.[46] The intelligentsia/planters interviewed and approved potential divines for the planned colony. Although Isaac Johnson referred to Reverend White's "call" for ministers for the infant settlement, it is
significant that in the same missive Johnson implied that the choice of ministers
heeding that call was in the hands of Winthrop and his colleagues.[47] This implication
became explicit one week after the Winthrop group took control of the company. On
October 27, they sent a circular letter to several prominent divines requesting their
presence in London on November 9 to help "judge of the persons and corses of such
of their brethren of the Ministry whom we shall desire to single out for this employ."[48] The two ministers who accompanied the Winthrop fleet, John Wilson and
George Phillips, had both been approved by the assistants prior to their departure.
Wilson had been a personal acquaintance of Winthrop's for some time, and Phillips
came strongly recommended by John Maidstone.[49]

Nor is there a lack of evidence that Winthrop and his colleagues had resolved prior
to their departure to continue to enhance the system of cultural domination. They certainly did not hesitate to make that purpose clear to prospective emigrants. In November of 1629, Arthur Tyndal, who desired to immigrate to the new colony, wrote
to Winthrop after a meeting between them to express his anxiety that "I came short,
in giveinge yow satisfacion concerninge that poynt, propounded by yow of so maine
importance, (vizt) whether I had absolutelie resolved to master my desires, and conversation, and to live under the Hierarchie of your church and civill government, pur-
posed and concluded among your selves."[50]

If in the summer of 1630 there was any question about the priorities of the newly
arrived government of Massachusetts, it was quickly laid to rest. At the first Court
of Assistants held in the colony, the magistrates commenced their new government
with the most pressing issue of the moment:

> Impr., it was propounded howe the ministers should be mayntayned, Mr. Wilson and
> Mr. Phillips onely propounded.
>
> It was ordered, that houses should be built for them with convenient speede, att the
> publique charge. Sir Rich: Saltonstall undertooke to see it done att his plantation for Mr.
> Phillips, and Mr. Governor, att the other plantation, for Mr. Wilson.

> It was propounded what should be their present mayntenance [they were extended the same terms as those enjoyed by their predecessors, Skelton and Higginson]. . . . All this to be att common charge, those of Maatapan and Salem onely exempted.[51]

Four days later, on August 27, Charlestown witnessed the same course of events that had transpired roughly one year before in Salem. After a day of fasting, an established and salaried minister, John Wilson, was "elected" and underwent lay ordination by the gathered congregants of the town.[52] The rituals of ecclesiastic cultural domination had been enacted.[53]

At the first General Court, held on October 19 at Boston, Winthrop and his associates applied the rituals of cultural domination, and with it the consent of the governed, to the civil government. In front of the assembled settlers, who had apparently been invited to attend the court, the magistrates "propounded" to henceforth limit the freemen to "the power of chuseing Assistants," who in turn would elect a governor and deputy governor from among themselves.[54] Once elected, the assistants and their chosen officers were vested with "the power of makeing lawes and chuseing officers to execute the same."[55] According to the charter, the enactment of such a proposal required the approval of the freemen, who in turn were the small number of planters holding shares of the company's joint stock. As J. T. Adams poignantly remarked, "While two thousand persons were settled in Massachusetts about the time of that October meeting, it is probable that not more than sixteen to twenty members of the Company had crossed the ocean, of whom a number had returned or died."[56] Yet here was no "Puritan oligarchy," for the Massachusetts founders characteristically eschewed all other forms of power save cultural domination.[57] The assistants, who held complete legal authority as a majority of present stockholders, turned to the assembled settlers and requested their consent. As the record of the court concludes, "This was fully assented unto by the generall vote of the people."[58]

At the next General Court the rituals of consent and cultural domination were further extended. On May 18, 1631, after the assistants/freemen reelected themselves to their positions, 116 male householders were made freemen of the colony and "sworn to this government."[59] The reasons behind this extension of the franchise, even if largely symbolic, are obvious. Charter rights aside, it would have proven no mean feat for the tiny handful of magistrates to enforce their political will in the face of a united majority of angry residents. Equally significant were the names of some of the people on the list. The first two names were those of the ministers of Dorchester, John Maverick and John Warham, and the fourth and fifth names were those of the pastor and the ruling elder of Watertown, George Phillips and Richard Browne. Also included were the remaining minister of Salem, Samuel Skelton (Francis Higginson having died), and his potential colleague, Mr. Roger Williams.[60] To deny this group any form of political enfranchisement and with it the fealty-creating rituals of oath taking might have irreparably damaged the legitimacy of Winthrop and his fellow magistrates.[61] By the same token, their inclusion in the political community afforded the magistrates the same cultural domination in the state that the ministers enjoyed in the churches. Once a magistrate was elected, his "only responsibility was to the Word of God," Harry Stout has claimed, "not to the people who called him to office."[62]

In fact, the assembled "commons" requested nothing more than the opportunity to register their consent to be governed: "[I]t was ordered nowe, with full consent of all the commons then present, that once in every yeare, att least, a Generall Court shalbe holden, att which Court it shalbe lawful for the commons to propounde any person or persons whome they shall desire to be chosen Assistants, and if it be doubtfull whither it be the greater parte of the commons or not, it shalbe put to the poll."[63] Nor did the commons use this power of election to replace any of the assistants or choose any additional ones. In the first three years of settlement, the same magistrates were elected to the same offices they had held the year before.[64] As in the churches, the purpose of civil elections was to confer political authority on an educated elite, in this case the legal intelligentsia. Godly elections would place men of "Humane Learning" in political office, claimed William Hubbard, "such as by the benefit of natural parts Experience, Education, and Study, have advantage above others to be acquainted with the affairs of the world abroad, as well as with the Lawes and Customes of their own people at home."[65] Since the fundamental law of Massachusetts was based on the word of God, magistrates also needed the biblicist hermeneutic skills shared by their thinking-class allies in the ministry.[66] As Thomas Cobbet observed, "Regulated Magistrates, ordered according to the Rules of God," should be "well versed in Scripture, Deut. 17. 18, 19, 20. men of choyce Abilities for wisdom and understanding; yea even in the things of God."[67] Here was a position for which none but the Puritan intelligentsia need apply.

The most profound result of this court was the establishment of an institutional precedent that was, at that point, unique in Western political history: "To the end the body of the commons may be preserved of honest and good men, it was likewise ordered and agreed that for time to come noe man shalbe admitted to the freedome of this body politicke, but such as are members of some of the churches within the lymitts of the same."[68] As Edmund Morgan has amply demonstrated, the preconditions for church membership in Massachusetts prior to the arrival of John Cotton were good behavior and a strong grasp of the fundamentals of Puritan religious theory.[69] Thus any non-"deviant" male having a reasonable facility in the sociolect of Puritanism could voluntarily join his local church by publicly giving ritual obeisance to the Puritan tradition and its bearers and subjecting himself to their "discipline." In so doing, he would become eligible to join the political community, in which the consent of the governed was the sine qua non of legitimate authority. He would have, in short, joined the party in a one-party state.[70]

This newly established Puritan regime was a two-tiered structure, containing an outer and an inner party.[71] The outer party consisted of respectable laypersons who were cultural virtuosos in Puritan religious theory. The inner party, staffed by members of the Puritan thinking class, consisted of ministers and magistrates, both ritually elected by the outer party.[72] If the cultural domination between the inner and outer party were to break down, the inner party would find its dominant position threatened, and both civil and ecclesiastic institutions might take on a purely representative character. It was vital to the interests of the Puritan thinking class to maintain this system of cultural domination over the outer party and to quickly suppress any challenges to it.[73] It is perhaps his greatest distinction that Roger Williams mounted the first major challenge to this system.[74]

Williams's arrival on February 5, 1631, must have seemed providential to the congregants of the church of Boston. Their own teacher, John Wilson, was returning to England shortly to attempt to cajole his wife into removing with him. Here was this earnest and devout young man of God, having matriculated at Pembroke Hall, Cambridge, A.B., not more than a few years ago, eminently qualified to assist the elder Wilson and fill in for him during his absence. Williams's troubles seem to have begun with a problem in historical ecclesiology, for when offered membership in the church, he refused unless they would "make a public declaration of their repentance for having communion with the churches of England."[75] Needless to say, the Boston congregants could hardly accede to such demands, and thus when teacher Wilson departed on March 29, he "commended to them [the congregants] the exercise of prophecy in his absence, and designed those whom he thought most fit for it, viz. the governour, Mr. Dudley, and Mr. Nowell the elder."[76]

Williams, undaunted by the "obstinacy" of the church of Boston, moved on to Salem. Once again, his clerical talents were quickly recognized and sought after. It is not known whether he required the Salem church to "separate" from the Church of England, as he had in Boston, but if he did they must have fulfilled this requirement to his satisfaction, for on April 12, 1631, he was formally called to the office of teacher. When news of this development reached Boston, a Court of Assistants was convened. It was not primarily his separatism that offended the magistrates, for he had been publicly tolerated on this regard in Boston. Rather, the real problem seems to have been "his opinion, that the magistrate might not punish the breach of the Sabbath, nor any other [religious] offence, as it was a breach of the first table."[77] Not only was Williams violating the second requirement of cultural domination (i.e., clerical unanimity of authorized expression), but he was also proposing that this requirement be made unenforceable.

That the Court of Assistants moved to "repress" Williams and the church of Salem is well known. More remarkable were the mildness and leniency of the measure actually taken. The assistants sent a letter to their erring colleague in the Salem congregation, Captain John Endecott. In light of Williams's dangerous opinions, "they marvelled they would choose him without advising with the council; and withal desiring him, that they would forebear to proceed till they had conferred about it."[78] This mild rebuke was apparently sufficient, for the congregation quickly revoked its offer. This seems to have been the extent of the "repression": the composition and sending of a mild admonition. Indeed, some five weeks later Williams was made a freeman of the colony, and his subsequent removal to Plymouth was entirely voluntary. This mildness, given the danger of Williams's doctrine, needs to be explained.

Such leniency cannot be attributed to a general policy of cultural toleration by the assistants. They had hardly been indulgent toward Thomas Morton of "Merrymount" when they cut down his maypole and sent him back to England in irons.[79] Nor were they any gentler to one of Craddock's servants, when he was summoned in front of them on June 14, 1631: "It is ordered, that Phillip Ratcliffe shalbe whipped, have his ears cutt of, Fyned £40, and banished out of the lymitts of this jurisdiction, for uttering mallitious and scandalous speeches against the government and the church of Salem."[80] Three months later, for "writing into England falsely and mallitiously against the government and execution of justice here," Henry Lynn was whipped and ordered out of the colony within one month.[81] When Thomas Dexter spoke "re-proachfull and seditious words against the government . . . sayeing this captious government will bring all to naught, adding that the best of them was but an attorney," he was disfranchised, fined £40, and "sett in the bilbowes."[82] Cultural crimes were palpably among the most serious and heavily punished offenses in Puritan Massachusetts.

The reasons behind the toleration extended to Williams lay in his status as a Puritan intellectual. To begin with, any public action against him would only further advertise divisions within the thinking class. This, in turn, would belie the algorithmic quality of the high culture and undermine the system of cultural domination. More important, Williams was protected by his opponents' class consciousness. Winthrop felt a particularly strong sense of identity and solidarity with both intelligentsia and intellectuals. As Cotton Mather remarked, "[H]is liberality unto the needy was even beyond measure generous . . . *but none more than those of deceased Ministers, whom he always treated with a very singular compassion* [italics mine]."[83] For both of these reasons, Winthrop and his colleagues were disposed to treat dissident members of the inner party indulgently. That this indulgence had limits, however, was shortly discovered by the elders of the church of Watertown.

If Williams had lacked charity in denying the validity of the Church of England, Pastor George Phillips and ruling elder (a lay office that declined in importance after the elimination of dual office holding in 1632) Richard Browne of Watertown erred similarly but in the opposite extreme. On July 21, Winthrop, Dudley, and Nowell confronted Browne and Phillips at Watertown "about an opinion, which they published, that the churches of Rome were true churches."[84] A debate over this remarkable position was promptly held "before many of both congregations," and the offensive doctrine "by the approbation of all the assembly, except three, was concluded an errour."[85] Browne was apparently one of the three dissidents.

A few months passed before further action was taken. Upon learning that Browne was still maintaining the legitimacy of the Catholic church (among other errors) "and being a man of a very violent spirit," the Court of Assistants took the same action that had succeeded so nicely with Salem. A letter was sent to the pastor and congregation of Watertown "to advise them to take into consideration, whether Mr. Brown were fit to be continued their elder or not."[86] Unlike their brethren in Salem, the congregation of Watertown (or at least the elements in it loyal to Browne) chose to ignore the admonition and "advice" of the magistrates. On November 23, an irate John Winthrop recorded their response: "[A]fter some weeks, they answered to this effect: That if we would take the pains to prove such things as were objected against him, they would endeavour to redress them."[87] What had Winthrop and his associates been doing in Watertown some four months before if not carefully and publicly refuting an error on the part of the ruling elder? What more "proof" could be required than Browne's continued and adamant refusal to recant and acknowledge his fault?

On December 8, Winthrop, Dudley, and Nowell returned to Watertown. The governor told the assembled congregation—a large faction of which had formed in opposition to Browne—that "being come to settle peace, & etc. they might proceed in three distinct respects: 1. As the magistrates, (their assistance being desired,) 2. As members of a neighbouring congregation. 3. *Upon the answer which we received of our letter, which did no way satisfy us* [italics mine]."[88] A pregnant pause must have fallen on the meetinghouse after Winthrop "laid down the law." Here, clearly expressed, were the limits of magisterial toleration. The assistants might indulge dissident church members in their heterodox opinions as long as they recognized the assistants' right to intervene and maintain unity when necessary. If this right was acknowledged, the assistants would assume the role of consociating brethren, extending brotherly advice in a spirit of reconciliation. But if this right was denied, the congregants would find themselves confronted by the prosecutorial might of the supreme political authority in the colony. Implicitly and prudently acknowledging the visitors' authority, Pastor Phillips asked that they "sit with them as members of a neighbouring congregation only," a request to which they graciously consented.[89] The storm over the church of Watertown had broken. Winthrop and his associates speedily arranged a truce between the aggrieved factions, after which "the pastor gave thanks to God, and the assembly brake up."[90]

The same year that theWatertown elders tested the limits of magisterial toleration of religious heterodoxy, they successfully established the limits of the assistants' authority in civil matters. Although Watertown's leaders acceded to the cultural censorship and judicial sovereignty of the intelligentsia, these leaders refused to allow the magistrates any disposition over their property. In 1631, when taxed for a fortification at Newtown (later Cambridge), Phillips and Browne convinced their fellow townsmen that "it was not safe to pay moneys after that sort, for fear of bringing themselves and posterity into bondage."[91] Ritual consent might legitimate cultural authority, but the power to tax required representation.

This protest left Winthrop in an awkward position. On the one hand, he could hardly deny the basic maxim that every good petit bourgeois church member recognized as self-evident—that taxation is illegitimate without representation. On the other hand, acknowledging their error would undermine the magistrates' prestige and might even appear as an admission on their part of a foiled attempt at arbitrary government. Some sort of agreement was reached with the elders of Watertown, for when summoned before the Court of Assistants, "they acknowledged their fault, confessing freely, that they were in an error, and made a retraction and submission under their hands."[92] Winthrop returned the gesture at the next General Court on May 9, 1632, by incorporating this "error" into the fundamental law of the colony and thus instituting a new principle of government: "It was ordered, that there should be two of every plantation appointed to conferre with the Court about raseing of a publique stocke."[93]

Admittedly limited in scope, this nonetheless was a principle of legitimation other than cultural domination. While the magistrates had a special public calling requiring extraordinary wisdom and orthodoxy, as Timothy Breen has shown in his landmark study of the Puritan ruler, "the deputies were surrogates for the many citizens who could not easily participate in the routine affairs of colonial government."[94] Once this principle had been created, it was inevitable that the new representatives would extend their powers beyond that of mere taxation. Indeed, the famed "revolution" of 1634, when the freemen demanded to see the charter and consequently gained for their representatives the right to deliberate and vote on all legislative matters, can be seen as a footnote to this momentous act. Here lay the real "mixed government" of Puritan Massachusetts, a polity combining two distinct legitimating principles as well as the two strata of the church/party. While the thinking-class elements of the inner party legitimated their rule through cultural domination, the political authority of the newly created deputies lay in their representative role as the spokesmen of the interests and concerns of the largely yeoman outer party.

The willingness to incorporate alternate modes of legitimate authority, as well as to share power and responsibility with those under their cultural domination, bespoke the most alluring aspect of the Massachusetts thinking class: recognition of the value of prudence in orienting human behavior and judgment.[95] It was prudence, or an awareness of the limitations of human judgment, that led the magistrates to institutionalize a check on their own power. It was prudence that prompted the church of Boston in July 1632 to inquire of "the elders and brethren of the churches of Plimouth, Salem, & c. for their advice" as to whether "one person might be a civil magistrate and a ruling elder at the same time."[96] Surely it was prudent to accept the unanimous opinion of these elders, an opinion that henceforth proscribed dual-office holding. Even the "resistance to the inventive propensity to the mind" that Theodore Dwight Bozeman has claimed underlay biblicist "primitivism" and the Protestant epistemology was evidence of "the immense value placed by precise Protestants upon acts of self-control."[97] It was this cultural disposition or intellectual "conservatism" that ensured that the one-party regime of Puritan Massachusetts never became totalitarian.

Once the relation between the inner and outer party had been established, only the relation between the two elements of the inner party remained unsettled. The situation that prompted the settlement of this relation was a quarrel between the two leading magistrates of the colony, John Winthrop and Thomas Dudley. Upon arrival in 1630, the assistants had pledged to reside together in a fortified town that later became Cambridge. Winthrop, however, shortly moved to Boston, which angered the volatile deputy governor.[98] No doubt his wrath was further incited by Winthrop's annoying habit of raising "questions" "about some bargains he [Dudley] had made with some poor men, members of the same congregation, . . . which the governour and some others held to be oppressing usury, and within compass of the state."[99]

Whatever the cause, the animosity between the two was interfering with the smooth operations of civil government. On August 3, 1632, Winthrop and Dudley presented their respective accounts of the dispute to the assembled ministers of Boston, Roxbury, and Dorchester. After conferring among themselves for one hour, the ministers "delivered their opinions, that the governour was in fault for removing of his house so suddenly, . . . The governour [prudently], professing himself willing to submit his own opinion to the judgement of so many wise and godly friends, acknowledged himself faulty."[100] Peace, if not tranquillity, had been restored to the government of Massachusetts at the hands of the clergy.

This was the first instance of ministerial mediation of a political dispute. In the years to come, such mediation would become increasingly common, as the elders' advice and opinion were sought in policy and constitutional struggles as well as personality conflicts. "The Ministers advise in making of Laws," reported Thomas Lechford, "especially Ecclesiasticall, and are present in Courts, and advise in some special causes criminally."[101] Indeed, on occasion such input was offered without necessarily being requested, a practice that created friction between the ministers and magistrates. With the establishment of this new role for the consociated clergy, the early polity development of the Puritan regime in Massachusetts was complete. A mixed government of culturally dominant magistrates and representative laymen, both subject to the binding advice and admonition of the ministerial intellectuals, had been created and would remain the institutional nucleus of the Massachusetts government for the remainder of the pre-Restoration period. Perhaps the greatest testament to its resiliency was its ability to both incorporate and survive the first substantial challenge it faced.

2

JOHN COTTON, ROGER WILLIAMS, AND THE PROBLEM OF CHARISMA

On September 4, 1633, the ship *Griffin* sailed into Boston harbor, bearing the most precious cargo yet brought to the Bay Colony. Two of the most stellar divines of the spiritual brotherhood of Puritan ministers, Thomas Hooker and John Cotton, had with great hazard ventured the journey to Massachusetts.[1] In cultural terms, their migration transformed the colony from a benighted outpost of exiles into a stronghold of Puritan theoretical and practical activity. As the Reverend Thomas Shepard later recalled, one of the "reasons which swayed me to come to New England" was that "I saw the Lord departing from England when Mr. Hooker and Mr. Cotton were gone, and I saw the hearts of most of the godly set and bent that way."[2] In short, they put Massachusetts on the high cultural map.

A fellow of Emmanuel College, Cambridge, Hooker received his A.B. in 1608/9 and his A.M. two years later.[3] Thereafter he served as the curate of Esher, Surrey, lectured at Chelmsford, Essex, and, after 1625, assisted Reverend Mitchell of Chelmsford. Hooker's "numerously attended" lectures spread his fame, particularly among "noblemen and others of high standing in English society."[4] Silenced by William Laud in 1630, Hooker taught school at Little Braddow, Essex, for the next year with his young assistant, John Eliot. Fearing further censure, Hooker immigrated to Holland in 1631 rather than hazard the wilderness of New England.[5] His experience in that country, particularly his stormy and brief tenure at Amsterdam, taught him the exigencies of ecclesiastic and civil power, making him an eminently practical, as well as theoretically acute, divine.[6] In 1633 he accepted an invitation from his former parishioners in Essex to serve them in New England. Here was a gem to be set in the crown of Massachusetts divines.

Even more precious was his colleague, the Reverend John Cotton. The son of an attorney, Cotton was sent to Trinity College, Cambridge, at the tender age of thirteen and received the degree of A.B. some eight years later. His intellectual abilities were quickly recognized, as testified by the Reverend Samuel Whiting:

The first time that he became famous throughout the whole University, was from a funeral oration which he made in Latin for Dr. Same, who was Master of Peter House;

26

which was so elegantly and oratoriously performed, that he was much admired for it by the greatest wits in the University. After that, being called to preach at the University Church, called St. Mary's, he was yet more famous for that sermon, and very much applauded by all the gallant scholars for it.[7]

From Trinity, Cotton moved on to Emmanuel College, where he received the A.M. in 1606 and served as dean, catechist, head lecturer, and fellow in the following years. In 1613 he received his B.D. from Emmanuel, thus completing his brilliant academic career.[8] The author of numerous works, Cotton was certainly the most famous and possibly the most profound theologian of early New England.

Cotton's subsequent ministerial career and the temperament it fostered contrasted sharply with those of Hooker. While Hooker's mettle was tempered in the fires of ecclesiastic persecution, Cotton was almost completely insulated from the episcopal courts. The result was an enduring naïveté (not to be confused with innocence) about practical issues of power. When he was first called to the office of vicar of St. Botolph's in Boston, Lincolnshire, in 1613, Bishop Barlow informed him that

he was a young man, and unfit to be over such a factious people. Mr. Cotton, being ingenuous, and undervaluing himself, thought so too, and was purposing to return to the College again. But some of Mr. Cotton's Boston friends, understanding that one Mr. Simon Biby [Simony and Bribery] was to be spoken with, which was near the Bishop, they presently charmed him; and so the business went on smooth, and Mr. Cotton was a learned man with the Bishop, and he was admitted into the place, after their manner in those days.[9]

Three years later, when Cotton formed a quasicongregational church within the parish, alderman Thomas Leverett and others complained of Cotton's nonconformity to the episcopal courts, resulting in a brief censure. Shortly thereafter, the same Thomas Leverett, no doubt converted by the young clergyman's brilliance and demeanor, "carried the appeal to the bishop's court in Lincoln, located a proctor who was susceptible to aldermanic charms, and arranged to have Cotton treated as a conformable man."[10]

Finally, in 1633 the repressive apparatus of the Laudian regime caught up with Cotton. After Cotton conferred with Hooker, the two divines fled together to the new colony. While Larzer Ziff and William B. Sprague have argued that Hooker was responsible for directing Cotton to Massachusetts, undoubtedly the various "letters procured from the church of Boston, by Mr. Winthrop, the governour of the colony, had their influence on the matter."[11] Cotton had every reason to assume that upon arrival he would be recognized as the leading intellectual in the colony. He was certainly not disappointed. Two weeks after his arrival, the magistrates convened a meeting with the ministers of the colony "to consider about Mr. Cotton, his sitting down." Although he was desired by numerous congregations, the "fittest place for him," the assembled inner party unanimously agreed, was the political and cultural capital, Boston.[12]

The acquisition of the eminent John Cotton, however, proved before long to be a mixed blessing for Massachusetts Bay. For all of his theoretical brilliance and personal charm, in the 1630s John Cotton was a decidedly dangerous man. Adopting a notion from Weber's sociology, David Hall has argued that the repressive crisis of the early 1630s fostered "a new charisma" on the part of certain ministers of the spiritual brotherhood.[13] Like cultural domination, charismatic authority is legitimated through public acts of recognition, such as elections. Again, as in the cultural domination at Salem, such elections need not, indeed, ideally ought not, have more than one candidate per office because such recognition is best if unanimous.[14] Of all of the orthodox clergy of the first generation, no one was more charismatic, in the technical Weberian sense, than John Cotton. For the next five years, Cotton slowly and subtly challenged the extant system of cultural domination, selectively replacing certain polity arrangements with alternative rituals, doctrines, and practices that served to institutionalize his own charismatic authority.

The first clear evidence that Cotton was dabbling in charisma concerns his rather novel financial arrangements. As Weber noted, "[C]harisma rejects as undignified all methodical rational acquisition" such as tithes, contractual stipulations, or state-funded benefices; rather, "it receives the requisite means through sponsors or through honorific gifts, dues and other voluntary contributions of its following."[15] Such informal, "irrational" forms of acquisition are meant to highlight the otherworldly nature of the charismatic calling. Following such an arrangement, Cotton insisted that the laity ought to maintain their clerics "not of constraint but freely, as brought by the givers as an offering to the Lord." The amount contributed should be left to the conscience of each individual "as God had prospered everyman."[16] Thus, after resolving Cotton's "sitting down" in Boston, the inner party further agreed that as compensation for his lecturing "he should have some maintenance out of the treasury." While Winthrop recorded that some of the assistants "upon their second thoughts" rescinded the offer, Cotton's writings and subsequent financial arrangements suggest that it was his aversion to this form of remuneration that squelched this offering.[17]

One month after his installation as teacher of the church in Boston, the congregation met to "take order for Mr. Cotton's passage and house," a consideration that Cotton refused. The point for Cotton was not that he objected to compensation in any form but rather that all contributions should be informal or voluntary.[18] Thus when the congregants raised £60 "(by voluntary contribution) towards his house" and another £100 for his "maintenance" he graciously accepted their munificence.[19] On December 5, "after much deliberation," Cotton informed the congregation that "the minister's maintenance, as well as all other charges of the church, should be defrayed out of a stock, or treasur, which was to be raised out of the weekly contribution; which accordingly was agreed upon."[20] Although Cotton was one of the highest paid clerics in Massachusetts, henceforth his maintenance was provided entirely by voluntary contributions.

Here was no small departure in ecclesiastic arrangements, for the first New England divines had contracted for fixed sums with the colonial government. Subsequent establishments varied widely in form. In some cases the town set a fixed rate on each settler; in others the General Court was required "to enforce the maintenance of the Ministrie." Only in Salem did a similar system emerge, whereby church members gave voluntary contributions in public while "the rest are required to give to the Ministrie, by collection, at their houses."[21] Nor was this voluntary scheme normative, at least in the eyes of the other clerics. John Fiske thought it was "not only Lawfull, but Safe & honourable" for the congregation "to maintain the Ministry by a certain set stipend."[22] Richard Mather heartily agreed. The minister's salary "is not to be allowed as almes and courtesie," he charged, "but as debt and duty, to bee paid according to the rule of Justice; the Labourer is worthy of his wages."[23] "The Elders are worthy of double honour, yea they must be given to hospitality: and therefore they must," claimed Thomas Hooker, "be able to give comfortable entertainment to strangers, as opportunity shall be offered."[24] Cotton's charismatic maintenance was a significant challenge to the financial interests of his established colleagues.

Not content with these pecuniary innovations, Cotton quickly attempted, with considerable success, to transform the church of Boston from a covenanted assemblage of cultural initiates into a charismatic community.[25] In theological terms, Cotton criticized the nature of the church covenant, and by implication the institution founded on that covenant, as he found it upon arrival. The requirements of cultural virtuosity and acceptable social behavior Cotton rejected as a covenant of works. As he informed the church of Salem in 1636, "The elders of the church propound it, will you renounce all your sinful pollutions? Will you keep covenant? And enter into a covenant with the church, and take Christ, and promise to walk after all God's ordinances? You answer, all this we will do; all this is no more than the old covenant."[26] The separatist obsession with formal covenant duties, Cotton argued, inevitably led to a scheme of works righteousness. Insofar as the congregants rested their hopes upon such a covenant, "their faith lay upon a curse." Only by recognizing that "the covenant of grace doth make a people, a joined people with God, and therefore a church of God," could the church members of Massachusetts avoid this curse and achieve salvation.[27]

In practical terms, this meant that the prerequisites for church membership would have to be supplemented with, if not entirely replaced by, a test of saving grace.[28] As Weber said, the charismatic community is constituted "on the basis of the charismatic qualification" of prospective members.[29] The church of Boston was not alone in imposing this new qualification, for Cotton seems to have won over most of his clerical colleagues to the practice. As his grandson, Cotton Mather, stated, "[U]pon his arrival, the points of church-order were with more exactness revived, and received in them, and further observed as such as were gathered after him."[30] When the recently arrived Thomas Shepard asked the inner party how to go about forming a new church in 1635, they replied that "such as were to join should make confession of their faith, and declare what work of grace the Lord had wrought in them."[31] On April 1, 1636, when Richard Mather attempted to gather a church at Dorchester, the assembled magistrates and ministers informed the congregants that they

> thought them not meet, at present, to be the foundation of a church; and thereupon they were content to forbear to join till further consideration . . . wherein they discovered three special errours: 1. That they had not come to hate sin, because it was filthy, but only left it, because it was hurtful. 2. That, by reason of this, they had never truly closed with Christ, (or rather Christ with them,) but had made use of him only to help the imperfection of their sanctification and duties, and not make him their sanctification, wisdom, &c. 3. They expected to believe by some power of their own, and not only and wholly from Christ.[32]

Admittedly devout, pious, and orthodox Christians, the congregants of Dorchester were told that they lacked sufficient religious charisma, or psychosocial intensity, to form a religious community.

This test of saving grace did far more than ferret out "inward hypocrites." It opened an avenue for lay expression and oral participation that would prove extremely contentious and controversial in the years to come. Cotton's charismatic innovation allowed the qualified brethren to offer "prophecy" in giving testimony to the movement of the spirit within their souls.

Many of the clergy had misgivings about this practice of lay oratory. Although "the confessions or speeches made by members to be admitted, have been by some held prophecying," noted Thomas Lechford, the view of "some of the most grave and learned"—presumably the clergy—was "that none should undertake to prophesie in publique, unless he intend the worke of the Ministery."[33] Cotton's charismatic arrangements certainly introduced novelties into the Bay religious scene.

How was Cotton, in a few short years, able to create a consensus on behalf of his ecclesiastic innovations? Granted his reputed oratorical and dialectical abilities, why did the majority of clergymen and magistrates endorse new practices that ran counter to the system of cultural domination? Any answer to this question must begin by noting the qualified nature of the consensus on the new polity arrangements. This consensus was qualified in two ways. First, it was limited by the extent to which various ministers chose to employ these innovations. While most clergymen supplemented the requirements for church membership with a test for saving grace (and even here the form and difficulty of the test varied widely), far fewer seem to have exchanged their stable, established benefices for voluntary contributions. Second, the consensus was hardly universal. A minority of ministers—most notably Thomas Hooker, Thomas Parker, and Peter Hobart—never acceded to these arrangements at all.

Given its qualified nature, the consensus of the inner party on behalf of charismatic authority was caused by the confluence of three factors. The first factor was alluded to above. The vast bulk of ministers used charismatic authority to supplement rather than replace their cultural domination.[34] And while charisma ultimately proved a dangerous threat to the cultural and political power of the thinking class, few ministers could perceive this consequence in the mid-1630s. The second factor, as we shall see, was instability within the magisterial element of the inner party as factional struggle limited the effective power and authority of the secular intelligentsia in this period. Finally, the most important factor supporting charismatic authority, and particularly that of John Cotton, was evidence of miraculous powers, which is essential for validating charismatic leadership.[35]

There could be no greater miracle or more convincing proof of divine favor toward a Puritan minister than being singled out as the special means of the Lord's dispensation of saving grace. Cotton's miracle was a religious revival that he sparked shortly after his arrival.[36] As Roger Clap poignantly recalled,

> O how did men and women, young and old, pray for grace, beg for Christ in those days. And it was not in vain. Many were converted, and others established in believing. Many joined unto the several churches where they lived, confessing their faith publicly, and showing before all the assembly their experiences of the workings of God's spirit in their hearts to bring them to Christ; which many hearers found very much good by.[37]

Nowhere was this revival more intense than in Cotton's church of Boston. Winthrop was quick to notice the "special testimony" of the Lord's presence "in the church of Boston, after Mr. Cotton was called to office there. More were converted and added to that church, than to all the other churches in the bay."[38] On September 8, 1633, when John Cotton joined the church of Boston, the congregation contained roughly 100 members after three years of existence. Within twelve months Cotton doubled the number of persons admitted to the church in Boston, and he added an additional hundred members in the two years after that.[39] Cotton's charismatic polity arrangements were sanctioned because they worked as an effective means for the widespread saving of souls.

For all of its allure, charismatic authority, even when fully recognized and effective, is associated with certain destabilizing problems. One of these problems became acute rather rapidly in the Bay Colony. Since charisma is grounded in extrarational "correctness" and certitude, any conflict between charismatic authorities implies error demanding punishment and/or ritual atonement.[40] John Cotton might ultimately be considered the preeminent divine of his generation in New England, but he certainly had no corner on the charisma market in 1633. As he was made painfully aware, Roger Williams had returned to Salem.

Even more than Cotton's, Williams's financial arrangements impressed his flock with "the starchtness [starkness] of his living in private."[41] Indeed, prior to his installation as teacher of the church of Salem, Williams may have had the symbolic upper hand in the struggle for status as a marginalized "prophet in sackcloth" because he exercised his ministerial talents by way of lay prophecy.[42] Indeed, the result of Williams's influence was a tradition of lay prophesying in the congregation, a tradition of rhetorical mass participation that was matched only by Cotton's congregants during the height of the Antinomian debacle.[43]

The tense, adversarial relationship between Cotton and Williams predated their arrival in Massachusetts. As Perry Miller noted, "[B]ack in Essex before the migration Williams had dared rebuke the great and much-esteemed Cotton for complying with the Book of Common Prayer."[44] In November 1633, Williams and his colleague Samuel Skelton objected to the newly instituted practice of biweekly clerical consociation, "fearing it might grow in time to a presbytery or superintendancy, to the prejudice of the churches' liberty."[45] This put Cotton and his colleagues in a difficult position, for if they allowed this protest to go unchallenged it might be perceived as an admission of the accuracy of the charge. On the other hand, pressing the issue publicly would only highlight and advertise a practice that some of the laity resented. The ministers and magistrates prudently chose to let the protest pass without remark.

Some of Williams's other public positions were received with considerably less toleration, however. On December 27, Governor John Winthrop convened what was apparently a private meeting (perhaps held at his house) of the magistrates and "some of the most judicious ministers" to consider "a treatise, which Mr. Williams (then of Salem) had sent to them, and which he had formerly written to the governour and council of Plymouth."[46] The most inflammatory passage of the treatise challenged the validity of the charter received from the king and thus the colonists' legal claim to their lands.[47] The ministers, most notably Cotton and Wilson, "much condemned Mr. Williams's errour and presumption," and consequently it was ordered "that he should be convented at the next court, to be censured."[48] Meanwhile, prudently attempting to minimize conflict and help his errant young friend, Winthrop sent a letter to Williams's fellow congregant John Endecott, warning him of the impending danger facing his minister.[49] Williams promptly wrote back to the governor, claiming that his intent was "only to have written for the private satisfaction of the governor," and appeared at the next court "penitently, and gave satisfaction of his intention and loyalty."[50] Hence, on January 24, 1634, the magistrates and ministers reconvened in Boston, and Cotton and Wilson, "weighing his [Williams's] letter [to Winthrop], and further considering of the aforesaid passages in his book, . . . found the matters not to be so evil as at first they seemed. Whereupon they agreed, that, upon his retraction, & c. or taking an oath of allegiance to the King, & c. it should be passed over."[51] Winthrop had succeeded, for the time being, in resolving the crisis and protecting Williams.

In the following months, relations between the established ministers of Boston and the church of Salem remained tense. On March 7, 1634, after his public lecture, the teacher of Boston was "propounded" a question about the wearing of veils by women. Cotton held that where "they were not a sign of the women's subjection, they were not commanded by the apostle."[52] Both Skelton and Williams were known to hold the contrary position, and in a show of support for his ministers the volatile Captain Endecott of Salem opposed Cotton's response.[53] As the ensuing debate became vociferous, "the governor, perceiving it to grow to some earnestness, interposed, and so it brake off."[54] Again Winthrop was able to avoid a public breach. As in the previous case, however, the result left the issue unresolved. Conflict could thus be avoided only as long as Winthrop was able and disposed to separate the contestants. While Winthrop's subsequent actions attest to his continuing protective impulses toward Williams, the governor's power and ability to protect his young friend abruptly ended.

On April 1, the famed revolution of 1634 began. At the General Court, the assembled deputies demanded to see the charter and, rightly "conceiving thereby that all their laws should be made at the general court, repaired to the governour to advise with him."[55] Winthrop, conceding that the charter granted legislative authority to the assembled freemen in the General Court, pointed out that "now they [the freemen] were grown to so great a body, as it was not possible for them to make or execute laws, but they must choose others for that purpose: and that howsoever, it would be necessary hereafter to have a select company to intend that work, yet for the present they were not furnished with a sufficient number of men qualified for such a business."[56]

Winthrop was in a precarious bind. Following the stipulations of the charter would weaken the cultural and political power of the inner party's intelligentsia and transform the polity of Massachusetts into a purely representative government of the outer party of church members. Ignoring the legitimate claims of the deputies, however, would undermine the consent that underlay the whole system of cultural domination. This consent was made all the more necessary by the perceived imperial crisis (from which the colony was spared by the English political crisis).[57] Indeed, the General Court had been convened at this time to address this crisis and ensure unity in the event of any military struggle.[58] Attempting to close party ranks, Winthrop offered a modest extension of the deputies' representative powers. Once a year, the deputies in the court would be empowered "to revise all laws, &c. and to reform what they found amiss therein," in addition to approving taxes. Winthrop was quick to point out that this added power was merely the right to a legislative veto, "but not to make any new laws, but prefer their grievances to the court of assistants."[59] The deputies, or representatives of the outer party, were decidedly unsatisfied with this offering.

When the annual Court of Elections met in Boston on May 14, John Cotton delivered the first election sermon. Probably aware of the displeasure vented at Winthrop by many of the deputies and freemen, Cotton claimed that "a magistrate ought not be turned into the condition of a private man without just cause."[60] Cotton's sermon had its desired effect, for while Thomas Dudley replaced him as chief executive, Winthrop was chosen to be an assistant and thus retained his membership in the inner party. A few years later, when Cotton was under intense public scrutiny, Winthrop returned the favor.

The reasons behind Winthrop's replacement as governor are not difficult to surmise. Clearly, the freemen and their deputies were not at all pleased by the concessions Winthrop had offered in April. Promptly after election, the deputies ordered that four General Courts be held annually (subsequently reduced to two), "and not to be dissolved without the consent of the major parte of the Court."[61] Henceforth, such courts would be the sole legislative authority, with the exclusive right to tax, appoint officers, and "dispose of lands, viz. to give and confirme proprietyes." The deputies further empowered themselves to meet "before every Generall Court, to conferre of and prepare such publique business as by them shalbe thought fitt to consider of att the nexte Generall Court."[62] Given the need for unity in the face of a potential imperial confrontation, the magistrates were hardly in a position to refuse these demands. The result was that the deputies, as the representatives of the godly brethren, acquired the right to a voice in all legislation, ecclesiastic as well as civil. "The Laws which Civill Authority do establish" in Massachusetts, stated Reverend Thomas Cobbet, "they must establish them, by, and with the consent of the people, either in themselves or their representatives, this strengthening their Politicall Laws, that they bind Scientes & Volentes."[63]

Equally significant was the personal rift between Winthrop and the man who replaced him, Thomas Dudley. Still miffed at Winthrop's desertion and his colleague's presumptuous inquiry into his business transactions, Dudley may also have been angered by Winthrop's toleration of the errant young divine of Salem.[64] Although the evidence showing that the deputies were merely "following Dudley's lead" in the General Court is somewhat less than decisive, certainly someone must have informed them that a perusal of the charter would demonstrate the "unconstitutional" nature of Winthrop's tenure.[65] Dudley's sole blunder was in trying to exact revenge for Winthrop's earlier financial inquest. Dudley instigated an investigation by the court, ordering "the Deputy Governour, Mr. Israell Stoughton, and Mr. Coxeall . . . to take an accompt of John Winthrop, Esquire, for such commodityes as hee hath receaved of the common stocke."[66] The account, delivered on September 4, revealed that Winthrop had lost a great deal of money during his tenure and had, in fact, been subsidizing the colony out of his own pocket.[67] This public vindication marked the beginning of Winthrop's slow but steady return to popular favor and political preeminence.

The same General Court that witnessed Winthrop's vindication was also rent by the first major political impasse between the deputed representatives of the outer party and the magisterial intelligentsia, a struggle that served to define the meaning of the events of the previous spring. The cause of the dispute was the desire of Newtown's residents to remove to Connecticut, on account of "their want of accommodation for their cattle, so as they were not able to maintain their ministers [Hooker and Stone]."[68] A majority of deputies approved the venture, but with the exception of Dudley and two others, the assistants were opposed to the exodus. Out of this difference of opinion "grew a great difference between the governour and assistants, and the deputies. They would not yield the assistants a negative voice, and the others (considering how dangerous it might be to the commonwealth, if they should not keep that strength to balance the greater number of the deputies) thought it safe to stand upon it."[69]

The assistants prudently drew the line at yielding their legislative veto. To relinquish this power would reduce the government to a representative "democracy" of church members since the assistants and deputies sat as a single body in the General Court. Nor was the particular issue at hand insubstantial. Given the magistrates' expectation of military conflict with the mother country—they showed a strong disposition to resist with what arms they had any abrogation of their charter rights—the dispersal of communities could greatly endanger those who remained in the Bay.[70]

Most important of all, though, was the real reason that Hooker's congregation was eager to leave—their minister's manifest displeasure with Cotton's polity innovations. Aware of the dangers of charismatic "enthusiasm," Thomas Hooker preferred the mechanisms of cultural domination.[71] In fact, Hooker was one of the most cogent and thoughtful defenders of cultural domination in the first generation. He had little sympathy with Cotton's charismatic system of voluntary maintenance. The laity's financial support of the ministry was "not a matter of liberty or curtesie which may be done or left undone," but rather "a duty and a work of justice, unto which the Church is called, and to the performance of which they are bound in conscience."[72] Failure to supply adequate provision for the ministry was thus a violation of "conscience" and an ecclesiastic sin. It was precisely to prevent such a "scandall," Hooker insisted, that "each man should know his proportion, according to rule, what he should do." The job of the deacon, then, was to "informe himselfe by advice and counsell from the body, what each mans free-will-offering should be."[73] Unlike Cotton's voluntary arrangements, Hooker insisted that "free-will-offerings" should be prescribed in sum and compulsory in form.

Hooker found even more objectionable the newly instituted test of saving grace for prospective church members. In 1637, R. Stansby informed Pastor Wilson that word had spread to England that the cause "which moved Mr. Hooker to remove" was the new strictness "in admission of members to your church, that more than one halfe are out of your church in all your congregations, & that Mr. Hooker before he went away preached against yt (as one report who heard him)."[74] Hooker opposed this innovation, in part at least, because, like Thomas Lechford, he recognized that some devout laypersons were "so bashfull, as that they choose rather to goe without the Communion, then undergoe such publique confessions and tryalls."[75] Again, like Lechford, Hooker bristled at the arrogance of those charismatics who held the bashful at fault for not being more forthcoming. "The fear of God, and Faith of those men, may be justly doubted," charged John Cotton, "Whose settled abode is in a place where Churches are gather'd and order'd according to Christ and yet are not after a convenient time joyned to them."[76] Such spiritual arrogance was all the more offensive because the required conversion narrative, in Hooker's view at least, lacked any biblical warrant whatsoever. Indeed, this "presumed kind of liberty" ran counter to the obvious fact that "there be many truly and savingly called, who never knew the time and manner of their conversion, and therefore cannot relate it to others."[77] Cotton and his charismatic disciples simply refused to realize that the invisible church of true believers "is not lyable to our eye, nor comes to be discerned visibly" and was therefore an object of faith rather than an institutional organization.[78]

Cultural domination, not charismatic authority, was the goal of Hooker's defense of New England's preexisting congregational polity. The religious experiences of the congregants were irrelevant to their status as church members. Unlike members of Cotton's charismatic community, who needed to certify each other's credentials as true saints, members of Hooker's visible church were satisfied with "visible Saints (leaving secret things to God)" who were so judged by "rationall charity, which can go no further, then to hopefull fruits."[79] As in Salem, nothing more was required than good behavior and a reasonable facility with the Puritan code of salvation. Thus, any person that "lives not in the neglect of any known duty, or in the commission of any known evill, and hath such a measure of knowledge as may in reason let in Christ into the soul" was fully qualified for membership.[80] Hooker never denied that such persons might turn out to be "hypocrites inwardly" but pointed out that as long as their behavior and profession of doctrine were "blamelesse and inoffensive" rational charity must conclude that they "are fit matter of a visible Church appointed and allowed by Christ."[81] By pegging church membership to "a measure of knowledge" of Puritan doctrine, Hooker was insisting on a community of the culturally virtuous dominated by a high cultural biblicist elite rather than by an antihierarchical charismatic community of "enthusiasts." The difference between Hooker's and Cotton's conceptions of the New England Way could not have been greater. If Hooker was allowed to leave under these conditions, as he ultimately was, it would damage Massachusetts and create a precedent whereby every dissident could demand the right to march off on a self-imposed exile into the wilderness.

Having reached this impasse, the General Court adjourned for the next two weeks. When it reconvened, once again John Cotton opened the session with a sermon. Therein he expressed in simple and straightforward terms his political philosophy, a philosophy that supported the magistrates' position. Cotton broke the civil polity into three elements, "the magistracy, ministry, and people," each with its own unique "strength" or power: "[T]he strength of the magistracy to be their authority; of the people their liberty; and of the ministry, their purity; and [he] showed how each of these had a negative voice, & c. and that yet the ultimate resolution, & c. ought to be in the whole body of the people."[82] Cotton's political theory has two notable features. The first is that the basis of ministers' veto power is their charismatic authority ("their purity") rather than their cultural expertise (their wisdom or learning). Second, the basis of the magistrates' authority is somewhat unclear, and while this does not rule out the possibility of their cultural dominance, given Cotton's subsequent activism on behalf of life tenure for assistants, he seems to have favored patriarchal domination by honoratiores, as found in the House of Lords.[83] On political questions, Cotton was remarkably traditional. Nonetheless, he carried the day for the assistants, for while "all were not satisfied about the negative voice to be left to the magistrates, yet no man moved aught about it," and the court resumed its business "cheerfully."[84] Hooker would have to remain in Newtown for the time being.

Two months later, controversy erupted again in Salem. On November 27, the magistrates were informed that "Mr. Williams of Salem had broken his promise to us, in teaching against the King's patent."[85] This time, however, Williams would have to contend with the bellicose Dudley instead of the tolerant Winthrop. The assistants promptly "granted summons" for Williams's appearance at the next court.[86]

An interesting contrast to the case of Williams and one that supplies valuable context is that of John Eliot. At the same Court of Assistants, the magistrates were informed that Eliot, the teacher of Roxbury, had been criticizing the government and ministry for their dealings with the Pequot Indians. The magistrates "took order, that he should be dealt with by Mr. Cotton, Mr. Hooker, and Mr. Welde, to be brought to see his errour, and to heal it by some publick explanation of his meaning; for the people began to take occasion to murmur against us for it."[87] The conference had its desired effect, for Eliot promptly and publicly acknowledged his mistake. Eliot must have been aware of, and indeed grateful for, the remarkably lenient treatment he was afforded as an intellectual. At a Court of Assistants held the previous month, John Lee had been summarily flogged and fined £40 for "speaking reproachfully of the Governor, sayeing hee was but a lawyer's clerke, & what better understanding hadd hee more than himself; also taxeing the Court for makeing lawes to pick men's purses."[88]

Lacking the restraining influence of their senior elder—Samuel Skelton had died on August 2—the congregation of Salem followed Williams down the dangerous path of dissent. In early 1635, Endecott, no doubt at Williams's behest, defaced the "idolatrous" cross in the ensign at Salem. On March 4, the General Court created a commission to look into this breach of public order by the errant magistrate.[89] At this juncture, the church of Salem took the most ill-advised and rash course imaginable. Presumptuously, it called and hastily ordained Williams, who was under the censure of the magistrates, to the office of teacher. The response of the colonial establishment was not long in coming, as the inner party attempted to combat Williams's new heretical views.

The most dangerous doctrine that Williams taught from his pulpit was "that a magistrate ought not to tender an oath to an unregenerate man," obviously a reference to the loyalty oath required by the previous year's General Court.[90] Since such oaths were made in the name of the deity, explained Williams, they formed a species of prayer. Requiring unregenerate men to pray would further compound their guilt with the sin of blasphemy. Clearly, if the magistrates could not enjoin residents to take an oath of loyalty, their power to require church attendance and thus privilege the cultural acts of the ministerial elite would be jeopardized. Williams had returned to the basic position that had gotten him in trouble before he left for Plymouth: the state-supported system of civil and ecclesiastic cultural domination was illegitimate and should be dismantled.

In response to Williams's call for disestablishment, the court ordered that any two magistrates could be empowered "to heare & sensure, either by ffyne or imprisonment," such persons as "doe usually absent themselves from church meetings upon the Lord's day."[91] To further clarify their position, the court also requested the ministers to "consult & advise of one uniforme order of dissipline in the churches, agreeable to the Scriptures, & then to consider howe farr the magistrates are bound to interpose for the preservation of that uniformity & peace of the churches."[92] The magistrates were looking for clerical sanction to interfere in ecclesiastic matters, for they could have had no doubt about the ministers' views in this regard. John Cotton held that a fundamental task of the state, one that greatly concerned "the civil peace," was "the establishment of pure religion, and the reformation of corruptions in religion."[93] On this point, Thomas Hooker was in complete agreement with his rival and colleague. A truly godly magistrate ought be a "nursing Father" to the church, forcing the church to "attend that wholesome dyet which is provided and set out, as her share and portion in Scripture."[94] In fact, Williams's separation of church and state was, according to Thomas Cobbet, "The Great Antichrists master-piece." "That liberty which suffereth the sheep of the Lord, in an ordinary way, to wander from their Fold and Pasture," he argued, "is not to be allowed off, by such as God calleth to be politicall Shepheards to them."[95] Nonetheless, when summoned before the assembled magistrates and ministers some six weeks later, Williams remained intractable. His colleagues argued vehemently and cogently against his absurd view.[96] All the more dismayed must the assembled inner party have been, then, when one of its number, John Endecott, attempted to defend Williams's damnable position. After earnest discussion, Endecott "gave place to the truth."[97]

At the next General Court, held May 6, Captain Endecott earned the dubious distinction of being the first magistrate in the young colony's history to fail of reelection.[98] The court then listened to the report of the commissioners appointed to inquire into Endecott's defacing of the flag. They charged that "hee had offended therein many wayes, in rashness, uncharitableness, indiscretion, & exceeding the lymitts of his calling; whereupon the Court hath sensured him to be sadly admonished for his offence, which accordingly hee was, & also disinabled for bearing any office in the common wealth, for the space of a yeare nexte ensueing."[99] Two months later, in response to a request by the town of Salem for some land at Marblehead Neck, Williams was summoned before the court.[100] The court expressed its displeasure in no uncertain terms that, while he was under censure from the government, "notwithstanding the church had since called him to the office of a teacher."[101] Williams was dispatched to "consider of these things" before the next court "and then either to give satisfaction to the court, or else to expect the sentence; it being professedly declared by the ministers, (at the request of the court to give their advice,) that he who should obstinately maintain such opinions . . . were to be removed, and that the other churches ought to request the magistrates so to do."[102] For the time being, the request for the land at Marblehead Neck had been denied.

Undoubtedly meant to chasten Williams and his flock, the combined rebuke and denial had the opposite effect. The Salem church was furious at the court's mixing of civil and church issues, as well as at the intrusion into their congregational independence; it dispatched a series of letters to each of the assistants' congregations, requesting that they admonish the magistrates for the "scandalous injustice" of denying their request.[103] This was the high-water mark of Salem dissent. While Williams continued on his giddy course, the majority of the congregation were gradually brought to their senses.

During the summer, the churches responded to the letters they received from Salem, taking "such happy pains" as "presently recovered that holy flock to a sense of his [Williams's] aberrations."[104] Williams, temporarily ailing and bedridden, wrote to his flock that as the other churches of the colony persisted in their sinful course, the church of Salem would have to renounce its fellowship with such bodies. He added that failure to do so would result in his own withdrawal from the congregation. This missive must certainly have given his parishioners reason to reflect.[105] For all of his earnestness, charm, and charisma, the congregation could clearly see that Williams's actions were becoming desperate and dangerous. Apparently undecided, the church let the issue hang fire as the summer came to an end.

On September 3, the General Court took steps to resolve the crisis once and for all. The deputies of Salem were dispatched "to fetch satisfaction for the lettres sent to the severall churches, wherein they have exceedingly reproached & vilifyed the magistrates & deputies of the Generall Court, or els the arguments of those that will defend the same with subscription of their names."[106] When Endecott protested against such heavy-handed measures, the court voted that he "should be committed for his contempt in protesting against the proceeding of the Court." At last, Endecott saw the "writing on the wall," and "upon his submission, & full acknowledgement of his offence, hee was dismissed."[107] To clarify the stakes at issue, the court ordered that the town of Salem be denied representation in the colonial government unless "the major parte of the ffreemen of Salem shall disclaime the lettres sent lately from the church of Salem to severall churches."[108]

The court then proceeded to deal with Williams himself. Charging him with "dyvers newe & dangerous opinions, against the authority of magistrates," as well as his "lettres of defamation," the court offered him a month to carefully consider his response. Williams promptly refused the offer. Thomas Hooker tried once more to reduce Williams from his erroneous ways and thus spare him the wrath of the court. Williams remained adamant, defending all of his acts and doctrines "without retraction."[109] Having failed to move Williams in the slightest, the next morning the court imposed the ultimate sanction short of death.[110] It exiled him from the orthodox Puritan community, ordering "that the said Mr. Williams shall departe out of this jurisdiction within six weekes nowe nexte ensueing."[111]

In an act of singular compassion, the court suspended sentence until the following spring, thus attempting to spare Williams the travail of a harsh New England winter in the wilderness, provided he would not "go about to draw others to his opinions."[112] Before long the magistrates came to regret this decision. While the majority of the Salem church members prudently removed Williams from office, admonished him, "openly disclaimed his errours, and wrote an humble submission to the magistrates," a small nucleus of devotees stuck by their charismatic leader. In January 1636 the magistrates learned that Williams, in violation of the clemency stipulation, continued "to entertaine company in his house, and to preach to them." Moreover, the magistrates also learned that "he had drawn above twenty persons to his opinion, and they were intended to erect a plantation about the Naragansett Bay, from whence the infection would easily spread into these churches, (the people being, many of them, much taken with the apprehension of his godliness)."[113]

Fearing this "infection," the magistrates decided to send Williams back to England. Although Winthrop never acknowledged the fact, he balked at this action. If Williams was dispatched to England, he could expect the worst that star chamber and episcopal courts could offer. Winthrop warned the young divine of the fate in store for him, so that when the magistrates came to arrest him, he had already embarked on his famed winter pilgrimage to Rhode Island.[114] Just as the assistants had feared, Williams built a religiously tolerant community of exiles and dissidents from the New England Way.

At least, however, he was gone. Shortly thereafter, Winthrop was rebuked by the assembled inner party for being soft on heresy. On January 19, the Massachusetts divines informed him that "strict discipline . . . was more needful in plantations than in a settled state, as tending to the honour and safety of the gospel."[115] Winthrop promptly acknowledged his fault and pledged "(by God's assistance) to take a more strict course hereafter."[116] At long last, the Puritan regime in Massachusetts had closed the book on the Roger Williams case.

The ministers and magistrates must have been relieved at the results of that court. The system of cultural domination had survived its first major challenge from a dissident intellectual. During the same period, the regime had successfully incorporated the political aspirations of the laity by ceding power to the deputies in the revolution of 1634. This cession of power was successful precisely because it fell far short of creating a democratic republic of the saints. Indeed, the rise of the deputies had been contained along lines that had been established in 1632. A cadre of Puritan divines of the very first rank had been settled and established, and the introduction of certain charismatic polity innovations had resulted in a religious awakening. With the final settlement of the struggle for charismatic authority between Williams and Cotton, the inner party could only have hoped that the last dangers of this "new charisma" had been put to rest. If so, such hope was decidedly premature. No sooner had the Williams issue been settled than an even more divisive and dangerous dissidence erupted. The year 1636 marked the beginning of the Antinomian crisis.

3

JOHN COTTON AND THE
DIALECTIC OF
ANTINOMIAN DISSENT

The most important and controversial figure in the Antinomian controversy was John Cotton. The movement was largely confined to the church of Boston, with a handful of supporters in neighboring Roxbury. When questioned, the leaders of the movement, particularly Anne Hutchinson, cited Cotton as their mentor and the source of their doctrines. Certainly Cotton's peers recognized him as the central figure in the controversy, and with good reason; as Larzer Ziff remarked, in "the private conferences and correspondences that took place in an ineffective effort to avoid public confrontation, he took the opinionists' side."[1] Moreover, without the institutional support of the prestigious church of Boston and its even more prestigious teacher, the Antinomian movement would have been short-lived and its leaders quickly disciplined.[2]

The most insightful and thought-provoking comment on the role of the preeminent divine of Boston in the movement was made by Cotton himself. On January 16, 1638, in the aftermath of the controversy, he complained that he had been used as a "stalking horse."[3] This statement raises several crucial questions. Who used Cotton and to what purpose? What did Cotton think he and his congregation were doing, and what did his ministerial colleagues make of the situation?

The answer to the first question is readily apparent: John Cotton was used as a stalking horse by the urban bourgeoisie of Massachusetts. As Bernard Bailyn noticed over thirty years ago, "[T]he merchants, with striking uniformity, backed the dissenters."[4] Indeed, in social terms the Antinomian controversy is a classic example of class conflict. In this case, the conflict was between the urban bourgeoisie and the thinking class, particularly the strata of ministerial intellectuals. The stakes at issue were nothing less than control of the colonial government and the continued existence of the system of cultural domination.

This class conflict, initiated by the urban bourgeoisie, is attributable to two interrelated causes. The first and most pressing was the arcane economic policy and philosophy of the inner party. In addition to their benefices, salaries, and stipends, the ministers and magistrates of the Bay Colony received substantial grants of land from the colonial government and the towns in which they resided. This agricultural interest qualified them for dual class membership in the agricultural grand bourgeoisie or gentry as well as the thinking class and led them to embrace an agrarian organic economic philosophy associated with the largely natural economy of the late feudal epoch.[5] The most important elements of this essentially medieval conception were a primitive version of so-called producer's ideology, the condemnation of usury, and a commitment to the notion of a just price and wage for each commodity or service.[6] As Bailyn noted, while such an economic theory "had a special appeal to a predominantly agricultural people," merchants and tradesmen quickly learned that "of all private occupations trade was morally the most dangerous."[7] Indeed, as Emery Battis has commented in his authoritative work on the Antinomians, "[I]f an organic economic philosophy was held to be a basic component of the Puritan moral code, then it would seem that the tradesman's soul was indeed in a perilous state."[8]

Even more problematic than this moral dilemma were the various policies and regulations imposed by the inner party to cope with the runaway inflation that accompanied the Great Migration. Since the first Court of Assistants on August 23, 1630, the magistrates had taken steps to limit prices and wages.[9] As the spiral of inflation intensified, the magistrates responded with increasingly coercive and unreasonable restrictions aimed at eliminating mercantile "profiteering." This draconian regulatory policy came to a head on March 4, 1635, when the General Court granted nine merchants (one from each town) the exclusive privilege of buying all incoming commodities at jointly agreed upon prices and then reselling such items at "five pounds per centum profitt, & not above."[10] As Bailyn noted, "[A] law that demanded of other buyers that they stand by idly while nine fortunate individuals monopolized the middleman's profit could not be enforced."[11] Although the General Court repealed this act some six months later, it added an ominous proviso:

> Whereas two former lawes, the one concerneing the wages of workmen, the other concerneing the prizes of commodyties, were for divers good considerations repealed this present Court, nowe, for avoydeing such mischiefes as may followe thereupon by such ill disposed persons as may take liberty to oppresse & wronge their neighbours, by takeing excessive wages for worke, or unreasonable prizes for such necessary merchandizes or other commodyties as shall pass from man to man, it is therefore ordered, that if any man shall offend in any of the said cases against the true intent of this lawe, hee shalbe punished by ffine or imprisonment, according to the quality of the offence.[12]

More than anathema, such restrictions threatened the prosperity and livelihood of the urban bourgeoisie. Predictably, they were attracted to Cotton's and Hutchinson's spiritist doctrines, for as Ziff has noted, "free grace above the legalistic restrictions of the moral law meant freer enterprise beyond the specific regulations of the state."[13]

The other cause of mercantile discontent, which underlay the first, was their perceived underrepresentation in the colonial government.[14] While hardly comprising a majority of the church members, much less the population at large, the merchants certainly did represent the bulk of the colony's liquid assets or capital. Moreover, without their vital marketing services the colony would most likely revert to the stage of a primitive natural economy.

In social terms, this class conflict took the form of an unabashed anti-intellectualism.[15] The Antinomian strategy was to "inveigh against learning, Scholars, and Colledges," claimed the author of *Good News from New England,* "and to cause others to admire them, they question the ancient truths taught by their ministers, and that before the whole congregation."[16] Indeed, in many respects the Antinomians were precursors of Gilbert Tennent in their attack on a pharisaical "unconverted ministry."

> Come along with me, sayes one of them [to the recently arrived Edward Johnson], i'le bring you to a Woman that Preaches better Gospell then any of your black-coates that have been at the Ninneversity, a Woman of another kinde of spirit, who hath had many Revelations of things to come, and for my part, saith hee, I had rather hear such a one that speakes from the meere motion of the spirit, without any study at all, then any of your learned Scollers.[17]

Such anticlerical and anti-intellectual sentiments were voiced in public gatherings as well as private "prayer meetings." "Now, after our Sermons were ended at our publike Lectures," recalled the Reverend Thomas Welde of Roxbury, "you might have seene halfe a dozen Pistols discharged at the face of the Preacher, (I meane) so many objections made by the opinionists in the open Assembly."[18] Such actions violated the code of deference surrounding the culturally authorized and privileged ministerial elite, subjecting them to the same sort of criticism one would vent on an equal or adversary. No wonder, then, Welde's lamentation: "Now the faithfull Ministers of Christ must have dung cast on their faces, and be no better than Legall Preachers, Baals Priests, Popish factors, Scribes, Pharisees, and Opposers of Christ himselfe."[19]

Why did John Cotton shelter and defend these anticlerical and anti-intellectual bourgeois insurgents? Larzer Ziff, apparently accepting Cotton's account of the controversy at face value, attributes his defense to his doctrinal affinity with the Antinomians as well as his political naïveté. "So long as the doctrine itself was under attack," claims Ziff, "he stood by them, but when it became clear to him—out of their own mouths, as he would have expressed it—that they aimed at a social revolution and were willing even to pervert doctrine to achieve it, he abandoned them."[20] No doubt his colleagues took a similar view of his behavior in the early months of 1636, when they first approached him about the novel opinions and practices circulating among his congregation.[21]

As the Antinomians became increasingly militant in late 1636 and 1637, however, such an interpretation of John Cotton's continued defense of the insurgents must have seemed absurdly charitable at best. Although his clerical colleagues were polite enough not to publicize it, they could hardly have failed to perceive that Cotton was indulging in a power grab vis-à-vis themselves in an attempt to emerge as the "first among equals."[22] In short, Cotton attempted to use the Antinomians in the same fashion that Mao Tse-tung used the Red Guards in his struggle for absolute preeminence against the other members of the inner party elite. The Antinomian insurgents were to delegitimize all or most of the other members of the thinking class while affirming Cotton's supreme charismatic authority. Only the class-conscious response of both ministerial intellectuals and magisterial intelligentsia was sufficient to quell early Massachusetts's cultural revolution.

The prospect of success for such a power play by Cotton must have been quite alluring in early 1636. Cotton's evangelical achievements in the previous two years had contributed to the growing importance and power of Boston in colonywide elections. In 1636, for the first and last time, the two chief magistrates were chosen from among Cotton's congregation in Boston. On May 25, 1636, John Winthrop, whose political life had been rescued two years prior by Cotton, was elected deputy governor. At the same time, gallant young Henry Vane, one of the most ardent friends and admirers of Cotton and Mistress Hutchinson, was chosen governor.[23] Among the assistants Cotton could count both Richard Dummer and William Coddington as firm and dependable allies. At least four of the thirty deputies were well-disciplined cadres in the Antinomian movement, while another four or five were sympathetic fellow travelers.[24] While certainly not a majority of either the magistrates or the deputies, the "core" and "support" groups of Antinomian merchants constituted a significant faction within the government.

Indeed, in many respects, the first half of 1636 was the period of greatest Antinomian success. As previously mentioned, Cotton's charismatic polity arrangements were imposed on the prospective congregants of Dorchester on April 1. This imposition may well have prompted Hooker's trek to the Connecticut Valley on May 31.[25] Hooker's emigration removed Cotton's most distinguished and outspoken opponent on polity issues as well as his greatest intellectual rival. When the General Court created a committee "to make a draught of lawes agreeable to the word of God, which may be the ffundamentalls of this commonwealth," the task naturally devolved upon John Cotton, who presented his "Moses His Judicialls" at the October session of the court.[26]

Nor were the Antinomians idle on the economic front. On the same day that the constitutional committee was created, the court repealed "the act of the last Generall Court that prohibited buyeing commodityes of shipps till leave be graunted."[27] However briefly, the tenor of commercial life would be determined by the three forces of supply, demand, and credit rather than by the exigencies of an outdated moral/economic theory. While this new economic policy liberated the urban bourgeoisie from the constraints of state intervention in trade, it was not intended to liberate other classes and sectors of the economy from such intervention. To make this point clear, at the autumn session of the General Court it was ordered "that the freemen of every towne shall, from time to time, as occasion shall require, agree amongst themselves about the prices & rates of all workmen, laborers, & servants wages; . . . & whosoever shall exceed shalbee punished by the discretion of the Court, according to the quality & measure of the offense."[28] This selective policy of governmental restraint, regulating wages but not prices, indicates a class-conscious economic agenda that Cotton seems to have been entirely unaware of.

Not content with a "free-trade" economic program and a few polity revisions of a charismatic nature, the Antinomians rallied around two basic theological positions that set them at odds with the orthodox thinking class. The more famous of the two by far concerns the Cotton/Hutchinson doctrine of free or unconditional grace. In his "Memoir," Thomas Shepard identified this doctrine as the "principal opinion and seed of all the rest," that is, that "a Christian should not take any evidence of God's special grace and love toward him by the sight of any graces, or conditional evangelical promises to faith or sanctification [what Miller called the federal theology], . . . but it must be without the sight of any grace, . . . by immediate revelation in an absolute promise."[29] In the strictly temporal "order of nature," John Cotton insisted, our justifying "Union with Christ" is complete "before our faith doth put forth itself to lay hold on Him."[30] Richard Mather saw the hand of Satan behind this doctrine, "instilling into the minds of some a conceit that they may be justified not only without their own works but also without the grace of faith."[31] This devilish delusion destroyed the wholesome symmetries of the "federal" covenant theology. Just as works preceded justification in the old covenant of works, claimed Peter Bulkeley, faith must "go before our justification" in the new covenant of faith. "There is a condition" to both covenants, he insisted; "the Lord doth not absolutely promise life unto any."[32]

By arguing that grace was a free or unconditional charismatic experience, the Antinomians challenged the conditional promises of grace that underlay the ethical preparationist preaching of the ministry.[33] In so doing, they earned the title of "antinomian," or opponents of the law. They "deny the use of the Law to any that are in Christ [the charismatically qualified]," averred Thomas Shepard, even as a "rule of Life."[34] Consequently, morally questionable business practices could not undermine the religious qualifications of one "sealed by the Spirit."[35] Indeed, the Antinomians were charged with holding that "to call into question whether God be my deare Father, after or upon the commission of some heinous sinnes, (as Murther, Incest &c) [much less sharp business practices] doth prove a man to be in the Covenant of workes."[36] This allegedly licentious conclusion was, according to the orthodox divines, the result of a false dichotomy between the two covenants. Christ had fulfilled rather than abnegated the covenant of works.[37] Thus the covenant of grace subsumed the old covenant without eliminating it, according to Peter Bulkeley, with the result that "even in the Covenant of Grace, life is promised unto good workes, and to welldoing."[38] Thomas Shepard agreed that "the fundamental error of Antinomians" was their failure to include legal behavior within the "gospel covenant"; "the gospel doth not only require doing, but also as much perfection of doing as the law doth."[39] Understandably, the orthodox divines considered such talk of free grace nothing more than an attempt, in Philip Gura's apt phrase, "to play the saint while knowingly remaining in sin."[40] Whatever its heretical implications, however, this doctrine was tailor-made for an urban bourgeoisie fettered by an agrarian moral code.[41]

If the Antinomians had been satisfied with this position, in addition to their economic agenda, their success might have been more enduring. The conferring of moral/spiritual respectability and increased economic opportunity upon the urban bourgeoisie hardly threatened the edifice of Puritan orthodoxy and the intellectual elite it privileged. Yet it was precisely this relatively privileged status of the thinking class that galled Boston's urban bourgeoisie. To undermine this status, the Antinomians rallied around their other, far more dangerous theological position, namely, that a real distinction existed between the word and spirit of God. "They would talk of the Spirit," recalled Roger Clap, "and of revelations by the Spirit without the Word, as the Quakers do talk of the light within them, rejecting the holy Scriptures."[42] This distinction "betweene the Word of God, and the Spirit of God," according to Edward Johnson, "was onely devised to weaken the Word of the Lord in the mouth of his Ministers, and withall to put ignorant and unlettered Men and Women, in a posture of Preaching to a multitude."[43] This distinction gave rise to the following four "errors" condemned by the Synod of 1637:

Error 9. The whole letter of the Scripture holds forth a covenant of workes. . . .

Error 39. The due search and knowledge of the holy Scripture, is not a safe and sure way of searching and finding Christ. . . .

Error 40. There is a testimony of the Spirit, and voyce unto the Soule, meerely immediate, without any respect unto, or concurrence with the word. . . .

Error 53. No Minister can teach one that is anoynted by the Spirit of Christ, more than hee knowes already unlesse it be in some circumstances.[44]

Such an assault on Puritan biblicism threatened to render the literary hermeneutical skills of the ministry irrelevant in the Protestant salvific scheme. In identifying the word, or logos, with the Holy Ghost, or spirit, orthodox ministers had asserted the indispensability of preaching the word as the necessary cause or "means" of salvation or grace.[45] By denying this identity, the Antinomians not only separated the word/logos from the spirit but also distinguished gracious religious experience—itself the result of the indwelling of the Holy Spirit—from religious culture.[46] This doctrine challenged the fundamental premise that legitimated the system of cultural domination, namely, that biblicist high cultural expertise was a necessary guide to the pious saint's pilgrimage.[47] The Antinomian position threatened the ministry's power and prestige. As King James had seen the truth of the slogan "no bishop, no king," so the orthodox divines understood "no biblicism, no cultural domination." How much more troubling was it, then, when such a damnable heresy was upheld by none other than the preeminent teacher of Boston, John Cotton, and several of his prominent congregants?

The orthodox ministers responded to the promulgation of the Antinomians' second position in early 1636 by attempting to convince Cotton of its dangers and enlist his aid in its suppression. Thomas Shepard, probably at the bequest of his colleagues, sent a polite missive to Cotton that tactfully raised critical questions about his public teaching on the relation between the word and spirit of God.[48] With all due humility, Shepard asked "whether this revelation of the spirit, is a thing beyond and above the woord" and further pointedly inquired "whether tis safe to say; because the spirit is not separated from the woord but in it and is ever according to it."[49] Cotton's response was not reassuring. While admitting that the two could never stand in opposition, he asserted that "above, and beyond the letter of the word it [the spirit] reacheth forth comfort and Power to the soule."[50] There was no acknowledgment of the "unsafety" of preaching such a doctrine, nor any promise to desist from doing so in the future.

Peter Bulkeley was even more direct than Shepard in pressing Cotton to place the preaching of the word of God in the etiology of salvation. Again, Cotton's response was decidedly unsatisfactory. Employing the Aristotelian causal nexus, Cotton stated that "the spirit of God is the principall and net Efficient cause, the word of Grace the Instrumentall Cause" of salvation.[51] Here was a troubling doctrine indeed. Although the "word of grace" was assigned an "instrumental" causal agency, obviously such a novel causal relation (instrumental causes are not part of the Aristotelian or any other causal nexus) was intended as a species of efficient causality.[52] And yet Cotton also stated that the spirit, and not the word, was the "principall and net Efficient cause." Cotton was trying to be conciliatory and offer some role for the cultural con-

tributions of his colleagues in the process of salvation while at the same time denying that they had any "real causal efficacy" in that process. Such a posture could
hardly have assuaged his peers' anxiety.

Apparently, the elders of the Bay Colony tried once more to recover Cotton from
his erroneous ways. Some six years later, in his own "official" account of his role in
the Antinomian controversy, Cotton recalled that in 1636 several of his colleagues
had "advertised me of the evil report that went abroad" of his congregation's heretical tenets.[53] When the particular congregants in question, presumably Hutchinson
and her disciples, were confronted by their teacher, they "utterly denied" the charge.
Consequently, Cotton reported their response and asked his brethren (no doubt assembled at one of their regular classical assemblies), "[W]hat course would you then
advise me to take?"[54] They desired that he preach against the doctrines at issue, which
he claimed to have promptly done to the satisfaction of his peers.

While Cotton's account must be used with great caution—at best he is selective
in his reportage, and at worst he is mendacious—many of the events he recounted
probably did occur. It was, after all, a common Puritan practice to reduce heresy and
error by public confrontation and admonition once private conferences (correspondence in this case) had proved ineffective. Particularly in the case of such a prestigious and preeminent divine, Cotton's peers would have taken great pains to forcefully state their objections to both of the novel doctrines circulating within the church
of Boston. The ministers may have tactfully ascribed these heresies to certain laypersons in Boston's congregation, as Cotton claimed in 1642. That Cotton preached
against these doctrines and their advocates, however, is made dubious by his colleagues' subsequent request that he "bear witness with us against those opinions
which shall appear to be false, and the defenders thereof: for we need, not only your
Consent with us in the truth, but your seasonable reproof of those that dissent."[55]

Having failed to reduce Cotton and enlist his aid, the Bay ministers had no recourse but to invoke the aid of the colonial government in the suppression of this
dangerous heresy. The ministers assembled at Boston during the October 1636 session of the General Court "and entered conference in private with them."[56] John Cotton and the Reverend John Wheelwright, a recent arrival and brother-in-law of Anne
Hutchinson, were present at this meeting. Both attempted to defend themselves and
"gave satisfaction . . . as they all did hold, that sanctification did help to evidence
justification." Although they continued to quibble on the more serious doctrine concerning "the indwelling of the Holy Ghost," it quickly became apparent that, at this
juncture at least, it was not Cotton and Wheelwright the ministers were after.[57] As
Hugh Peter later testified, the clergy told Cotton that they had come to Boston to
charge Hutchinson with fomenting Antinomian doctrines, "for the spring did then
arise as we did conceive from this gentlewoman, and so we told him."[58] No doubt
the ministers thought that Cotton might still be reclaimed by making an example of
this spirited woman.

At this point Cotton interceded on Hutchinson's behalf. Arguing that it was "not
according to God to commend this to the magistrates," he arranged for a private conference at his house between Hutchinson and her ministerial opponents.[59] While the
exact proceedings of this conference were the source of considerable controversy at
Hutchinson's subsequent trial, a few basic events were confirmed by all of the wit-

nesses. After a brief period of reticence and inhibition, Anne Hutchinson drew an invidious distinction between the covenant of grace held by Cotton and Wheelwright and the covenant of works espoused by the other Bay divines. Furthermore, she argued that the "ground" of this doctrinal error lay in their inadequate "sealing by the spirit." "I acknowledge using the words of the apostle to the Corinthians," Hutchinson claimed at her trial, "that they that were ministers of the letter and not the spirit [all of the ministers save Cotton and Wheelwright] did preach a covenant of works."[60] Finally, Cotton recalled expressing his sorrow that Hutchinson was so uncharitable in her characterization of his peers: "I told her I was very sorry that she put comparisons between my ministry and their's, for she had said more than I could myself, and rather I had that she had put us in fellowship with them and not have made the discrepancy. She said, she found the difference."[61]

While the exact wording and intonation of these statements remain uncertain, there could be no doubt as to the meaning and implication of this confrontation. Hutchinson's decision to take the offensive against her clerical opponents rather than retract her objectionable views signaled the final break between the thinking class and the Antinomian bourgeois insurgents. Even more portentous was Cotton's response, or rather lack of response, to Hutchinson's overt challenge to their legitimacy. Given the repression that had been threatened and eventually invoked against Roger Williams, one of their colleagues, Cotton should have been aware that anything less than a public denunciation and censure would be interpreted by his clerical brethren as giving aid and comfort to the enemy. In the ensuing class conflict between the dominant thinking class and the Antinomian bourgeoisie of Boston, there could be no neutral third parties. From that point on, Cotton could no longer be considered part of the forces of orthodoxy by his ministerial peers.

Once the battle lines had been drawn, the Antinomians quickly moved to strengthen their position within the church of Boston. On October 30, less than a week after the aforementioned conference with Hutchinson, several members of the congregation nominated John Wheelwright to the office of pastor. As David Hall has noted, this move was not simply an attempt to ordain another minister sympathetic to the bourgeois insurgents but was "clearly meant to insult—and replace—Wilson."[62] No doubt aware of the dangerous implications of this nomination, Winthrop interceded on Wilson's behalf. Pointing out the obvious fact that they already had a pastor (the collective wisdom of the colony did not sanction having more than one clergyman per office), Winthrop could not accede to Wheelwright's nomination, "seeing he was apt to raise doubtful disputations."[63] Given the unanimity required to confer charismatic authority, there was nothing the vast majority of congregants could do in the face of Winthrop's determined dissent.[64] Realizing that they could not supply him with a clerical office in the church of Boston, the Antinomians proffered Wheelwright "for the preaching for a church gathering at Mt. Wallystone."[65]

After the failed attempt by the opinionists to "pack the pulpit" in Boston, the Antinomian controversy moved to the political arena. On December 7, Governor Henry Vane informed the General Court that pressing business required his immediate presence in England. The orthodox majority accepted his resignation, politely noting the reluctance with which they parted with such a distinguished chief executive.[66] Suddenly the emotional young Vane lost his composure:

> [T]he governour brake forth into tears, and professed, that howsoever the causes propounded for his departure were such as did concern the utter ruin of his outward estate, yet he would rather have hazarded all, than have gone from them [the court] at this time, if something else had not pressed him more, viz. the inevitable danger he saw of God's judgement to come upon us for these differences and dissensions, which he saw amongst us.[67]

Given Vane's recent vocal support of Anne Hutchinson's heresies, this confession "contained the implication," as Hall put it, "that her indictment of the ministers was correct."[68] The court responded to this barb by declaring that "it would not be fit to give way to his departure upon these grounds."[69] Vane promptly pulled himself together, apologized for his rash emotional outburst, and reiterated the urgency of the private business that beckoned in England. Once again, the court graciously "consented to his departure."[70] Not only were they rid of this heretical magistrate, but also they had succeeded in teaching him, and hopefully his fellow opinionists, a lesson in manners.

When news of Vane's rash and somewhat cowardly resignation—he was, after all, deserting his allies in the heat of battle—reached the Antinomians in the church of Boston, they hurriedly met to undo the governor's blunder. No doubt realizing the immense advantage that control of the colony's chief magistracy afforded them, they sent a note to their errant young cohort informing him that they "did not apprehend the necessity" of his departure.[71] Presumably John Cotton had been a party to this counsel, for Vane informed the magistrates and deputies that "notwithstanding the license of the court, yet, without the leave of the church, he durst not go away." The court resolved that "the best way for avoiding trouble" was to allow Vane to remain in office until the Court of Elections in May.[72] In the meantime, at least, the Antinomians would continue to control the chief magistracy.

At this point, the ministers made one last effort to recover John Cotton or at least to clarify their differences with him. They carefully drew up a list of sixteen questions, mostly concerning the relationships between faith and salvation and sanctification and justification, and requested that he reply in writing. It was not Cotton's inflexibility that was most alarming but rather the pugnacious tone of his response. He began by noting that "though I might without Sinne referre you (as our Saviour did the High-Priest when his doctrine was Questioned) to what I have ever taught and spoken openly to the world," yet he would deign to answer their "interrogatories."[73] His colleagues could hardly fail to respond to such a pointed remark. "The truth is," they wrote back, "we have been tender of your honour, and have made conscience of dissenting in the least from you, wherein Truth might not be wounded."[74] Even this mild rebuke failed to budge Cotton from his position on the relation between sanctification and justification in his "rejoynder." Only the charismatic "seal of the Spirit," independent of any sanctifying graces, could give evidence of one's elect status.[75] This position was not only spiritually arrogant—Cotton was, after all, denying any "encouragement" to weak Christians "who gather the evidence of their safe estate from the work of Christ in them"—but also thoroughly illogical. If, as

Cotton and his allies implied, one could acquire sanctifying graces "under the Covenant of workes," noted Peter Bulkeley, "then must we of necessitie change the Articles or promises of the Covenant of Grace, and make the promise of sanctification no part of it." On the other hand, if sanctification was indeed "a blessing of the Covenant of grace," then it followed logically that "it is a warrantable and safe way for a man by and from his sanctification to take an evidence of his justification, and of his estate in Grace before God."[76]

Having failed in all of their private efforts, the elders then turned to the General Court "to advise with them about discovering and pacifying the differences among the churches in point of opinion."[77] No sooner had the deliberations begun than Vane erupted in a fit of anger. He objected that the ministers had already commenced a correspondence with Cotton on these very issues, and without the governor's knowledge and permission at that. This time it was the fiery Hugh Peter who cut Vane down to size. Peter told the excitable governor "how it had sadded the ministers' spirits, that he should be jealous of their meetings, or seem to restrain their liberty."[78] Vane, realizing that Peter had turned the tables on him by making him appear to be the enemy of Christian liberty, promptly apologized for his outburst. Peter, however, declined to let Vane off so easily. He told him that "before he came, within less than two years since, the churches were in peace" and "besought him humbly to consider his youth, and short experience in the things of God."[79]

This turn of events emboldened Pastor John Wilson, who had undoubtedly been infuriated by the recent attempt of his congregation to replace him. Wilson took to the offensive, lamenting the sad condition of the Bay churches and "the inevitable danger of separation." Wilson blamed this state of affairs "upon the new opinions risen up amongst us" and, by implication, the opinionists who espoused them. Not surprisingly, Wilson's speech was met with approval from all of those assembled with the exception of Cotton, Wheelwright, and their Antinomian allies in the court.[80] The court ended its session by calling for a public fast to consider these dissensions the next month.

Once outside of the friendly confines of the General Court, Wilson was subjected to the wrath of his foes in the church of Boston. Cotton was particularly incensed by his colleague's speech and brought the issue up to the congregation for censure. Wilson blandly defended his right to speak the truth as he saw it when requested by the political authorities. Vane was not at all assuaged by this argument and, as Winthrop put it, "pressed it violently against him."[81] Once again Winthrop interceded, claiming that he "could see no breach of rule" in Wilson's behavior. Lacking the unanimity necessary for a formal church censure of Wilson, Cotton was limited to delivering a sharp rebuke, and "not without some appearance of prejudice" at that.[82]

The next and most vociferous public attack on the forces of orthodoxy occurred on January 19, 1637. On the very fast day appointed by the General Court for healing the dissensions in the churches, John Wheelwright ascended the pulpit of Boston and delivered an incendiary sermon calling for Antinomian militancy in the ongoing struggle with the orthodox. He began by noting that the call for a fast was often a tactic used by the most backward of Christians. "Many tymes those that are the least acquainted with the Lord Jesus are given most of all to fasting," stated Wheelwright, adding that "the Papists are given much to fasting and punish themselves by whipping."[83] After drawing this decidedly unflattering comparison with his enemies, he issued a stirring call to action: "The second action we must performe and the second way we must take is, When enimyes to the truth oppose the wayes of God, we must lay load upon them, we must kill them with the word of the Lord."[84] To the objection that such action would "cause a combustion" in the civil and church polities, Wheelwright answered, "I must confesse and acknowledge it will do so, but what then? did not Christ come to send fire upon the earth?"[85] With this manifesto, the gauntlet was thrown down by Boston's insurgents.

The Antinomians of Boston were hardly reticent in their response to Wheelwright's call to action. Shortly thereafter, recorded Winthrop, "the members of Boston (frequenting the lectures of other ministers) did make much disturbance by publick questions, and objections to their doctrines."[86] In "laying load upon" the orthodox ministry with "the word of the Lord," the Antinomians violated the ritual code of deference that surrounded the clergy and supported their system of cultural domination. Such an assault on the clergy's culturally privileged status threatened their legitimacy and hence their claim to power. With this assault, the bourgeoisie of Boston declared class war on the dominant ministerial intellectuals.

The thinking class's response was not long in coming. At the March session of the General Court the orthodox ministers and magistrates set in motion the slow but inexorable machinery of ecclesiastic repression. The court commenced by exonerating Wilson in his dispute with the church of Boston.[87] Vane and his allies strongly dissented from this resolution, at which point the other magistrates requested the opinion of the ministers on the subject. The ministers closed ranks with their magisterial class allies, stating that "no member of the court ought to be publicly questioned by a church for any speech in the court, without the license of the court."[88] Recognizing the likelihood that Boston's church would remain intransigent and refuse to cooperate with the General Court, the ministers strengthened the magistrates' hand. "In all such heresies or errours of any church members as are manifest and dangerous to the state," declaimed the clergy (with, of course, the notable exception of John Cotton), "the court may proceed without tarrying for the church."[89] Indeed, it was the unavoidable "dutie of highest civil authoritie," wrote Thomas Cobbet, "to restrain and punish corruptions and abuses in religion."[90]

Before dealing with Wheelwright, the court decided to make an example of one of his cohorts, perhaps to make clear to him the gravity of his situation. Stephen Greensmith, a merchant of Boston, was charged with "affirming that all the ministers (except Mr. Cotton, Mr. Wheelwright, & hee thought Mr. Hooker) did teach a covenant of works."[91] Greensmith was duly convicted and sentenced to pay a substantial fine and give ritual penance for his cultural crimes.[92] Requiring such an act of obeisance not only repaired the cultural deference and prestige of the beleaguered ministry but also humiliated and debased the urban bourgeois rebel. After passing sentence, the court adjourned until the next morning, thus giving Wheelwright time to consider the meaning of the day's events.

Whatever message the trial of Stephen Greensmith was meant to send, it fell on deaf ears. At about the same time that Wheelwright arrived at the court on the morning of March 10, the magistrates were presented with a petition from the church of

Boston. The church members requested first that "as free-men they might be admitted to be present in the Court in causes of judicature." The court responded that while all judicial proceedings were by custom public, pretrial investigations would be held in private at the discretion of the court. The petitioners also questioned "whether they [the court] might proceed in cases of conscience, without referring them first to the Church." Having received a vote of confidence from the ministers on this very question the day before, the magistrates curtly replied that "when any matter of conscience should come before them, they would advise what were fit to be done in it."[93] This, however, was not an infringement on conscience, perhaps because, as Thomas Cobbet held, when heretics maintained positions "manifestly crosse to the Word" and after "due means of conviction," such dissidents "become sinners against their own consciences."[94] Wheelwright, for his part, was as defiant as ever and refused to answer any questions that might incriminate him. Unable to gather any damaging evidence from his testimony, the court dismissed him until his trial later that day.

When Wheelwright returned to the court that afternoon, he may well have been surprised to find, assembled among the court, the other elders of the colony, who had been summoned to offer their counsel. If so, he was probably not half as surprised as they were when he was followed into the room by a large throng of supporters from the church of Boston.[95] Emboldened by the presence of his fellow opinionists, Wheelwright openly acknowledged that he had meant his doctrinal opponents when he spoke, in his sermon, of "Herod, who would have killed Christ so soon as he was born; Pilate, who did kill Christ when he once came to show forth himself."[96] No doubt flabbergasted by Wheelwright's defiant posture and the vociferous support of his allies in the gallery, the court prudently adjourned the day's proceedings and requested that the ministers consider the following question for the next day: "Whether by that which you have heard concerning Master Wheelwright's Sermon, and that which was witnessed concerning him, yee doe conceive that the Ministers in this Country doe walke in and teach such a way of Salvation and evidencing thereof, as he describeth, and accounteth to be a Covenant of workes?"[97]

As expected, all of the ministers save John Cotton agreed with the statement that it was, in fact, their wholesome doctrines that Wheelwright had slanderously labeled a "covenant of workes." They further testified, again with the notable exception of the teacher of Boston, to "the great dangers that the Churches and Civill State were falne into, by the differences which were grown amongst us in matters of Religion."[98] With the legitimating sanction of the ministers in hand, the court promptly found Wheelwright guilty of contempt of civil authority and sedition.[99] His sentencing, however, was deferred until the next court so that he might still recant his errors and receive the clemency of the inner party. Vane and his co-opinionists in the court asked that their dissent from these proceedings be entered in the records of the court. Their request was curtly denied.

Vane then proffered a petition/remonstrance signed by over forty members of the church of Boston, "which, because it wholly justified Mr. Wheelwright, and condemned the proceedings of the court, was rejected."[100] The incendiary nature of Boston's Antinomian dissent is revealed in certain thinly veiled threats in the remonstrance: "We have not drawn the sword, as sometimes Peter did, rashly, neither have we rescued our innocent brother, as sometimes the Israelites did Jonathan, and yet they did not seditiously." Nor was their tone toward the constituted authorities any less truculent and unflattering. "Farther, we beseech you, remember the old method of Satan, the ancient enemy of free grace in all ages of the churches," they wrote in an obvious reference to their opponents, "who hath raised up such calumnies against the faithful prophets of God."[101] Perceiving the unabated and incendiary Antinomian sentiment in Boston, the court agreed to hold the upcoming Court of Elections in Newtown.[102]

In the following months, the Antinomian forces remained defiant in the face of imminent repression from the orthodox inner party elite. On April 6, the church of Concord held a fast day for the ordination of their chosen elders, Peter Bulkeley and John Jones. Conspicuous in their absence from this gathering of church emissaries were the Antinomians of Boston: "The governour, and Mr. Cotton, and Mr. Wheelwright, and the two ruling elders of Boston, and the rest of that church, which were of any note, did none of them come to this meeting. The reason was conceived to be, because they accounted these as legal preachers, and therefore would give no approbation to their ordination."[103] Yet as alarming as this ecclesiastic boycott was, it paled in comparison to the wild antics and bizarre putsch attempt of the Antinomians at the Court of Elections!

Winthrop recorded that the Antinomians "expected a great advantage that day" in the colonywide elections.[104] If so, when they arrived in Newtown in the early afternoon of May 17, they must have been bitterly disappointed. The orthodox ministry had campaigned actively and with great effect outside of Boston. Seeing the likelihood of imminent electoral defeat, Vane attempted to forestall, if not forego, the outcome. He moved that the remonstrance submitted by the church of Boston, which had been rejected at the last session of the court, be read aloud and discussed before any ballots were cast. Winthrop objected to this ploy. The purpose of this assembly was "a court for elections," he stated, "and those must first be despatched, and then their petitions should be heard."[105] Vane and his supporters were adamant and attempted an electoral filibuster by refusing to "proceed to election, except the petition were read."[106]

In the face of this unprecedented stance, the orthodox majority of electors milled about the open field where the election was to be held in a state of confusion. Before control of the day's events slipped away, Pastor John Wilson dramatically seized the moment. Climbing upon the limb of a large oak tree, Wilson addressed the assembled freemen and their representatives, "advising the people to look to their charter and to consider the present work of the day, which was designed for the chusing the governor, deputy governor and the rest of the assistants for the government of the commonwealth."[107] The crowd responded warmly to Wilson's call with cries of "election." Winthrop then called for a vote to decide whether they ought to proceed to election or first read the remonstrance, and "the greater number by many were for election."[108]

Vane and his allies nonetheless refused to participate in the elections unless they were first allowed to read their petition. Having reached the end of his tether, Winthrop pointedly informed Vane that "if he would not go to election, he and the rest of that side would proceed" without him.[109] Once their bluff had been called, the Antinomians had no choice but to participate and make the best of a bad situation.

Even so, they could hardly have been prepared for the drubbing they received. Not only was Vane replaced as governor by Winthrop, but also all three of the Antinomian magistrates—Vane, Coddington, and Dummer—were, in the words of the newly elected chief magistrate, "left quite out" of office in the new court.[110]

Incensed by their humiliating defeat, the Antinomians showed no sign of accepting the results of the election. They "grew into fierce speeches," no doubt declaiming the nefarious nature of their opponents. Apparently, this show of self-righteous spleen escalated into an attempted putsch, as the insurgents "laid hands on" their opponents. This was a most furtive and desperate move, for they were at best a sizable minority, and upon "seeing themselves too weak, they grew quiet."[111] Yet for all its opéra bouffe absurdity, the import of this violent fit of pique was hardly lost on the newly elected orthodox regime.

Why was the Antinomians' electoral campaign so singularly unsuccessful outside of their urban stronghold? In class terms, the election results are a clear example of conflicting economic interests between the mercantile bourgeoisie and the rural yeoman majority. Like all merchants, the grand bourgeoisie of the seaports derived their middleman's profit in two transactive "moments," one in the purchase of agricultural products for export and the other in the sale of imported commodities.[112] In both of these moments, their profits presumably came at the expense of the rural yeomanry, who produced the vast bulk of the agricultural products and consumed the lion's share of the imported articles. This sharp conflict of interests in transactive terms stood in stark contrast to the apparent identity of interest among the yeomanry and the thinking class. It was their dual class membership—that is, as noted earlier, that many members of the thinking class held their wealth in the form of large tracts of land—that dictated that they would stand in the exact same trade relations with the urban merchants as their yeomen fellow townsmen. Hence their unique ability to claim to "represent" the interests of the small farmers who made up a vast majority of the freemen. It should come as no surprise that one of the first substantive acts of the new General Court was to resolve that "[t]he former order of selling corne at five shillings the bushell, for the time to come, is revoked, & the price of corne is set at liberty."[113]

That the colonywide election had resulted in the utter defeat of the Antinomians and the complete vindication of their political opponents was undeniable, yet the forces of insurgency and dissent continued to be as intransigent as ever. When the previously convicted Wheelwright was summoned before the newly elected magistrates and deputies, they graciously deferred his sentencing until their next session so that he might have time "to bethink himself, that, retracting and reforming his errour, &c. the court might show him favour."[114] Wheelwright remained as truculent as before, stating that "if he had committed sedition, then he ought to be put to death." Furthermore, he declared that if the orthodox regime "did mean to proceed against him, he meant to appeal to the king's court, for he could retract nothing."[115] Before adjourning the session of the court, the deputies and magistrates passed an antialien act designed to quarantine the Antinomian infection by not allowing any more like-minded immigrants to settle in the colony.[116]

Nor was Wheelwright alone in his continued defiance. The honor guard from Boston that had previously attended Governor Vane refused to extend the like courtesy to the newly elected Winthrop. Indeed, Winthrop was increasingly isolated in both the church and town of Boston. On May 24, Vane and Coddington refused to sit with Winthrop on the bench reserved for the magistracy, even after he personally invited them to sit there. Furthermore, on a day appointed for a public fast, they "went from Boston to keep the day at the Mount with Mr. Wheelwright."[117] Less than two months later, in early July, Vane not only refused an invitation to a dinner given by Governor Winthrop but also had the audacity and bad manners to carry away the intended guest of honor, the visiting Puritan Lord Ley.[118]

The Puritan regime had reached a fundamental impasse. Measures that had succeeded in dealing with previous dissident movements had utterly failed against the Antinomians. While clerical conferences and cajoling had recovered ministers George Phillips and John Eliot from their errors, Cotton proved far more recalcitrant. In the case of Salem's separatists, state repression of a clerical ringleader and censure of a prominent layman—Roger Williams and John Endecott, respectively— brought the town and its congregation into line. Similar actions against John Wheelwright and Stephen Greensmith left Boston's opinionists as defiant as ever. The Antinomians were clearly a far more formidable foe than anything the regime had faced before. Largely protected and sanctioned by the colony's most famous intellectual, John Cotton, the bourgeois insurgents of Boston drew on the élan and self-assurance that come with charismatic authority. Such a thoroughly pugnacious and self-confident group could not be recovered through the relatively tolerant and patient use of civil authority that had characterized previous religious conflicts. This case demanded an unprecedented level of repression in the Bay. In order to legitimate this exercise of power, the magistrates sought a source of cultural sanction far in excess of anything that had been offered or available previously. The suppression of Antinomian dissent required the authority of New England's first full-blown synod.

4

ANTINOMIANISM DEFEATED

The unabated truculence of the Antinomian insurgents left the General Court little choice when it met in early August. No doubt with the concurrence of the clerical elders who had converged at the court, it ordered the first synod in the history of New England to be convened in Newtown on August 30. Careful preparations were required to confer upon this dramatic ecclesiastic exercise the desired cultural-sanctioning effect. An invitation was extended to all orthodox ministers throughout New England, including the recently arrived John Davenport.[1] Moreover, all ruling elders and magistrates could attend, thus turning the synod into a virtual party plenum or convocation of the entire inner party.

For this assemblage to have sufficient cultural authority to silence such determined opinionists as the Antinomians of Boston, all resolutions would have to be unanimous. While Wheelwright's dissent might safely be ignored because he had recently been convicted of sedition and was thus an interested party, Cotton's could not; hence, as Hall put it, "reconciliation between Cotton and the other ministers became imperative."[2] Shepard had begun this process at the Court of Elections, where he "preached a sermon in which he reduced the points at issue."[3] Specifically, Shepard stated three propositions to which both Cotton and his orthodox peers could agree. The first was that "justification and sanctification were both together in time," thus averting the question of causal precedence in the "order of nature." The second proposition was a concession to Cotton's religious psychology, which stated that "a man must know himself to be justified, before he can know himself to be sanctified." The third proposition was the most important, at least to the orthodox majority. In agreeing that "the spirit never witnesseth justification without a word and a work," John Cotton had been forced to acknowledge the indispensability of the hermeneutical skills that underlay cultural domination and the religious significance of preparatory "work."[4] In the weeks before the synod, the ministers held several meetings to resolve the personal differences between Wilson, on the one hand, and Cotton and Wheelwright, on the other. These meetings were relatively successful, as Wilson politely stated that "by his speech in the court, he did not intend the doctrine of Mr. Cotton and Mr. Wheelwright" but rather other opinions held by private persons in and around Boston. The teacher of Boston accepted the gesture graciously, "and accordingly Mr. Cotton declared so much in the congregation the Lord's day following."[5] While the theological issues had not been entirely "reduced," at least amicable relations had been restored.

Shepard published a fairly rosy account of the synod's proceedings in his memoir: "[B]y the help of all the elders joined together, those errors, through the grace and power of Christ, were discovered, the defenders of them convinced and ashamed, the truth established, and the consciences of the saints settled; there being a most powerful presence of Christ's spirit in that Assembly, held at Cambridge anno 1637, about August, and continued a month together, in publick agitations."[6] In fact, however, the synod was far more rancorous and tumultuous.

No sooner had the aforementioned "errors" been presented (eighty-two in all) than the Antinomian messengers of Boston took offense "at the producing of so many errours . . . and called to have the persons named, which held these errours."[7] The moderators, Thomas Hooker and Peter Bulkeley, declined to name anyone since the synod was to deal with doctrinal issues, not persons. The Antinomians were not mollified and continued to express their dissatisfaction, even after the moderators had enjoined their silence.

At this point the magistrates stepped into the breach, no doubt led by Winthrop, and warned that "if they would not forbear [speech], it would prove a civil disturbance, and then the magistrate must interpose." The Antinomians objected that the magistrates lacked any authority in such ecclesiastic affairs and thus "the magistrate has nothing to do in this assembly." Winthrop pointedly responded that "if he would not forbear, but make trial of it, he might see it executed."[8] Having come upon an immovable object in the person of John Winthrop, the assembled Antinomian delegates "contemptuously with[drew] themselves from the generall Assembly," never to return.[9]

This defiant ecclesiastic boycott apparently had a chastening effect on Cotton. In his "Way of the Congregational Churches Cleared," he recalled being shocked at this juncture "that some of the members and messengers of our church, were ready to rise up, and plead in defense of sundry corrupt opinions, which I verily thought had been far from them."[10] Be that as it may, Cotton's willingness to conform to the judgment of his peers was sharply attenuated. While he openly acknowledged "some of the opinions to be blasphemous: some of them heretical, many of them erroneous," when the synod took up the relationship between the habit of faith and the act of justification, Cotton proved somewhat less accommodating.[11]

The very "marrow of Puritan divinity," according to the venerable Perry Miller, was a "federal" or covenant theology.[12] This theology, which found expression in the "preparationist" preaching of the orthodox majority, stipulated that if unregenerate man would but engage in a sincere and solemn quest for the "habit of faith," God would respond by "justifying" the sinner as part of a contractual agreement known as the covenant of grace.[13] Even such spiritistically inclined ministers as John Norton acknowledged that while the decree of election was absolute, "yet the Dispensation of the Decree in the Gospel is conditional. That indefinite Proposition, *Whosoever believes, shall be saved.* is equivalent unto that conditional, *If you believe, you shall be saved."*[14] This was no abstruse question of theological niceties as Miller well knew, for this agreement had profound implications for polity issues. It was precisely because God usually bestowed his justifying grace on those who sincerely sought the habit of faith that the cultural virtuosity that evidenced this yearning could be used as evidence of election and hence church membership and political enfranchisement. The practical result was, in the words of Miller, that "[t]he proof of election will be in the trying, not the achieving."[15]

Clearly this doctrine was an important theological legitimation of the system of cultural domination. Underscoring its importance, Cotton Mather employed graphic, if somewhat melodramatic, language in his description of that "dark day in the synod, wherein Mr. Cotton, with the great Chamins, seemed to assert, 'that the habit of faith in us, is the effect of our justification' and solemn speeches were made with tears, lamenting it that they should in this important matter dissent from a person so venerable and considerable in the countrey."[16] Cotton, in effect, reversed the terms of Norton's conditional proposition so that it now read: "If you are saved, then you shall believe." Since the opinion of "so venerable and considerable" a divine could not be ignored or dispensed with, a compromise was reached (no doubt after interminable wrangling) whereby neither justification nor the habit of faith was temporally, and hence causally, precedent to the other.[17] While Cotton, unlike Wheelwright, was gracious enough to withhold his dissent from this and the other theological compromises reached at the synod, he was conspicuous among the established divines in his refusal to sign the assembly's report.[18]

Nonetheless, his failure to dissent ensured the fulfillment of the second requirement of cultural domination, that is, that officially authorized bearers of the cultural tradition must always agree in their public formulations or at least not disagree. Issues dealing with other requirements of cultural domination, as well as general polity questions, were left until the final day of the synod.[19] In order to limit unauthorized and possibly challenging venues of cultural expression, a resolution was passed to curb a particularly threatening Antinomian practice:

> 1. That though women might meet (some few together) to pray and edify one another; yet such a set assembly, (as was then in practise at Boston,) where sixty or more did meet every week, and one woman (in a prophetical way, by resolving questions of doctrine, and expounding scripture) took upon her the whole exercise, was agreed to be disorderly, and without rule.[20]

To further guarantee that the minister's speech acts were afforded the greatest deference and ritual respect available, the synod agreed:

> 2. Though a private member might ask a question publickly, after sermon, for information; yet this ought to be very wisely and sparingly done, and that with leave of the elders: but questions of reference, (then in use,) whereby the doctrines delivered were reproved, and the elders reproached, and that with bitterness, &c, was utterly condemned.[21]

The synod then considered the potential case of a congregant who engaged in an "ecclesiastical boycott" of church authority by simply refusing to attend a given church meeting and participate in the "cultural charade," a tactic employed with some frequency by the Antinomians. The orthodox majority agreed that such a person "might be proceeded against, though absent; yet it was held better, that the magistrates' help were called for, to compel him to be present."[22] Finally, to curtail the "excessive" invocation of conscience, the assembly agreed to one last proviso:

> 4. That a member, differing from the rest of the church in any opinion, which was not fundamental, ought not for that to forsake the ordinances there; and if such did desire dismission to any other church, which was of his opinion, and did it for that end, the church whereof he was ought to deny if for the same end.[23]

On September 22 the synod at long last concluded its sessions at Newtown and dissolved.[24] The orthodox inner party elite had to feel gratified; the Antinomians' disruptive practices and heretical tenets had been roundly condemned, and consensus had been achieved around several important theological compromises. While the proceedings were far from idyllic, Winthrop later recalled that "there was great hope, that the late general assembly would have had some good effect in pacifying the troubles and dissensions about matters of religion."[25] Indeed, according to Joseph Felt, "the country at large" expected that "the late synod would calm the controversy of the Legalists and Antinomians."[26] If so, the continued truculence of the forces of dissent in Boston must have been the cause of bitter disappointment.

Not only did the Antinomians fail to acknowledge and recant their errors—despite the fact that they "had been clearly confuted and confounded in the assembly"—but they also resolutely "persisted in their opinions, and were as busy in nourishing contentions (the principal of them) as before."[27] The orthodox inner party had employed every means at its disposal against the Antinomian insurgents, all to no avail. When the General Court assembled on November 2, they had no choice but to reach for the weapon of last resort and purge the dissidents from the party and the body politic. In a most disarmingly frank passage in his *Journal,* Winthrop recorded the orthodox majority's decision to purge the Antinomians and the forthright manner in which they went about it:

> [T]he general court, being assembled . . . and finding, upon consultation, that two so opposite parties could not contain in the same body, without apparent hazard of ruin to the whole, agreed to send away some of the principal; and for this a fair opportunity was offered by the remonstrance or petition, which they preferred to the court the 9th of the 1st month [March 9], wherein they affirm Mr. Wheelwright to be innocent, and that the court had condemned the truth of Christ.[28]

Seizing upon this pretext, Winthrop and his colleagues "dismissed from being a member of the Courte" the two merchant Antinomian deputies of Boston, William Aspinwall and John Coggeshall, and "order was given for two new deputies to bee chosen by the towne of Boston."[29] Apparently, the Antinomian electoral majority in Boston was unimpressed by the court's purgative measures, for "they intended to have sent the same men again." Now Cotton, for the first time in the controversy, restrained his disciples and convinced them to send two other deputies to Newtown.[30] Even then, however, they remained defiant; one of their two new deputies, Sergeant John Oliver, had signed the petition on behalf of John Wheelwright. He was summarily dismissed by the court.[31]

The ensuing wave of repression that the orthodox court sent crashing upon the Antinomian dissidents has received ample historical treatment and analysis. On the whole, the interpretations have been fairly sympathetic to the Antinomians and have viewed the purge and repression initiated by the court as a slightly hysterical over-reaction.[32] Be that as it may, what seems most remarkable was the extreme, almost dangerous leniency of the court's actions, a leniency that suggests the guiding hand of John Winthrop. The Antinomians had continually defied the will of the duly elected government of the colony (and, indeed, had attempted violence against it during the Court of Elections) and subsequently refused to honor the most important symbolic and ecclesiastic assemblage in the brief history of the colony. In short, they remained unwilling to accept the existing system of cultural domination and continued to attempt to undermine it.[33] It is therefore all the more impressive that the court continually offered to all of the dissidents the option to recant and retract their errors and thus earn the clemency of the court. And yet, quite sensibly, the elite were also firm in their resolution; failure to sufficiently recant would result in censure and banishment.

Hence when John Wheelwright was summoned before the court on that November 2, if he had confessed his seditious ways and promised to atone for his past errors, he most likely would have escaped punishment. Instead, he chose to justify "himselfe & his former practise" and even threatened to appeal his conviction to the king. Consequently, Wheelwright was "disfranchized & banished, haveing 14 dayes to settle his affaires."[34] The court then turned to the two ex-deputies of Boston. John Coggeshall, for "disturbing the peace"—he had earlier stated "that Mr. Wheelwright is innocent, & that he was persecuted for the truth"—was "disfranchized, & enjoyned not to speake anything to disturbe the publicke peace, upon paine of banishment."[35] Next was William Aspinwall, who refused to learn from the examples of his immediate predecessors and continued to justify his course and vilify the court. Such behavior, in addition to "his insolent & turbulent carriage," resulted in his disfranchisement and banishment within a month's time.[36] Having dispatched the Antinomians' political and ideological advance guard, the court then summoned their lay "ringleader," Anne Hutchinson.

The trial of Anne Hutchinson is one of the most infamous events in early American history. More than any other proceeding, event, or document, the trial reveals the inner dynamic between the challenge of Antinomian dissent and the response of the orthodox regime. Faced with an unyielding dissident movement that threatened the very foundations of cultural domination, the General Court, like subsequent one-party states, resorted to the dramaturgical rite of a political show trial. The purpose of this show trial was to vindicate the cultural authority of the ministry and the political rectitude of the court.[37] For her part, Hutchinson stoutly challenged the legitimacy of the court and the doctrine of the clergy. Outnumbered and outmatched by New England's assembled dialecticians, however, Hutchinson was eventually forced in desperation to assert her own charismatic authority by way of immediate revelation from the divinity against the superior learning and cultural authority of the ministers and magistrates of the inner party. At that juncture the focus of the trial turned to Cotton's relationship to Hutchinson and his judgment regarding her revelations.

As in all show trials, the guilt of the accused was a foregone conclusion.[38] Winthrop and his fellow elder statesmen were fully aware of Hutchinson's activities and, as the proceedings were to shortly prove, had gathered more than enough evidence to justify, in their minds at least, banishment. In fact, Winthrop never actually accused her of anything in his opening remarks. Instead he simply asserted as a matter of known fact that she had "troubled the peace of the commonwealth and the churches here" and told her that "you are known to be a woman that hath had a great share in the promoting and divulging of those opinions that are causes of this trouble." The purpose of the inquest was not to prove her guilt but rather, he told Hutchinson, to "reduce you that so you may become a profitable member here among us, otherwise if you be obstinate in your course that then the court may take such course that you may trouble us no further."[39] Had Hutchinson recanted, she would have vindicated the position of the ministers and magistrates by acknowledging that her views were erroneous and her practices unwarranted. Her failure to recant allowed the assembled inner party to publicly demonstrate their superior forensic, dialectical, and biblicist skills.[40] Either by acknowledgment or by demonstration, the cultural authority of the ministers and magistrates could only benefit.

Hutchinson's crime was starkly political. Troubling the "peace of the commonwealth and churches" was the seventeenth-century Puritan equivalent of sedition. In his opening statement, Winthrop adduced three particulars of this crime. The first was that she had aided and abetted other dissidents whom "the court had taken notice of and passed censure upon." The reference here was to her "affinity and affection" for Wheelwright and his supporters who had signed the remonstrance in his behalf. Since Wheelwright's fast-day sermon had been condemned as seditious, those who continued to support and befriend him were guilty by association. Hutchinson was also charged with holding an illegal conventicle in her house despite the ban on such meetings by the synod. Such unauthorized cultural expression was not only "not tolerable nor comely in the sight of God" but also inappropriate "for your sex." The most serious particular, however, was that of traducing the ministry. "You have spoken divers things," he stated, "very prejudicial to the honour of the churches and ministers thereof."[41] By denying them their due honor and deference, Hutchinson threatened to desacralize and delegitimize the privileged position of the ministerial intellectuals.

Hutchinson's response to this opening remark was in many ways paradigmatic of what was to follow for much of the trial. "I am called here to answer before you," she stated, "but I hear no things laid to my charge."[42] Fully aware of the political nature of the trial, Hutchinson attempted to highlight it by pointing out the absence of any legal wrong doing on her part. There was, in fact, no written law banning fraternization with condemned criminals, holding private meetings (with or without synodic sanction), or even showing contempt toward the ministry. While no state needs a written law banning seditious activities in order to legally protect itself, the charges against Hutchinson did not amount to sedition in any obvious sense. The Antinomians had never tried to subvert the charter—the supposed constitutional framework— or even change the institutional structure of the government. Rather, they attempted to challenge the regime or party that controlled the government. Hutchinson's point in her opening statement was that she was on trial simply for organized opposition to the ruling regime. Her problem, however, lay in the fact that in a political community without the notion of legitimate or loyal opposition, the distinction between political dissent and sedition is tenuous at best. Her case was hardly made any stronger by the recent electoral victory of the orthodox. Indeed, the strange putsch attempt of the Antinomians during that election, coupled with their inaction during the Pequot campaign, raised serious doubt about just how loyal the Antinomian opposition really was.

Winthrop may well have been shocked that, once charged, this plucky woman proceeded to defend her own actions and question the wisdom of the General Court and the recently convened synod. It was not long into the proceeding when he was forced to remind her, "[W]e are your judges, and not you ours."[43] Despite her determined defiance, the magistrates and ministers were able to direct the proceedings to right where they wanted. The sequence of events is fairly straightforward, and the whole "trial" can be reduced quite easily to five distinct "stages." The first three stages comprised the "proof" of Hutchinson's errors in theory and practice. It was precisely because these innings were dominated by the cultural expertise of the regime that Hutchinson tried to derail the proceeding in the fourth stage. This unsuccessful attempt ultimately served to further legitimate the position of the orthodox and raise serious questions about Cotton's role and position within the colony.

In the first stage (directly after the opening remarks), Winthrop questioned Hutchinson about her relationship with Wheelwright and others convicted of sedition by the court. To the charge of aiding and abetting such enemies of the state—"[Y]ou did harbour and countenance those that are parties in this faction," Winthrop pointedly informed her—she blandly replied, "That's matter of conscience, Sir." No doubt stunned by the audacity of her reply, Winthrop attempted to remind her of the important nature of the proceedings. "Your conscience you must keep or it must be kept for you" he said, no doubt hoping that this warning would intimidate her and force her to recant. His threat was in vain. The first stage ended without any recantation on Hutchinson's part.[44]

In the second stage, Winthrop and Hutchinson discussed the two public lectures held weekly at her house "whereto sixty or eighty persons did usually resort."[45] Although such assemblies, and hers in particular, had been condemned by the synod roughly two months previously, she not only admitted to persisting in such forbidden practices but also attempted to justify them on biblical grounds. A standard account of this exchange accurately states that "she quoted two passages of Scripture: Titus II, 3–5, which indicated that the elder women should instruct the younger, and Acts XVIII, 26, wherein Aquila and Priscilla 'tooke upon them to instruct Apollo, more perfectly, yet he was a man of good parts, but they being better instructed might teach him.'"[46] But as Winthrop quite clearly saw, the citation from Acts could hardly be used to justify her gatherings. "See how your argument stands," he said, patiently trying to reason with her: "Priscilla with her husband, tooke Apollo home to instruct him privately, therefore Mistris Hutchinson without her husband may teach sixty or eighty."[47]

While Hutchinson's venomous reply showed no lack of wit—"Must I shew my name written therein?"—she was quite mistaken if she thought she had the better of the argument. Winthrop's comment was quite accurate and to the point. Indeed,

Hutchinson quickly recognized this and cleverly dropped the argument from Acts and claimed instead that the custom of private gatherings between neighboring women "was in practice before I came" and "therefore I was not the first."[48] For the first time in the proceedings, Endecott interjected: "You say there are some rules unto you. I think there is a contradiction in your own words. What rule for your practice do you bring, only a custom in Boston."[49] Hutchinson, realizing that neither her citation from Acts nor the appeal to custom could legitimize her practice, retreated from her earlier arguments and staked her claim entirely on the citation from Titus: "No Sir that was no rule to me but if you look upon the rule in Titus it is a rule to me. If you convince me that it is no rule I shall yield."[50]

Here was a great opportunity to reduce and perhaps reclaim this strong-willed woman, for the citation from Titus was remarkably patriarchal in nature and in no way sanctioned the sort of activities that Hutchinson engaged in during her meetings.[51] Winthrop carefully built the argument with her. "You know that there is no rule that crosses another," he told her, "but this rule crosses that in the Corinthians." On this point Winthrop knew he had her, for Corinthians 14:34–35 is quite specific in its injunction:

> Let your women keep silence in the churches; for it is not permitted unto them to speak: but they are commanded to be under obedience, as also saith the law.
> And if they will learn any thing, let them ask their husbands at home: for it is a shame for women to speak in the church.

Winthrop then went on to explain the obvious "surface" meaning of the citation in Titus, namely, that "elder women must instruct the younger about their business, and to love their husbands and not to make them to clash."[52] If Winthrop thought such careful reasoning would have an ameliorating effect on Hutchinson he was sorely mistaken. She dryly answered that she "did not conceive but that it is meant for some publick times." No doubt taken aback by the aplomb with which she pronounced such a "strong misreading," the befuddled Winthrop blurted, "Well, have you no more to say but this?" "I have said sufficient for my purpose," she curtly replied.[53] While the second stage had been no more successful than the first in bringing a recantation, on both particulars the court had been able to make its case and display its superior training and rectitude.

In the third stage of the examination, Deputy Governor Thomas Dudley pressed Hutchinson on the most serious charge against her, "traducing" the ministry of Christ in Massachusetts.[54] "She in particular," he told the court, "hath disparaged all our ministers in the land that they have preached a covenant of works, and only Mr. Cotton a covenant of Grace."[55] Not brooking any of her tangential evasions, the grim Dudley stated, "I will make it plain that you did say that the ministers did preach a covenant of works."[56] In the face of her abrupt denial, he went further, threatening to prove, he told her, "that you said they were not able ministers of the new testament, but Mr. Cotton only." In a fit of uncontrolled pique, Hutchinson defiantly retorted, "If ever I spake that I proved it by God's word!"[57] It very quickly dawned on her, however, that Dudley could indeed prove these allegations on the basis of statements she made in "conference" with the ministers in October of the previous year. "If one shall come unto me in private, and desire me to tell them what I thought of such an one," she stated warily, "I must either speak false or true in my answer." Attempting to draw a distinction between "privileged" private discourse and open public proceedings, she urged that "[i]t is one thing for me to come before a public magistracy and there to speak what they would have me to speak and another when a man come to me in a way of friendship privately there is difference in that." This distinction had little impact as Winthrop pointedly responded that "though things were spoken in private yet now coming to us, we are to deal with them as public."[58] All of the cards were in his hand, and he could interpret the rules in any way that facilitated his goal.

Hugh Peter was the first minister to testify about the proceedings of that October meeting. After noting her initial reticence, Peter recalled that

> she told me that there was a wide and a broad difference between our brother Cotton and our selves. I desired to know the difference. She answered that he preaches a covenant of grace and you the covenant of works, and that you are not able ministers of the new testament and know no more than the apostles did before the resurrection of Christ. I did then put it to her, What do you conceive of such a brother? She answered he had not the seal of the spirit.[59]

Peter's account was directly corroborated, with occasional embellishment, by the Reverends Thomas Weld, George Phillips, Zechariah Symmes, John Wilson, and Thomas Shepard, respectively.[60]

Although she remained defiant in her response—"Prove that I said so"—Hutchinson must certainly have been discomfited by the untoward turn the proceedings had taken.[61] She could hardly expect to gain much credibility or sympathy by simply contradicting the testimony of six established and respected divines. She thus employed two separate maneuvers to wriggle out of her bind. First she tried to undermine the ministers' testimony by subtly changing its wording: "Whereas they say I said they were under a covenant of works [which they in fact never said] and in the state of the apostles why these two speeches cross one another. I might say thay might preach a covenant of works as did the apostles [precisely what they did in fact say], but to preach a covenant of works and to be under a covenant of works is another business."[62] When this ruse failed to impress the colony's assembled dialecticians, she raised an objection about the order in which various speeches were made. Hugh Peter promptly put an end to this quibble. "We do not desire to be so narrow to the court and the gentlewoman about times and season, whether first or after," he interjected, "but said it was."[63] Having failed in both maneuvers, Hutchinson found herself in the precarious bind of being unable to defend herself against the charge of "traducing the ministry" without contradicting the ministers' testimony and thus further traducing them.

Perhaps sensing her vulnerability, Dudley went for the kill. He alleged and threatened to produce testimony to prove that she had publicly professed that most dangerous doctrine of the Antinomians that a real distinction existed between the word and spirit of God.[64] Finally, Hutchinson began to crack under the intense strain of her interrogation. "I acknowledge using the words of the apostle to the Corinthians unto him [Ward]," she confessed, "that they that were ministers of the letter and not the spirit did preach a covenant of works."[65] She further recalled that when asked by

Ward whether their orthodox doctrines might "bee a way too [in addition to her own way] wherein we may have hope," she had replied, "[N]o truly if that be a way it is a way to hell."[66] After this confession Winthrop adjourned the court until the following morning, and as Edmund Morgan has noted, "[W]hen the court adjourned for the day, the evidence against her on this charge looked overwhelming."[67]

When the court convened the next morning, Anne Hutchinson commenced her desperate last stand. Not willing to go down without a fight—much less recant—she questioned the legitimacy of the ministers' testimony, given their "interest" in the controversy: "The ministers come in their own cause. Now the Lord hath said that an oath is the end of all controversy; though there be a sufficient number of witnesses yet they are not according to the word, therefore I desire that they may speak upon oath."[68] Hutchinson placed the ministers in a difficult position. Refusing to testify under oath might imply that their testimony was not sincere and that she had been falsely accused. On the other hand, acquiescing in her request might suggest that at least the grounds existed to question the veracity of their previous statements.[69] It was this latter suggestion that Thomas Shepard took particular exception to, averring that "I know of no reason of the oath but the importunity of this gentlewoman."[70] Given the controversial nature of Hutchinson's request, the court was unable to reach any consensus on the ministerial oath for some time.

Impatient with this impasse, Hutchinson produced three "friendly" witnesses: John Coggeshall, the recently disfranchised deputy of Boston; Thomas Leverett, the ruling elder of the church of Boston; and, of course, the teacher of the church of Boston, John Cotton. Cotton's testimony was potentially the most damaging of all. Should he contradict the other ministers' testimony, such a public breach of clerical unity, particularly by such a preeminent and popular divine, would sorely undermine the legitimacy of the whole proceeding. Thus, when Coggeshall "desired that the elders would confer with Mr. Cotton before they swear," John Endecott turned on him with unconcealed anger. "I will tell you what I say," he replied. "I think that this carriage of your's tends to further casting dirt upon the faces of the judges."[71] But while the court could easily abuse and intimidate an unrepentant lay dissident like Coggeshall, the great John Cotton would have to be handled somewhat more gingerly.

Coggeshall was the first to testify, and his testimony is an excellent, if somewhat stark, reminder of the inquisitorial and largely ritual nature of the proceedings. Coggeshall began by, at least in part, contradicting the testimony of the ministers: "Yes I dare say that she did not say all that which they lay against her."[72] If Coggeshall thought this was a normal English trial, in which he might freely offer his own account of the meeting between the clergy and Hutchinson, instead of a show trial, in which the accused could either confess to her cultural crimes or be purged, he was sorely mistaken. "How dare you look into the court," bellowed the Reverend Hugh Peter, "to say such a word?" At last Coggeshall saw the proverbial "writing on the wall." "Mr. Peters takes upon him to forbid me," he replied. "I shall remain silent."[73] Indeed, that was the end of Coggeshall's testimony.

While the court might peremptorily silence the condemned dissident Coggeshall, Thomas Leverett, who was the next to testify, was the leading lay figure in the church of Boston and heretofore had been thoroughly orthodox. Fortunately for the authorities, his testimony was quite brief and equivocal in impact. Though he corroborated most of the ministers' previous account, he differed from them in his recollection that Hutchinson had only claimed that "they did not preach a covenant of grace so clearly as Mr. Cotton," itself an invidious distinction but not necessarily warranting censure for traducing the ministry. He did, however, remember that the reason she ascribed for their inability was that "as the apostles were for a time without the spirit so until they [all the ministers save Cotton] had received the witness of the spirit they could not preach a covenant of grace so clearly." While this statement gave some limited credence to the contentions of the clerics, Leverett failed to respond to Winthrop's gentle reminder that Hutchinson had claimed that "they were not able ministers of the new testament."[74] Although his testimony did not clear Hutchinson of the charges against her, it did somewhat undermine the more damaging contentions of the ministers on the previous day.

Cotton's testimony was the most important offered until this juncture, and from the moment it commenced until the end of the trial, his role in the proceedings became increasingly pivotal. For the last year he had effectively shielded Hutchinson from the censure of his clerical brethren and their magisterial allies. In the interim, however, a synod had been held that had clearly and publicly condemned her doctrines and practices, and his own potential colleague John Wheelwright had been convicted and banished. Nonetheless, Cotton continued to try to protect her from what everyone else at the court must have clearly seen was her ineluctable fate, conviction and banishment. He recalled that she had distinguished between himself and his colleagues on the ground that "[y]ou preach of the seal of the spirit upon a work and he upon free grace without a work or without respect to a work, he preaches the seal of the spirit upon free grace and you upon a work." While this account might not sound particularly helpful to Hutchinson's defense, Cotton somehow thought it would clear her, for he concluded his opening remark by saying, "I must say that I did not find her saying they were under a covenant of works, nor that she said they did preach a covenant of works."[75]

Morgan has claimed that Cotton "stood his ground" on this account in the face of his colleagues' obvious displeasure, and consequently "the case against Mrs. Hutchinson was about to collapse."[76] On the contrary, not only was Cotton's testimony insufficient to clear Hutchinson—the difference between preaching a covenant of works and what Cotton called preaching the seal of the spirit upon a work was purely semantic—but also he was almost immediately forced to "give ground" by Hugh Peter:

> Mr. Peters. I humbly desire to remember our reverend teacher. May it please you to remember how this came in. Whether do you not remember that she said we were not sealed with the spirit of grace, therefore could not preach a covenant of grace, and she said further you may do it in your judgement but not in experience, but she spake plump we were not sealed.
>
> Mr. Cotton. You do put me in remembrance that it was asked her why cannot we preach a covenant of grace? Why, saith she, because you can preach no more than you know, or to that purpose, she spake.[77]

While Cotton continued to try to defend and help his disciple throughout the rest of the trial, in the exchange quoted above he had been forced to admit that Hutchinson had denied that the ministers preached a covenant of grace and that the reason was that they had no gracious experience. Thus, contrary to Morgan's interpretation, the third stage of the trial ended on a despondent and desperate rather than a victorious note for Hutchinson. Quite probably it was this very desperation that prompted Hutchinson's confession of revelations in the trial's fourth stage.

The penultimate stage was the briefest and has remained the most famous part of the entire proceedings. At last cracking under the strain of the inquest, Hutchinson claimed a prophetic authority for her biblical interpretations. "The Lord knows that I could not open [interpret] scripture," she stated. "[H]e must by his prophetical office open it to me." Specifically, the Lord had taught her, in Hebrews 9:16, "which was the clear ministry [Cotton's] and which the wrong [the other ministers']. Since that time I confess I have been more choice and he hath let me to distinguish between the voice of my beloved and the voice of Moses, the voice of John Baptist and the voice of antichrist."[78] More than just a case of divine inspiration, Hutchinson claimed, God had informed her of the proper reading of this and other texts by the same communication he had used with the ancient Hebrew patriarchs, "by an immediate revelation."[79]

Here lay the very essence of the Antinomian threat, for if the Lord continued to offer direct revelations to his latter-day prophetesses, then there was nothing uniquely special about his revelations in the New Testament. It was precisely because the Lord had ceased to directly reveal his will to intermediaries since the death of Christ that the Bible took on its privileged role in Puritan tradition and that the ministers justified their exalted role as the premier exegetes of that tradition. No one was more keenly aware of this danger than Winthrop, who brilliantly summed up the situation for the court:

> [T]he grand work of her revelation is the immediate revelation of the spirit and *not by the ministry of the word* [italics mine], and that is the means by which she hath very much abused the country that they shall look for revelations and are not bound by the ministry of the word, but God will teach them by immediate revelations and this hath been the ground of all these tumults and troubles, and I would that these were all cut off from us that trouble us, for this is the thing that hath been the root of all the mischief.

With telling unanimity, the court responded to Winthrop's charge by stating, "[W]e all consent with you."[80] Hutchinson's "inspired" declarations dramatized for all of the spectators the giddy heights of enthusiasm that threatened to undermine Puritan biblicism and the orthodox one-party state it legitimated in Massachusetts.

Not content with such a bold claim to divine authority, Hutchinson proceeded to employ her prophetic abilities to warn the assembled court about the disastrous sin they were close to committing. Citing a passage from Daniel 6:4–5, she claimed that the Lord had told her that

> though I should meet with affliction yet I am the same God that delivered Daniel out of the lion's den, I will also deliver thee.—Therefore I desire you to look to it, for you see this scripture fulfilled this day and therefore I desire you that as you tender the Lord and the church and commonwealth to consider and look what you do. . . . [I]f you go on in this course you begin you will bring a curse upon you and your posterity, and the mouth of the Lord hath spoken it.[81]

In short, she threatened that if they dared convict God's beloved prophetess, he would ruin them and their colony in retribution. Whatever sympathy she might have had until this point among both spectators and participants was quickly dissipated, as the moderate Israel Stoughton spoke for the vast consensus: "Behold, I turn away from you."[82]

With this confession of personal divine revelations, Anne Hutchinson sealed her fate. In the fourth stage of the trial not only did she remove all scruples from the minds of moderate deputies like Stoughton concerning her banishment, but also she embarrassed, if not shocked and horrified, those sympathetic to her cause. The court had heard more than enough to justify her banishment. The court did, however, further require her testimony in the final stage of the trial. At this juncture, however, it was not her future in the colony that was at issue but that of her teacher, John Cotton.

It is not clear that at any point in the fifth stage of the trial John Cotton was in imminent danger of banishment, but as he was remarkably slow to realize, he had raised the censorious suspicions of the assembled ministers and magistrates by justifying Hutchinson. Her bizarre outburst, which could only have confirmed their worst fears about her, hardly reflected well on her protector, John Cotton. Captain John Endecott of Salem, whose own teacher had been banished largely at the behest of John Cotton, was the first to politely but pointedly ask "her reverend teacher . . . whether he doth condescend to such speeches or revelations as have been here spoken of."[83] At last Endecott would have his satisfaction, for just as he had reluctantly been forced to turn his back on Roger Williams, now Cotton would have to denounce his most fervent disciple, Anne Hutchinson. Of this necessity, however, John Cotton seems to have been completely ignorant. He proceeded to draw a distinction between immediate revelations and revelations "in a word of God and according to a word of God." The former, of course, were erroneous "and tending to danger more ways than one," while the latter type, presumably that of Hutchinson, "are not only lawful but such as christians may receive and God bear witness to it in his word."[84]

No doubt bemused by Cotton's scholastic logic chopping, Endecott politely thanked the teacher of Boston for the fine distinction between the two senses of "revelation." Not willing to let him wriggle off the hook too easily, Endecott again asked Cotton "to give your judgement of Mrs. Hutchinson; what she hath said you hear and all the circumstances thereof." For the second time in as many opportunities, Cotton reached into his dialectical bag of tricks and pulled out a distinction. This time he distinguished between the two senses of the word "miracle": "I would demand whether by a miracle she doth mean a work above nature or by some wonderful providence for that is called a miracle often in the psalms."[85] Sensing that her teacher was trying to save her by moderating her meaning, Hutchinson offered a supportive caveat, alleging that "I would not have the court so to understand me that he will deliver me now even at this present time."[86]

At this point Deputy Governor Thomas Dudley, who had been a parishioner of Cotton's in Lincolnshire, took up the dialogue with his old minister. The conversation, which is quoted below, is a testament not only to Dudley's inability to communicate the intention or purpose of his inquiry but even more to the outright political foolhardiness of John Cotton:

Dep. Gov. I desire Mr. Cotton to tell us whether you do approve of Mrs. Hutchinson's revelations as she hath laid them down.

Mr. Cotton. I know not whether I do understand her, but this I say, if she doth expect a deliverance in a way of providence—then I cannot deny it.

Dep. Gov. No Sir we did not speak of that.

Mr. Cotton. If it be by way of miracle then I would suspect it.

Dep. Gov. Do you believe that her revelations are true?

Mr. Cotton. That she may have some special providence of God to help her is a thing that I cannot bear witness against.

Dep. Gov. Good Sir I do ask whether this revelation be of God or no?

Mr. Cotton. I should desire to know whether the sentence of the court will bring her to any calamity, and then I would know of her whether she expects to be delivered from that calamity by a miracle or a providence of God.[87]

Apparently, Cotton thought that the court had solicited his opinion as to how they ought to judge Hutchinson's revelations and prophecies. The court, of course, had nothing of the kind in mind. Rather, they were interested in discerning Cotton's judgment, or apparent lack thereof, in order to gauge his orthodoxy and perhaps legitimate their sentence. Presumably, they assumed he would join them in their condemnation of Hutchinson's "enthusiastic" threats. Cotton seems to have been entirely unaware of this expectation and of the fact that his continued advocacy was only likely to damage his own reputation and raise the suspicions of the assembled inner-party elite.

While the entire court was undoubtedly disgruntled with Cotton's equivocating distinctions, it was Endecott who pugnaciously pursued the errant divine. "I speak in reference to Mr. Cotton," he began. "I am tender of you Sir and there lies much upon you in this particular." Cotton's distinction had failed, in Endecott's judgment at least, to clear Cotton "from that which his last answer did bring upon him." Endecott therefore desired that Cotton state clearly and unequivocally "[w]hether do you witness for her or against her."[88] By stating the question in such stark terms— basically, "Do you side with her or with us?"—Endecott must have thought he left Cotton no choice at all.

Cotton, however, was oblivious to the increasing danger in which he was placing himself. He reiterated his equivocating distinctions. If the revelation was "in a word" and the divine deliverance was by an act of providence, then "that I cannot deny." If, on the other hand, the revelation was "without the word" and deliverance was by a miracle, then he looked upon it "as a delusion, and I think so doth she too as I understand her." To continue to equivocate, much less take her side, after Endecott had stated the issue so bluntly was an extremely dangerous practice. Given the obvious consensus in the court concerning Hutchinson and her revelation, Cotton's continued dissent was an act that might well call for public recantation. That Cotton was on thin ice was made painfully clear by Dudley's pointed rejoinder: "Sir, you weary me and do not satisfy me."[89]

Cotton continued to compound his problems. Begging leave to express himself, he forthrightly stated that "[i]n that sense that she speaks I dare not bear witness against her." At last Cotton had gone too far. In continuing to justify Hutchinson's revelations, he was undermining the legitimacy of the court's contrary judgment.

Such a course of action could only provoke the anger of the court, as Cotton was soon to discover. Specifically, Increase Nowell made his displeasure known by disagreeing with Cotton's assessment in the strongest possible terms: "I think it is a devilish delusion." Even the normally conciliatory Winthrop expressed his strong disagreement with his errant teacher. "Of all the revelations that I ever read of I never read the like ground laid as is for this," he said, adding that even the "Enthusiasts and Anabaptists had never the like."[90]

Still, Cotton refused to denounce Hutchinson and her revelations. Unlike Hutchinson, Cotton argued, the Anabaptists and Enthusiasts "[b]roach new matters of faith and doctrine." "So do these," replied Winthrop, "and what may they breed more if they be let alone."[91] At this point the inquisitorial treatment of Cotton began to pick up momentum. Dudley concurred with Winthrop in finding Hutchinson's revelations even more objectionable than those of the Anabaptists and said that he was "sorry that Mr. Cotton should stand to justify her." Hugh Peter was even more forthright, stating that "I can say the same and this runs to enthusiasm, and I think that's very disputable which our brother Cotton hath spoken."[92] Winthrop ominously added, "[I]t overthrows all." Such revelations had been the cause of all of the infamous carnage at Münster, claimed Dudley; "they that have vented them have stirred up their hearers to take up arms against their prince and to cut the throats one of another."[93] Finally the chorus of disapproval reached a crescendo. Deputy Richard Collicot of Dorchester put Cotton in the "hot seat" and expressed the court's suspicion and hostility toward him: "It is a great burden to us that we differ from Mr. Cotton and that he should justify these revelations. I would intreat him to answer concerning that about the destruction of England [a prophecy attributed to Hooker by Hutchinson]."[94]

Winthrop clearly perceived where the proceedings were headed. By his refusal to side with the rest of the orthodox inner party elite, Cotton had succeeded in making himself the subject of the assembly's censorious deliberations. The governor quickly interceded to break off the court's pursuit of the dissenting divine, stating that "Mr. Cotton is not called to answer to any thing but we are to deal with the party here standing before us." In so doing, Winthrop repaid a debt to Cotton, who had saved his political career with an election sermon some three years before. But while Cotton was spared public censure or admonition, his performance at the court had severely damaged his reputation with both the magistrates and his clerical colleagues. The great John Cotton had raised and justified the regime's worst suspicions, and only his public recantation and confession, something he had never heretofore been required to do, would repair the damage he had done. The first such recantation came almost two months later, and another, fuller, confession came roughly a year after that.

With his intercession, Winthrop had ended the fifth stage of the examination. Quickly he brought the entire proceeding to a close. Welde, Eliot, and Peter reiterated their previous testimony under oath, and the General Court with great dispatch banished Anne Hutchinson and ordered her confined until her departure.[95] After Winthrop pronounced the sentence of the court, Hutchinson raised the question that had animated her for the last two days: "I desire to know wherefore I am banished?" What was her crime? Where was her jury? Could her prosecutors and accusers also legitimately stand as her judges? Where was the equity in this trial? She understood the political nature of the proceedings against her and wanted to force such an acknowledgment on the court. The time for explanation, however, had long since passed. She had been given the opportunity to confess, recant, and beg the clemency of the court. She had the chance to give public penance for her assaults on the privileged position of the ministers and their cultural domination. She had forgone these opportunities, at least in the eyes of her judges, because of her truculence, obstinacy, and inflated sense of self-importance. Gravely, Winthrop ended the affair with his final response: "Say no more, the court knows wherefore and is satisfied."[96] Anne Hutchinson would trouble Massachusetts no more.

Having disposed of the Antinomians' lay political and theoretical ringleaders, the General Court proceeded to deal with their most prominent supporters. With this group the goal was not to purge and banish, as with the ringleaders, but rather to cajole recantations and confessions so that such persons might be "recovered" by the community. On November 15, the court summoned "Captain Underhill, and some five or six more of the principal [all from Cotton's congregation], whose hands were to the said petition [on behalf of Wheelwright]."[97] When they arrived at the court, however, the seven remonstrants refused to recant and "stood to justify" the petition. Reluctant to banish them, the court instead disfranchised them and stripped them of whatever offices they held.[98] But while these seven prominent Antinomians of Boston remained recalcitrant, several remonstrants from neighboring Charlestown saw the error of their ways and offered public recantations. William Larnett approached the court and acknowledged "his fault in subscribing the seditious writing, and desiring his name to be crossed out, it was yielded him and crossed."[99] Six of his fellow Charlestown residents—Ralph Mousall, Ezekiel Richardson, Richard Sprague, Edward Mellows, and William Frothingham—quickly followed suit.[100] Apparently, the spirit of the Antinomian movement had been broken outside of Boston.

On November 20, the General Court ordered all of those who had signed the remonstrance on behalf of John Wheelwright, fifty-eight in all, to surrender their arms or be disarmed by the local authorities. The court justified its act on the grounds that, like the Anabaptists in Münster, the Antinomians might "make some suddaine irruption upon these that differ from them in judgement."[101] As James F. Cooper has noted, this charge was preposterous. The real intent of the disarmament order, as Cooper has argued, was "to embarrass the offenders, not annihilate them."[102] Such embarrassment was in turn intended to prompt the "offenders" to recant their remonstrance. Indeed, to encourage and facilitate such recantations, the court ordered "that if any that are to bee disarmed acknowledg their sinn in subscribing the seditious libell, or do not justify it, but acknowledg it evill to two magistrates, they shalbee thereby freed from delivering in their armes according to the former order."[103] This order had its desired effect, as a rush of recantations immediately ensued.[104]

Finally, to ensure the end of such defiant outbursts as those of Captain Underhill and his fellow congregants, the court ordered that "whosoever shall hearafter openly or willingly defame any court of justice, or the sentences or proceedings of the same, or any of the magistrates, . . . shalbee punished for the same by fine, imprisonment, or disfranchizement, or banishment, as the quality & measure of the offence shall deserve."[105] Now literally beyond reproach, the General Court had mandated its privileged status. In singling out the magistrates in particular for such privileged status, the court had also reestablished the cultural domination of the intelligentsia-assistants. The court's action against the Antinomians had been quick, thorough, and generally effective. Within two months the church of Roxbury "dealt with divers of their members" who had signed the remonstrance and "proceeded to two or three admonitions, and, when all was in vain, they cast them out of the church."[106] Massachusetts had been made safe from the Antinomian threat.

Totally isolated within the colony, Boston's dissidents nonetheless remained defiant. While they had been purged from the political community, they were still a majority within the church of Boston. Several congregants, "highly offended with the governour" for the court's measures, approached their ministers and asked them to initiate church proceedings against Winthrop.[107] Cotton may at last have come to see the recklessness of his zealous parishioners, for he refused to fulfill their request. Apprised of his opponents' intentions, Winthrop took matters in his own hands on the next Sabbath. After the sermon, Winthrop announced that the church of Boston, as an ecclesiastic institution, lacked the secular authority "to inquire into the justice and proceedings of the Court."[108] While his private and religious actions might be the subject of church censure, as Battis aptly put it, "the church must not presume to call a magistrate to account for his official acts, however unjust they might seem."[109] Winthrop had stood his ground in the church of Boston. The Antinomians were rebuffed in their own stronghold.

Winthrop remarked in his *Journal* that in the aftermath of Hutchinson's examination a plethora of "foul errors were discovered, which had been secretly carried by way of inquiry, but after were maintained by Mrs. Hutchinson and others."[110] Winthrop claimed that the airing of these "errors" was decisive in turning Cotton away from his heretical parishioners and toward his orthodox colleagues. No doubt such doctrines—now of a clearly Gnostic nature—played some part in Cotton's decision to desert his disciples.[111] Other considerations, however, probably had equal if not greater impact on his thinking. Cotton could hardly have failed to recognize that the Antinomian movement had been defeated everywhere outside of Boston and that the church of that town could not hold off the forces of orthodoxy forever. Moreover, he must have been keenly aware of how his advocacy of Hutchinson's cause at the court had alienated him from his colleagues.

Indeed, Cotton had gone so far with the court that the only thing that could restore his position as an orthodox and trustworthy divine was an act of public recantation. Thus, on January 16, 1638, Winthrop recorded that the great John Cotton, "finding how he had been their [the Antinomians'] stalking horse, (for they pretended to hold nothing but what Mr. Cotton held, and himself did think the same,) did spend most of his time, both publickly and privately, to discover those errours, and to reduce such as were gone astray."[112] While Cotton would perform a more thorough and complete recantation almost a year later, he had at long last distanced himself from and denounced his erstwhile Antinomian allies.[113] Cotton's defection to the ranks of the orthodox signaled the end of Antinomian dissent. In the next few months he purged those few stalwarts in the church of Boston who refused to recant.

Anne Hutchinson was the first to go. On March 15, 1638, Hutchinson was summoned before the church and admonished for her various and sundry errors. One week later, after a halfhearted and unsuccessful recantation and at the insistent prodding of Cotton and his attendant colleagues, at long last she was "[c]ast out of the Church for impertinently persisting in a manifest lye then expressed by her in open Congregation."[114] Judith Smith followed shortly thereafter. On April 15, after having been "formerly in private admonished of Sundry Errors," she was excommunicated for maintaining said errors in addition to, like Hutchinson, "sundry lyes then expressed by her and persisted in."[115] Two weeks later the same fate befell Anne Walker. While she had been privately admonished for various private failings—"Drunkenish, Intemperate, and unclean or wantonish behavior, and likewise of Cruelty towards her Children"—like Hutchinson and Smith before her she was cast out of the church for "manifold lyes and still to this day persisting impenitently therein."[116] These three excommunications, all within a period of two months, are all the more impressive in light of the fact that in the previous seven years only one person had been excommunicated in the church of Boston, and he was re-admitted after seven months.[117] An example had been made of them. Antinomian dissent in the church of Boston had come to an end. As Cooper has noted, in the aftermath of Hutchinson's excommunication, "even most Boston Antinomians—strongly influenced by their own church authorities—eventually had been brought into line."[118]

The merchant Antinomian dissidents of Boston had been defeated. The system of cultural domination and the one-party state it supported had been secured by the class-conscious response of both ministerial intellectuals and magisterial intelligentsia. The most dangerous merchant dissidents had been purged and banished, and the yeoman freemen had overwhelmingly supported the orthodox thinking class. In the process, however, the balance of power had subtly been altered, and a host of new issues faced the architects of the New England Way. The political demise of the merchant community also represented the ascendancy of the yeomen freemen as represented by the deputies. What would be their role in the one-party state, and what would be their relationship to the magisterial intelligentsia? The Antinomian movement had been defeated at the hands of the General Court. On the other hand, the ministers had been extremely influential in their role as political advisers and mediators. What would be the relationship between the state and the churches or, more to the point, between the magisterial intelligentsia and the ministerial intellectuals? How could orthodoxy be fostered within the ranks of the ministers? What role could the state have in this process? Finally, the colony still had to contend with the legacy of Cotton's charismatic polity revisions. Was the system of voluntary contributions sufficient for ministerial maintenance outside of the wealthy church of Boston? Even more problematic was the institutionalization of Cotton's test of gracious experience. Religious charisma is extremely unstable and rarely persists from generation to generation. What would happen when the next generation of devout Puritan laymen ceased to be gripped by such profound religious experiences? This last problem would continue to plague Massachusetts well beyond the famous Half-Way Synod of 1662. All of the others would be resolved within the next decade.

5

ORDERING THE
ONE-PARTY REGIME

The suppression of Antinomian dissent had required the concerted effort of all of the orthodox elements of Massachusetts's one-party state. In the spring of 1637 the culturally virtuous freemen of the outer party, with the urgent blessing of the ministerial intellectuals, had purged those deputies and assistants suspected of dissident sympathies during the Court of Elections in Newtown. In the late summer, the magistrates prompted the elders to condemn the theory and practice of Antinomianism in New England's first full-blown synod. Finally, in early winter all three elements of the one-party regime—ministerial intellectuals, magisterial intelligentsia, and representatives of the culturally virtuous outer party—cooperated at the General Court in banishing the Antinomians' ringleaders and extracting recantations from the bulk of the dissidents. Only with such cooperation and unity had orthodoxy been secured in Massachusetts. In the decades ahead, every significant threat to orthodoxy and the system of cultural domination, either from dissidents within the colony or from heterodox forces without, was met by a unified and determined regime.

On most other issues, however, consensus and cohesion proved far more elusive. Particularly divisive were issues dealing with the precise delineation, distribution, and disposition of power within the orthodox regime. Indeed, in the decade following the Antinomian controversy, Massachusetts was gripped by internecine struggles between the three aforementioned elements of the regime, each attempting to increase and consolidate its hold on power. This struggle was punctuated by a series of shifting alliances between these elements—first among the magistrates and deputies, then briefly between the deputies and ministers, and finally the famed and enduring alliance of the two strata of the thinking class, the ministers and magistrates. When this struggle was finally resolved—roughly around the time of the Cambridge Platform—Massachusetts emerged with a tripartite mixed government.

In the immediate aftermath of the Antinomian controversy, the deputed representatives of the outer party may well have appeared more politically powerful, in a de jure sense, than either the ministers or the magistrates. In the early 1630s these representatives gained a deliberative voice in the levying of taxes and quickly extended

that voice to all legislation. By the late 1630s they were a large and cohesive majority of the General Court, the sole legislative body authorized by the colony's charter. Moreover, the charter stipulated that the deliberations of the General Court
should be decided by a simple majority vote, thus making the unified political will
of the deputies the law of the land. Indeed, the magistrates' demand and practice of
a legislative veto in 1634 was an unconstitutional innovation that the deputies had
tolerated in order to avoid a political crisis at a dangerous moment. In the eyes of the
deputies it was decidedly not, as subsequent events would prove, a legitimate precedent for what they perceived as an arbitrary grasp of power by the magistrates.

By contrast, in a strictly de jure sense the ministers were politically impotent.
Since they were barred by custom and agreement from dual-office holding, their ecclesiastic callings precluded any official participation in the General Court. In fact,
however, their influence was substantial. Perhaps their most striking exercise of
power was in the role of counselors and mediators in political crises and disputes.
According to David Hall, the ministers consulted with the magistrates at least seventy times between 1633 and 1649: "All other channels of influence were insignificant compared to their direct consultations with the government."[1] Although the clerics could not be elected to civil office, the various standing committees created by
the General Court to deal with pressing concerns (e.g., inflation, the construction of
a code of laws, the oversight of Harvard, etc.) were ubiquitously staffed and generally dominated by a sizable proportion of ministers. Equally impressive was their influence over the electorate. At the very beginning of each annual Court of Elections,
a duly appointed member of the ministry would preach a decidedly political and
often factionally partisan election sermon to the assembled freemen. In addition, in
the early 1630s the clergy established a traveling midweek lecture circuit, moving
among Boston, Roxbury, Dorchester, and Cambridge.[2] Harry Stout has argued that
these highly popular "occasional" sermons were largely political in content; upon as-
cending the pulpit, the ministers "would become social guardians telling the nation
who they were and what they must do to retain God's special covenant interest."[3]

The lion's share of political power, however, was clearly held by the magistrates.
Like the ministers, the magistrates enjoyed the respect and deference due high cultural initiates. But whereas the ministers used the midweekly sermons to influence
the political behavior of the community as a whole, the magistrates' exercise of cultural domination was restricted to the deputies in the General Court. Prior to 1644,
the deputies and assistants met and deliberated together. If the few transcripts and
accounts of particular courts are at all representative, then the proceedings of the
General Court were dominated by the magistrates' superior rhetorical, legal, and dialectical skills. Moreover, in those rare cases where the deputies remained intractable
in the face of such forensic feats, the assistants, in their own judgment at least, retained the right to a legislative veto.

Even more effective than their legislative role (which was, after all, subject to the
deputies' legislative veto) was the magistrates' extraordinary judicial power. As jus-
tices of the peace or assistants at the Quarter Courts in Boston, the magistrates
presided over all criminal cases, and as John Murrin has shown, if the crime in question was not a capital offense, the magistrates almost always dispensed with the use
of juries in favor of summary justice.[4] Murrin has characterized the criminal trial pro-

cedures of Massachusetts Bay in this period as "inquisitorial": "[T]he magistrates themselves compiled evidence, prosecuted, questioned witnesses and the accused, judged, and passed sentence." Not surprisingly, Murrin notes that these magistrates achieved "a truly phenomenal rate of conviction, perhaps somewhere in the 90 percent range."[5] This judicial power appears all the more formidable when it is recalled that, perhaps as a result of the magistrates' legislative veto, the General Court had failed to pass any substantial body of criminal law. Not only did the magistrates serve as both prosecutor and judge, but also they convicted and sentenced on the basis of their interpretation of the word of God and their own best judgment.[6] Indeed, the magistrate's duty as "a publique politicall Nurse-father to the Church" required him, according to Thomas Cobbet, "to judge what is, or is not according to the Word." Without such discretionary judgment, the magistrates could never "rescue the church from noysom milk provided" by errant divines or "such as should be Nurses."[7] Finally, the assistants collectively acted as the administrative or executive arm of the colony in the absence of the General Court and in emergencies.[8]

Although ministers, deputies, and magistrates had been important in the defeat of Antinomianism, it was the latter two that proved decisive in November 1637. Perhaps as a result, the magistrates and deputies seem to have developed a particularly amicable relationship in the period directly after Hutchinson's banishment. On March 12, 1638, the magistrates acceded to one of the perennial demands of the deputies by creating a committee to compile a set of laws and statutes.[9] This desire on the part of the court for a legal code may well have carried some slight rebuke to the ministers, for they had, in response to a similar request, compiled a code submitted by John Cotton, known as "Moses His Judicialls," in 1636. The creation of this subsequent committee obviously signaled the court's displeasure with the ministers' previous effort. Presumably the flaw with "Moses His Judicialls," was its emphasis on the delineation of powers within the government and their theological legitimation. The deputies, on the other hand, wanted a code of specific laws, rather than a code of "fundamental law," to bind the judicial decisions of the magistrates.[10]

Implicit rebukes aside, both deputies and magistrates (and Winthrop in particular) were frustrated with the ministers' uncooperative stance in the late summer of 1638. At issue was "the great disorder general through the country in costliness of apparel, and following new fashions."[11] Duly concerned, the court summoned the ministers and requested them "to redress" such conspicuous consumption "by urging it upon the consciences of their people," no doubt in their midweek occasional sermons. While the ministers promised to preach against this excess, they seem to have failed to fulfill this pledge, prompting Winthrop's bitter explanation that "divers of the elders' wives, & c. were in some measure partners in this general disorder."[12]

The ministers for their part were concerned about the power of the magistrates, particularly that of Governor John Winthrop. Winthrop recorded that several of the ministers lobbied heavily against his reelection as governor at the next Court of Elections. The explanation they offered to Winthrop was that although "they all loved and esteemed him," they feared "lest it might make way for having a governour for life."[13] Ostensibly, this fear was prompted by Cotton's recent grab for preeminence among the ministers. Perhaps more significant was Winthrop's unparalleled popularity among the freemen throughout the colony. Indeed, of all the magistrates of the first generation, Winthrop was the only one whose popularity rivaled that of the ministers. The most palpable evidence of this popular favor was the fact that despite the maneuvering of the ministers, Winthrop was once again chosen governor on May 22, 1639.[14]

Winthrop's popularity notwithstanding, the concerted political will of the ministerial intellectuals was hardly to be taken lightly. Jealous of their "church liberties," they lobbied against an order passed during the height of the Antinomian controversy. This order stated that "persons which have stood excommunicate above 6 months should be presented" to the government for punishment. The ministers were successful, and the act was repealed by the General Court on September 4, 1639.[15] No doubt flushed with this success, in the following months the ministers became increasingly active in political matters. In particular, they attempted to win the favor of the deputies so as to use them as a bulwark against the magistrates' political preeminence. The ministers quickly found two issues on which they could appeal to the concerns of the deputies: the discretionary basis of the assistants' judicial decisions (ostensibly due to the lack of written statutes) and the perceived economic oppression practiced by the merchants.

On November 3, 1639, Ezekiel Rogers, the pastor of Rowley who was henceforth to enjoy a particularly adversarial relationship with the magistrates, sent Governor Winthrop a letter. In it Rogers apprised the governor of the "expectation of the Country" concerning the upcoming session of the General Court. Rogers claimed that the people were particularly concerned about the merchants' practice of economic "oppression, & what wilbe done against it." The most propitious way of dealing with the problem, he argued, was to find a few particularly notorious offenders and summarily make an example of them: "For my part, I beleeve that if there were a Law to hang up some before the Lord; they deserve it, & it would to him be a sacrifice most acceptable." Ominously, Rogers added his prayer that the Lord would protect Winthrop "from partaking at all in other mens sinnes (especially of such a nature) by the least indulgence." Rogers concluded with mention of a second expectation of the court with a lightly veiled threat: "A body of Lawes is now of all much desired; and matureness of proceeding therein wished. Your forwardness to communicate to the Elders such things as they may be capable of, doth as much indeare you to them (who must be a great meanes of your strength) as honour you."[16]

Not surprisingly, when the General Court convened on November 5, Winthrop recorded that "great complaint was made of the oppression used in the country in sale of foreign commodities."[17] As per Rogers's instructions, an example was made of a particularly notorious merchant, Robert Keayne of Boston. Some disagreement arose, however, over his sentence. The deputies wanted to fine him a staggering £200, while the magistrates thought half that sum would suffice.[18] They compromised and fined Keayne £200, with the stipulation that he pay half the fine before the year's end, "the other £100 to be respited till the next General Court, whereby the Court may have liberty to shewe favor to him if they see cause."[19]

While the dispute over Keayne's sentence may have slightly alienated the deputies, the magistrates attempted to recoup their losses with the representatives by their handling of the request for a legal code. Not only did they pledge to expedite its compilation, but they further agreed to submit the code to the freemen for ratification.[20] This magisterial pandering to popular sentiment angered some of the ministerial intellectuals, especially the author of the new legal code, Nathaniel Ward. On December 22, he complained to Winthrop of the "ill consequence" of this gesture to the outer party in fostering a "creeping democracy": "I suspect both Commonwealth and Churches had desended to lowe already. I see the spirits of people runne high and what they gett they hould. They may not be denyed their proper and lawfull liberties, but I question whether it be of God too interest the inferiour sort in that with should be reserved."[21]

Although this referendum and the court's failed attempt to curtail fashion may have created some tension between the two elements of the inner party, it took a further action by this session of the General Court to cause a breach between the elders and magistrates. At issue was the ministers' frequent preaching of occasional sermons. These political sermons were quite popular and attracted many of the less affluent residents who, according to Winthrop, "would usually resort to two or three in the week, to the great neglect of their affairs, and the damage of the publick."[22] Therefore, the court ordered a conference with the ministers "about the length and frequency of church assemblies."[23]

This time the court, no doubt at the prompting of the magistrates, had gone too far. While not clearly politically motivated—as the only authorized public political speech, the occasional sermon was a powerful tool for swaying public opinion—the magistrates were nonetheless infringing on the ministers' domain. Any such state regulation of midweek preaching would "enthrall them to the civil power" and "cast a blemish upon the elders, which would remain to posterity, that they should need to be regulated by the civil magistrate, and also raise an ill savour of the people's coldness, that would complain of much preaching."[24] In a collective huff, the elders practiced their version of a "negative voice" by refusing to accede to the court's wishes.

When the magistrates learned of the offense taken by the ministers, they quickly tried to make amends. The order was intended as a respectful request, they explained, and not an imperious command. Moreover, they had asked for nothing more than a conference, which would "be rather an argument of the zeal and forwardness of the elders." One of their explanations, however, contained a thinly veiled barb. They argued that since the order did not specifically mention occasional sermons, "it might be taken for meetings upon other occasion of the churches, which were known to be very frequent."[25] Such "other occasion" may well have been a reference to the classical meetings of the ministers that many laymen, like Williams and Skelton some years before, deeply resented as signs of a "creeping presbyterianism" on the part of the elders.

Nevertheless, the magistrates were hardly in a position to contest the issue, for, as Winthrop remarked, "the elders had great power in the people's hearts, which was needful to be upheld, lest the people should break their bonds through abuse of liberty, which divers, having surfeited of, were very forward to incite others to raise mutinies and foment dangerous and groundless jealousies of the magistrates."[26] Winthrop may have exaggerated the extent of "mutinous" sentiment, but he was right in recognizing the ministry's crucial role in supporting the authority of the magisterial intelligentsia. John Norton, in his *Brief Catechisme,* informed the laity that the

Fifth Commandment demanded "that we walk orderly in our callings, inwardly acknowledging, and outwardly according to Rule, expressing that honour which is due to Superiours, Inferiour, Equalls, according to their several relations."[27] John Fiske went even further in his catechism, stressing the outward expression of reverence for one's superiors, "and that readily upon all occasions, both in word & deed, in such wise as may both testitfie our esteem of them, as our betters, and our care to deserve well of them." Indeed, the Fifth Commandment also required the godly "to procure likewise unto them like honourable esteem & respect from others."[28] It was thus understandable when the assistants, "finding how hardly such propositions would be digested" by the ministers, let the matter of excessive sermonizing drop.[29]

The damage had been done, however. The fragile peace between the assistants and elders was shattered. For the next few years the ministers' primary political goal would be to limit the power of the magistrates. The magistrates, for their part, would attempt to hold onto their prerogatives and their privileged position. The significance of this feud was not overlooked by the deputies, who saw their chance to increase their power within the General Court at the expense of the assistants. In the following months a tacit alliance was reached between the ministers and the deputies that would last until the aftermath of the Goody Sherman's sow affair.

This alliance bore its first fruits at the Court of Elections. On May 23, 1640, Thomas Dudley replaced John Winthrop as governor, and Richard Bellingham, one of the leaders of the antimagisterial movement, was elected deputy governor.[30] Winthrop, who remained one of the assistants, claimed that Dudley's election "was obtained with some difficulty, for many of the elders laboured much in it." The ministers, who had convened in Boston, sent a delegation to mollify Winthrop. They professed "their sincere affections and respect towards him" and explained that they were solely motivated by the fear "lest the long continuance of one man in the place [governor] should bring it to be for life, and, in time, hereditary."[31] A gentleman in the full sense of the word, Winthrop graciously accepted their explanation and his reduced political role.

While Governor Dudley did pass legislation certain to please the deputies and elders—he ordered that the ratification of Ward's legal code be expedited and repealed the previous order about midweek lectures—he quickly proved that he was not their tool.[32] Particularly galling to the deputies was his handling of Robert Keayne's fine abatement. In addition to being the foremost economic "oppressor" in Boston, Keayne was also Dudley's brother-in-law. As if that were not enough reason to prompt the governor's clemency, Dudley himself had been accused of "oppression" in the early 1630s when he attempted to corner the vital corn market. Thus, when the issue of Keayne's fine abatement came up, Dudley proffered and passed an order remitting the substantial sum of £120 to Keayne. The deputies were furious, for they wanted a far smaller abatement, and because Dudley failed to bring their request to a vote, "they charged the governour with breach of order." Dudley, as was his wont, "grew into some heat, professing that he would not suffer such things." The deputies took great offense at Dudley's imperious threats, and a major political crisis seemed in the offing. The next day, Dudley offered an explanation of his intentions (*not* an apology or retraction), and peace, if not amity, was restored to the General Court.[33]

The elders were also indirectly involved in the imbroglio over Keayne's fine abatement. On August 23, Ezekiel Rogers wrote to inform Winthrop that "many of God's people did thinke that some of the court were very sharpe in dealing with Mr. Hawthorne," the speaker of the deputies. Although Rogers didn't mention the particular order, presumably it was the Keayne issue that prompted Hawthorne to consult with the ministers. When he attempted to inform the court as to the elders' counsel, Winthrop reportedly told him that "his so advising with the Elders would be to the overthrowe of you all." Certain that Winthrop suffered "in the minds of many for this," Rogers stated that it was his Christian duty to "let you understand this much."[34]

Winthrop promptly responded to Rogers, thanking him "for his faithfulnesse." He claimed no recollection of the incident in question with Hawthorne and "was sure I used no suche expression, it being against my judgement and practice." Winthrop did not, however, back down. He categorically stated that "for a man to oppose the Judgement of some elders to the Judgement of the Court openly in Civill matter (which might be the Case) was worthy reproofe, and I thinke likely I might saye something to that purpose." Winthrop then went on the offensive, challenging Rogers "to produce my accusers that I might be cleared or justly condemned." Knowing full well that Rogers had overstepped his bounds, Winthrop stated that if he did not hear from Rogers shortly, he "would cleare myselfe publickly."[35]

Winthrop did not have to wait long for his response. On August 31, Rogers wrote to him, agreeing that "your judgement concerning consultation with the Elders in waighty cases, is sound and according to the worde." But Rogers, like Winthrop, refused to back down. "Godly wisdome should teach us," he warned, "both not to intermeddle where we have no call."[36] It was precisely the substance of this "Godly wisdome," that is, the respective legitimate domains of church and state, that was at issue in the next major showdown between the ministers and magistrates.

At the October 1640 session of the General Court, the ministers submitted a document delimiting the powers of the ecclesiastic and civil institutions. While the document itself has been lost, it apparently urged an expansion of church power at the expense of the "civil magistrate." The magistrates found several of the proposed restrictions on their power unacceptable, but they were particularly alarmed by the ministers' contention that "the civil magistrate should not proceed against a church member before the church had dealt with him."[37] This proposition directly contradicted the elders' previous contention that "[i]n all such heresies or errours of any church members as are manifest and dangerous to the state the court may proceed without tarrying for the church." Presumably this proviso was intended solely for heretics or other "cultural criminals" who were church members and thus liable to ecclesiastic censure. Indeed, the purpose of this stipulation was to ensure the preeminence or cultural authority of church censures, thus assuring their power to thwart heterodoxy. Nonetheless, this was not only a sharp restriction of magisterial power but also potentially an extremely dangerous proposition for the stability of the regime. The assumption on the ministers' part seems to have been that a united and orthodox ministry would be able to root out any dissident movements within their churches. What they ignored was the possibility that one or more of the ministers might stray from the path of orthodoxy and shield errant laymen, as John Cotton had during the Antinomian controversy in Boston. A congregational church led by a dissident minister could hardly be expected to discipline its heretical members. As in the case of Anne Hutchinson, the court would have to make the first move because the principle of congregational independence left the other orthodox churches without any ecclesiastic jurisdiction over their dissident neighbor beyond mere peer pressure. Naturally, the magistrates balked at these proposals, and so "the matter was referred to further consideration," or, in modern parlance, it was tabled.[38]

Tensions between the magistrates and ministers were at an all-time high as a result of the elders' "suggestions." Angered by the clerics' political meddling, the magistrates vented their wrath on Ezekiel Rogers, the cantankerous minister of Rowley. Rogers made an appearance at the same October session of the court in order to obtain a grant of land for Rowley. Rogers quickly discovered that the acreage of his initial request was inadequate and asked for an additional parcel of land. Unfortunately, the desired piece of land had previously been promised to a "plantation at Cochitawit." When the court consequently felt obliged to deny Rogers's request, the divine erupted in a fit of self-righteous indignation: "Whereupon he pleaded justice, upon some promises of large accomodations, &c. when we desired his sitting down with us, and grew into some passion, so as in departing from the court, he said he would acquaint the elders with it."[39] The magistrates would hardly tolerate such threats, even from an orthodox minister like Rogers. They promptly dispatched one of Rowley's deputies to summon Rogers before the court to give satisfaction for his offensive speech. Apprised of the magistrates' angry response, Rogers sent Governor Dudley an apologetic letter "wherein he confessed his passionate distemper, declaring his meaning in those offensive speeches, as that his meaning was that he would propound the case to the elders for advise only about the equity of it, which he still defended." This written apology, however, was insufficient to clear Rogers, for Thomas Dudley, unlike Winthrop, had a stern, uncharitable, and unforgiving temperament and was not to be threatened or challenged lightly. Rogers was forced to undergo the public humiliation of a recantation before the General Court. As compensation, and in prudent recognition of the fact that Rogers "would not yield from the justice of his cause," the court at last granted his town the desired parcel of land.[40]

The heightened tensions with the magistrates served to reinforce the ministers' tacit alliance with the deputies. This alliance resulted in the election of a new governor at the Court of Elections on June 2, 1641. Dudley, who on most political issues was of the same mind as John Winthrop, was replaced as chief executive by one of the principal leaders of the deputies in their struggle against magisterial power, Richard Bellingham.[41] Bellingham's election had required considerable effort, including a highly irregular election sermon by Nathaniel Ward and an allegedly fraudulent vote count.[42] Once elected, Bellingham was immediately authorized by the court to review all standing orders and statutes and "take notice what may bee fit to bee repealed, what to bee certified, & what to stand, & to make returne to the next Generall Court."[43]

As governor of Massachusetts, Bellingham did achieve an important goal of the ministers and deputies. After three years of indecision and consultation, on December 10, 1641, the General Court passed into law Nathaniel Ward's code of fundamental law.[44] As previously mentioned, the "Body of Liberties" was hardly the legal code that the deputies had wanted, but at least it was something. For their part, the ministers must have been quite pleased with Bellingham's ratification of Ward's code, for, as David Hall has argued, "the weight of the Massachusetts 'Body of Liberties' fell upon the 'Liberties the Lord Jesus hath given to the churches.'"[45] Particularly significant in this regard was section 11 of article 95—there were ninety-eight articles in all—which for the first time gave legal sanction to the ministers' controversial classical assemblies:

> It is allowed and ratified, by the Authorities of the Generall Court as a lawfull libertie of the Churches of Christ. That once in every month of the yeare (when the season will beare it) It shall be lawfull for the ministers and Elders, of the Churches neere adjoyneing together, with any of the bretheren with the consent of the churches to assemble by course in each severall Church one after an other.[46]

For the most part, however, Bellingham proved to be an embarrassment as governor. Shortly after his election, Bellingham married a young woman who had been "ready to be contracted to a friend of his"; Bellingham had, in fact, been negotiating the marriage arrangements. Bellingham compounded his error by presiding over the ceremony himself, "contrary to the constant practice of the country." In addition, he failed to publish his intentions or the wedding contract, as required by the court.[47] The July session of the General Court "presented him for the breach of the order of court." The governor, however, refused to leave the bench, "as the manner was." The rest of the magistrates refused to proceed with the inquest because they were "unwilling to command him publicly to go off the bench, and yet not think it fit he should sit as a judge, when he was by law to answer as an offender." The inquest was permanently derailed by the bellicose Bellingham, who said "he would not go off the bench, except he were commanded."[48]

Winthrop claimed that Bellingham's bellicosity was motivated by jealousy because "some other of the magistrates bore more sway with the people than himself, and that they were called to be of the standing council for life, and himself passed by." Consequently, Winthrop argued, Bellingham "set himself in an opposite frame" to the magistrates "in all proceedings."[49] While such jealousy might explain Bellingham's overzealous prosecution of Dudley in a civil case before the December session of the General Court, the governor's assault on magisterial power was more likely the result of his previous tenure as a member of the deputies.[50] Nor was Bellingham alone in his quest to limit the assistants' power. At the same December session of the General Court, Captain William Hawthorne, the speaker of the deputies, moved "to have some certain penalty set upon lying, swearing, & c." The point of such set penalties was to eliminate the discretionary basis of the magistrates' judicial decisions. When Deputy Governor Endecott, speaking for the bulk of the magistrates, objected to this suggestion, "Mr. Hathorne charged him with seeking to have the government arbitrary, & c. and the matter grew to some heat."[51] Given the magistrates' practice of the "negative voice," however, there was nothing the deputies could do.

Such challenges from Hawthorne and Bellingham did not pass without response. Both Bellingham and Hawthorne received their comeuppance at this session of the court. Bellingham's rebuke came in the form of a slight by the court. After Bellingham's legal machinations against him, Thomas Dudley threatened to resign his post as magistrate and retire from political office. The court "entreated him, with manifestations of much affection and respect towards him," to continue in his public calling. Seeing the display of public affection evoked by Dudley's threat to resign, Bellingham also threatened to leave the magistracy. The governor quickly changed his mind, however, "for no man desired him to keep [his position as a magistrate], or to consider better of it."[52]

The speaker of the deputies was cut down to size by one of the magistrates' staunchest allies among the elders, John Cotton of Boston. At the court, Hawthorne suggested to the deputies that they "leave out" of office "two of their ancientest magistrates, because they were grown poor [Winthrop and either Dudley or Endecott], and spake reproachfully of them under that motion." Having been apprised of Hawthorne's suggestion, Cotton delivered an occasional sermon on the next lecture day "to refute, and sharply (in his mild manner) to reprove such miscarriage, which he termed a slighting or dishonouring of parents."[53]

This session of the General Court marked a subtle but significant transition in the political history of early Massachusetts. Henceforth, the tension between the ministers and magistrates, though still existent, ceased to be the predominant division within the orthodox one-party regime. Instead, the court was gripped by a deepening struggle between the deputed representatives of the outer party and the magisterial intelligentsia.[54] For the next three years the deputies and assistants vied for judicial, executive, and legislative power. The ministers' legitimating counsel proved decisive in this struggle within the court. Initially sympathetic to the deputies' cause, they finally sided resolutely and unequivocally with the magistrates, thus ending the conflict and fixing for its duration the separation of powers in the Puritan one-party regime.

Tension between the deputies and magistrates came to a head on two issues during 1642, the magistrates' Standing Council and their claim to a negative voice.[55] The first issue was raised by a treatise written anonymously by Richard Saltonstall that argued that the Standing Council was a "sinful innovation."[56] At the May session of the General Court the document was brought to the attention of Winthrop (who had been reelected governor after Bellingham's less than auspicious tenure) by Thomas Dudley, who received it from a freeman.[57] Incensed at this challenge to magisterial power, Winthrop sought to have the author of the work presented to the court to answer for his erroneous expressions.

The deputies, who knew the author was their ally, Richard Saltonstall, refused to discuss the book unless Saltonstall was first cleared of any wrongdoing by the court. This Winthrop refused to do, and he offered to present the treatise to the elders for their critical commentary on its content. The deputies balked at this offer and proposed instead that "the whole cause"—including the content of Saltonstall's work, his liability for writing it, and the legitimacy of the Standing Council—be presented to the ministers.[58] Perhaps fearing that a ministerial exoneration of Saltonstall might make them look petty and overly zealous in defense of their privileges, the magistrates agreed to "discharge him [Saltonstall] from any censure or further enquiry by this or any other Court" on account of his treatise.[59] The text and issue of the Standing Council were then referred to the judgment of the elders, and the present Standing Council and its members were vindicated "from all dishonour & reproach cast upon it or them in Mr. Saltonstall's booke."[60]

On October 1, 1642, the ministers, who had assembled at Ipswich, gave their judgment on Saltonstall's book and the Standing Council.[61] Aware of the depth of the division between the magistrates and deputies, they offered a conciliatory compromise in their counsel. In accord with the deputies, they cleared Saltonstall of any wrongdoing and even endorsed his fundamental principles. Nonetheless, they endorsed the institution of the Standing Council, albeit with one interesting proviso. They proposed that the council be comprised of the prominent magistrates and "other freemen," presumably the leaders of the deputies.[62] This last proviso proved to be a major bone of contention between the magistrates and deputies.

The second issue dividing the deputies and assistants, the magistrates' negative voice, was raised by the infamous case of Goody Sherman's sow. The facts of the sow case, arguably the most important judicial proceeding in early colonial history, are fairly straightforward. In 1636 Goodwife Sherman lost a sow that she had left to forage for the winter on Deer Island in Boston harbor. At around the same time Robert Keayne, the notorious oppressor of Boston, advertised his recovery of a stray sow. Although she subsequently claimed that the stray sow was her own, she never came to collect the pig from Keayne's pen. When Keayne slaughtered a swine the following October, Goody Sherman visited his pen and, not finding her lost sow, accused Keayne of having just killed her pig. When she finally brought suit in 1640, a jury found in favor of Keayne and ordered Goody Sherman to pay the defendant £3 for court costs.[63]

Despite the facts, two extenuating circumstances complicated the case. Perhaps the most important circumstance was the social status of the accused. As previously mentioned, Robert Keayne was a hated and notorious merchant oppressor in Massachusetts. Having been convicted by the court, he had avoided paying a substantial fine through the good offices of his brother-in-law, Governor Thomas Dudley. To make matters worse for himself, Keayne had vengefully sued Goody Sherman and her legal associates for slander and won an award of £20 from the jury.[64] The yeomen of the colony could not help but feel sympathy for the poor woman who had suffered at the hands of Massachusetts's most vilified economic offender. Such sympathy was compounded by the efforts of George Story, Sherman's boarder and legal representative, who had "worked hard to build up the general hostility to Keayne."[65] Keayne found that his business reputation and sharp legal dealings were perhaps more important in this case than the facts surrounding the disappearance of Goody Sherman's sow.

The other circumstance complicating the case was the highly irregular path it had taken through the courts. The plaintiff, Richard Sherman, petitioned the General Court in May 1642 to hear their appeal of the original decision in favor of Keayne.[66] The court granted Sherman's request, albeit with great misgivings by the magistrates. Normally, the assistants served as the appellate court in all cases, and the judicial judgment of the General Court might be appealed to only after the magistrates had heard the case. Winthrop feared that such a precedent might be used by the deputies to seize a share of judicial power. Winthrop, of course, felt that judicial power ought to be restricted to the magisterial intelligentsia. Winthrop argued to the elders that the deputies had no "ordinary" calling in "judging private Causes." Since the deputies were only the representatives of the freemen and since the freemen "cannot exercise Judicature in their owne persons," "their deputyes are not Judges in waye of such an Ordinance."[67]

The eyes of the freemen were focused on the General Court when it heard the sow case in June 1642. After the evidence was presented, the vote of the court revealed a deep division between the deputies and magistrates: fifteen deputies and two magistrates (probably Saltonstall and Bellingham) found for the plaintiff; seven magistrates and eight deputies voted to acquit Robert Keayne, the defendant.[68] While a majority of the deputies and the General Court as a whole had voted in favor of Sherman, the magistrates' negative voice served to uphold Keayne's previous acquittal. The public outcry, no doubt fueled by the deputies, against what seemed to be another case of magisterial protection of a wealthy offender was not lost on Winthrop:

> There was great expectation in the country, by occasion of Story's clamours against him, that the cause would have passed against the captain [Keayne], but falling out otherwise, gave occasion to many to speak unreverently of the court, especially of the magistrates, and the report went, that their negative voice had hindered the course of justice, and that these magistrates must be put out [of office], that the power of the negative voice might be taken away.[69]

At issue was the magisterial intelligentsia's status as the culturally dominant political authority in the one-party state.

The ministry was decisive in the struggle between the magistrates and deputies over the sow case and the negative voice. On October 14, Winthrop wrote to the elders to inform them that the leaders of the deputies were using the anti-Keayne sentiment among the freemen to urge that "diverse of the magistr[ates]" who defended the negative voice ought to be replaced at the upcoming Court of Elections. Trying to rally the ministers to the magistrates' cause, Winthrop argued that such an electoral revolution would be both dangerous and dishonorable: "Dishonorable it would be to take the power from those whom the Countrye picks out, as the most able for publ[ic] service, and putt it into the hands of others, whom they passe by, as the more weake: dangerous allso it wilbe, for it will raze the foundation of our Government."[70] Winthrop claimed, with some validity, that the elimination of the magistrates' negative voice would turn the General Court into a representative democracy of the outer party.

The deputies took an even more direct and effective tack toward the ministers. In the spring of 1643, just prior to the Court of Elections, they presented Goody Sherman's side of the case to the elders.[71] The ministers were understandably incensed at this apparent miscarriage of justice on behalf of the notorious Robert Keayne. Consequently, the magistrates found themselves isolated within the one-party regime, as both deputies, elders, and freemen sided with Goody Sherman. This juncture represents the high-water mark of the antimagisterial movement. The deputies had found a remarkably popular case to rally the freemen against the magistrates' legislative veto. In addition, they had gained the legitimating authority of the ministers' judgment on their behalf. The situation could hardly have been more dire for the magisterial intelligentsia.

Winthrop acted swiftly to salvage the situation. His first move was to try to distance the ministers from the deputies and reverse their previous decision against Robert Keayne. In early May he published his "Summary of the Case Between Richard Sherman and Robert Keayne" and presented it, with his fellow assistants, to a conference of the elders and the leaders of the deputies. The re-presentation of the case had the desired effect, as the ministers were forced by the ambiguous nature of the evidence to revoke their previous decision: "[T]he elders there declared, that notwithstanding their former opinions, yet, upon examination of all the testimonies, as they did not see any ground for the court to proceed to judgement in the case, and therefore earnestly desired that the court might never be more troubled with it." Indeed, even the leaders of the deputies who had pled on behalf of Goody Sherman "seemed now to be satisfied."[72] The meeting appeared, or so thought Winthrop, to resolve the struggle within the General Court. Such appearances, however, proved to be deceptive.

When the newly elected General Court convened on May 10, 1643, George Story petitioned the court on behalf of Goody Sherman for a new hearing. Much to the magistrates' surprise, the deputies voted to grant the petition and retry the case.[73] The deputies protested that they were merely representing their constituents' anger over the disposition of the case.[74] The court had reached an impasse, as the assistants understandably refused to rehear the case. Once again, the freemen saw Goody Sherman's plea for justice go unheeded because of the magistrates' negative voice. Aware that they had the bulk of the freemen, if not the ministers as well, behind them, the deputies pushed in "earnest to have it [the negative voice] taken away."[75] Winthrop quickly dispatched a treatise justifying the negative voice with the prescriptions of the colony charter and the previous acts of the General Court. Almost immediately a countertreatise attacking the institution of the negative voice was produced by either Richard Bellingham or Israel Stoughton.[76] This rebuttal further emboldened the deputies, who, with the popular support of the freemen on their side, felt that at long last victory over the magisterial intelligentsia was at hand.

Governor Winthrop seems to have shared the deputies' view of the situation in terms of their likelihood of success, for his explanation of his actions betrayed a sense of despair. In his *Journal* Winthrop frankly acknowledged that "it was the magistrates' only care to gain time, that so the people's heat might be abated, for then they knew they would hear reason, and that the advise of the elders might be interposed; and that there might be liberty to reply to the answer [of Bellingham or Stoughton] which was very long and tedious."[77] Accordingly, Winthrop proposed that the court request the ministers' judgment on the negative vote for their upcoming October session and that in the interim "it shalbee no offense" for any freemen to "deliver their minds soberly & peaceably therein, or to deliver the same in writing, in any modest or briefe way."[78] The deputies, who, as Robert Wall puts it, "had no reason to think the ministers would be prejudiced against their cause," agreed to Winthrop's proposal and let the issue of the negative vote rest until the following session of the General Court.[79] The magistrates' status as the culturally dominant force within the government hung in the balance over the summer.[80]

In the meantime, Winthrop prepared and circulated a "Defense of the Negative Vote" in June 1643. This treatise, presumably intended to influence the ministers as well as the freemen, consisted of two parts. The first attempted to legalistically prove the legitimacy of the negative vote from the language of the colony charter as well as subsequent acts of the General Court. In the second part, Winthrop offered scriptural and theoretical arguments on behalf of the legislative veto.

The most important and controversial argument made by Winthrop was that without the negative voice the government of Massachusetts would be transformed from a mixed aristocracy/democracy into a "meere Democratie."[81] While using the language of the classical Aristotelian taxonomy of pure and mixed forms of government to describe the General Court, Winthrop gave an innovative sense to the peripatetic theory. Though these forms of government were clearly pure archetypes, the classical tradition had held that the prevailing pure and mixed forms of government stood in a teleological, "organic" relation to the societies and social structures from which they arose. Thus societies dominated by a strong warrior caste would naturally tend toward an aristocratic form of government, while societies dominated by a class of wealthy merchants would tend toward oligarchic government. This conceptualization still passed muster in early modern England, where the nobility—in theory, at least, the descendants of the medieval warrior caste—represented a large proprietary interest in society and were thus appropriately represented in the upper house of Parliament. In Massachusetts, however, the case was somewhat more problematic. The Bay magistrates lacked both noble forebears and the large-scale proprietary interest in their colony that the English lords enjoyed. Indeed, as we have seen, the deputies had considered not nominating two of the chief magistrates on account of their poverty. As the leaders of the deputies were quick to point out, "[O]ur magistrates are not of the Nobility, as the upper house their [England] is."[82]

Winthrop's answer to this objection was his greatest innovation in classical political theory, an innovation that reveals the principle of cultural domination in the Bay government. The magistrates were not an aristocracy of land or martial status, argued Winthrop, but rather a cultural elite or "natural aristocracy" bestowed with "the gifts of God, [such] as wisdome, learninge etc." While he acknowledged "that there are of the Deputyes men of wisdome and learninge sufficient," nonetheless, "in Common repute (especially in forreine parts) the magistrates be looked at, as men precedinge in gifts and experience."[83] This was no small innovation, for nowhere in Aristotelian political tradition is theoretical or cultural expertise recognized as a legitimate principle of political representation or authority. Apparently without intentional irony, Winthrop used the language of Aristotle's political theory to argue for a Platonic political regime, for the magistrates were far more a guardian class of "philosopher kings" than a landed warrior caste.

Winthrop must have been delighted with the effect his treatise had on the elders. Before the end of the summer the elders circulated a work, subsequently attributed to John Norton, that supported the negative vote and Winthrop's arguments on its behalf. This ministerial treatise differed from Winthrop's in that it did not attempt to support the legality of the negative vote from either the earlier acts of the court or the provisions of the charter. Instead it focused on the major theoretical question raised by the governor in his work: "Whether a mixed forme of goverment viz: of Aristocracy and Democracy or a popular forme of goverment as that consisting of the Deputies be fitter for this common wealth."[84] Implicit in this question were two of Winthrop's most central assumptions, namely, that Massachusetts's government was, in fact, a mixed aristocracy/democracy and that the elimination of the magistrates' legislative veto would reduce it to a "meer democracy." The author agreed with Winthrop that, on general grounds, such a transformation was decidedly undesirable and cited three results of Protestant political scientific research on governmental forms to prove his point:

1: That no simple forme is safer than an Aristocracy, nor so unsafe as a Democracy, a meere monarchy excepted.

2: That a mixed forme of goverment is more safe than a simple.

3: Amongst mixt formes that which is tempered of an Aristocracy, and a popular state, to excell.[85]

In the case of Massachusetts, this proposed change in government was even more unfortunate because the magistracy did not represent an aristocracy of military or proprietary status but rather a cultural elite possessing superior wisdom, learning, and experience. The loss of this "natural aristocratic" element in the fundamental frame of government, argued the ministerial treatise, "in effect puts out one of the eyes (if not the right eye) of the common wealth, *exposing it unto the losse of the reason of its whole magistracy* [italics mine] (the most fit men for that service as chosen by, and out of the whole country)."[86] On September 7, Cotton delivered the ministers' official decision on the negative vote.[87] The elders had upheld the assistants' legislative veto. Henceforth the magistrates could be assured in their exercise of power and would enjoy an enduring and cohesive alliance with the ministerial intellectuals.

What prompted the ministers to unequivocally side with the assistants on the question of the negative vote? No doubt a part of the explanation lies in their class interest. Once Winthrop identified the magistrates' claim to political prerogatives with their high cultural training, the ministerial intellectuals had an interest in seeing that legitimating principle honored. If the magistrates' cultural expertise did not warrant their legislative veto within the state, then it would be difficult for the ministers to justify their negative voice within the church on the same basis.[88] This identification of cultural expertise as a legitimating principle in both church and state polities must have been reinforced by the presence of Samuel Gorton. Gorton, who was captured and convented before the September session of the court, had written several bileful letters to the Bay government from his heretical outpost in Rhode Island. While accepting the legitimacy of the deputies, Gorton apparently earned some sympathy with his anti-intellectual assault on the privileged position of Massachusetts's "mandarin" magistrates and ministers. Thus the ministerial response may have been a perfectly rational class-conscious defense of the principle of cultural domination.

Although class concerns are certainly a part of the explanation, there is nonetheless evidence to suggest the influence of "ideal" factors, at least in the arguments of the ministerial treatise. Although undifferentiated oneness within the regime was never a goal of this Aristotelian scheme, the institution of mixed government was meant to foster unity insofar as significant interests in the society were represented in the state. The negative voice, however, as Winthrop clearly stated in his treatise, was intended to register and institutionalize division within the General Court, not unity. Using the organic and teleological language of the Aristotelian theory, Winthrop offered a novel consequentialist argument on behalf of such division: "[H]erein would the Lord our God, have his excellent wisdome and power appeare, that he makes (not the disparitye onely but) even the contrarietye of partes, in many bodyes, to be the meanes of the upholding and usefullness thereof."[89] The Lord's wisdom did not consist in the creation of a unified political will but rather in the conservative influence of what we would call a system of checks and balances. As Winthrop put it, "I cannot liken it [the negative vote] better to anything than to the brake of a windmill: which hath no power, to move the runninge worke: but it is of speciall use, to stoppe any violent motion which in some extraordinary tempest might otherwise endanger the wholl fabricke."[90]

This incipient conservatism was a poetical expression of the profound sense of human limitation and imperfection that underlay the "Augustinian strain of piety." Given the debased state of human nature and judgment, itself the result of original sin, Winthrop argued for prudence or caution in recognizing the fallibility of political institutions. This sense of human limitation, particularly in questions of government, was profoundly, if bluntly, expressed in the ministerial treatise: "The best humane administration is uncapable of perfection."[91] Godly wisdom dictated that the institutions of government ought to be arranged to check and eliminate potential mistakes rather than to pursue with unanimity some ideal or perfect regime. Winthrop's appeal to political prudence struck a resonant chord in the divines or at least in the ministerial treatise. One of its principal arguments on behalf of the negative vote was the paradigm case of the virtue of caution, the "lesser of two evils": "In case of error the hurt is negative, it can delay a good it can doe not positive evill. . . . The nocent whom a negative voyce keeps from just punishment one court, may be punished the next but the limmes, life, etc of the innocent which plurality of votes takes away, can never by men be restored."[92]

Thus both godly wisdom and class interest led the Massachusetts ministers to side with the magistrates over the negative voice. Speculation as to which of these factors was ultimately decisive is pointless. Suffice it to say that the confluence of both interest and belief made the case doubly convincing to the Bay divines. The result was a decisive victory for the magistrates and an enduring alliance and sense of class-conscious unity between the ministerial intellectuals and magisterial intelligentsia.[93] Henceforth the deputies would find themselves isolated in their unsuccessful struggle against the assistants. The issue of the magistrates' legislative veto had finally been laid to rest.

The deputies tried to salvage what they could from their defeat on the negative vote. If the magistrates were indeed a separate body within the General Court, then the deputies demanded a complete bicameral separation. Consequently, on March 7, 1644, the General Court ordered that henceforth the deputies would sit and deliberate apart from the magistrates.[94] Wall has argued that this was a "feeble" move that merely removed "the domination of the great gentlemen's physical presence."[95] Yet if the trial of Anne Hutchinson is at all representative, it was the magistrates' superior legal, dialectical, and rhetorical skills that allowed them to dominate the court's deliberations. Nor was their procedural power insignificant, for it was the exclusive right and responsibility of the chief magistrate to order the business of the court and bring all questions to a vote. Sitting apart from the magistrates, the deputies not only were spared the influence of the magistrates but also acquired the right to initiate and deliberate on legislation of their own. The institutionalization of a complete bicameral separation within the General Court significantly increased the deputies' legislative power within the Bay government.

In the following year the struggle between the deputies and magistrates took on an anticlimactic character. The deputies engaged in one last-ditch effort to curb the magistrates' executive power. This initiative bore some likelihood of success, for they had the legitimating authority of a previous clerical decision on their side. As long as the ministers continued to support the magisterial intelligentsia, however, the deputies' attack was doomed to fail.

The deputies' assault on magisterial executive power came in June 1644. Meeting on their own, the deputies sent the magistrates an order setting up a committee "whereby power was given to seven of the magistrates and three of the deputies and Mr. Ward (some time pastor of Ipswich, and still a preacher) to order all affairs of the commonwealth in the vacancy of the general court."[96] This proposal was not entirely unreasonable, for in 1642 the ministers had endorsed the notion of including prominent freemen in the Standing Council. Nonetheless, the magistrates balked at this suggestion, arguing that they were the executive branch of the government in the absence of the General Court. As the court was about to adjourn, the deputies requested that the magistrates refrain from acting in their executive capacity until the next session of the court. Once again the assistants refused, and they told the speaker of the deputies that "if occasion required, they must act according to the power and trust committed to them." The deputies' leader responded ominously, "[Y]ou will not be obeyed."[97]

As fate would have it, on June 23, two days after the court had adjourned, news of an impending Indian emergency reached Boston. An ad hoc committee of local ministers, deputies, and magistrates was convened and agreed to request Governor Endecott to summon the court promptly. Military commissions were drawn up "from the council of the commonwealth, but who were this council was not agreed."[98] On June 28, the magistrates drew up a document declaring and justifying their right to rule in the absence of the court and sent it to the deputies.[99] Apparently it was quite convincing, for the deputies agreed that if the magistrates would forbear publishing their declaration, they would "consent, that the governour and assistants shall take order for the welfare of this commonwealth in all sudden cases that may happen within our jurisdiction, until the next session of this Court, when we desire this question may be determined."[100] It was presumably at this point that Endecott addressed the court with a speech bewailing the questioning of the magistrates' authority, "as if they had none out of court but what must be granted them by commission from the General Court." To resolve the dispute Endecott requested that the elders be empowered to "be mediators of a thorough reconciliation, and to go about it presently, and to meet at Boston two or three days before the next court to perfect the same."[101]

When the General Court convened in late October, the ministers were summoned to Boston to give their counsel. Initially, they were given one question to answer: "Whether the magistrates are by patent and election of the people, the standing council of this commonwealth in the vacancy of the general court . . . [and] in cases where there is no particular express law provided, there to be guided by the word of God, till the general court give particular rules in such cases."[102] On the very next day the elders arranged a time when they could attend the court and deliver their response. When they arrived, they found, in addition to the magistrates, a committee of a mere four deputies to hear their counsel. Perhaps the deputies suspected the ministers would not take their side; if so, they were correct. Notwithstanding their previous counsel, Cotton delivered the ministers' answer "on the magistrates behalf, in the very words of the question."[103] Isolated within the regime, the deputies had no choice but to acknowledge and accept the legitimating judgment of the Bay divines. Consequently, on November 13, "all the answers given in by the reverend elders to the severall questions were approved just & true answers to satisfaction" by vote of the General Court.[104] Once again the ministers had sided squarely with their magisterial allies, and the result was another decisive victory for the assistants.

Although they sporadically sniped at the magistrates in the following years, most noticeably in the Hingham militia affair, such shots were increasingly futile and more often than not backfired on the deputies. For all intents and purposes, the institutional pattern of the orthodox one-party regime was set and would remain essentially intact until just prior to the loss of the charter in the 1680s. The delineation and balance of power between deputies, assistants, and ministers had evolved into a fixed form and, having reached that form, was ossified and remained unchanged for almost forty years. The system of authority known as the New England Way had come of age.

6

ESTABLISHING ORTHODOXY

The primary task facing Massachusetts's ministerial intellectuals in the decade following the Antinomian controversy was to preserve the fruits of their victory by firmly establishing their interpretation of Puritan doctrine as the official orthodoxy. Three obstacles stood in their path, two of which had emerged only after the suppression of Antinomian dissent. The defeat of Anne Hutchinson had sorely undermined the charismatic authority of her mentor, John Cotton, within the ministerial community. Indeed, the whole affair had raised suspicions and doubts about the safety of charismatic authority. In the years directly following the Antinomian controversy, a new informal leadership structure emerged among the clergy in Boston and its neighboring towns (Roxbury, Dorchester, Charlestown, Watertown, and Cambridge), a structure I have called the "big six pulpits." The Antinomian controversy had also revealed significant disagreements among the ministerial intellectuals on questions of theology and church polity. While such differences had been smoothed over for the time being by the various compromises struck at the Synod of 1637, there could be no doubt that new issues would arise in the future from which debates and controversies could ensue. To ensure that such controversies would never assume the crisis proportions of the Antinomian fiasco, the orthodox regime created an educational system, with Harvard College at its apex, that would foster cultural cohesion among the thinking class through a common, hegemonic core curriculum. Finally, of course, the Bay divines faced various dissidents among the laity and clergy who threatened to undermine the system of cultural domination. All three obstacles had to be cleared before the Massachusetts thinking class could compile the canonical document of the New England Way, the Cambridge Platform.

The problem of ministerial leadership only arose as a result of the suppression of Antinomian dissent. Although the ministry was officially a collegial community, by the mid-1630s de facto leadership within the ranks of the clergy had clearly devolved on the two preeminent divines in the Bay Colony, John Cotton of Boston and Thomas Hooker of Newtown. Of the two, Cotton's star had shone a bit brighter, and that, in addition to his dabbling in charismatic authority, had undoubtedly played a large part in Hooker's removal to the Connecticut Valley. Hooker's departure left Cotton as the dominant figure among the Bay ministers: it was Cotton who gave the critical election sermon of 1634; it was Cotton who was authorized to prepare the legal code of the new colony, "Moses His Judicialls"; and it was Cotton who played the central ministerial role in the suppression of Roger Williams. It may well have been the novel experience of such exalted preeminence that led Cotton to aspire to the status of first among equals within the ministry during the Antinomian controversy. Whatever the cause, one result of the Hutchinson affair was that Cotton's prestige and leadership position within the clerical community suffered irreparable damage. No one was more aware of this than John Cotton himself, who felt obliged to publicly recant and confess his errors twice within a year of Hutchinson's trial and even seriously considered emigrating out of the colony. With Cotton under suspicion, if not in outright disrepute, a leadership vacuum emerged within the ministry.

The structure that arose to fill this vacuum in the years directly following the Antinomian controversy—a structure that seems to have persisted well into the third generation and perhaps beyond—was informal and never officially created or sanctioned by the General Court or a synod. Nonetheless, there is tangible evidence that the ministers occupying the big six pulpits (Boston, Cambridge, Charlestown, Dorchester, Roxbury, and Watertown), all within close distance of each other and the General Court, quickly became the leaders of clerical opinion and practice. In the years between the end of the Antinomian affair and 1642, the General Court authorized the creation of four select committees with ministerial representation, two on the governance of Harvard, one on wage and price regulation, and one to compile a legal code. Of the thirty-two ministerial committee positions created by the court, twenty-one, or roughly two-thirds, of the positions were filled by the ten ministers occupying the big six pulpits at that time.[1] This political overrepresentation by the big six pulpits is all the more striking when it is considered that the Bay Colony contained some twenty churches at that time that were served by thirty-four ordained ministers.[2] Fewer than one-third of the colony's ministers and pulpits had over two-thirds of the duly authorized power.

George Selement has discovered a very similar pattern in his study of publication among the Puritan ministry. Selement has shown that in colonial New England "an elite group of only twenty-seven pastors (out of a total of 531) wrote 70 percent of all ministerial treatises: five men of 122 in the first generation, two of 84 in the second, two of 88 in the third, seven of 117 in the fourth, and eleven of 120 in the fifth."[3] While Selement's study is of New England as a whole, his evidence from Massachusetts is striking; all four "prolific ministers" in the first generation occupied big six pulpits.[4] Part of the explanation of this geographic publication pattern—and it is a pattern that persisted throughout the colonial period in Massachusetts—Selement finds in the location of printing facilities in Cambridge (and later Boston), the heart of the big six pulpits. This location also explains why the big six pulpits supplied the censors for the press.[5] Although Selement is unsure whether the geographic determination of ministerial publication in the Bay Colony was a fortuitous "fringe benefit of being the pastor" of the right congregation at the right time or whether, on the contrary, "the best speakers and writers held the choicest pulpits," the political machinations by the General Court surrounding Cotton's call to teach the church of

Boston and the court's maneuvering in securing John Norton to replace him after his demise suggest that the latter possibility was the operative one. In any event, those ministers occupying the big six pulpits clearly stood in a privileged and dominant position with respect to clerical publication in the 1640s and beyond.

In addition to leading the ministry in publication and political consultation, the divines of the big six pulpits also represented their colleagues' interest in the inculcation and establishment of high cultural training. On September 27, 1642, the General Court specifically stated that, in association with the Bay magistrates, "the teaching elders of the sixe next adjoyning townes, that is, Cambridge, Watertowne, Charlestowne, Boston, Roxberry, & Dorchester, & the president of the colledge [Henry Dunster at the time] for the time being shall have from time to time full power & authority to make & establish all such ordinances, statutes, & constitutions as they shall see necessary."[6] Equally significant in this regard was the General Court's decision on November 15, 1637, to locate Harvard under Shepard's watchful gaze in Newtown, later renamed Cambridge on behalf of the beloved alma mater.[7] While Shepard's explanation of this choice bears some weight—"this town, then called Newtown, was through God's great care and goodness, kept spotless from the contagion of the [Antinomian] opinions"—it seems somewhat less than decisive given the fact that the alternate and original site was not Cotton's heretical Boston but rather Hugh Peter's newly disciplined and orthodox Salem.[8] Harvard's location in Cambridge was probably just as much the result of that town's geographic position among the big six pulpits as it was a consequence of the town's reputed orthodoxy.

There were several reasons why the big six pulpits, as opposed to some other leadership structure, emerged in the aftermath of the Antinomian controversy. The immense advantage of being in close physical proximity to the General Court in a period when overland travel and communication were inconvenient at best cannot be overstated. Such proximity made mutual consultation with and attendance upon the General Court something of a social obligation for the ministers in the big six pulpits. Another advantage held by the ministers of these pulpits was their control over the weekly lecture circuit of political "occasional sermons" created by the General Court in the early 1630s; all four towns in the lecture circuit (Boston, Cambridge, Watertown, and Roxbury) contained big six pulpits. Finally, of course, the big six were blessed in the early years of settlement with a particularly choice set of divines, a blessing that no doubt resulted in the tradition of filling those pulpits with the best available talent in the colony and, occasionally, beyond. Not only Cotton and Hooker but also the prolific Mather and Welde, the earnest and evangelical Eliot, the solid and safe Phillips, Wilson, and Symmes, and the "soul ravishing" Thomas Shepard left a legacy for the big six pulpits that set them apart from all of the others in the Bay Colony. Here was a body of divines to be reckoned with.

The fact that the ministers of the big six pulpits assumed a significant degree of de facto leadership does not mean that they exercised unlimited and hegemonic power over their clerical brethren. The leadership of the big six pulpits was limited in three important ways. The clerical community was officially collegial, as evidenced by the various synods, and the principle of congregational independence ensured that consensus among the ministry would generally be the result of bland compromises and tacit ambiguity. The most this leadership could reasonably hope for in the majority of cases was the bare minimum of agreement necessary to ensure political and class cohesion. It should also be remembered that the big six pulpits offered only a core or nucleus of leadership, not a definitive and closed list of movers and shakers. Thus in the first generation of settlement the leadership of the big six was supplemented by the skills of Hugh Peter of Salem and Peter Bulkeley of Concord. Each generation created its additional leadership cadres outside of the big six. The third factor limiting the big six's influence was geographic distance. Just as the difficulties of travel and communication had rendered their proximity to the General Court and each other a distinct advantage, so the ministers on the northern frontier or the Connecticut Valley enjoyed a significant degree of autonomy as a result of their isolation. The eventual consequence of this stretching of the lines of communication was the emergence of a rival locus of ministerial leadership for the Connecticut Valley in Stoddard's Northampton at the end of the century.

Although the emergence of the big six pulpits filled the leadership needs of the Bay ministry, it also created certain untoward consequences. When death or emigration created a vacancy within the big six pulpits, the congregation and the General Court naturally looked to fill the position with the most qualified available talent in New England. If, however, the desired candidate was presently employed by another church, then the fulfillment of this wish might be impeded by the principle of congregational independence, particularly if the congregation declined to dismiss or release its prized minister. When such conflicts of interest arose, as John Norton's Ipswich and John Davenport's New Haven were to learn, it was the principle of congregational independence that was ultimately sacrificed.[9] Similarly, when a new church was created in any of the big six towns it was imperative that its ministers be fit for the leadership and attention that would befall them. Thus in the early 1650s, when the newly formed second church of Boston called to the ministry Michael Powell, a man without any university training, the church quickly found its congregational independence thwarted, as the General Court effectively blocked his ordination. Nonetheless, these problems were a small price to pay for the leadership supplied by the big six pulpits.

The other major obstacle facing the Massachusetts ministry subsequent to the Antinomian controversy was the heterogeneity of religious opinion and practice among the clerics of the first generation. While this issue only emerged as a practical problem during the Hutchinson affair, Hall attributes this lack of cohesion to "the breakdown of recruitment" of Bay divines. "The consequence was," he argues, "the assembly of an ill-assorted group of preachers in the 1630s, a group that ranged from Hansard Knollys, later to become a founder of the English Baptists, to James Noyes, who quickly proved an enemy to congregationalism."[10] To address this problem, the Bay ministry, in conjunction with the General Court, created an educational establishment with Harvard at its apex. The result was that "unlike the experience of the first generation ministers," the second generation of Harvard-educated clergymen "were homogenous in background and outlook."[11] As Harry Stout has put it,

> Harvard College played an indispensable role in supplying cultural cohesion and hierarchical control. The college collected a common cultural core which, through the minis-

ters, would be exported to every settlement in the land. By 1660, there were 135 college-trained leaders among the second generation, of whom 116 were Harvard graduates. . . . Inevitably these ministers' words were similar in matters of personal salvation and the meaning of New England because they emerged from a common education in Cambridge.[12]

Harvard produced a remarkable degree of unanimity of opinion and feeling among Massachusetts's rising generation of ministerial intellectuals.

Harvard's role in producing a well-educated and cohesive ministry has been well documented. Indeed, the principal goal of the college mentioned in "New England's First Fruits," Harvard's premier pedagogical manifesto, was "to advance Learning, and perpetuate it to posterity, dreading to leave an illiterate Ministery to the Churches, when our present Ministers shall lie in the Dust."[13] But Harvard's cultural boon was not restricted to the Bay clergy. Harvard also trained teachers for the various Latin grammar schools required by the General Court's educational legislation of 1647.[14] Between 1659 and 1677, Harvard produced eleven grammar school teachers for the Massachusetts towns.[15] The purpose of these schools was not merely to help students qualify for Harvard but also, as the General Court stated in 1642, to teach children "to read & understand the principles of religion & the capitall lawes of the Country."[16] Such schoolmasters inculcated their charges in the basic rudiments of the "canonical" orthodox tradition they had received at Harvard. For the future generations of Massachusetts residents, they were the teachers of the New England Way.

Far more important than its training of teachers, however, was Harvard's contribution to the magisterial intelligentsia and the political leadership of the Bay Colony. Even with literate clergy, there was no more frightening prospect for the Puritan one-party regime than an uneducated and uncultivated magistracy. As Jonathan Mitchell, one of the leaders of the second generation of divines, put it, "It sufficeth not to Have supplyes for the ministry, for time will shew that unlesse we Have the Helps of Learn[in]g & education to accomplish persons for the magistracy & other civill offices, things will languish & goe to decay among us." Thus, Mitchell pleaded in 1663, if additional public funds were supplied to maintain poor worthy scholars at Harvard, the issue would be "such as may possibly be fit for speciall service in the Commonwealth." Indeed, it was his hope that "some [graduates of humble origins] of singular Integrity & Ability may Have the eyes of the Country upon them of the magistracy besides others employed in Inferiour Civill offices."[17] While Mitchell's plea for additional public support came to naught, his wish for a Harvard-educated magisterial intelligentsia was amply fulfilled. By 1677, Harvard had graduated seventeen young men who went on to serve the Bay Colony in the General Court or as local magistrates.[18]

Educated in the same mores and high cultural tradition, such Harvard graduate legislators could be expected to be of one mind with each other and the Bay divines on most important issues. More than thirty years later, Thomas Shepard, Jr., saw the hand of a benevolent providence leading the founders "to provide Nurseries for Church and Commonwealth, in their ordering Schools of Learning, and in particular the Colledge." The fruits of such labors had been "a constant supply of a godly, learned Magistracy and Ministry (persons fitted for publick service both in Church and Common-wealth) and we have had experience of the blessing of God upon that endeavour."[19] Harvard afforded the Bay thinking class, both magisterial intelligentsia and ministerial intellectuals, a greater degree of class consciousness and unanimity of opinion than the first generation had enjoyed.

Nothing great is achieved without sacrifice, and the creation and maintenance of Harvard was no exception. While the education of orthodox divines and magistrates may have been invaluable for the Puritan regime, it had a very real price for the residents of Massachusetts. The cost of erecting and supporting an institution of orthodox higher learning sorely tapped the financial resources of the fledgling community at a time of deep economic strain. Indeed, perhaps the most impressive fact about Harvard was not its pedagogical success but its very existence and persistence. Building institutions for the dissemination and creation of high culture is rarely the first, and generally the last, priority of a newly established colonial outpost struggling to achieve a reasonable subsistence. It would be roughly sixty years before the older colony of Virginia took decisive steps to follow the Bay Colony's pedagogical lead.

The financial burden of the initial outlay for Harvard rested squarely on the shoulders of the Massachusetts taxpayers. On October 28, 1636, the General Court appropriated £400 "towards a schoole or colledge" and left the site of the institution unspecified.[20] As Samuel Eliot Morison has aptly remarked, the tidy sum of £400 represented a prodigious proportion of the colony's meager tax revenues: "more than half the entire colony tax levy for 1635, and almost one-quarter of the tax levy for 1636."[21] While this fund, which took the form of a credit, was not drawn on in the following year due to the emergence of the Antinomian affair, at the cessation of that controversy the orthodox regime renewed its pedagogical mission with a rekindled zeal. In November 1637, by order of the General Court, the college was founded in Newtown under the tyrannical rule of Nathaniel Eaton.[22] In short order, in part due to Eaton's financial malfeasance, the college found itself in need of additional support.

Although the General Court played an indispensable role, its subsidies were not the only source of funds for the newly created college. Harvard also benefited from the largesse of private persons. The most famous bequest was that of the college's namesake, the Reverend John Harvard of Charlestown. Harvard died of consumption on September 14, 1638, just over a year after his arrival, and left half of his estate, valued at £1,600, and his private library of some 400 volumes to the college at Newtown.[23] Although John Harvard's bequest was the largest and most famous, he was by no means alone. Between 1645 and 1653 various residents of the Bay Colony donated some £334 to the infant institution of higher learning.[24] Additional support was sought and received from English and Continental sources. On June 2, 1641, the General Court authorized Thomas Welde, Hugh Peter, and William Hibbins to travel to England and, ostensibly, "congratulate the happy [political] success there," but in fact their real purpose was to solicit funds for Harvard.[25] Their mission was largely successful. Lady Anne Mowlson of London donated £100 for a scholarship for poor students, various merchants and gentlemen subscribed £150 for the library, and "some gentlemen of Amsterdam gave towards the furnishing of a Printing-Press" about £49.[26]

While such private beneficence offered some relief to the Massachusetts taxpayers, it did not come without a price. The various bequests by Bay residents represented financial resources that were not being used in other, perhaps more pressing economic ventures. Nor was the foreign funding an unmixed blessing. Once in England, both Welde and Peter, two of the most eminent Massachusetts ministers, were lured into prominent positions in their native land, and they never returned to the Bay Colony. The loss of two such ministers was a large price to pay for the financial support of a college in a "howling wilderness." The cost was particularly high in the case of Hugh Peter's Salem, whose congregation "was unwillingly drawn to give leave to their pastor to go."[27] Not only did the church of Salem lose its revered minister, but also its presumed congregational independence was violated in the process.

As helpful as such private donations were, they were certainly less than sufficient. Harvard's survival continued to depend on the support of the New England governments. In addition to a complete tax abatement on all income and holdings, Harvard was awarded the revenues from the Charlestown ferry, one of the principal routes of travel to Boston. Morison called this steady source of income "a good beginning," but it was by no means adequate in itself.[28] Thus Thomas Shepard appealed to the commissioners of the newly formed New England Confederation assembled at Connecticut "for some contribution of help towards the maintenance of poor scholars in the college." The commissioners in turn "commended to the deputies of the general courts and the elders within the several colonies" a tax of 12 pence or one peck of corn per family each year.[29] Although the bulk of the revenue for this college levy came from Massachusetts, all four of the United Colonies complied, and between 1645 and 1653 over £259 was raised.[30] Whatever Harvard expenses were not covered by such intercolonial rates were borne by the General Court of Massachusetts. While the records of the Bay Colony's financial support of Harvard are sketchy in the first decades, Lawrence Cremin states that between 1669 and 1682 "52.7 per cent of Harvard's annual income came from the government and government-sponsored subscriptions."[31] No doubt the Massachusetts thinking class felt that such support was a small sacrifice for the great boon of Harvard College.

If Harvard was to be a pillar of the Puritan regime, more than financial support was required. Harvard's role in creating orthodox members of the thinking class necessitated a particularly careful governance of the college by the regime's inner party. Placed under Shepard's watchful eye, the college was initially ordered by a committee of six magistrates and six ministers. Authorized to "make & establish all such ordinances, statutes, & constitutions as they shall see necessary" for the college's well-being, this committee, known as the overseers, was reorganized by the General Court on September 27, 1642, to include the ministers of the big six pulpits and "the Governour & Deputy for the time being, & all the magistrates of this jurisdiction."[32] Unlike the English universities, which were self-governing guilds of fellows and instructors, Harvard was governed by the magisterial intelligentsia and the leaders of the ministerial intellectuals.[33] This anomalous situation persisted even after the college charter of 1650 was granted. Even though the General Court incorporated the president, treasurer, and five fellows with power to govern Harvard and choose their own successors, this authority could only be used in "the presence of the Overseers of the Colledge and by their counsell and consent."[34] Far more so than perhaps any other institution of higher education in its time, Harvard was dominated by and served the state.

Whereas the inner-party elite on the board of overseers was responsible for the governance of Harvard, day-to-day administration and instruction naturally devolved on the president and his tutors. It was therefore imperative that the faculty and especially the president be thoroughly orthodox in doctrine and pedagogy. While this did not create any problems for the first president, Nathaniel Eaton, his successor, Henry Dunster, ran afoul of this requirement. Indeed, the circumstances surrounding Dunster's resignation from Harvard provide one of the most revealing stories of Harvard College and the Massachusetts thinking class in the pre-Restoration period.

Nathaniel Eaton, Dunster's predecessor, distinguished his brief tenure at Harvard with remarkable maladministration and brutality. After Eaton physically abused and malnourished his charges for over a year, the General Court dismissed him from his post "for cruell & barboros beating of Mr. Naza: Briscoe [an usher or tutor in the college], & for other neglecting & misuseing of his schollers," and he was fined over £95.[35] Without a president, the college lapsed out of existence. When the Reverend Henry Dunster arrived in the Bay Colony on August 6, 1640, Harvard was thus at the absolute nadir of its brief institutional history. All nonbuilding operations had been suspended for over a year, and Nathaniel Eaton had escaped from the Massachusetts jurisdiction and had absconded, deeply in debt, with much of Harvard's assets.[36] As Samuel Eliot Morison observed, "[T]he financial prospect [of Harvard], forlorn at best, became so desperate when the economic depression of 1641 set in as to daunt anyone without the faith, courage, and youth of Henry Dunster."[37] Before the month was over the thirty-year-old Dunster was offered and had accepted the presidency of Harvard.

Dunster promptly fixed his residence at the college and resumed classes in the autumn term. Two years later, on September 22, 1642, those students lured back from Eaton's maladministration graduated with great pomp and circumstance before the overseers.[38] Dunster successfully stretched the college's meager revenues and put Harvard on a sure and sound footing. In 1641, Dunster married the widow of the Reverend Josse Glover and thus acquired the first printing press in the colony.[39] Although the widow Glover died within a year, her brief union with Dunster afforded to him the means to subsist as well as the first functional printing facility for the Puritan regime. Indeed, while the court offered Dunster the salary of £56 per annum, they only paid him in his first year. Thereafter he lived off his own estate and "got what he could from the Charlestown ferry rent, student's tuition fees, Commencement fees, and an occasional special grant."[40] The fruit of Dunster's labor was the graduation of over a dozen classes of orthodox ministers and legislators for the young colony. Dunster's remarkable achievements distinguished him as one of the most prominent and probably popular heroes of the orthodox thinking class.

Given Dunster's critical importance and contributions to the one-party regime, his failure to present his newborn son for baptism in 1653 signaled the beginning of a tragic and dangerous episode in Massachusetts's history.[41] Reluctant to lose so valuable a pedagogue, the Reverend Jonathan Mitchell of Cambridge attempted to reclaim his ex-teacher and present member of his flock from his erroneous dalliance with antipedobaptist scruples. When Mitchell failed in his purpose—he found himself being slowly converted by Dunster—the General Court arranged a conference with the leading elders to convince Dunster of his error and extract a recantation.[42] After this conference was in turn unsuccessful, the General Court on May 3, 1654, had little recourse but to

> commend it to the serious consideration & speciall care of the overseers of the colledge, & the selectmen in the severall townes, not to admitt or suffer any such to be contynued in the office or place of teaching, educating, or instructing of youth or child, in the colledge or schooles, that have manifested themselves unsound in the fayth, or scandelous in there lives, & not giveing due satisfaction according to the rules of Christ.[43]

Henceforth there could be no doubt in Dunster's mind as to the inevitable consequence of his continued dissent.

The court did not have to wait long for Dunster's response. On June 15, the General Court acknowledged receipt of the president's resignation and instructed the overseers to confer with Dunster and, if he should remain resolute in his decision to leave his office, to then take steps to secure an adequate replacement.[44] The overseers pleaded with Dunster to remain as president and keep his scruples to himself. Dunster remained intransigent, and on July 30 he publicly proclaimed his views during a baptism at Cambridge.[45] Dunster's speech left the General Court with no choice. Nearly a decade earlier they had passed a piece of legislation mandating banishment for any person that should "openly condemne or oppose the baptizing of infants, or go about secretly to seduce others from the approbation or use thereof."[46] Dunster's resignation was accepted, an account was taken to compensate him for services rendered, and he was replaced as president of Harvard by the Reverend Charles Chauncy. Dunster at last had fallen victim to the intolerant repression of the orthodox regime.

What is most remarkable about this episode, however, was the extreme leniency shown toward the errant pedagogue. Twice prior to passing their "orthodoxy in education" order of May 1654, the inner party attempted to convince Dunster of his heretical failings. Even after this legislation was passed, the overseers tried to retain Dunster in his office, asking only that he remain publicly silent about his antipedobaptist scruples rather than undergo a public recantation. Although Dunster declined this option with his outburst in the church of Cambridge, he was not dismissed from office until October 24, and he was allowed to remain in the president's house through the winter of 1654–1655.[47] Neither banished from the colony nor excommunicated from the church of Cambridge, Dunster removed to Scituate in Plymouth Colony in March 1655 and continued to hold property in Cambridge until his death some four years later. He was buried in Cambridge in accord with his wishes.[48] This leniency is all the more striking considering the floggings and heavy fines normally afforded Massachusetts Baptists in this period.[49]

Three mitigating factors helped prompt the leniency shown toward Henry Dunster in the face of his Anabaptist tendencies. Undoubtedly the gratitude and debt felt by the thinking class toward the savior of higher education at Harvard influenced the actions of the General Court. More important, however, was Dunster's status as a fully accredited intellectual in the Puritan regime. Like Wheelwright and Williams before him, Dunster benefited from the incipient class consciousness of the inner party as well as its obvious reluctance to draw public attention to a rift within its ranks. But while all three dissident intellectuals persisted in their heterodox views after an initial period of leniency by the General Court, only Dunster avoided the ultimate wrath of the Puritan regime.

The third and all-important factor mitigating the court's repression of the errant president was Dunster's singularly amenable behavior. Although he continued to entertain antipedobaptist scruples, unlike Williams and Wheelwright he never questioned the legitimacy of the orthodox regime or its system of cultural domination. Thus, when the Middlesex County Court ordered him to undergo a public admonition for his outburst in the church of Cambridge, Dunster humbly and duly complied and consequently publicly accepted the legitimacy of the magistrates' right to decide such questions of orthodoxy. By politely undergoing this public admonition, Dunster signaled his acceptance of the system of cultural domination and, as William McLoughlin put it, "[b]y holding his peace he probably proved an embarrassment rather than a help to the Baptists, for he gave truth to the Puritan claim that uniformity and conformity were not insisted upon by them so long as dissenting opinions were 'not vented.'"[50] Here lay the key to Puritan toleration and repression: orthodox unanimity was sought not as an end in itself but as a means to cultural domination. While Dunster's heterodox views on infant baptism rendered him unfit to preside over the colonial college, his unwillingness to undermine the system of cultural domination—and his acceptance of public rebuke for his violations of that system—signified to the inner-party elite that once he was removed from power there was no reason other than sheer vindictiveness to penalize him further. His gracious decision to emigrate from Massachusetts was probably motivated as much by the desire to spare the regime further embarrassment as by the desire to find a more tolerant and hospitable environment for his views.

Part of the remarkable success of the Massachusetts thinking class in creating Harvard and empowering the big six pulpits was a consequence of an immense tactical advantage they enjoyed. The inner party held the initiative throughout. In both cases, they perceived a pressing structural problem, devised a strategy to fulfill their goals, and successfully adopted sufficient means. The situation was totally reversed when the inner party faced their third obstacle on the path to the Cambridge Platform, lay and clerical dissent. It was the dissidents who enjoyed the initiative for the most part, deciding when and where to launch their forays against orthodoxy.

The thinking class also lacked the advantage of a clearly defined position. While the Antinomian controversy produced a renewed commitment to orthodoxy, it did very little to define or delimit exactly what was and was not orthodox. The Synod of 1637 devoted most of its attention to denouncing Antinomian heresies and banning lay activities that threatened the ministers' cultural domination. The few bland theological compromises struck at the synod were far from a complete and unified doctrine, much less a whole system of church governance and teaching. Such a complete system was not forthcoming until the synod that produced the famous Cambridge Platform, the official codification of the New England Way. The fundamental issues addressed by that synod arose as a result of the various lay and clerical dissidents that challenged the ministerial intellectuals and their cultural domination in the years following the Antinomian controversy. Their practical experience with the various heretical movements of the 1640s profoundly influenced the ministerial intellectuals' decisions in drawing up the Cambridge Platform and the nature of the polity arrangements it legitimated.

The first phase of the suppression of heretical error by the orthodox regime was the least taxing and dangerous. Essentially confirming their victory over the Hutchinsonians, the Massachusetts thinking class vigorously quashed any movement or discourse that bore even a faint resemblance to "familism" or Antinomianism. While this phase in the struggle against heterodoxy lasted only a few years, from 1638 to 1641, remarkably it resulted in the exposure of no fewer than three heterodox would-be divines. All three aspiring ministers were carefully scrutinized and examined by the orthodox inner-party elite and found doctrinally lacking. Only one of their recantations was successful in gaining the clemency of the thinking class.

The most famous potential minister suppressed for heterodoxy was Hanserd Knollys. Knollys arrived in Boston during the summer of 1638.[51] A graduate of St. Catherine's College, Cambridge, he had served as vicar of Humberston, Lincolnshire, in the early 1630s. A combination of Laudian repression and nonconformist scruples led Knollys to resign his clerical position and, ultimately, seek refuge in New England.[52] Pious and well-educated, Knollys was a potentially valuable member of the clerical community. There was, however, one small problem. Apparently, Knollys had been profoundly influenced in his nonconformity by his cousin, the Reverend John Wheelwright.[53] Not necessarily finding Knollys guilty by association, the orthodox inner party nonetheless thought it was only prudent to inquire into the soundness and safety of his theological judgment.

While the details of Hanserd Knollys's examination(s) are sketchy at best, an extant letter from Hugh Peter to John Winthrop confirms that Knollys was interviewed in the fall of 1639 at Boston, presumably by the ministers of the big six pulpits.[54] Their interrogation of Hanserd Knollys substantiated the inner-party elite's suspicions and fears about the errant divine. Although no record of the examination remains, it did not go very well for Knollys, for on January 21, 1640, he wrote to Winthrop to express his regret, "sorrow," and "shame"

> that I who professe love to Christ and to the brethren, should pearce him, and his members by that my sinne, The roote of which sinne was the Relicts of that Cursed Enmity in my heart against the Lo[rd] Christ and his people, for certainly had not the Devill (that old accuser of the brethren) fyered his temptation upon the tinder of that Corruption, he could not (I thinke) have caused my wretched heart to conceave nurrish and bring forth such a monstrous Imp soe like himselfe (to witt) an Accusation of the Brethren.[55]

While the exact nature of Knollys's accusation and heretical opinions is unclear, it was sufficiently dangerous to render his effusive recantation superfluous. On February 20, 1640, Winthrop recorded that Hanserd Knollys, "being suspected and examined, and found inclining" toward "familistical" doctrines, "was denied residence in the Massachusetts."[56] Nor did the judgment of the orthodox regime prove precipitate, for after returning to England Knollys eventually found his calling as a Baptist minister in London.[57]

A somewhat greater, if less famous, threat to orthodoxy was Robert Lenthall. A graduate of All Souls College, Oxford, Lenthall arrived in Massachusetts in 1638 and settled in Weymouth.[58] Lenthall found in Weymouth a town deeply divided. Before his arrival, a delegation of elders had convened in Weymouth on January 9, 1638, to patch over a falling-out between certain members of the yet ungathered church and its intended pastor, the Reverend Thomas Jenner.[59] The cause of the dispute at Weymouth was the congregation's failure to give Jenner, in Cotton's words, "satisfaction answerable to his pains." This lack of adequate compensation prompted the would-be divine to appeal to the magistrates for help.[60] Further complicating matters was the fact that a sizable portion of the congregation of Weymouth had been under Lenthall's ministry in England prior to his censure for nonconformity. Thus, while the gathering of this church was met with the "approbation of the magistrates and elders"—presumably the question of ministerial maintenance had been resolved for the town—the pro-Lenthall faction unsuccessfully attempted to disrupt the proceedings.[61] When this tactic failed due to the presence of the magistrates, the dissident faction quickly moved to gather a second church in Weymouth under the ministry of Robert Lenthall. Upon learning of these machinations, the magistrates "thought it needful to stop it" and summoned Lenthall and his principal supporters to appear before the March session of the General Court.[62]

Prior to his appearance at the court, Lenthall was examined by a delegation of ministers and magistrates. The result was that, as Winthrop put it, Lenthall "was found to have drank in some of Mrs. Hutchinson's opinions, as of justification before faith."[63] The case was even more complicated, for while Cotton was able "upon conference" to reduce Lenthall from his Antinomian heresies (and who could know better of such errors than Cotton?), Lenthall continued to oppose "the gathering of our churches in such a way of mutual stipulation as was practised among us."[64] Lenthall held that "the covenant of baptism gives being to the church," a stipulation that Winthrop interpreted as favoring a presbyterian or parishional church government.[65] This was no run-of-the-mill variant of presbyterianism, however, for Lenthall's other formulations of the nature of the church were extremely reminiscent of Cotton's proto-Antinomian views in his 1636 sermon at Salem. "The Covenant of Grace and Baptism is the internal form of a church," Lenthall insisted, "and their meeting together in God's name to worship God in one place gives an outward form of a church." Like Cotton before him, Lenthall was more than capable of displays of charismatic self-righteousness. "Upon this distinction," he solemnly proclaimed, "I will lay down my life."[66] The virulent anticlericism of some of his supporters, as revealed in their sentences by the General Court, is far more typical of Antinomian than presbyterian sentiment: "Mr. Ambros Marten, for calling the church covenant a stinking carryon & a humane invention, & saying hee wondered at God's patience, feared it would end in the sharpe, & said the ministers did dethrone Christ, & set up themselves; hee was fined £10, & counselled to go to Mr. Mather to bee instructed by him."[67] In any case, Lenthall's supporters had signed their names to a blank sheet of paper on which Lenthall was to write whatever church covenant stipulations he desired. Such an unauthorized course, which Lenthall himself "did openly maintain," threatened to bypass the collegial safeguards of orthodoxy.[68] The dissidents of Weymouth shortly found their fledgling church squelched.

Sometime before his court appearance, Lenthall was brought to see the enormity of his transgressions and the dangerous predicament in which they had placed him. Accordingly, on March 13, 1639, Lenthall offered the General Court a complete written recantation "of his errour in judgement, and of his sin in practice to the disturbance of our peace."[69] The court ordered Lenthall to present his recantation and thus "give satisfaction" to the church of Weymouth and then report to the next court.[70] Having duly and humbly performed these acts, Lenthall was excused by the General Court. His lay supporters did not fare as well. Drawing even harsher punishment than Ambros Marten, John Smith was imprisoned and fined £20 "for disturbing the publicke peace by combining with others to hinder the orderly gathering of a church at Waymoth, & to set up another there, contrary to the orders heare established & the constant practise of all our churches, & for undewe procureing the hands of many to a blank for that purpose."[71] For assisting Smith, Richard Silvester was fined £2 and disfranchised, while a Mr. Britton who "had sided with Mr. Lenthall, & C. was openly whipped, because he had no estate to answer, & c."[72] Wisely, Lenthall quickly immigrated to Newport, Rhode Island.

Perhaps as a response to Knollys, Lenthall, or both, the ministerial intellectuals attempted to codify their doctrines of salvation and the morphology of conversion. On September 23, 1640, the ministers of the big six pulpits drew up a list of eleven statements titled "Propositions Concerning Evidence of God's Love." While generally bland, the propositions were a useful checklist for distinguishing Antinomian from orthodox views. The first proposition concerned the morphology of conversion and warranted the "preparationist" preaching of the Bay divines: "A Ch[ristia]n may have (upon the manifestation of Gods free grace in the offer of the Gospell) some comfort and staye of heart, by restinge upon it: although he hath as yet no grace in himself."[73] The next three propositions placed belief or faith in Christ temporally, causally, spiritually, and invariably prior to salvation or any "testimony of Gods sp[iri]t touching a mans good estate."[74] Propositions 5 through 9 waffled on the relation between sanctification and justification. Proposition 6, a small concession to Cotton's salvific scheme, stated that a Christian "takeinge it for granted that he hath grace in himself" might find his assurance of salvation by the testimony of the spirit "without present actuall reasoninge or mindenge of his Graces." On the other hand, proposition 7 affirmed that a Christian "doubtinge of his Grace" can and ought to seek evidence of his salvation in "the truth of his Graces" or sanctified behavior. The balance of judgment lay in favor of the latter proposition, for proposition 9 stated unequivocally that justification without sanctification "is not the witt[ness] of Gods Sp[iri]t but a delusion." Finally, and most important, the last two propositions clearly delimited the "test[imony] of the Sp[iri]t" by the word of God, "either in the lettre or sence thereof." Indeed, so crucial was Puritan biblical exegesis that even when "the Sp[iri]t witt[nesse]s Gods love by the word in the sence of it, yet this test[imony] is to be tryed by the written word: that so it may be discerned to be indeed a test[imony] of the Sp[iri]t, and not a delusion."[75] The ministerial intellectuals had at last defined their position with respect to Antinomian opinion.

Ironically, the last minister to fall victim to Antinomian opinion was Jonathan Burr, one of the authors of the "Propositions Concerning Evidence of God's Love." A graduate of Corpus Christi College, Cambridge, Burr had served as rector of Rickinghall Superior, Suffolk, until 1639, when he was silenced for nonconformity and immmigrated to Massachusetts.[76] Burr settled in Dorchester in 1640 and became a member of Mather's congregation. In short order the eager divine gave "good proofs of his gifts and godliness to the satisfaction of the church" and was duly called to join Mather in the pulpit.

While Burr considered the offer, he preached a series of sermons in Dorchester that Winthrop described as "savouring of familism."[77] When Burr failed to satisfactorily answer the congregation's questions about his dubious doctrines, a conference was arranged between himself and Richard Mather, who was in turn to report to the church. Burr's written account of his opinions clearly troubled Mather. While some of Burr's stated views were sufficiently vague and qualified to "admit of a charitable construction," others were so dangerous and baldly stated that "no other [conclusion] could be gathered but that he was erroneous."[78] For his part, Mather uncharitably reported all of Burr's errors to the church without mentioning any of his "qualifications" or ambiguous evasions. To compound matters, Mather failed to apprise his potential colleague of the substance of his report before he presented it to the church. The incensed Burr denied the heretical views attributed to him, and Mather responded by selectively reading to the congregation the more dangerous passages of Burr's treatise. The congregation quickly divided into pro-Burr and pro-Mather factions, and despite various attempts at peacemaking, the divisions grew deeper.[79] Like Lenthall before him, Burr had dabbled in Antinomian beliefs and succeeded in dividing his church.

Yet things turned out well for Jonathan Burr, unlike Lenthall and Knollys before him. His ensuing examination did not result in silence, censure, or exile but rather recantation, reconciliation, and ordination. The inner party were able to recover Burr from his Antinomian errors because they had a clearly defined orthodox position to present him with—Burr had, in fact, signed the doctrinal statement—and because Burr did not use his dissident position to challenge the orthodox regime or its system of cultural domination. Quite the contrary, on February 2, 1641, Burr and Mather agreed to submit their differences to a meeting of "the governour and another of the magistrates, and about ten of the elders of the neighbouring churches [the big six pulpits]." What followed was a textbook case of successful reconciliation. After four days of deliberation, the assembled representatives of the inner party wisely concluded that both sides were at fault, "more particularly Mr. Burr for his doubtful and unsafe expressions, and backwardness to give clear satisfaction, & c. and Mr. Mather for his inconsideration both in not acquainting Mr. Burr with his collections before he had published them to the church, and in not certifying the qualifications of those errours which were in his writings." Mather and Burr pacified their supporters by humbly acknowledging the rectitude of the judgment rendered and meekly "took the blame of their failings upon themselves." For his part, Burr tearfully and manfully recanted "those erroneous opinions of which he had been suspected, confessing that he was in the dark about these points, till God, by occasion of this agitation, had cleared them to him." So sweet and thorough was the reconciliation in the church of Dorchester that Winthrop was moved to remark that "God was much glorified in the close thereof."[80] Jonathan Burr was ordained before the end of the month.[81] The orthodox position against Antinomianism had been secured.

The second phase of the suppression of heresy in the early 1640s was pointed in the opposite direction of the first. Having secured their "left" flank against the Antinomians, the orthodox inner party turned against those presbyterian/Arminian sympathizers on their "right."[82] There were several good reasons why the orthodox regime took measures against the colony's tiny presbyterian presence after it had seemingly ended the threat of "enthusiastic" familism. If the Hutchinsonians had offended theologically by transcending orthodox Calvinism, the presbyterians clearly violated the congregational polity scruples of the Puritan regime by extending membership on a parishwide basis. Such differences over church governance had profound political implications in a society where the franchise depended on church membership. Moreover, such polity differences might in turn lead to theological disputes. In a religious landscape dominated by congregational "gathered" churches, those who favored local presbyterian church government must have found a "soft" Arminian view of salvation and the morphology of conversion a singularly compelling justification for their charitable policy on church membership. As early as November 3, 1639, Ezekiel Rogers urged Winthrop to move against "Arminian, & the like fowle errors . . . if not to sett a brande on such a[s] have so offended already, yet to prevent the like, by calling to account any that shall dare so to offende."[83] Perhaps Rogers felt it was best to nip such a contagion in the bud.[84]

The most important reason for suppressing the handful of practicing presbyterians, however, was to establish some difference or distinction between them and the "orthodox" majority. It was particularly important to dramatize this distinction to the culturally virtuous laymen of the outer party, because from their perspective the clerical leaders must have seemed remarkably presbyterian in the years following the Synod of 1637. They had eliminated lay prophesying, curtailed postsermonic questions, and regularly practiced clerical consociation. While the churches remained gathered in form and the powers of admission and excommunication were still vested in the church as a whole, the ministers had made significant advances in their formal powers, and their constant and often intimate consultations with the magistrates certainly did not escape the attention of those lay members jealous of their "church liberties." But nothing raised their censorious suspicions more than the specter of an established ministry. Sensible yeomen, they realized that one of the keys to church power lay in the purse, and that as long as they could dictate the financial disposition of the church and its officers at their will, they would hold a powerful check on the aspirations of the elders.

The ministers for their part made a conscious effort to avoid any public action that might be interpreted as calling for or mandating their establishment. Thus, when Winthrop suggested to the Synod of 1637 just before it closed that they choose a preferred and gospel-warranted form of "maintenance," the elders declined "lest it should be said, that this assembly was gathered for their private advantage."[85] Some two months later the General Court reiterated this request "that some order may bee taken hearin according to the rule of the gospel," and once again the ministers demurred.[86] But while the ministers studiously avoided such self-interested public improprieties, the magisterial intelligentsia was free and eager to secure a stable and secure income for their clerical comrades. On September 6, 1638, the first steps toward ministerial establishment were taken by the General Court. The legislation was ostensibly directed at residents who were not church members and therefore declined to contribute to the ministers' salary and other church expenses. The court ordered that

> every inhabitant in any towne is lyable to contribute to all charges, both in church & commonwealth, whereof hee doth or may receive benefit; & withall it is also ordered, that every such inhabitant who shall not volentarily contribute, proportionably to his ability, with other freemen of the same towne, to all common charges, as well for upholding the ordinances in the churches as otherwise, shalbee compelled thereto by assessment & distres to bee levied by the cunstable or other officer of the towne, as in other cases.[87]

Such legislation could hardly fail to draw the attention of a yeomanry committed to the maxim "no taxation without representation."

Naturally, not all of the ministers approved of or even allowed such formal and rational financial proceedings. On May 2, 1639, John Cotton preached on behalf of voluntary "charismatic" contributions, arguing that all other sources of income "have always been accompanied with pride, contention, and sloth." While the clergy were not to blame, the very fact that the magistrates had been "forced to provide for the maintenance of ministers" was unimpeachable evidence that "the churches are in a declining condition."[88] It was thoroughly typical of Cotton to fail to realize that what worked in the uniquely affluent church of Boston was unlikely to succeed anywhere else in Massachusetts. When the church of Boston wanted to build a new meetinghouse in 1641, it simply raised £1,000 "out of the weekly voluntary contributions without any noise or complaint, when in some other churches which did it by rates, there was much difficulty and compulsion by levies to raise a far less sum."[89] Of course, it was not the voluntary form that made the church of Boston's finances so felicitous, but rather the fact that Boston had a preponderance of wealthy merchants with a disproportionate amount of the colony's disposable income.

Far more representative of the average was the church of Concord. The congregants there found "the maintenance of two minsters too heavy a burden for them" and consequently requested a ministerial visitation. When a small delegation of clerics arrived at Concord, "they found them [the congregants] wavering about removal, not finding their plantation answerable to their expectation." In addition to urging a further empowerment of the deacons of the church, the elders advised the congregants to tighten their belts and "continue and wait upon God, and be helpful to their elders in labour and what they could." The two ministers of Concord, Peter Bulkeley and John Jones, were enjoined "to be content with what means the church was able at present to afford them" and to keep their colleagues informed if they received a better offer.[90] It was therefore entirely understandable if ministers like Bulkeley and Jones of Concord should find some form of legally established maintenance preferable to Cotton's voluntary system of support. As William Hubbard would later argue, "[I]f Ministers by divine Institution may expect maintenance and encouragement, who would take care to see it done but the Rulers of Christian commonwealths." "They will have a hard task," he concluded, "that will undertake to prove that Tithes in some sence are not moral."[91]

Given the likelihood of such clerical preferences, the lay congregants were understandably concerned to thwart any perceived "creeping presbyterianism" on the part of the ministers. Thomas Lechford noted that clerical "set meetings to order Church matters" had led some of the laity to conclude that the ministers "bend towards Presbyterian rule."[92] Thus on November 22, 1642, the members of the newly gathered church of Woburn insisted on performing lay ordination on their pastor, Thomas Carter. The assembled divines, who witnessed the ceremony, had urged them to "desire some of the elders of the other churches to have performed it [the ordination]," but the members, fearing such clerical ordination "might be an occasion of introducing a dependency of churches, & c. and so a presbytery, would not allow it."[93] Even more direct was the displeasure of one Mr. Briscoe of Watertown. Briscoe wrote and circulated a treatise in which he objected that he and other residents of the town were taxed to support a church in which they were not members. The text, which Briscoe published anonymously, must have been provocative because Winthrop reported that it "occasioned much stir in the town." It must also have been persuasive, for while the Court of Assistants fined Briscoe £10 for publishing the text before he acquainted "the court or magistrates with his grievance" in violation of his duty and "some slighting of the court," the actual arguments presented by him were passed over without comment or censure.[94] The existence of such strong anti-establishment sentiment must have been a powerful motive for the elders in their effort to root out presbyterianism.

The ensuing Synod of 1643 was one of the most important nonevents in early New England history. The synod of some fifty ministers convened at Harvard on September 4 and dined at the public charge. After Thomas Hooker and John Cotton were chosen moderators, the assembly took up its sole issue, namely, what to do about the presbyterian churches of Newbury and Hingham. Thomas Parker of Newbury recalled that his fellow presbyterians "proposed our arguments, and answered theirs; and they proposed theirs, and answered ours."[95] According to Winthrop, the ministers "concluded against some parts of the presbyterial way." Before the synod broke up, the two ministers of Newbury requested "time to consider the arguments" presented against their polity.[96] What makes this second synod in New England's history a nonevent is the curious fact that there is almost no surviving evidence about it. The only known mention of it is a brief paragraph in Winthrop's *Journal* and another brief paragraph in a published letter from Thomas Parker, the presbyterian minister of Newbury.[97] Yet surely here was a significant ecclesiastic gathering that reached several prejudicial conclusions concerning a burning polity issue. The reasons for this strange silence on this synod are unknown, but there can be no doubt that part of the explanation lies in the fact that the results of the synod quickly became a "dead letter." Given the very principle of congregational independence the synod had been called to defend, such an ecclesiastic gathering could only have a consultative and not a coercive authority. It remained for the state to actually enforce the ministers' conclusions. This it declined to do.

Part of the magistrates' reluctance to prosecute the presbyterians might have been the result of their affinity for "establishment" as evidenced by their order of 1638. Parker particularly noted "much conjunction" with regards to his position on "admission of Members," namely, that "the rule must bee so large, that the weakest Christians may bee received."[98] Thomas Lechford noted the same trend in opinion.

"Of late some Churches are of opinion, that any may be admitted to Church-Fellowship, that are not extremely ignorant or scandalous," he claimed, "but this they are not very forward to practice, except at Newberry."[99] A far more important reason why both the magistrates and ministers dropped the presbyterian issue was because they were faced with a much more pressing and dangerous threat. Indeed, at that very moment when the inner party was poised to strike against their right flank, a powerful assault from their "familist" left began the third and final phase of the suppression of lay dissent in the early 1640s. In the process, the orthodox majority soon embraced quasipresbyterian positions themselves.[100] On September 7, 1643, just three days after the antipresbyterian synod had convened, the General Court sent a military company to bring Samuel Gorton to Boston.

Samuel Gorton was one of the most colorful, formidable, and dangerous heretics the Puritan regime ever faced. His theology was a fascinating hodgepodge of every available enthusiasm: large doses of Antinomianism and familism, some antipedobaptist and even antibaptist scruples, a hint of proto-Quaker inspiration, and heaping portions of anti-intellectual and anticlerical bile. Overshadowed by his predecessor Anne Hutchinson, Gorton broached even more theological errors and was probably every bit as charismatic, pugnacious, and obnoxious to the orthodox regime. The magistrates and ministers soon found that they had more than they could handle with Samuel Gorton and his band of disciples.

Gorton first reared his head in Massachusetts during the height of the Antinomian controversy. Gorton had not been in Boston long before he concluded that the political climate was inhospitable to his views. During a brief stay at Plymouth, "his behaviour was so turbulent and offensive both to the magistrates and others, as they were necessitated to drive him out of their jurisdiction."[101] From there he went to Portsmouth, Rhode Island, where, after a short sojourn, he and his newfound disciple John Weeks were publicly flogged and banished by the local authorities.[102] Naturally, Gorton and his followers—they soon numbered five men—found their way to Providence, the hotbed of heresy. By the autumn of 1640, even the tolerant Roger Williams was complaining to Winthrop that Gorton was "now bewitching and bemadding poore Providence, both with his uncleane and fowle censures of all the Ministers of this Country, (for which my self have in Christs name withstood him) and also denying all visible and externall Ordinances in depth of Familism."[103] Although granted only temporary leave to rest at Pawtuxit (Pawtucket), outside of Providence, Gorton soon had attracted a large and vociferous following. Eventually the Gortonists grew to such a number that "it was beyond the power of Mr. Williams and his party to drive them out," and an armed battle between the two factions was only averted by the pacific intercession of Roger Williams.[104] Gorton was clearly a difficult and trying neighbor.[105]

On November 17, 1641, thirteen members of Williams's faction, themselves dissident exiles from the Bay Colony, petitioned the General Court of Massachusetts to help them in their struggle against Gorton. In particular, they wanted "a neighbor-like helping hand" in the form of a military contingent "to help us to bring them [the Gortonists] to satisfaction, and to ease us of our burthen of them at your discretion." The Massachusetts authorities pointedly responded that since Providence was not within their jurisdiction there was nothing they could legally do.[106] Almost a year passed before a handful of Providence residents took the court up on its oblique suggestion. As Winthrop recalled, on September 8, 1642, "four of Providence, who could not consort with Gorton and that company, and therefore were continually injured and molested by them, came and offered themselves and their lands, &c. to us [the General Court], and were accepted under our government and protection."[107] Winthrop offered three reasons why the General Court annexed Pawtuxit. Of doubtful significance was the claim of humanitarian intercession, namely, that Winthrop and others moved to liberate these four men from the oppression and "unjust violence" of the Gortonists. Somewhat more plausible was the desire to gain a forward base for military operations against the Narragansett Indians. Most important, however, was the desire "to draw in the rest in those parts, either under ourselves or Plimouth, who now lived under no government, but grew very offensive."[108] The Bay authorities were trying to eliminate the last refuges and outposts of heterodoxy in New England.

Upon learning of this turn of events, Gorton and eleven of his most ardent disciples moved to Shawomet, a site south of Pawtuxit and Providence that was outside of the area being claimed by Massachusetts. Before leaving, however, they fired a parting salvo at the Bay government. On November 20, 1642, they sent a letter to the General Court that Winthrop aptly described as "full of reproaches against our magistrates, elders, and churches, of familistical and absurd opinions."[109] While this letter, like the rest of Gorton's writings, was largely convoluted and occasionally incoherent, he proved quite adept at turning a venomous phrase or casting a bileful aspersion.

In addition to denying that the court had any jurisdiction in Rhode Island, Gorton was careful to lambaste the hireling, pharisaical Massachusetts ministry. He was particularly irate about the divines' constant "bowing of the backes of the poore, going forth in labor to maintain it, and in the spirit of that hireling, raising up your whole [state?] structure and edifice; in all which, you bring forth nothing but fruit unto death." Gorton was scandalized that the common people of the Bay were actually forced to pay "a price to give for the keeping of their souls in peace and safe estate" in order that the clergy might be "furnished with riches, honor, and ease."[110] Indeed, the Bay regime's obsession with mandarin ministers and overeducated magistrates led them to "kill the other witness" of the Lord, Jesus Christ: "[Y]ou kill the other witness, the death or weakness of the Lord Jesus; for you must have man to be honorable, learned, wise, experienced and of good report, else they may not rule amongst you; yea, and these things are of man, and by man, as peers."[111] In addition to these notorious errors, Gorton warned his erstwhile foes about their superstitious practice of the sacrament of baptism, "so that if you be ashamed of the cross in baptism, be ashamed of the baptism also; for such as the cross is, such is the baptism."[112] Having discharged their invective barrage, the Gortonists retired to the safety of their refuge at Shawomet.

Much to their chagrin, the Gortonists discovered that they were not safe from the Massachusetts authorities even at Shawomet. Gorton and his followers had purchased their land from Miantonomo, the sachem of the Narragansetts. Unfortunately, two of his subsachems who resided in the locality, Pumham and Sacononoco, objected to the sale. In the spring of 1643, the two traveled to Boston to place themselves and their followers under the Massachusetts jurisdiction and thus regain control of the land occupied by the Gortonists. When Gorton and his followers declined to travel to Boston to resolve the issue, the court acceded to Pumham and Sacononoco's request. On September 7, 1643, the delegates of the United Colonies, who were assembled in Massachusetts, sanctioned the court's annexation of the Shawomet area and authorized them to take whatever actions they felt appropriate toward Gorton.[113] On that very day, the General Court, having already had their offer of safe passage rebuffed by Gorton, dispatched three commissioners to Shawomet "to requir & see satisfaction made with security, or to bring their persons" back to Boston.[114] The Gortonists, who boasted of their military prowess and ability to defend themselves, belligerently refused to comply with the commissioners' wishes. Naturally, they compiled a written response to the court and gave it to the commissioners to deliver.

This second missive was even more provocative than the first. Dated September 15, the letter was addressed "[t]o the great and honoured Idol Generall, now set up in the Massachusetts." The opening passage was a venomous assault on the General Court, "whose pretended equity in distribution of Justice unto the souls and bodies of men, is nothing else but a meer device of man, according to the ancient customes & sleights of Satan, transforming himself into an angel of Light, to subject and make slaves of the species of kinde that God hath honoured with his own image."[115] The residents of Shawomet warned the magistrates not to try to take them by force, "for we are come to put fire upon the earth, and it is our desire to have it speedily kindled."[116] The Gortonists even took the time and effort to vilify the Bay clergy and their superstitious and anti-Christian dispensation of the sacrament of the Lord's Supper: "You are about your dished up dainties, having turned the juice of a poore silly Grape that perisheth in the use of it, into the blood of our Lord Jesus by the cunning skill of your Magicians, which doth make mad and drunke so many in the world."[117] The radical fringe at Shawomet had hurled vitriolic defiance at the orthodox one-party regime.

Not to be trifled with, the General Court took immediate and direct action against the Gortonists. Captain George Cook, Lieutenant Humphrey Atherton, and Edward Johnson were duly commissioned "with a guard of 40 able men to attend them" to descend on Shawomet and bring Gorton and his followers back to Boston with as "much of their substance [property] as should satisfie our charges."[118] After Gorton sent the commissioners a defiant message on September 28, the officers laid siege to the dissident band, which had taken refuge in a well-fortified house. After a protracted firefight—strangely, nobody was injured—the Gortonists capitulated and were seized. Gorton later recalled the festive spirit of the march back to Boston, particularly once they entered the Massachusetts jurisdiction: "[I]n some towns their minister which the soldiers brought along with them against us, gathered the people together, in the open streets, went to prayers, that the people might take notice, what they had done, was done in a holy manner, and in the name of the Lord." Apparently, the celebratory tour came to a head in Dorchester, where a large throng "placed us at their pleasure, as they saw fit to have us stand, and made vollies of shot, over our heads in sign of victory."[119] On October 13, 1643, Gorton and his band of ten followers arrived in Boston, along with their confiscated property, as prisoners of the Puritan regime.[120]

If the ministers and magistrates thought their impressive show of force would intimidate Gorton and induce him to recant and sue for pardon, they were sadly mistaken. The very next Sunday, Gorton struck back at the orthodox regime. Forced to attend Cotton's service—the text was "out of Acts 19 of Demetrius pleading for Diana's silver shrines or temples"—Gorton asked to speak after the sermon. Foolishly, his request was granted. After summarizing Cotton's sermon, Gorton gave his own interpretation of the significance of the "silver shrines": "[H]e said that in the church there was nothing now but Christ, so that all our ordinances, ministers, sacraments, & c. were but men's inventions for show and pomp, and no other than those silver shrines of Diana."[121] Undaunted by the insurmountable forces arrayed against him, Gorton went right for the jugular, namely, the "show and pomp" that "sacralized" the culturally dominant expressions of the ministerial intellectuals. Gorton had joined the battle.

The trial or examination of Samuel Gorton and his disciples began on October 17, 1643. After one day of preliminary questioning and posturing, the court charged that Gortonists were "a blasphemos enemy of the true religion of our Lord Jesus Christ & his holy ordinances, & also of all civill authority among the people of God, & particularly in this jurisdiction."[122] Gorton naturally denied the charge. For the next three weeks the General Court examined the Gortonists, largely one at a time and often behind closed doors. The Gortonists' basic defensive strategy was largely evasion and equivocation. Careful not to say anything to the court that even hinted of heterodoxy, the defendants stated that their bileful letters had been uncharitably misinterpreted. A careful and sympathetic reading, which they supplied, showed that they had been in no way disrespectful or heretical. While their performance must have been quite impressive, the best they could hope to do was frustrate their interrogators. Ultimately, nothing the Gortonists said could clear them of the charge. The General Court still had their letters, and the Gortonists repeatedly refused to recant them. The only question was the sentence.

Throughout the trial, recalled Gorton, the ministers of Boston used their pulpit to urge "the magistrates and the people to take away our lives."[123] It is quite likely that other ministers in the Bay promoted the same course in their occasional sermons. For the ministerial intellectuals, Gorton was more than an anathema; he was their very nemesis. An articulate and sharp-tongued anti-intellectual, Gorton systematically attacked the foundations of the ministers' cultural domination, urging in its stead the antiformal "democratic enthusiasm" of a charismatic religious community. Unlike the Antinomians, Gorton could not be portrayed to the common folk as the aggressor in this conflict. Because the magistrates had gone out of their way to confront Gorton, he could plausibly claim to be persecuted for his conscience. Gorton's truculent public outbursts had probably already tarnished the aura of unflinching deference and respect surrounding the clergy. Predictably, the ministers, who were present throughout the trial, advised the General Court to sentence the Gortonists to death.[124]

The magistrates agreed with the ministers that the Gortonists ought to be executed for their heinous cultural crimes. Like their clerical brethren, the magisterial intelligentsia realized that Samuel Gorton's danger lay in his potentially powerful appeal to the culturally virtuous outer party. Fundamentally, Gorton's goal was to liberate the church members from the cultural domination of the thinking class of the inner party and thus create a truly democratic Puritan regime. Given Gorton's public condemnation and reproach of the Puritan thinking class, he could not safely be allowed to survive this confrontation without recanting. Such a precedent was unthinkable and would only lead to the further promulgation of public defiance of the proper order of things. Since neither Gorton nor any of his followers were willing to recant their offensive writings, the magistrates concluded that they could not be allowed to survive. All but three of the magistrates—presumably the Bellingham faction—voted for the death penalty.[125]

Much to the shock and dismay of the magistrates and ministers, the elected representatives of the culturally virtuous laymen of the outer party refused to accede to the execution of Gorton and his disciples. Their decision came hard on the heels of a bitter and protracted struggle with the magistrates over the "negative voice," which had ended on September 7 with the elders unequivocally siding with the assistants. No doubt, the ministers' decision to reach a class-conscious alliance with the magisterial intelligentsia served to mitigate, if not excuse, Gorton's anti-intellectual diatribes. While the deputies' decision may have been partially motivated by frustration over having finally lost the struggle against the magistrates, they would also prove reluctant to execute Quakers and even banish baptists in the following decades. In any event, their vote had a profound effect on the inner party. Not only did it help cement the ministerial-magisterial axis, but also the deputies' decision had a profound and enduring effect on ministerial judgment. A growing sense of suspicion toward the deputies and the laymen they represented spurred a "conservative" and antipopular thrust to clerical convictions.[126] The decisive moment in this change of sentiment was the case of Samuel Gorton and his followers in 1643. When Gorton arrived, the ministers had been in the process of cracking down on their "rear-guard" presbyterian elements. By the time the whole affair had ended, the ministers of Hingham and Newbury were off the hook, and the Bay divines were looking to incorporate significant portions of the presbyterian system of church government. When the deputies chose to spare the lives of men who had publicly and vociferously attacked the privileged position and cultural domination of the orthodox thinking class, the ministerial intellectuals finally concluded that the culturally virtuous laymen of the outer party could not be trusted. No single person had a more profound impact on setting the terms and conditions of the Cambridge Platform than Samuel Gorton.

Although the Gortonists were spared their lives, they did not escape punishment. On November 3, the General Court sentenced each of the dissidents to be sent to a separate town,

> there to bee set on worke, & to weare such boults or irons as may hinder his escape, & to continue dureing the pleasure of the Court; provided that if he shall breake his said confinement, or shall in the meantime, either by speach or writing, publish declare, or maintaine any of the blaphemos or abominable heresies wherewith hee hath bene charged by the Generall Court, . . . upon his conviction thereof shalbee condemned to death & executed.[127]

After having sentenced the Gortonists to an indefinite term of forced servitude, the inner party must have thought that it had finally broken the back of this dissident movement. It hadn't, of course. In the spring of 1644, John Endecott of Salem informed Winthrop that "[w]e have heere divers that are taken with Gorton's opinions, which is a greate griefe unto us." Randall Holden, the Gortonist confined at Salem, had not only found a group of converts among the townspeople but also "reviled Mr. Norrice [the minister of Salem] & spoken evill of the Church." Endecott advised Winthrop to request the death penalty for Holden so "that others might feare, ffor assuredly both with you & with us, & in other places that heresie doth spread which at length may prove dangerous."[128]

Winthrop declined to take Endecott's advice. Executing Holden would only make a martyr of him in the eyes of his followers. Nor was the time propitious to raise the issue with the deputies, who, still smoldering over their defeat on the negative voice, were now assaulting the magistrates' monopoly of executive power. Perhaps the deputies were still unwilling to invoke the ultimate sanction of the state on the heretical dissidents, for Winthrop claimed that the court couldn't agree "what to do with them," and we can only suppose that the vast majority of the magistrates favored the death penalty. Winthrop had few options. "Finding that Gorton and his company did harm in the towns where they were confined," on March 7, 1644, the General Court released the Gortonists and gave them fourteen days to leave the colony "upon pain of death."[129] The Gortonists wisely returned to Shawomet. At least for the foreseeable future, the Gorton affair had come to a close.[130] It remained for the synod that produced the Cambridge Platform to register the effect of Gorton and his dissident predecessors on the polity arrangements known as the New England Way.

7

FROM THE CAMBRIDGE PLATFORM TO THE HALF-WAY COVENANT

The impression received from reading a standard account of the period between the synods that produced the Cambridge Platform and the half-way covenant is that the Puritan project declined in Massachusetts. The churches became increasingly tribal in their concerns, the clerics became sacerdotal in their ministry, and a broad "declension" undermined the religious culture and practice of Christian piety. While there is much to be said for each of these claims, taken together they depict a distinctly misleading portrait of the Massachusetts scene, particularly if they are not placed in the context of the larger institutional practices of both church and state in this period. Assuredly, by most obvious measures, the orthodox one-party regime was more firmly entrenched in the years 1646–1662 than at any time before or after. The word was widely preached to forced attendance, the number of orthodox gathered churches grew, three intercolonial synods were held, remonstrants were imprisoned and heavily fined, baptists were banished, and Quakers were flogged and executed. How much more Puritan could the Bay Colony be?

The problem with these claims is not that they are incorrect but rather that they are disjointed when examined out of perspective. Each of these phenomena—tribalism, sacerdotalism, and declension—was symptomatic of a deeper, more pervasive conjuncture. Here, as often is the case, David Hall has been the trailblazer. It was precisely this period, he has urged, that was suffused by "a coolness between the preachers and their audience that extended beyond the General Court into society as a whole."[1] In his *Farewell Exhortation* of 1657, Richard Mather warned church members of the dangers of such "coolness" on their part toward their clerical elders. "If through profaneness, or worldliness, or high flown imaginations of excellent attainments, you shall once think an able ministry, & Christs ordinances to be of no great necessity," he informed his congregation, "believe not that your hearts are in a right frame in such a case."[2]

Yet even this "coolness" must be placed in its ecclesiastic context. When the focus is narrowed from the audience as a whole to the full members of the churches, their relation to the clergy in this period was clearly tense and occasionally adversarial.

Nor were the ministers for their part sanguine about their congregants. In early 1650, Peter Bulkeley offered John Cotton his frank assessment of the problem with the laity:

> Shall I tell you what I think to be the ground of all this insolence, which discovers itself in the speech of men? Truly I cannot ascribe it so much to any outward thing, as to the putting of too much liberty and power into the hands of the multitude, which they are too weak to manage, many growing conceited, proud, arrogant, self-sufficient, as wanting nothing. And I am persuaded that except there be some means used to change the course of things in this point, our churches will grow more corrupt, day by day; and tumult will arise hardly to be stilled.[3]

As Bulkeley's comment suggests, the cause of the tension between the clergy and congregations was the delineation of power within the churches. In the years between 1646 and 1662, the ministerial intellectuals clashed with the culturally virtuous members of the outer party over the question of ecclesiastic power and its relationship to lay consent. As was so often the case in Puritan Massachusetts, the issues most worthy of serious contention were those that involved church polity.

An essential prerequisite of cultural domination, consent had been an important feature of the parallel institutions of church and state, both of which emerged with "mixed" governments. In the state, the culturally dominant magisterial intelligentsia of the inner party ruled with the consent and concurrence of the culturally virtuous members of the outer party and their deputed representatives in the General Court. Similarly, the ministerial intellectuals governed the churches with the consent and concurrence of the full members of the congregations (and therefore members of the outer party). In both cases, the requirement of lay consent afforded the members significant power, often enough to constitute a de facto negative voice on most important issues. And yet in one crucial respect, the separate lines of development in church and state polities in Puritan Massachusetts were almost entirely antithetical. While both developed into mixed governments containing a minority of culturally dominant thinking-class members of the inner party juxtaposed with a majority of culturally virtuous laymen of the outer party, the paths they took in this development led in opposite directions.

At the outset, the Bay Colony was governed by a ruling junta of the magisterial intelligentsia who were endowed with autocratic powers. In a structural sense, the story of the subsequent fifteen years of Massachusetts's political history (1630–1645) was one of gradual but constant accretion of power by the virtuous laymen of the outer party. Early on they acquired the right to register their consent to be governed and participate in the election of the magistrates. Next came the right to representation on issues concerning taxation. Shortly thereafter followed the power to participate, via their representatives, in all legislative matters, political trials, and the judicial review of highest appeals. With the institution of a complete bicameral separation in the mid-1640s, in which both magistrates and deputies were endowed with a legislative veto, the polity development of the General Court reached a mature, completed phase. Indeed, government at the local level had become even more "democratic," for the General Court had passed a law in 1647 that enabled select non–church members "who have taken or shall take the oath of fidelity to this government" to vote in town elections and hold a variety of local offices.[4] While the Bay Colony had remained an orthodox one-party state throughout, there can be no doubt that the General Court of Massachusetts had become increasingly republican in character and that the power of the freemen had expanded dramatically.

Just the opposite was the case with the development of church polity. Initially, the Bay churches had been independent gathered congregations of covenanting laypersons. All power within the church—admission, admonishment, censure, excommunication, election, and ordination—was predicated on the active consent and participation of the laity. It was the ministers, not the church members, who introduced ecclesiastic "innovations" to increase their power and ensure their cultural domination. They instituted clerical consociation during the first half decade of settlement in the face of significant lay opposition and received legal sanction for that practice in the early 1640s. The first intercolonial synod—an anomalous church practice in a society dedicated to the decentralization of ecclesiastic power within particular churches—was held in response to the Antinomian controversy, and some six years later a second synod was held to contend with the presbyterian minority.[5] And, of course, an educational system was established with a colonial university to facilitate the training of orthodox ministerial intellectuals at the public's charge. In sharp contrast to the growth of lay power in the Puritan state, the first decade and a half of Massachusetts's church history was characterized by small but significant accretions of ministerial power at the expense of the laity. Culturally dominant from the beginning, the ministers became more and more of a speaking aristocracy in the face of an increasingly silent democracy.

This dichotomy in the secular trend of development in church and state—the laity gaining power in the state and losing it in the church—highlights another important difference in the tempo of polity development. From a purely institutional point of view, after the first churches established a pattern for subsequent gatherings, almost all of the Puritan regime's energies were directed at differentiating and delimiting power within the General Court. Only after this process was complete in the mid-1640s did the regime turn its institutional attention to the delineation of church power between the laity and clergy. The result was that, even with the few clerical "innovations," by 1646 church power was still decentralized and largely vested in the laymen of the particular quasi-independent congregations. Almost every exercise of church power and initiative required the concurrence of the lay members. While deference toward the ministerial intellectuals was always an important stipulation, apparently it required supplementation in the Synod of 1637. Remarkably, the power of repression vested in the clergy was almost nonexistent, and the ministers were forced to rely on lay consent and state interference to squelch heterodox dissent. Indeed, it was precisely because the clergy, as a separate interest or "estate," held little, if any, ecclesiastic power that the General Court was forced to uphold orthodoxy within the churches. The consequence was that they were able to do so only on an ad hoc basis, largely in response to particular dissident movements. Without the magistrates' constant vigilance and "nursing" care, the Bay churches might well run rife with heterodoxy and anarchic "independence." It was in part the fear of this potential "Babel" in the religious culture that induced the ministers to attempt to undermine the importance of lay consent and increase their own church power in the years between 1646 and 1662.

The remarkable stress placed on lay consent in the Bay churches and the concomitant absence of clerical means of repression were legacies of the Puritan movement in Stuart England. As the repression of the English church forced the Puritan movement underground, it underwent a drastic decentralization, ceding power and authority to local "cells" or congregations. This afforded a degree of protection for the clerical leadership insofar as they were only implicated in the dissident activities of their local cells and thus could not all be taken by the authorities in one fell swoop. In Stuart England, as in all societies where dissent is forced underground, this decentralization had a profoundly democratic effect on the distribution of power within the movement or party. As the local congregation increasingly became the locus of power and sovereignty within the movement, the power of the laymen within the movement expanded dramatically. This was precisely because the influence of the small number of ministerial intellectuals was diffused and diluted among the various particular congregations. Within each congregation, itself an "independent" party cell, the ministerial intellectuals were a small and isolated minority. Such an "egalitarian" empowerment of the lay membership, which clearly occurred in Stuart England and early Massachusetts, is an extremely common phenomenon within radical underground political movements.

Once the Puritan movement achieved state power in Massachusetts, there was a natural tendency, as with other revolutionary movements, for the leadership to attempt to increase and solidify its control by centralizing power within the party. The locus of sovereignty moved from the various Jacobin clubs to the Committee of Public Safety, from the soviets to the Central Committee, from the party cells to the revolutionary tribunal, and, in the case of the American Revolution, from the independent states to the federally constituted government. It was only in extracongregational assemblages such as synods or Central Committee meetings that the revolutionary intellectuals were able to achieve a "critical mass" and assume mastery or a "vanguard" relationship to the following. Thus the more sovereignty and power afforded synodic gatherings within the Puritan movement, the more influence and power were enjoyed by the ministerial leadership.

Such centralization of power and authority within the party was accompanied by a "dilution" and thus devaluation of the consent and participation of the culturally virtuous members of the outer party. Like the ministerial intellectuals, the laity needed particular conditions of concentration to achieve a critical mass. If the number of persons within an ecclesiastic or political body was too great to afford a face-to-face dialogue among them, the influence of the nonelite mass following was diminished. The result was that membership in the outer party would become relatively comprehensive in the sense of including a significant percentage of the population in excess of the culturally virtuous. This process of the centralization of power and the dilution of lay consent and influence was a powerful force in the polity maneuvers of 1646–1662 in Massachusetts. Hence Edmund Morgan's brilliant insight into the dialectic of polity development in the early Bay churches: "Historically the magnification of the minister's office has often gone hand-in-hand with a comprehensive policy of church membership, while a limited membership, emphasizing purity, has been associated with a restriction of clerical authority."[6]

In Puritan Massachusetts, the ministerial intellectuals attempted to centralize power within the churches by means of clerical consociation and synodic fiat, while trying to devalue lay consent by diluting and thus expanding the conception of church membership. Given the limited formal and independent power vested in the ministry within the churches/party cells, their task represented a prodigious, almost Herculean challenge. That they met with only limited success in the years 1646–1662, however, is testament not only to the difficulty of the task but also more specifically to the resistance of the culturally virtuous laymen of the outer party.

Yet an element in the polity of the Bay churches eludes the sociology of revolutionary parties. As previously mentioned, John Cotton irrevocably complicated the internal politics of Massachusetts's churches by introducing religious charisma in the mid-1630s. Cotton's presence and activism resulted in the widespread incorporation of two significant charismatic polity features that further empowered the laity within the churches. The more famous, of course, was his institution of a test of saving grace, or charismatic religious experience, as a prerequisite for church membership. This requirement resulted in a culturally and charismatically elite lay membership, a membership that could be virtually guaranteed not to grow beyond its optimum size for "critical mass."

While widely adopted and incorporated in the late 1630s, this charismatic conception of membership was controversial from its first appearance and had induced the immigration of Thomas Hooker and his comrades to Connecticut. The ministers of Hingham and Newbury had apparently refused to comply with the stipulation, and by the mid-1640s many Bay divines began to question the safety of placing so much ecclesiastic importance on such experiential confessions, particularly when they excluded otherwise culturally virtuous laymen from church membership. Nor were all such otherwise culturally virtuous non–church members enamored of this stipulation; it necessitated their ecclesiastic exclusion. The Child Remonstrants specifically listed the exclusive charismatic nature of the Bay churches as one of their three grievances:

> 3. Whereas there are diverse sober, righteous and godly men, eminent for knowledge and other gracious gifts of the holy spirit, noe wayes scandalous in their lives and conversation, members of the church of England (in all ages famous for piety and learning) not dissenting from the latest reformation of England, Scotland, &c. [i.e., presbyterianism] yet they and their posterity are deteined from the seales of the covenant of free grace.[7]

While the remonstrants only succeeded in raising the ire of the General Court, their desire "to be taken into your congregation and to enjoy with you all those liberties and ordinances Christ hath purchased for them" may well have coincided with the wishes of a growing segment of the ministry.[8]

The other legacy of Cotton's charismatic influence in the Bay churches concerned the financial compensation of the clergy. In both his preaching and practice, Cotton had advocated a charismatic voluntary maintenance of the clergy whereby members and nonmembers alike would contribute whatever each felt appropriate to their minister's salary. Like the test of saving grace, this innovation stirred significant controversy among the elders and seems not to have been universally adopted. Indeed, in the early 1640s the General Court passed legislation to redress the problem of an "insufficient" voluntary maintenance. Nonetheless, there is clear evidence that as late as 1646 this compensatory stipulation was still widely practiced. Even the Child Remonstrants, who complained that non–church members were "forced to contribute to the maintenance of those ministers who vouchsafe not to take them into their flock," were forced to admit that such forced payment only occurred "in some places" and thus, by implication, not in most.[9] While the control of the purse strings is not the only (nor necessarily the most potent) power within an institution or organization, it is most certainly considerable and not to be reckoned with lightly. As long as the financial well-being of the ministers depended on the goodwill of the congregants, a powerful force existed to induce the clergy to accede to their wishes. In the period between 1646 and 1662, the ministerial intellectuals not only had to contend with the legacy of decentralized lay empowerment inherited from the dissident past but also had to undo the further lay empowerment that had resulted from John Cotton's dalliance with religious charisma.

The subtle but intense power struggle between the clergy and laymen of the outer party during this period has eluded the attention of historians because, from our perspective, the stakes at issue were remarkably, almost absurdly, low. Orthodoxy having been established in the early 1640s, at no point thereafter did the culturally virtuous laymen encourage or brook heterodox expression or dissent. Indeed, when a handful of merchants petitioned the General Court on October 18, 1645, to suspend the enforcement of legislation from the previous year that had banned baptist dissent and the extended residence of aliens, seventy-eight laymen from various churches submitted a counterpetition at the next court "for the continuance of such orders, without derogation or weakening, as are in force against Anabaptists, & other errorious persons."[10] Naturally, the court acceded to the antibaptist wishes of the laymen. When it came to the suppression of heterodox dissent and the enforcement of orthodoxy, the ministers and lay members were most assuredly of one mind.

That the Cambridge Platform represents the first official codification of the New England Way is so well known as to constitute conventional wisdom among historians. John Norton told the assembled freemen of the colony in 1661 that the Cambridge Platform was "that for which we are Out-casts at this day; that (for the substance of it) is it that sheweth what New-England is."[11] What is less well known is that the synod that produced this "identity-creating" document was surrounded by controversy. Indeed, the very calling of the synod caused dispute. In May 1646, "a bill was presented by some of the elders [to the General Court] for a synod to be held in the end of the summer" for the avowed purpose of reaching a widespread "agreement upon one uniform practice in all the churches."[12] While the magistrates were more than willing to comply with the ministers' request, the deputies raised two critical objections.

Unlike the Synod of 1643, the call for this assemblage was to emanate from the General Court, and the deputed representatives of the outer party "were not satisfied of any such power given by Christ to the civil magistrate over the churches in such cases."[13] Simply put, the deputies asked what ecclesiastic right the government had to command the independent churches to participate in an extracongregational assembly. Some divines, like John Eliot, argued that the public and thus civil nature of synods gave the state "influence, by Law and Command, to give allowance unto such

Assemblies," and even "an Extrinsicall Efficiency in calling Councils."[14] In the face of this argument the deputies might easily have quoted the great John Cotton, for some eight years earlier he had warned of the danger of "giving the Spiritual Power, which is proper to the Church, into the hands of the Civil Magistrate, as Erasmus would have done in the matter of excommunication. If any Magistrate should presume to thrust himself by his Authority or otherwise, into a work which properly belongs to a Church-Officer, let him remember what befell Saul."[15]

The deputies' second objection was that such an ecclesiastic gathering would inevitably centralize power away from the local congregations. Since the synod's conclusions were to be submitted to the General Court for approval, "this seemed to give power either to the Synod or the court to compel the churches to practise what should so be established."[16] The deputies' logic was flawless. If the synod's results were, in themselves, binding on the churches, then the lion's share of power within the church/party would devolve on the ministerial intellectuals who attended and dominated such assemblies. Alternately, if the General Court could enforce synodic conclusions, the locus of sovereignty within the churches would be shared by the state and the ministers who composed such conclusions. In either case, ecclesiastic power would be "centralized" from the particular churches and thus removed from the hands of the outer party. Why should the deputies agree to a practice that could only result in the loss of their own power as laymen within their "independent" decentralized congregations?

Fortunately for the elders, the magistrates were able to reach a compromise with the deputies and issue the call for a synod. According to Winthrop, the deputies on their part assented to the magistrates' proposition "that the civil magistrate had power upon just occasion to require the churches to send their messengers to advise in such ecclesiastical matters, either of doctrine or discipline, as the magistrate was bound by God to maintain the churches in purity and truth."[17] The magistrates responded by graciously declining to exercise that power "because all members of the churches, though godly & faithfull, are not yett clearly satisfyed" that such magisterial authority was indeed legitimate.[18] Instead, on May 15, 1646, the General Court simply chose to "express our desire" that the ministers and "other messengers of the severall churches" meet in a synod at Cambridge toward the end of the summer. Once the synod finished its business, its report was to be sent to the magistrates so that "it may receive from the said Generall Courte such approbation as is meete, that the Lord being thus acknowledged by church & state to be our Judge."[19]

The deputies' ojections pointed to an even more critical question. What was the reason for calling the synod in the first place? That some variation existed in the practice of the churches was hardly a very compelling justification. Such variation had been part of the Bay ecclesiastic scene from the very outset and had not, to that point at least, proved any real abiding threat to orthodoxy. Certainly reasonable men could agree to disagree about details that were not fundamental or essential. If a particular heterodox movement or opinion should arise that could not be handled by an individual congregation, the General Court could intervene. If such intervention in turn proved ineffective, a synod could then easily be justified and convened. Unlike the previous Synods of 1637 and 1643, which had been convened under "crisis" circumstances to contend with dissident movements, in 1646 no significant doctrinal danger loomed over the Massachusetts landscape. What heterodox opinion or controversial question warranted this extracongregational assembly?

The ministers did, in fact, seize upon a controversial issue as justification for the assembly. The principal reason the General Court offered for the synod was to resolve the question of what persons were eligible for the ordinance of baptism. The ministers had chosen wisely, for, as the court noted, on the issue of baptism

> the apprehensions of many persons in the country are knowne not a little to differ; for whereas in most churches the ministers do baptize onely such children whose nearest parents, one or both of them, are settled members, in full communion with one or other of these churches, there be some who do baptize the children if the grandfather or grandmother be such members, though the immediate parents be not, & others though for avoyding of offence of neighbour churches, they do not as yet actually so practice, yet they do much incline thereto, . . . ; on the other side there be some amongst us who do thinke that whatever be the state of the parents, baptisme ought not to be dispensed to any infants whatsoever.[20]

Although the question of baptism had indeed presented the churches with a quandary and had even given rise to the heterodox dissent of antipedobaptists, the issue was an ironic justification for the synod. First of all, the Bay baptists had already been roundly denounced as heretics, and the appropriate repressive legislation had been enacted and upheld. More important, however, the synod itself never reached any conclusions on this topic. While the bulk of the ministers, apparently led by Norton and Mather, favored instituting what was later derisively called the half-way covenant, a handful of important elders protested vigorously, and the majority declined to force the issue.

The ministers were not disingenuous in their expressed concern over variant practices and the issue of baptism. Undoubtedly a large part of their motivation was indeed their wish to resolve these problems, and in fact they did take some steps toward resolving them with the Cambridge Platform. The point is, rather, that there was another, perhaps more important, purpose in calling for the synod. Not that this purpose was part of a conspiratorial hidden agenda, for the only difficulty in discerning it is posed by its very obviousness. As the deputies clearly and rightly perceived, if the ministerial intellectuals could hold an extracongregational assembly at a relatively pacific moment in the religious culture and succeed in enforcing a uniform code of practice and polity, that in itself would represent a significant centralization of ecclesiastic power away from the particular churches.

This was not a paranoid fear for their liberties by the laity, for one of the principal architects of the Cambridge Platform, Richard Mather, had raised precisely this point against platforms in his justification of the New England Way some years earlier. "Christians have liberty from God to search the Scriptures and try all things, and hold fast that which is good," he asserted, "but the foresaid imposing of platformes and confessions compiled by men, doth seeme to abridge them of that liberty." Whatever unity might be achieved by such platforms, it came at the cost of "shutting the doore against any further light which god may give to his best servants, and more discerning, beyond what they saw at First." Mather claimed to speak for the clerical community when he concluded that "therefore we doubt such imposed platformes are not lawfull, or at least not expedient."[21] By 1646, Mather and his colleagues had apparently changed their views on the legality and expediency of such platforms and pressed on for a synodic gathering to create one of their own. Given such a precedent, subsequent synods could (and in fact did) follow in which lay consent might be further diluted and power might be removed from the laymen of the outer party. That a minor setback had occurred in the form of the deputies' protest was no cause for clerical anxiety. If the synod could nonetheless reach a mutually acceptable code and have it enforced, the elders' purpose would be achieved.

The ministers ultimately achieved some degree of success in their purpose, but, as they were soon to learn, they had a long, hard road ahead of them. As the time for the synod drew near, the various churches received the court's "request" to send their messengers to Cambridge on September 1. Three Massachusetts churches chose not to comply. While the refusal of Hingham to participate might well be attributed to bitterness over its recent humiliation in the Hingham militia affair, the recalcitrance of Boston and Salem was certainly troubling. Both congregations had been hotbeds of religious charisma (and, on occasion, heterodox dissent) and now acted as the self-appointed champions of congregational independence and lay power. Winthrop records that the leaders of some thirty or forty members of the church of Boston offered a particularly critical but cogent assessment of the situation: "[T]his synod was appointed by the elders, to the intent to make ecclesiastical laws to bind the churches, and to have the sanction of civil authority put upon them, whereby men should be forced under penalty to submit to them." Naturally, these members protested "that they should betray the liberty of the churches, if they should consent to such a synod."[22]

For two weeks the church of Boston discussed and debated the issue. The lay protesters could hardly have been either impressed or convinced by the arguments with which they were presented. To their objection that the court had already given the ministers the "liberty" to convene at their pleasure in the early 1640s and that hence there was no reason or legitimation for the General Court to call the synod, the lay recalcitrants received the disingenuous response "that that liberty was granted only for a hold in case of extremity, if in time to come, the civil authority should either grow opposite to the churches, or neglect the care of them, and not with any intent to practise the same, while the civil authority were nursing fathers to the churches."[23] But the ministers had, in fact, exercised that power, both in their clerical consociation and in the Synod of 1643. The real objection that the laymen were raising was that given this practice of clerical consociation, the only purpose of this synod could be to use the power of the state to enforce the ecclesiastic will of the ministerial intellectuals. Understandably, the dissenting laymen of Boston remained unmoved in their refusal to allow their elders to participate in the assembly at Cambridge. For their part, pastor Wilson and teacher Cotton refused to give in to their troublesome congregants. Reputedly "much grieved in spirit," the Boston ministers warned their flock "that they thought it their duty to go notwithstanding, not as sent by the church, but as specially called by the order of court."[24] Aside from its obvious inaccuracy— the court had specifically "requested," not ordered, the elders' presence—this statement contained the thinly veiled threat that the elders would attend the synod with or without the blessing of the church.

When the synod convened at Cambridge on September 1, John Cotton and John

Wilson were not there. The church of Boston had called their bluff. Not daring to participate in the synod without the approval of their congregants, the ministers of Boston were forced to remain at home. Upon hearing of Boston's ecclesiastic boycott, the ministers at Cambridge "wrote letters to the elders as brethren of the church of Boston, inviting them and pressing them also by arguments to send their elders and other messengers."[25] The Boston brethren, however, remained adamant in their opposition.

The next day, September 2, John Norton delivered Boston's biweekly "lecture" or occasional sermon. Addressing the assembled throng (which included most of the synod) from the most prestigious pulpit in the colony, Norton chose a text that was, in Winthrop's words, "suitable to the occasion, viz. of Moses and Aaron meeting in the mount and kissing each other." Noting that the power of synods, like the one Boston was boycotting, was only "consultative," he nonetheless insisted that the magistrate had the legitimate authority to call such assemblies and that it was "the duty of the churches in yielding obedience to the same."[26] Norton had expressed the collective judgment of the orthodox regime; Boston's brethren would have to carefully consider their response.

The following Sunday the church of Boston once again took up the issue of their participation (or lack thereof) in the synod at Cambridge. Apparently, the ministers opened the meeting by asking the members to vote, by show of hands, whether they "would hold communion with the other churches." While a majority of the congregation expressed their consent, "some of the opposite party resisted and gave this reason, that they did assent to the proposition, yet they could not vote it, because they did not know what would be inferred upon it." The recalcitrant brethren proved prescient in their reservations, for the ministers informed them that, having agreed to hold communion with the other Bay churches, they could express this communion in one of two ways. Either the church could send their elders as "messengers to the Synod" or the whole congregation could "go themselves" en masse. The opposing brethren protested "at this way of doing a church act by the major part, which had not been our practice in former times."[27] They were informed that the stipulation of unanimity was not operative in this particular case.

Trying to make the best of a bad situation, the oppositionists then suggested that if the church had to participate in the synod, it should participate en masse, with the entire congregation in attendance. This would have been no small innovation, for previous synods had never had such a mass participation. Rather, the conventional wisdom, at least according to John Eliot, was that the messengers sent by the churches "ought to be Elders, of both Orders, Teaching and Ruling, to represent the whole Church." This elite representation was necessary "because, as the temptation of Learned men, is to affect a Prelacy over the people," Eliot reasoned, "so the temptation of the Fraternity is to affect a Morellian Democracy."[28] Not only would such a course "savour of disorder and tumult," objected Cotton and Wilson, but also "it were impossible any business could proceed in due order" under such anarchic conditions. Although they were unable to achieve a consensus, the ministers finally had their way: "In the end it was agreed by vote of the major part, that the elders and three of the brethren [a sop to the dissenters] should be sent as messengers."[29]

While they had failed to halt the synod in its tracks, the recalcitrant laymen of

Boston did succeed in slowing down its progress. As a result of Boston's ecclesiastic boycott and the absence of Thomas Hooker and John Davenport, the synod adjourned after only two weeks, to reconvene the following June. The ministers had failed, in this first session at least, to produce the desired code of practice. This failure does not mean, however, that—as Wall has claimed—"the synod sessions of 1646 accomplished nothing of importance."[30] While they had not produced a full-fledged platform, the ministers did reach an agreement on certain fundamentals, an agreement that was subsequently published under the title, "The Tentative Conclusions of 1646."

"The Tentative Conclusions" dealt with the two most pressing issues for the ministerial intellectuals gathered at Cambridge. These issues were the very ones that Norton had addressed in his occasional sermon at Boston: what was the nature of synodic power, and did the magistrates have the legitimate authority to convene such an assemblage? To the latter question, concerning the magistrates' authority in "matters of the first table," the "Conclusions" answered in the affirmative but with the following important proviso: "[H]e [the magistrate] is not to mould up and impose what Erastian forme of Church polity he pleaseth; because if there be but one form commanded now of God, he cannot therefore command what forme he will."[31] The test also toed Norton's line on the question of synodic power. "The Synods declaration of the truth binds not politically, but formally onely," the ministers explained; "it binds the conscience, and that by way of the highest institution that is meerly doctrinall."[32] Finally, the text ended with a summation that included the same image that Norton had invoked at Boston: "The Churches desire, the Magistrate Commands; Churches act in a way of liberty, the Magistrate in a way of authority. Moses and Aaron should goe together, and kiss one another in the Mount of GOD."[33] In short, the synod pronounced itself lawfully gathered and ecclesiastically legitimate.

Nor should this session's impact be sought solely in dialectical feats and rationalizations. The very act of gathering in a synod seems to have emboldened the clerics to exercise their "presbyterial" power. According to Winthrop, just before the synod broke up, the husband of a recent excommunicant requested the intercession of the assembly. His wife had been "cast out [of the church of Weymouth] for some distempered speeches, by a major party" despite the dissent of "the ruling elder and a minor party."[34] The ministers informed the husband that since they were about to disperse, they could not hear his wife's case as a body. They must have offered him some sound tactical advice, however, for before long "complaint was made to the elders of the neighbouring churches, and request made to them to come to Weymouth and to mediate a reconciliation." When the elders in turn informed their flocks of this request, the laymen balked at this violation of congregational independence, "seeing the major party of the church did not send to the churches for advise." To this impertinent objection the ministers pointedly replied that "it was not to be expected, that the major party would complain of their own act." Apparently, this accurate observation had some effect on the laymen, for while only "some of the churches approved their [the elders'] going," none actually banned or officially disapproved of the clerical council.[35]

Perhaps emboldened by their recent meeting at Cambridge, the elders descended on Weymouth with this lukewarm lay blessing. When the church of Weymouth asked if they came in the name of their churches—"they objected this, that except they had been sent by their churches, they should never know when they had done, for others might come still, and require like satisfaction"—the elders boldly replied in the affirmative. As in the late session of the synod, the ministers came in a consultative way "of brotherly communion" to offer their counsel. Using their cultural influence and pressure to its fullest effect, they quickly secured a reconciliation, "whereupon the woman who had offended was convinced of her failing, and bewailed with many tears, the major party also acknowledged their errour, and gave the elders thanks for their care and pains."[36] Such a fulsome peacemaking could only bolster the prestige of the elders and legitimate their "consociated" exercise of power.

The most profound effect of the synod session of 1646, however, was on the General Court. Sanctioned by the synod to order matters of the first table, on November 7, 1646, the court passed a flurry of ecclesiastic legislation. Since the synod had stipulated that such legislation must be warranted by the Bible, and since the elders were the official interpreters of that text, it must be inferred that these acts were passed with the concurrence, if not at the bequest, of the ministerial intellectuals. That most of this legislation was clearly meant to bolster the clerics' cultural domination only serves to confirm that inference. The first order levied a fine of 20 shillings per month for the first six months (raised to 40 shillings per month if a recantation was not forthcoming) for any person found guilty of the following heresies: "deniing the imortality of the soule, or the resurrection of the body, or any sinn to be repented of in the regenerate, or any evill done by the outward mann to be accounted sinn, or deniing that Christ gave himselfe a ransome for our sinns, or [denying] that we are justified by his death & righteousnes, but by the perfection of our owne works, or deniing the morality of the 4th commandment." The penalty for spreading such errors was a hefty £5 per offense.[37]

The rest of the legislation was a bit harsher and more clearly focused on cultural domination. The death penalty was prescribed for blasphemy and, more pointedly, for any person who dared "reproach the holy religion of God, as if it were but a politicke devise to keep ignorant men in awe."[38] The same sentence was set for adults, who, like the Quakers in years to come, attempted to undermine the principle of Puritan biblicism and the political empowerment of the ministers' literary critical skills it supported: "Itt is ordered, that if any person of age of discretion professing or having professed Christianity, shall deny the Holy Scriptures to be the word of God, or not to be attended to by illuminated Christians, & shall continew obstinate after dew meanes of conviction, shall be putt to death."[39] Failure to attend the ministers' public exercises—"the ordinary meanes to subdue the harts of hearers not onely to the faith, & obedience to the Lord Jesus, but also to civill obedience, & allegiance unto magistracy"—would draw a fine of 5 shillings for each such occurrence "without just & necessary cause." A more substantial fine of 40 shillings per month was imposed on all who "shall go about to destroy or disturbe the order of the churches established in this country, by open renouncing their church estate, or their ministry."[40]

The last piece of ecclesiastic legislation passed by this session of the General Court mandated public deference toward the ministerial intellectuals. Seeing that "the open contempt of Gods word & messenger thereof is the desolating sinn of civil churches," the court ordered that any person who "shall contemptuously behave himselfe toward the word preached, or the messengers thereof called to dispense the same in any congregation, . . . either by interrupting him in his preaching, or by charging him falsely with any error . . . shall for the first scandale be convented, & reproved openly by the magistrates, at some lecture, & bound to their good behaviour." A second offense would result in either a fine of £5 or the following humiliating public ordeal: "to stand two houres openly upon a block 4 foote high, on a lecture day, with a paper fixed on his breast, with this, A WANTON GOSPELLER, written in capitall letters, that others may fear & be ashamed of breaking out into the like wickedness."[41] Given the deputies' scruples about calling the synod some six months earlier, such a deluge of ecclesiastic legislation would have been unthinkable without the synod's sanction and the approval and probable prompting of the elders.

When the synod reconvened at Cambridge on June 8, 1647, it once again failed to produce a platform of church discipline. Nonetheless, this second session was not without effect. On the first morning of the session, Ezekiel Rogers of Rowley staked out the ministerial "high ground" and roundly denounced the obnoxious "practice of private members making speeches in the church assemblies to the disturbance and hindrance of the ordinances."[42] While the General Court proved slow to follow the elders' lead in this regard, on other, more important matters it was more than willing to oblige.[43] On November 11, 1647, the court took its first halting steps, no doubt at the elders' urging, toward ensuring an adequate and regular "maintenance" for the ministers. The stipulated purpose of the act was to make certain that "their may be a convenient habitation for the use of the ministry in every towne in this jurisdiction, to remaine to posterity." To that end the court ordered that the town lots granted to the elders were to be held by them and their successors in perpetuity. Thus the minister's "deed of purchase & the deed of gift thereupon" would accrue "to the use of a present preaching elder, & his next successor, & so from time to time to his successors." Far more important was the law's stipulation concerning the minister's maintenance. The General Court authorized the towns to set a fixed rate on each of the householders—church members and nonmembers alike—toward their minister's salary; "the particular summe upon each person asseased by just rate shalbe due, to be paid accordingly, as in other cases of towne rates."[44] While this act did not actually command the towns to "establish" their ministers, it was the first in a series of enactments that attempted to reverse the lay empowerment initiated by John Cotton's charismatic maintenance mechanisms.[45]

On August 15, 1648, the synod convened for its third and final session. Within less than a fortnight the delegates unanimously approved the famed "Cambridge Platform of Church Discipline." The platform itself has received ample scrutiny from historians, who have pronounced it a model and manifesto of congregational church polity. By most measures it certainly was just that. In each period of religious history, the ministers stated, there had been one and only one divinely sanctioned form of religious polity, "before the law, Oeconomical, that is in families; or under the law, National: or since the coming of Christ, only congregational."[46] Such congregations were made up of visible saints who had mutually entered into "a Visible-Political-Union amongst themselves, or else they are not yet a particular church."[47] This much was certainly congregational and unlikely to raise the suspicion of the lay brethren.

What the elders deduced from these premises, however, was somewhat more controversial. It was this "mutuall covenant," argued the clerics, and "not faith in the heart, nor the profession of that faith, nor cohabitation, nor Baptisme" that constituted a visible church.[48] This, of course, contradicted Cotton's popular claim of 1636 that the true church covenant was, in fact, the covenant of grace. "Build a church upon any other foundation but faith and the profession of faith," Cotton had warned, "and it will break into manifold distempers."[49] In short, the ministers insisted that the outward legitimacy of congregational churches rested on their cultural virtuosity and *not* on their charismatic qualifications. Far from an egalitarian charismatic community, the congregational churches were, in fact, "mixed" polities, with Christ as the titular and spiritual monarch. In the sensible realm, the church "resembles a Democracy" in that the brethren have the right of election and consent, but "in respect of the Presbytery & power committed to them, it is an Aristocracy."[50]

Mixed as it might be, the precise delineation of power within the churches, according to the platform, was decidedly asymmetrical, with the bulk of power invested in the "aristocrats." Although a congregation "cannot become subject to any" without its consent, once "such a people do chuse any to be over them in the Lord, then do they become subject, & most willingly submit to their ministry in the Lord."[51] Apparently, the lay brethren only enjoyed their democratic powers when they elected their elders and thereafter were reduced to obedience, if not subjection. "Church government, or Rule, is placed by Christ in the officers of the church," explained the ministers, "who are therefore called Rulers, while they rule with God." The list of specific powers accorded the ministerial officers was quite impressive:

> to call the church together upon any weighty occasion, when the members so called, without just cause, may not refuse to come: nor when they are come, depart before they are dismissed: nor speak in the church, before they have leave from the elders: nor continue in so doing, when they [the elders] require silence, *nor may they oppose nor contradict the judgment or sentence of the Elders, without sufficient & weighty cause* [italics mine].
>
> It belongs also unto the Elders to examine any officers, or members, before they be received of the church: to receive the accusation brought to the Church, & to prepare them for the churches hearing.[52]

According to the platform's provisions, it appears that after the election of their elders the lay brethren were limited to offering their consent to the ministers' initiatives.[53]

Not content with claiming the lion's share of ordinary ecclesiastic power, the ministers also undermined the lay brethren's control over the churches' purse strings. There could be no question that a "necessary & sufficient maintenance is due unto the ministers of the word: from the law of nature and nations, from the law of Moses, the equity thereof, as also the rule of common reason [not, apparently, from the New Testament]." The laymen, brethren and nonbrethren alike, were sorely mistaken if they believed themselves "at liberty to doe or not to doe, what & when they pleas in this matter." Quite the contrary, such ministerial compensation was "a bounded duty, & due debt, & not as a matter of almes, & free gift," but rather like "any other commanded duty, & ordinance of the Lord." If such a commanded duty failed to move the churches "through the corruption of men," the synod insisted that the magistrate was to intervene and "establish" those ministers denied their just recompense: "[T]he magistrate is to see ministry duely provided for, as appeares from the commended example of Nehemiah. The Magistrates are nursing fathers, & nursing mothers, & stand charged with the custody of both Tables."[54] These stipulations went a long way toward undoing the damage caused by Cotton's institution of voluntary ministerial maintenance. Although the synod did not preclude such voluntary arrangements, it ensured that they could not be used as a coercive power against the elders. If the lay-men should attempt to do just that, then the magistrates had the ministers' sanction and command to intervene and secure a "just" salary for their thinking-class colleagues.

The synod failed, however, to achieve one of its purported objectives. The ministers failed to authorize the practice of the half-way covenant. As the Reverend John Allin later recalled, the majority of elders intended to pass the measure, but one of the more prominent elders (presumably John Davenport) "professed He would oppose it with all his might: by reason whereof, and the Dissent of some few more, it was laid aside at that time."[55] In fact, the platform's stipulations neither endorsed nor precluded the half-way measures. While the half-way covenant will receive ample analysis before long, it is worth noting at this point that one of its central assumptions was articulated in the Cambridge Platform of 1648. It was one of the basic tenets of the Synod of 1662 that, although ineligible for the Lord's Supper, the children of the visible saints were themselves members of the church as a consequence of their baptism. In the words of the Cambridge Platform, "these church-members that were so born, or received in their childhood," were, unless otherwise excommunicated, "in covenant with God."[56] While it failed to foreshadow all of the provisions of 1662, the Cambridge Platform went half the distance in that direction.

When the ministers finally adjourned the Cambridge Synod in the summer of 1648, they had ample reason to be pleased with their work. It had taken three years, but at long last they had compiled the official platform of the New England Way. This platform deleted or abated some of Cotton's more dangerous charismatic innovations and located the bulk of ecclesiastic power in the hands of the ministerial intellectuals and the magisterial intelligentsia. All that remained was to submit their report to the General Court for its approval. A large-scale ecclesiastic victory must indeed have seemed imminent to the elders. If so, they were to be frustrated. It would be more than three years before the General Court of Massachusetts finally endorsed the Cambridge Platform as the official church document of the Bay Colony.

The General Court was divided about what action to take in reference to the platform. Indeed, it was not until October 17, 1649, over a year after the synod had concluded, that the Cambridge Platform was finally "commended to the judicious & pious consideration of the several churches within this jurisdiction." The government requested "a return from them [the churches] at the next Generall Court how far it is suiteable to their judgements & approbations."[57] This was certainly an "innovation," for neither of the two previous synods' conclusions had been submitted to the laymen of the churches for their approval. This policy could only have come from the deputies, who had been ambivalent from the outset about the synod. Such ambivalence was undoubtedly shared by the lay members of the outer party, for they failed to perform the request of the court in delivering their judgment to its next session. Thus on June 22, 1650, the court once again issued a request to the churches, this time in the form of an order: "[T]hat the said book be duely considered of all the said churches within this pattent, and that they, without faile, will retourne their thoughts and judgements, touching the perticulars thereof, to the next session, of this Court, to the end that the said worke maybe perfected to Gods praise."[58] The magistrates had had enough of the lay brethren's stalling.

The response of the churches was hardly enthusiastic. The lay members submitted to the autumn session of the General Court "several particulars against the said confession of discipline, or severall particulars therein." No doubt at the insistence of the deputies, "the Courte judged it convenient, and conducing to peace, to forbeare to give their approbation thereto, unless such objections as were presented were cleared and removed." To that end, on May 13, 1651, the court ordered that the objections be submitted to John Cotton "to be communicated to the elders of the severall churches, who are desired to meete and cleere the said doubts." While this might well be seen as another attempt at lay stalling, somewhat more ominous was the deputies' claim that they "cannot see light to impose any formes as necessary to be observed by the churches as a binding rule."[59] If the deputies persisted in such scruples, the whole synod would have been for naught.

Fortunately for the elders, the deputed representatives of the outer-party laymen did finally acquiesce. Whether the pressures that the ministers and magistrates brought to bear on the deputies were political, dialectical, or other is not clear. But change their mind they did, and on October 14, 1651, the General Court ratified the Cambridge Platform: "The Courte, having perused the said answer [of the elders to the lay members' objections], doe thankfully acknowledge their paines therein, accounting themselves called of God, especially at this time, when the truth of Christ is so much opposed in the world, to give their testimony to the said booke of discipline, that for the substance thereof it is that we have practised and doe believe."[60] Yet even this belated clerical victory was far from unconditional. For one of the first times in Bay history, some fourteen deputies insisted that their dissent be recorded.[61] Nonetheless, after more than five years and no small effort, the ministers had at last achieved their purpose.

The Bay religious scene in the ensuing half decade was deceptively peaceful. It was peaceful in that there was very little in the way of large-scale heterodox dissent. With the notable exceptions of Marmaduke Mathewes and the church of Malden and a handful of baptists in Lynn, heterodox expression was limited to individual "heretics" who were easily handled by the magistrates.[62] What was deceptive about this peace was that within the orthodox churches the tension between the clergy and the lay brethren was unabated. This tension was focused on two issues left ambiguous by the Cambridge Platform. The first issue was the importance of lay consent in church acts, specifically in the election of ministers. The platform had stated that such consent was a necessary condition for both the constitution of a church and the election of its officers. What the platform did not state was whether such consent was also a sufficient condition. In short, could an orthodox gathered congregation elect any officers it chose? Was lay consent the only binding criterion in the "calling" of the ministerial intellectuals?

The "test case" that resolved this question involved the second church of Boston.

After having gathered in 1650, the lay brethren of that congregation sometime in 1652 "invited Michael Powell, of Dedham, to become their pastor, and he had accepted of their call."[63] Although orthodox and pious, Powell lacked university training and thus represented a dangerous precedent for the ministerial intellectuals. On October 26, 1652, the magistrates, "having receaved credible information that the new church in Boston have chosen Mr. Powell to be theire minister, and that he hath accepted of theire choice," took immediate measures to block his ordination. The court "lovingly" advised the congregation "to desist from any further proceeding therein." While the reasons for this advice were "too long to be inserted heerein," the magistrates pledged that they would "not be wanting in their endeavours" to see that the second church of Boston "maybe competently furnished with an able minister." Apparently the lay brethren of the second church of Boston were unmoved by the magistrates' advice, for they sent the court a petition requesting that the court lift its ban on Powell's public preaching in their congregation. The magistrates protested that they had never discouraged, much less banned, "the church or Mr Powell from exercising in publicke, till it please God to provide better for them; but our advice is against proceeding to establish Mr Powell as a teaching elder." At this point the General Court was far less reticent in supplying its reasons: "[T]hat notwithstanding the judgement of the church concerning Mr Powells abilities and fitnes, yet the Courte are not sattisfied of the expediency of their proceeding in respect of this place of such publicke resort, and considering the humor of the times in England, inclining to discourage learning, against which wee have borne testimony this Courte in our petition to the Parliament."[64]

The lay brethren of Boston had raised an important issue for the elders. There was no legal restriction preventing any Bay congregation from choosing clerical officers who lacked formal high cultural training and expertise. Surely the principles of congregational independence and lay consent did not go so far as to allow for an uneducated or illiterate ministry! Some eight years earlier, Thomas Shepard had argued that such a policy betrayed the "spiritual drunkenness" of "Rigid Separatists," "either edifying themselves by their own Gifts onely, chusing Unlearned Ministers, abhorred in Bishops: challenging a licentious liberty to speak, and rule, and do, and not be ruled."[65] Clearly, this potential danger required legislative action, and it was forthcoming at the next General Court. On May 18, 1653, the Bay government took the extreme measure of banning all unauthorized lay preaching. Noting that some of the newly gathered congregations "are destitute of persons fitly qualified to undertake the worke of the ministrie" and that bold heretics took advantage of this situation to spread their errors, the court passed the following unheralded act: "[I]tt is ordered by this Court, that no person shall undertake any constant course of publicque preaching or prophesying within this jurisdiction without the approbation of the elders of the fower next neighboring churches, or the County Court to which the place belongs."[66]

This time the General Court and the ministers had gone too far. In the next three months the court received angry letters from several of the churches demanding that the ban on lay preaching be repealed. The ban was unnecessary, argued the lay brethren of Salem, because most of these new churches, like the second church of Boston, were "branches of churches who watch over their members, and have power to reforme any such doctrinall evills among them without calling on Elders or courte to suppress them." Moreover, the act was a clear violation of the lay members' church liberties and thus not to be tolerated: "[I]f a breach be once made into these liberties, we know not how farre it may proceed in time, there being such a leading example as this." Unaware of any scriptural warrant for such legislation, the Salem congregants informed the court that "wee are not clair nor can judge it to be right and according unto the rules of Christ."[67] A letter from the church of Woburn contained the exact same arguments.[68] If the Bay thinking class was to avoid the ire of the outer party, the ban on lay prophesying would have to be lifted.

On August 30, the General Court of Massachusetts rescinded the ban on lay preaching that it had passed some three months before. Acknowledging that the law was "dissatisfactory to divers of the inhabitants whom the Court hath cawse to respect and tender," the magistrates and deputies repealed the measure so "that all jealowsies maybe remooved." In its stead, the General Court passed a law empowering the county courts to prosecute "every person that shall publish and maintaine any heterodoxe and erronious doctrine."[69] The protest of the lay brethren had succeeded in protecting their precious church liberties, and their political initiative had been vindicated.

This is not to say that the more extreme and radical expressions of lay protest had passed without the censorious attention of the magistrates. At the same session, Lieutenant Robert Pike of Salisbury was presented to the court for "defaming" the Bay government. Upon learning of the ban on lay preaching some months previously, Pike had apparently broken into what the Puritans called "manifold distempers":

> [H]e replied that such persons as did act in making the lawe did breake their oath to the countrey, or acted contrary expressing the ffreemans oath; for, said he, it is against the libertie of the countrey, both eclesiasticall and civill, and that he stood there ready to make it good; and farther said divers of the severall churches had called theire member to accompt which did act in that lawe making, and that some places were about to shew theire minds to the Generall Court about it.

For his insolent outburst Pike was disfranchised, fined £20, and forced to post an additional £10 to "be bound to the good behavior during the Courts pleasure."[70] Some two weeks later, the court showed a good deal more leniency to John Baker. Like Pike, Baker had responded to news of the ban on lay preaching with "abusive & opprobrious speeches . . . against the ministers & ministery." Charged with such speeches and "upholding private meetings, & prophesyings, to the hindrance & disturbance of publicke assembling," Baker prudently saw the error of his ways and "tendred voluntaryly to desist from prophesying publickly any more." Although he escaped without any fine or punishment, he was required to post bond of £20 "to his good behavior."[71] While the lay brethren's church liberties were not to be trifled with, neither were the honor and reputation of the ministerial intellectuals and magisterial intelligentsia.

This same session of the General Court received another, final petition from the second church of Boston. Like the first, it requested "the taking away an injunction of the Court, forbidding them to proceede to call or ordaine Mr. Powell to office amongst them." The magistrates responded that they had not banned the church from calling Powell to office "but only to the office of pastor or teacher." The court insisted that the church could call Powell to the office of ruling elder and that he might continue to preach in the absence of a minister. He could not, however, dispense the sacraments, for he was not and could not be a minister: "[T]hey [the General Court] are not satisfied that he hath such abilities, learning and quallifications as are requisite and necessary for an able minister of the gospell, whereby he might be able rightly to divide the word of trueth, and be able to convince gainesayers."[72] Here was the basis for a reasonable compromise. Powell could continue to preach to the second church of Boston as a ruling elder rather than as a cleric. Until they found a proper minister to fill the pulpit, the congregation could continue to receive the sacraments in Boston's first church. The congregation could enjoy Powell, and there would be no dangerous precedent of an uneducated minister. The second church of Boston embraced the opportunity; indeed, it was another two years before it hired its first minister, John Mayo, from separatist Plymouth, and even then Powell continued to preach and was even paid for it.[73] For their part, the elders had established something far more significant. Lay consent may have been a necessary condition for ministerial election, but it was decidedly not sufficient. That far, at least, the principle of congregational independence did not go.

It was only after this first issue was resolved that the ministers and their magisterial allies took up the second issue dividing the churches in these years. Just as they had required state action to decide the role of lay consent in clerical election, the thinking-class elite of the inner party now sought legislation to ensure that the lay brethren dutifully afforded the ministerial intellectuals a sufficient salary. Such legislation was passed on August 22, 1654. On that day, the General Court acknowledged its duty "to use all lawfull meanes" to make sure that the elders were "comfortably maintained." Much as the Cambridge Synod had desired, the court ordered that

> the County Court in every shire shall, upon information given them of any defect [in their financial support of the clergy] of any congregation or touneship within the shire, order and appointe what maintenance shallbe allowed to the ministers of that place, and shall issue out warrants to the select men to assisse, and the connstable of the said toune to collect, the same and to distreine the said assessments uppon such as shall refuse to pay. *And it is heereby declared to be our intention, that an honorable allowance be made to the ministrie respecting the abillitie of the places* [italics mine].[74]

The Bay Colony had taken another stride toward a fully established clergy. Whereas the previous act of 1647 had only empowered the towns to ensure the ministers an honorable salary, this act shifted the locus of that authority to the magistrates. Far more than the selectmen, the magisterial intelligentsia could be depended on to see to the financial well-being of the elders.

Such acts of ministerial establishment can be very deceptive in that they imply that the ministers were poorly paid. Peter Bulkeley accused the brethren of "a streightheartednesse, and close-handednesse towards the Lord." Such "close-handednesse" was evidenced by "not ministring to the things which concern his worship," especially the maintenance of his ambassadors, the clergy. "The least portion is enough, and the worst is good enough," Bulkeley observed, "for those things that concern his honour."[75] While the ministers and magistrates undoubtedly felt that the clergy was undercompensated, the facts suggest otherwise. On May 6, 1657, the General Court established committees in each of the Bay counties to investigate the "many complaints of the great suffering of the familyes of divers reverend ministers of Gods word within this jurisdiction, for want of such suitable supply as theire state & condition doe require." While the court never mentioned who made such complaints, it requested that the committees return their findings to the next session of the General Court, "so this Court, which are, by Gods promise, nursing ffathers to the churches, may see that there be meate in Gods howse, and the Lord may still delight to dwell amongst us, and to blesse both us & our poore posteritie, and the said scandall taken of & prevented for the future."[76] These complaints of "great suffering" leave the impression of impoverished clergymen and starving families.

The reports of the committees paint a rather different portrait. While the court never published the reports, the findings on some twelve clergymen in eight different towns are available. According to the admittedly small sample, the average town of some fifty-nine families paid its minister(s) the rather handsome salary of £65 per year. In addition, the clergymen were granted comfortable tracts of land and a goodly number of cattle.[77] The results of this rather limited survey are consistent with Hall's findings on the subject of clerical compensation:

> The average size of their estates placed the ministers within the wealthiest 15 percent of the colonists. Marriage patterns confirmed the high rank of the group. The richest men in New England, the merchants of Boston, agreed to frequent marriages between their daughters and young parsons, while often marrying themselves into ministerial families. Altogether, a Harvard education paid off in the seventeenth century.[78]

The magistrates' efforts on behalf of ministerial establishment were not a result of misinformation so much as high aspirations for clerical income and status. These reports of substantial clerical compensation led the court to conclude that "some ministers are not so well provided for as they ought to be." On October 14, 1657, the General Court "fully authorized" the magistrates of the County Courts to "take the best & speediest opportunitie & meanes to relieve the said wants."[79] The process of ministerial establishment continued apace.

By 1657, however, the issue of clerical maintenance was dwarfed in importance by the first major dissident movement in roughly a decade. In July 1656, Anne Austin and Mary Fisher arrived in Boston and were promptly arrested.[80] On August 7, they were joined by their comrades William Brend, Thomas Thurston, Christopher Holder, John Copeland, Richard Smith, Mary Prince, Dorothy Waugh, Sarah Gibbons, and Mary Witherhead.[81] They, too, were shortly apprehended and imprisoned. The Quaker assault on the orthodox one-party regime in Massachusetts had begun.[82]

Historians have had an almost morbid fascination with the Quaker invasion and the remarkable repression it met. Indeed, the often barbaric cruelty of the orthodox regime and the eager, almost masochistic, thirst of the Quakers for such punishment are fascinating.[83] The Quakers undeniably displayed great élan with their self-conscious and public lack of deference, naked testimonials, and violent and unsolicited harangues before church and court. Nor was the orthodox regime lacking in dramatic and vigorous action. When a group of Quaker missionaries tried to disrupt a church service in Salem on September 20, 1657, one of them was seized by the hair and gagged with a glove and handkerchief.[84] On October 14, 1656, the General Court had ordered that "what Quakers soever shall arise in this country . . . shalbe forthwith committed to the house of correction & at their entrance to be severely whipt, & by the master thereof to be kept constantly to worke, & none suffered to converse or speake with them."[85] Seeing that such leniency had failed to break the dissidents' resolve, on October 14, 1657, exactly one year after the first anti-Quaker act, the General Court stepped up their repression.

Since severe whippings and forced labor proved insufficient to deter the return of previously banished Quakers, the court ordered that "every male Quaker shall for the first offenc [of returning after banishment] have one of his eares cutt off." (The Puritans' tender sensibilities led them to limit the punishment for women to severe floggings.) Another return visit would cost his other ear. Finally, if the loss of both ears or three whippings did not deter a Quaker's return, the court ordered that the offender be silenced in a most grotesque manner: "[F]or every Quaker, he or she, that shall third time heerin againe offend, they shall have theire tongues bored through with a hot iron, & kept at the house of correction, close to worke, till they be sent away at their owne charge."[86] As is well known, these measures were ultimately successful in keeping the Quaker dissidents from infesting the Bay Colony. The notorious "cart and whip" act of 1661 and the execution of four previously banished Quakers, in Jonathan M. Chu's words, "seemed to have stemmed the tide of the more seditious forms of Quakerism."[87] Such measures also afforded a stage for the more "radical" Quakers to act out their macabre drama of martyrdom and a gruesome, albeit fascinating, spectacle for the orthodox audience.[88]

While the reign of orthodox terror may tell us something about the perceived magnitude of the Quaker threat, it is silent about the quality or significance of this threat. At first sight, the Quaker dissidence bears a strong resemblance to the Antinomian movement. In theological terms, both believed in an "inner light" or divine inspiration that transcended the revealed word. Both also downplayed the significance of sin—and therefore works or graces—for those within the covenant of grace. Their tactical similarities are also striking. While the Quakers were a bit more extreme, like the Antinomians they frequently violated the code of ritual deference surrounding both ministers and magistrates, disrupted church meetings with dissident speeches, offered "alternative" lay sermons, decried an overeducated and unconverted ministry, and hurled defiance at the General Court.[89] In short, like the Hutchinsonians of some twenty years before, they engaged in a headlong frontal assault on the system of cultural domination.

In one important aspect, however, the Antinomian and Quaker movements in Puritan Massachusetts were almost diametrical opposites. The constituency of the Antinomian movement had been the urban bourgeoisie, and its lay leadership came from the wealthiest mercantile families. Moreover, both leaders and followers were church members and, in some cases, very prominent public figures. In structural terms, the Antinomian movement was a bid for power from within the churches, not an assault on the churches per se. Just the opposite was the case with the Quakers. Not only was the Quaker leadership "drawn from the lower levels of English Society," but as Carla Pestana has shown, "those who listened to their message [in

Massachusetts] were equally marginal."[90] Unlike the Antinomians, who appealed to a small economic elite, the Quakers drew upon "the tumultuous nature of the discontented and irregenerate multitude."[91] This comment by John Norton in the official orthodox denunciation of the Quaker heresy, *The Heart of New England Rent*, reveals the distinct ecclesiastic threat of the Quakers: they appealed to the increasing majority of unchurched residents. Norton was not at all surprised at "[h]ow potent a temptation, the opening of an opportunity to the irregenerate & hungry multitude, of changing places with their Superiors," was to the unchurched majority.[92] As Norton eloquently, if uncharitably, put it, "[T]heir Doctrine carryeth meat for its followers in the mouth of it."[93]

The problem with this unregenerate multitude was that it was also, in Norton's words, "hungry." That is to say, although the unchurched majority were "irregenerate" insofar as they were unwilling/unable to undergo the test of charismatic religious experience that Cotton had instituted, they were otherwise largely pious and sincere Christians who desired church fellowship. Part of the historical significance of the Quaker movement in Massachusetts, then, was that it dramatized to the Bay divines the plight of these unfranchised and unchurched residents. While the elders had become increasingly sensitive to this problem—itself the result of Cotton's charismatic innovation—it was not until the onset of the Quaker invasion that they took any decisive steps to resolve it. Indeed, in previous years the elders, and Cotton in particular, had been rather uncharitable and harsh in their estimation of the Bay nonmembers: "The fear of God, and Faith of those men, may be justly doubted, whose settled abode is in a place where Churches are gather'd and order'd according to Christ and yet are not after a convenient time joyned to them."[94] Some twenty years later the ministers were, perhaps by force of circumstances, far more sympathetic to the religious needs of this segment of the population.

The ultimate significance of the Quaker movement for the orthodox Bay regime was that it thus forced the magistrates and ministers to neutralize the danger of an unchurched majority that might easily be induced to support heterodox dissent. The best way to neutralize this danger would be to somehow bind the majority of such nonmembers to the churches in obedience. This in turn could be accomplished either by inducing such persons to offer oaths of fealty to the churches or by actually bringing them within the church itself and thus giving them an interest in its well-being. The Bay divines opted for both alternatives by means of a single polity innovation. That innovation was, of course, the half-way covenant.

The half-way covenant was one of the most complex and brilliant ecclesiastic innovations the Bay divines ever devised. Ostensibly concerned with the subjects and significance of the ordinance of baptism, the "covenant" served several distinct purposes. From the perspective of the overall religious culture, the purpose of the half-way covenant was clearly inclusive. That is to say, the stipulations of the covenant served to draw into the church a large proportion of the unchurched population.[95] Such inclusion would in turn help neutralize the Quaker threat and, in particular, their appeal to the otherwise "irregenerate multitude." Once within the church, even as half-way members, the new brethren would have an interest in the church's well-being and orthodoxy. They would also be subject to the educational, disciplinary, and pastoral care of the elders and the congregation. "Discipline is our great Interest," claimed Increase Mather in defense of the half-way covenant, and it was that "which we are ingaged to assert and plead for."[96] Most important, adult half-way members would be expected to "own the covenant" and thus, upon a sacred oath, pledge fealty and obedience to the church and its culturally dominant tradition.

Although the effect of the half-way covenant was not necessarily a complete "parishional" inclusion, such a possibility was by no means precluded by the synod's findings. Indeed, this "creeping parishionalism" was one of the charges laid against the covenant by its clerical and lay opponents. Understandably, the majority of orthodox elders took great offense at this charge, as John Allin vividly expressed in his *Animadversions Upon the Antisynodalia Americana*: "But if it be meant of inlarging the Church to the bounds of a Parish, it is a meer Slander: I do not believe that he [John Davenport] can prove that any two Elders of these Churches have so declared their judgement; much less so many as are of the Synods minde."[97] But of course, as Robert Pope has shown, in many Connecticut towns the half-way covenant did in fact lead toward, and ultimately give way to a comprehensive system of church membership.[98] Although the provisions of the covenant did not mandate such a parish system, they certainly did not preclude it. The covenant held that half-way or federal membership in the churches was a privilege of all who had been baptized—"the Seal of Membership in the Church the body of Christ"—in a "true church."[99] Because the Bay congregationalists were nonseparating, they held that the English churches were, in fact, "true." Presumably, anyone who had been baptized in England was eligible to subscribe to the church covenant and thus become a half-way member. Indeed, the church of Salem yielded to its minister's wishes and dispensed with the requirement of "visible sainthood" for church membership within six months of its adoption of the half-way measures.[100] The possibility of a parish system was very real and tangible. In and of itself, however, such a system may not have been so controversial, for the covenant still limited the franchise in church and state to members in full communion. To understand what made the half-way covenant so unsavory to the lay brethren, it is necessary to assess its potential impact on the ecclesiastic balance of power within the churches.

With respect to ecclesiastic polity, the half-way covenant effected a dramatic centralization of church power from the lay brethren to the ministerial intellectuals. The covenant achieved this centralization in three ways. Not least of these was the ecclesiastic mechanism that formulated and authorized it. The half-way covenant was passed by two separate synods, one in 1657 and the other in 1662. As in the Synod of 1646–1648, this noncrisis ecclesiastic assembly was itself a significant centralization of power. Nor was the importance of this assembly lost on its participants. One of the two questions answered by the Synod of 1662 was "[w]hether according to the Word of God there ought to be a Consociation of Churches, and what should be the manner of it."[101] Not surprisingly, the elders found scriptural warrant not only for congregational and clerical consociation—both at the expense of congregational independence—but also for "the more solemn Meetings of both Elders and Messengers in lesser or greater Councils [i.e., synods], as the matter shall require."[102]

The second way in which the half-way covenant centralized ecclesiastic power was by diluting lay consent and initiative. This would occur because the church was opening its doors to a host of new half-way members. As previously mentioned, when the number of persons within an ecclesiastic or political body is too great to afford face-to-face dialogue and discussion among them, the influence of the nonelite mass following is diminished. This was, in part, exactly what the half-way covenant achieved. In effect, the membership of the churches was to be expanded from an elite cadre of charismatic communicants to an amorphous mass of the "culturally correct" (undoubtedly the bulk of the lay population). Under such conditions, there were too many congregated laymen for them to achieve consensus and, thus, a critical mass. Not surprisingly, the bulk of lay brethren and their handful of clerical allies preferred a "stricter course" in terms of church membership. As John Davenport put it, "[T]here is danger of great Corruption and Pollution creeping into the Churches, by the Enlargement of the Subject of Baptism."[103]

The most important way in which the half-way covenant centralized church power was by devaluing lay consent. This devaluation was responsible for much of the lay opposition to the covenant, and it was in this regard that the ministers were indeed guilty of "innovation."[104] There had been no consensus in the founding years warranting the baptism of the grandchildren of full members. "It belongs not to any Predecessors, either neere or further off removed from the next Parent," Thomas Hooker had claimed, "to give right of this priviledge [baptism] to their Children." Should the children of members fail to join the church as full communicants upon achieving adulthood, Hooker concluded, "their apostacy takes off the federall holinesse of the Children." In such a case where "both the next Parents were apostates, its not the power of all former Predecessors to bring the Childe to the enjoyment of this priviledge."[105] Even Richard Mather, one of the principal proponents of the half-way covenant, had written in the early 1640s that the grandchild of a full member was left unbaptized in Massachusetts if the child's "Father and Mother were neither of them Believers, and sanctified." In such a case the parents were considered "not faederally holy, but uncleane, what ever their other Ancestors have been." Mather concluded with the classic slippery-slope argument: "And if we should goe one degree beyond the next Parents, wee see not but we may goe two, and if two why not 3, 4, 20, 100, or 1000? For where will you stop?"[106]

The most important innovation was not, however, that the half-way covenant allowed the grandchildren of full members and their descendants to be baptized. That practice seems to have been followed in several congregations by the late 1630s. The innovation was that such otherwise unregenerate progeny were, by virtue of their baptism, granted membership themselves. "The membership of Children confederating in their Parents is a distinct membership from the membership of their Parents," claimed John Norton, and "this distinct membership gives them a proper right unto Baptisme, so as they are baptized by their own right, and not by the right of their parents."[107] Yet as late as the early 1640s Richard Mather had acknowledged that the membership of such children upon reaching maturity was still uncertain in the collective judgment of the ministry: "[B]y Reason of the Infancy of these Churches, we have had no occasion yet to determine what to judge or practise one way or other."[108]

Even Increase Mather's *First Principles of New-England*, a collection of documents whose sole purpose was to prove that the half-way covenant was *not* an innovation, contains clearly damaging evidence to the contrary. The first document that

Mather presented was a letter from John Cotton and the church of Boston to the brethren of Dorchester. The letter, dated December 16, 1634, contained advice as to whether the grandchild of a church member whose immediate parents were ineligible for the Lord's Supper could be legitimately baptized. While the church of Boston did, in fact, warrant such baptism, the grounds it offered for so doing were decidedly not those of the Synods of 1657 and 1662: "Upon due and serious discourse about the point, it seemed good unto us all with one accord, and agreeable (as we believe) to the word of the Lord, that the Grand-Father may lawfully claim that priviledge to his Grand-child in such a Case." Although the child could be baptized, it was only the grandfather that could "claim that priviledge to his Grand-child" and only then with "two Cautions." The first "caution" was that "the Grand-child baptized by right of the Grand-fathers Covenant, be committed to the Grand-fathers education." In essence, this implied the nonmembership of the "next parents" since they could not be entrusted with the religious instruction of their child. The other stipulation or "caution" made this implication even more obvious: "that the Parents of the Child, do not thereby take occasion to neglect the due and seasonable preparation of themselves for entrance into Covenant with God and his Church."[109] The inescapable implication of this passage is that the parents of the infant in question were not, in spite of their own baptism, in "covenant with God and his Church." While baptism was undoubtedly dispensed in such circumstances in the first decades, it clearly did not confer membership in the churches, as it did in the half-way covenant.[110] In short, baptism was a church ordinance but not a "seal of the covenant."

The consequences of this new basis of church membership for lay consent were profound. Part of what served to legitimate lay consent in the first Bay churches was the fact that membership was restricted to a relatively small group of cultural virtuosos. High standards of virtuosity among the laity meant that their judgment represented a cultivated and informed viewpoint and not a merely democratic nose counting (the Puritans most assuredly did not ascribe to the dictum "vox populi vox dei"). The institution of an additional test of religious charisma, in the form of Cotton's test of saving grace, made the lay brethren an even more elite and accomplished group. This in turn legitimated an even greater emphasis on lay consent and initiative. The half-way covenant had just the opposite effect. By dramatically lowering the standards for church membership, it reduced the cultural significance of such membership and thus delegitimized and devalued the importance of lay consent. Such consent and initiative were less worthy precisely because their source was relatively "common" and undistinguished. This had clearly not always been the New England Way. John Davenport was reputedly offering the collective wisdom of his colleagues when he responded to English questions about the Bay churches' restrictive baptismal policies in 1639: "As a Citie priviledge belongeth onely to Citizens and their children; so Baptisme and the Lords Supper" belong only to the charismatically qualified members of the churches. Extending baptism and membership to those less qualified devalued both the seal and the membership, just "as a Seale of a Corporation is abused . . . to one that being no freemen of that Corporation is uncapable thereof."[111] This devaluation was a major cause of much of the controversy and opposition the half-way covenant evoked, particularly among the lay brethren.

Although the long fight over the half-way covenant is the subject of subsequent chapters, it is worth noting now that the opponents of the half-way covenant found themselves in a difficult rhetorical position. While the covenant's revision of church membership was undeniably an innovation, it was also completely consistent and logical. As John Allin chose to put it, the half-way covenant was not a "falling from our former practice, as is Objected, our Principles are the same; this is onely a progress in practising according thereunto, as the encrease of the Churches doth require."[112] The covenant's opponents were faced with a series of disjunctions that led either to heterodox absurdity or to the half-way covenant.

To begin with, baptism itself either was or was not a seal of the covenant. If it was, then it might confer membership, but if it was not, then the opponent was forced to agree with the notorious Samuel Gorton that baptism itself is just an anti-Christian piece of superstitious magic or necromancy. The next set of alternatives concerned whether church membership required the consent of a culturally virtuous prospective member. If such consent was required and, as previously established, baptism conferred membership, then the position of the heretical antipedobaptists was confirmed and vindicated.[113] As Increase Mather noted, "[T]here is hardly any Argument produced against such Inlargement as is by the Synod asserted, but what the Antipaedo-Baptists make use of to serve their turn."[114] If, on the other hand, such consent was not required, then the church membership stipulations of the half-way covenant were warranted and correct. Finally, given that baptism conferred church membership on children incapable of expressing culturally informed consent, either such membership continued into adulthood, when it could be confirmed through an oath of fealty, or it did not. This latter option was fairly popular with the opponents of the half-way covenant; they often held that a prospective member's failure to achieve a regenerating religious experience resulted in an implicit and de facto dismission from the church. But, of course, if that were the case, responded the proponents of the half-way covenant, then one could be excommunicated without the consent of either the clergy or the lay brethren, a clear violation of church liberties.[115] In short, the opponents of the half-way covenant found themselves between a dialectical rock and a hard place.

The half-way covenant thus represented a stark conflict of interests between the lay brethren and the ministerial intellectuals. It was in the interest of the lay brethren to maintain an elite corps of members through rigorous admission criteria. This would not only allow them to maintain a "critical mass" but also legitimate or justify the great significance attached to lay consent and initiative in the Bay churches and thus result in their own continued decentralized empowerment. The elders' interest, on the other hand, lay in the opposite direction. They wanted to centralize ecclesiastic power away from the lay brethren by both opening the gates of membership and devaluing lay consent. They did, however, share one overarching purpose, a purpose highlighted by the previously mentioned perspective of the overall religious culture. Equally committed to religious orthodoxy, both the clergymen and lay members wanted to defuse the Quaker threat, preferably by binding the unchurched majority to the will of the churches.

With this shared purpose in mind, the half-way covenant can be seen as a lay/clerical half-way compromise. Their shared purpose would be achieved in that a significant proportion of the unchurched would henceforth come under the churches' disciplinary care and would be bound by an oath of fealty. After that, the two sides "split the difference." For the ministers, the newly bound residents were granted church membership, albeit of a slightly attenuated nature. The lay brethren in full communion, alternately, were granted a continuation of their monopoly on the franchise. As the Synod of 1657 stated, "Concerning the power of voting, it is not rational that they [the half-way members] should exercise a Church-power as to the administration of Church-Ordinances, which voting implies, who themselves are unfit for all Ordinances."[116] Some three years later the General Court extended this franchise stipulation to secular elections as well. On May 31, 1660, the deputies and magistrates ordered that "no man whosoever shall be admitted to the freedom of this body politic but such as are members of some church of Christ, and in full communion."[117]

If the foregoing analysis supplies much of the half-way covenant's final, formal, and material causes, what was its efficient cause? Why did the ministers, who had been interested in the innovation at least since the Synod of 1646–1648, wait until 1657 and 1662 to push for its institution? Alternately, why did the laymen yield to their elders, to the extent that they did, at these particular moments? There were essentially two efficient causal agencies involved in the promulgation of the half-way covenant. The first was the danger of heterodox dissent from the orthodox system of cultural domination, and the second was the potential political threat represented by the English Empire. To retrace our steps then, the half-way covenant first reared its head at the Synod of 1646–1648. That synod came hard on the heels of the dissent of the Gortonists. In addition to these dissidents, the recent ascendancy of the presbyterian party in Parliament left many orthodox thinking-class members in the Bay Colony anxious lest the English authorities attempt to enforce their church order or restructure the colonial government. Such anxieties were not allayed by the emergence of the Child Remonstrants, who clearly intended to appeal to their fellow presbyterians in the English government to eliminate the congregational one-party domination of Massachusetts. While the court was largely able to preclude this appeal, it was less successful in the case of a similar appeal by the Gortonists. Thus in early 1646 Gorton and his cohorts received a letter of safe passage from the Commission for Foreign Plantations to their officially recognized and legal residence in Rhode Island.[118] It was at precisely this moment that the elders requested and the deputies agreed to the calling of a synod to institute the half-way covenant.

By the third session of the synod in 1648, however, the scene had changed dramatically. The Child Remonstrants had been heavily fined and rebuked, the Gortonists were just an unpleasant memory, and, most important of all, the congregational party was on the rise in the persons of Oliver Cromwell and the New Modell Army. As the danger from within and without waned, the justification for the half-way covenant seemed (probably to ministers as well as laymen) far less compelling and pressing. Thus, when presented with a handful of dissenters, the elders at the synod chose not to force the issue and let the innovation "lie on the table" for the time being. This is not to suggest that such dissent in itself precluded the passage of the half-way covenant, for each of the synods that subsequently established its stipulations contained prominent dissenters, and the majority simply passed the measure on a purely majoritarian basis.

The first of these synods followed closely the onset of the Quaker invasion of Massachusetts. The first Quakers arrived in the summer of 1656, and on October 14 of that year the General Court responded favorably to a call for a synod on the half-way covenant from its counterpart at Hartford, Connecticut. Yet the Quaker threat, by itself, was not cause enough to induce the lay brethren and their deputed representatives in the General Court to adopt the conclusions of the Synod of 1657. What was necessary in this regard was the dissolution of the Protectorate in the following years, culminating with the death of Oliver Cromwell.

With the restoration of Charles II, the orthodox regime found itself in an even more precarious imperial position than in 1646. On May 22, 1661, John Norton addressed the assembled freemen at the annual Court of Elections. In addition to urging a thorough acknowledgment of the king, Norton also argued for synodic action. Granting that every believer had "a judgement Directive" and that each congregation had "a judgement Authoritative," Norton nevertheless insisted that "also there is a judgement Decisive, which belongs unto the Council."[119] Yet the judgment of the council of 1657 had not been "decisive," and the stakes at issue, for both the ministry and the laity, had grown dramatically in the subsequent years. "Let us acknowledge the order of the Eldership in our Churches in their way," Norton implored, "and the order of Councils in their way, duely backed and encouraged." Without such backing and encouragement, Norton warned, "[e]xperience will witnesse that these Churches cannot long consist."[120] Thus on December 31, 1661, the General Court of Massachusetts issued the call for the Half-Way Synod of 1662.[121] Less than a year later, the court recommended the half-way covenant to the "consideration of all the churches & people of this jurisdiction."[122] The clerical innovation had finally gained the sanction of the one-party state.

Ironically, the ministers' victory proved hollow in the short run. The reports of the imminent demise of the Massachusetts one-party state proved to be greatly exaggerated. The regime lasted for roughly another twenty years before it was eventually abolished by the imperial authorities. Once this threat declined, the members of the particular churches refused to implement the half-way covenant. Although the political fallout from this fight over the half-way covenant is the subject of subsequent chapters, ultimately the ministerial intellectuals were successful. When the Puritan regime in Massachusetts finally lost its hegemonic grip on state power, the bulk of the unchurched were incorporated into the churches by means of the half-way covenant and mass covenant renewals. The result of this clerical empowerment was that the tradition of Puritanism became an enduring part of the cultural mores of provincial New England and early America.

What, at long last, does all of this ecclesiastic and political "perspective" portend for tribalism, sacerdotalism, and declension? Actually, quite a bit. Tribalism was not so much a self-absorbed obsession on the part of the churches as it was the result of a tradition of lay empowerment that was self-consciously embraced by the culturally virtuous laymen. It was, in a perverse way, a strange sort of spiritually elitist ecclesiastic populism. While sacerdotalism is a genuine historical phenomenon, its importance has been somewhat exaggerated. Throughout the seventeenth century the ministers' authority was based on their cultural prestige and domination. In the first decade, the elders supplemented this authority by dabbling in charisma. When such charisma proved dangerous to orthodoxy and church polity, the ministers looked to sacerdotalism to replace such charisma as a supplement to their cultural domination. Sacerdotalism was thus merely a supplement to the overriding source of ministerial authority, the system of cultural domination.

Finally, of all of these claims, declension would seem to fare the worst. The foregoing analysis suggests that, in practical terms, the Puritan project was very much alive and well in the Bay Colony. Even the declining rate of full church membership has been shown by Pope and others to be the result of a more rigorous introspection of religious experience rather than a decline of piety. An equally likely explanation of these declining rates might be that succeeding generations who fervently shared the doctrinal commitments of their forebears simply did not see warrant for Cotton's charismatic test of gracious experience.

The reality, of course, was much more complex. Declension did occur in Massachusetts in at least two distinct respects. The first and most obvious respect was a relative decline in ministerial status and influence. As we shall see, this is one of the recurring leitmotivs of the jeremiads and the reforming synods. As a wealthy and mature mercantile bourgeoisie emerged in Boston in the years after the depression of the early 1640s, they gradually began to compete with the ministers as economic and political authorities. The ministers did not fall into disrepute or disrespect. In fact, they remained the most important authorities on almost all issues relevant to life in the Bay Colony. In the first decades of settlement, the ministers had an almost unlimited amount of prestige and influence; ministerial declension occurred because they were no longer the only important authorities on all issues.

The second respect in which the Bay Colony underwent declension was the inescapable fact that the succeeding generations failed to share their ancestors' powerful and charismatic religious experiences. This was not a decline in piety per se, for the succeeding generation sincerely shared the faith of their fathers. The point is that powerful charismatic religious experiences are not conjured by the will. Rather, like the one-party state itself, such experiences seem to come in "generational waves" that respond to periods of social and personal chaos. Whereas the one-party state serves to create social order and cohesion in a masterless environment, profound religious experiences have the same effect on the individual, steeling him or her for actions in an otherwise anarchic personal or social context. The very success of the orthodox Puritan one-party regime in supplying order and cohesion to the Bay Colony precluded religious charisma and made it unnecessary in the succeeding generations. That the second and third generations were expected to undergo a psychological transformation that was alien to their experience was, as Emory Elliott has shown, a source of profound spiritual anxiety and intergenerational tension.[123]

8

THE RESTORATION AND THE
POLITICS OF DECLENSION

The collapse of the Puritan Protectorate and the restoration of the Stuart monarchy in 1660 shook the very foundations of the Puritan Bay regime and initiated a prolonged time of troubles for the orthodox thinking class. The Restoration threatened the regime's de facto political independence and challenged its ideological self-conception as the vanguard of the militant Protestant internationale. The changed imperial climate deepened the preexisting tensions between the laity and clergy. More ominously, for the first time in Massachusetts's history, significant, enduring, and public divisions emerged among both the magistrates and ministers. These divisions reached critical proportions in the years surrounding the formation of the third church of Boston. The inevitable result of these divisions was a loss of cultural authority by the thinking class in general and the ministerial intellectuals in particular. The spectacle of orthodox divines citing biblical sanction for diametrically opposed positions—and with some heat at that—led the laity to suspect that the clergy's biblicism was not as univocal as had been advertised. Indeed, some concluded that the ministers were sophistic masters of the word rather than its humble servants. Such conclusions came to the fore in the late 1660s when the deputies denounced the clergy as the source of innovation and backsliding. By the time of King Philip's War in the mid-1670s, the Bay clergy had been sorely buffeted by the winds of the Restoration.

The inner party divided over two distinct but associated issues. One issue was whether the regime should adopt the same defiant and militant posture toward the Stuart government that Winthrop and others had struck before the Revolution or instead try to reach an accommodation with the king. The other, ultimately more divisive issue was the so-called half-way covenant. While ministerial dissent over the stipulated extension of baptism and church discipline had emerged as early as 1648, public clerical division had been minimized by the majority's decision not to press the issue without unanimity and the dissidents' polite refusal to publish their dissent. Fear that the Bay government might be lost to the Restoration monarchy made it seem imperative to the ministerial majority that the provisions of the half-way covenant be enacted and enforced despite the dissent of a handful of divines. To the dissidents, such fears betrayed an accommodating, backsliding spirit that threatened the very foundations of the New England Way. In a sense, the divisions within the regime and its inner party in the 1660s and 1670s were a dispute over the essence of Puritanism.

The Restoration further complicated these divisions by sending nonconforming congregational divines rushing to the Bay Colony for refuge. Two such ministers were James Allen and John Oxenbridge, both of whom adamantly opposed the half-way covenant and any accommodation with the English government.[1] Unlike the bulk of the Bay clergy, Allen's and Oxenbridge's first loyalties were to the independent ideal rather than the society and community to which they had fled. The same could be said for John Davenport, whose decision to remove from New Haven to Boston and resume the fight against the half-way covenant was ostensibly prompted by the loss of his settlement's political independence to the government of Connecticut. Admittedly orthodox members of the congregational movement, these men were relative "outsiders" in the colony and within the clergy. Indeed, almost all of the clerical opponents of the half-way covenant were outsiders in one sense or another. Although they were not refugees from Restoration England, both John Mayo of the second church of Boston and Harvard president Charles Chauncy initially chose to settle in separatist Plymouth rather than in Massachusetts.[2] Even the sole exception to this rule, Eleazar Mather of Northampton, was minister to a fledgling congregation in the remote Connecticut Valley.[3] None of these dissident outsiders, however, had quite the impact of the twenty-two-year-old refugee divine that arrived in Boston on September 1, 1661. Massachusetts-born, this young man spent a year at Trinity College, Dublin, followed by a three-year stint in the pulpit at Great Torrington in England that filled him with distaste for the rustic surroundings of Boston and an overweening sense of self-importance.[4] Shortly after his arrival, Increase Mather would insert himself into the center of every political controversy of both church and state. The Massachusetts ministerial intellectuals would not recover from this blow for another thirty years.

O n May 22, 1661, John Norton delivered the most important public address of his career. The most prominent divine in the colony—he had succeeded John Cotton as teacher of the first church in Boston and had led the campaigns against the Quakers and on behalf of the half-way conclusions of 1657—Norton was the obvious choice to give this most critical election sermon. The political community Norton faced was anxious and uncertain. In a colony still shaken by the Quaker invasion and recent polity struggles, news of the Restoration had raised fears about the colony's cherished political independence. Perhaps more damaging was the blow to the regime's self-conception.

As an ideological community, the Bay Puritans had seen themselves as the advance guard of a world historical "gospel" congregational movement destined for ultimate victory. This conception found validation in the English Revolution and the ascendance of the independents in the 1650s. Nor were the Bay godly alone in this belief, as evidenced by the high regard with which New Englanders were held in England. "It is with the honestest on both sides a matter of high account to have been a New-English man," reported Nathaniel Mather from London in the spring of 1651.[5] Nine months later Mather was unchanged in his assessment: "'Tis a notion of mighty great and high respect to have been a New-English man, 'tis enough to gayne a man very much respect yea almost any preferment."[6] All of that changed with the Restoration. From a city upon a hill, New England had become, in Norton's phrase, "Sion the Outcast." The godly orthodox, like subsequent revolutionaries, could not help suspecting that history had passed them by as they changed overnight from a light to the reformed churches of the world to "a subject of contempt."[7]

Norton's doctrine was clearly intended to reassure his auditors. Although rejected by the world of men, Massachusetts was still "acknowledged" and "beloved" by God. It was God's purpose in afflicting New England "to give her Repentance" for her sins "so he may bring her the Blessing of his own people." Indeed, even the enemies of the godly "are instrumental to their prosperity."[8] Massachusetts need merely repent "from her backsliding," and she would, through God's mercy, be healed of her wounds.[9] The precise means of such repentance and reformation formed the core of Norton's counsel.

The program John Norton presented to the electors on that spring day proved to be the basic position of the bulk of the Bay clergy and roughly half the magistrates for some years to come. Implicit in this program was a particular interpretation of what was necessary to the Puritan way in New England and what was merely incidental. For Norton and his colleagues, the essence of Puritanism was a commitment to biblicist exegesis and a clerically dominated order and discipline in the churches. The two were obviously related, for biblicism helped keep order in the churches by restricting the democratic urges of the laymen within the bounds of what Norton called "Scripture liberty": "If you ask what Liberty is? you may look at it as a Power, as to any external restraint, or obstruction on mans part, to walk in the Faith, Worship, Doctrine, and Discipline of the Gospel, according to the Order of the Gospel."[10] The order of the gospel could be found, according to Norton, in the Cambridge Platform. "'Tis that for which we are Out-casts at this day," he told the freemen, and that very same gospel order "sheweth what New-England is."[11]

According to Norton, the order of the gospel sanctioned a centralization of ecclesiastic power from the local congregations to the consociated clerics. He acknowledged that individual congregations retained the authority to judge in matters of religious controversy, just as individual believers enjoyed a "judgement Discretive." Only a council of consociated clerics, however, had the ultimate power or "a judgement Decisive." It was such a "ministeriall judge" that had the final say "when a Controversie ariseth in a Church" since "differences must not always continue."[12] Norton further insisted that such consociated power extended to the actions of individual ministers. Citing 1 Corinthians 14:32—"the Spirits of the Prophets are subject to the Prophets"—he argued that unless clerical councils had the power to censure errant divines, "there can be no Administration, or else there needs be a meer rixation and chiding-Administration."[13]

That Norton and the majority of his colleagues would urge a centralization of ecclesiastic power as well as a continued commitment to biblicist policy is hardly surprising. Biblicism had always been the foundation of the Puritan epistemology as well as an important support for clerical cultural authority, and the clergy had been attempting to centralize church authority since before the Cambridge Platform. Yet it was also a well-conceived response to the implications of the Restoration. A commitment to biblicism would keep the churches "Puritan" and ensure the continued importance of the ministerial intellectuals' literary critical skills. Placing ecclesiastic power in the hands of the presbytery would allow the clerics to maintain order in the churches in the event that the Puritan party lost its monopoly on political power in the colony. "Let us acknowledge the Order of the Eldership in our Churches in their way," Norton pleaded, "and the Order of Councils in their way duely backed and encouraged." Without this order, he warned, "[e]xperience will witnesse that these Churches cannot long consist."[14]

Given the fact that the last clerical council in 1657 had expressed a "judgement decisive" on behalf of the half-way covenant, the overall thrust of Norton's program was clear. The New England Way could be preserved in the face of the Restoration's threat to the Bay government by transforming the local cells of the Puritan party into religious institutions controlled by the presbytery of clerics and administering to the religious needs of the bulk of the community. In short, Norton and his colleagues were trying to turn the independent congregations of a sect into the quasiparishes of an established church. Since it was this church order that exemplified the New England Way and protected the brethren's "scripture liberties," the best way to ensure that the church remained established and thus secure those liberties was to reach an accommodation with the royal authorities: "Attend we the Example of the godly wise, for the continuing of our Liberty, in like cases. You will say, What is that? I answer, An Address to the Supreme Authority [the king], and a just Apologie."[15] Considering the success of John Winthrop, Jr.'s, diplomacy on behalf of Connecticut in these years, there is some reason to believe that Norton's policy might well have achieved its purpose.

Norton's program was logical and coherent. It was also extremely controversial. The bulk of the godly brethren and their deputed representatives had ardently resisted the centralization of ecclesiastic power implicit in the half-way covenant and the consociation of churches for the last dozen years. They also did not perceive the necessity of reaching an accommodation with the king. Their charter, the vast Atlantic Ocean, and their own steadfast truculence would protect them from the clutches of king and council, just as it had in the 1630s.

Like the clerical majority, the laity had their own interpretation of Puritanism, although it did not gain clerical expression until the fight over the third church of Boston. While sharing a commitment to biblicism, they stressed the principles of informed lay consent, voluntary fellowship, and political and ecclesiastic participation, all of which were proto-republican. From the lay point of view, the New England Way was inconceivable without the apparatus of the one-party state. "The prosperity of Church and Commonwealth are twisted together," Urian Oakes would argue some twelve years later. "He is a madman that will hope for the Continuance of our Spiritual Liberties, if the Wall of our Civil Government be once broken down."[16] If Massachusetts's Puritanism was to be preserved, the encroachments of imperial authority would have to be resisted at all costs.

The lay majority was not alone in its judgment, particularly with respect to imperial policy. A minority of magistrates, led by Governor Endecott and Deputy Governor Bellingham, agreed that the policy of intransigence that Winthrop had followed in the first decade of settlement should be resumed. Accordingly, in the summer of 1661 the General Court dispatched a defiant letter to the king, insisting on the colony's practical independence by virtue of the charter granted by his royal father.[17] The deputies must have thought that, on this issue at least, the die had been cast and Massachusetts had been irrevocably committed to a policy of complete independence. If so, they were mistaken.

The receipt of a royal response dated September 9 gave the momentum back to the clergy and their moderate allies. The king demanded, among other things, that the most violent anti-Quaker legislation be immediately suspended, and the General Court duly complied on November 27.[18] A delegation of clergymen, in consultation with the magistrates, urged that messengers be dispatched at once to disavow the court's letter of the previous June and offer "a just apologie." After some wrangling, a special session of the court was convened on December 31 and named moderate magistrate Simon Bradstreet and John Norton agents to represent the colony to the Crown.[19] This same session of the court issued a call for a synod to settle the issues of the half-way covenant and the consociation of churches.[20] After a rocky start, Norton's program seemed to be finally on course. Events, however, proved otherwise. The Half-Way Synod of 1662, coupled with the fruits of Norton's embassy, would inaugurate a period of bitter public division within the Bay thinking class.

In many ways, the Synod of 1662 represents the high-water mark of clerical power in Massachusetts Bay. Never again would the majority of the ministers be able to impose their will on the godly brethren of the outer party. While prominent laymen like Henry Bartholomew and William Hawthorne of Salem opposed their own minister by voting against the synod's report, the majority of brethren in attendance endorsed the half-way covenant and the consociation of churches.[21] The result had not been easily obtained. The first two sessions of the synod had deadlocked over the controversial fifth proposition, which contained the half-way provisions.[22] It was not until the third session in September, four months after the synod had first convened, that a sufficiently large majority was procured to sanction the judgment of the clergy. Four ministers—John Wilson, Richard Mather, John Allin, and Zechariah Symmes—presented the synod's conclusions to the General Court which on October 8, 1662, ordered that these conclusions be printed and commended to "the consideration of all the churches & people of this jurisdiction."[23] The official organs of centralized authority in Massachusetts had endorsed the half-way covenant and the consociation of churches.

Despite this apparent victory, the deliberation of the synod gave the clergy cause for concern. Lay support, lukewarm as it was, had been gained by means of a studied ambiguity and latitude. "The reason why there were soe few, not above 10 or 12 that appeared to act contrary to what the Assembly voted," reported Eleazar Mather, "was because they would allow every one his interpretation in the debate." The result, according to Mather, was that "sundry inconsiderately voted for that which when it was too late they wished they had not done."[24] Jonathan Mitchell's preface to the synodic report stressed this theme of latitude with respect to the assembly's conclusions. Since this matter "wherein the godl-wise are not like minded" was both abstruse and "remote from the foundation," Mitchell claimed that it was a religious duty "to bear one with another."[25] Eleazar Mather had a different impression of clerical attitudes toward dissent, no doubt a result of his conversations with his colleagues. "All dissenting is esteemed intollerable," he reported to John Davenport, "& dissenters are accoumpted & charged to be the Breakers of the peace of the churches."[26] That the clerical majority had to resort to such ambiguity and dissimulation was hardly a propitious sign for their continued cultural domination.

The most troubling feature of the synod's deliberation, however, was the nature of the ministerial dissent that emerged. Previous synods had not been without clerical disagreement. James Noyes and Thomas Parker had declined to join their colleagues in denouncing the presbyterial way in 1643, for example, and John Cotton had similarly refused to sign the results of the Synod of 1637. Yet all three conscientiously avoided undermining their fellow ministers by publishing their disagreement. Such clerical unity dissolved in 1662, as the handful of dissenting divines chose to go public with their views and continue the fight against the half-way covenant.

The central figure in this campaign was Increase Mather. Through his brother in Northampton, Increase had maintained a running correspondence with John Davenport, whose dissent, according to John Allin, had blocked the inclusion of the half-way measures in the Cambridge Platform.[27] During the third session of the synod, Increase attempted to read a letter of dissent he had procured from Davenport, but John Norton, the moderator, "advised them not to suffer me." Undaunted, Increase submitted this and other writings from New Haven to the General Court with "a preface subscribed by Mr. Ch[auncy], Mr. Mayo, my Brother & myselfe, in the name of others of the Dissenting Brethren in the Synod." Mather proposed publishing these documents and urged Davenport to enter the fray in print, "many that are true to the cause desiring us soe to doe."[28] Mather's proposal found fruition in the London publication of Chauncy's *Antisynodalia Americana* that very year and the Cambridge printing of Davenport's *Another Essay for the Investigation of the Truth* in 1663.[29] Increase Mather had exposed the clerical breach for all to see.

Increase Mather's motivation in inciting public dissent over the half-way covenant was complicated. Much has rightly been made of the twenty-three-year-old's identity-creating rebellion from his father, Richard Mather, one of the principal architects of the half-way measures. Equally important was Increase's marginal position within the clergy. Not yet an ordained minister, he had entered into an agreement in the summer of 1662 with the second church of Boston to preach for pay. Mather's pedigree and temperament, however, filled him with a desire for a position of leadership and importance. Such a position was inconceivable within the ministerial majority that supported the half-way covenant. Men such as Richard Mather and John Norton, on the one hand, and Jonathan Mitchell, on the other, had nailed down the clerical leadership of their respective generations. Faced with the prospect of playing a bit part in the ministerial establishment, Increase opted instead for a leading role among the handful of dissenting "outsiders." His strategy was successful, for he shortly became a darling of the opponents of the half-way covenant among the deputies.[30] Increase had indeed become popular, but only at the price of breaking from his colleagues in the pulpit.

Whatever his motivations, the results of Increase Mather's actions were disastrous for the ministerial majority. Both *Antisynodalia* and *Another Investigation* characterized the half-way covenant as a backsliding abandonment of the purity of the original principles. "There is danger of great Corruption and Pollution creeping into the Churches," warned Davenport, "by the Enlargement of the Subject of Baptism."[31] In his unsigned preface to the same work, Increase Mather described the half-way "profanation" of the seal of baptism as "sacriligious impiety, as if a man should take the Blood or Body of Christ, and prostitute it to dogs."[32] Such "unjust aspersions" upon the synod and its clerical proponents, complained John Allin of the majority, "do tend much to weaken the Authority of their Ministry and Dispensations."[33]

Aside from its particular content, the very existence of published clerical dissent undermined the cultural domination of the clergy by suggesting that there was more than one way to legitimately interpret the sense of Scripture. Even worse were the dissenters' appeals to popular judgment. Such appeals, warned Richard Mather and Jonathan Mitchell, "introduce a strange and destructive Confusion, and evacuate a special end of the Lord's appointing Pastors and Teachers." It was the clergy's special responsibility and privilege "to study and search out the Truth, and recover it from the fallacies of gainsayers." Having done so, they could then "deliver it in a plain and positive manner to the People suitable to their understanding."[34] This end was jeopardized by the antisynodists' public dissent and invocation of popular lay opinion. The dissenters not only were guilty of doctrinal error but also had violated the basic rules of clerical congeniality that supported the system of cultural domination by stirring up controversy. At least that was the view expressed by Richard Mather and Jonathan Mitchell:

> Had Divine Providence so disposed, that the lot of our Dissenting Brethren had been Ours in a case circumstanced as this is; we are ready to think, that after our Reasons given, and Arguings in a Synod (the most proper place of Publick Disputation where Churches walk in order, Acts 15. 17.) we should have looked at it as our Duty to sit down in silence, and not to amuse and trouble the People by Printing a Dissent.[35]

Unfortunately, Increase Mather and his cohorts seemed oblivious to their "Duty to sit down in silence."

The clerical majority continued to press for their ecclesiastic program. John Higginson of Salem took up the cause in his 1663 election sermon, *The Cause of God and His People in New-England*. Not surprisingly, God and New England's cause was "to keep Gods Commandments in matters of Religion."[36] This entailed a "duty to press forward still to the mark," particularly in "reforming whatever is amiss or defective amongst us, as in those the late Synod hath pointed unto, about the Subjects of Baptisme, and consociation of Churches."[37] That same year Thomas Shepard published *The Church Membership of Children and their Right to Baptisme* in support of the half-way covenant. Despite such offerings and the endorsement of the General Court, the extension of baptism fared poorly in the Bay churches. Although several churches officially endorsed the synod's result in deference to their elders, very few were willing to actually practice its provisions. As Robert Pope has noted, few half-way members in Massachusetts owned the covenant and had their children baptized in the 1660s. The result was a smoldering feud between the bulk of the laymen and the dissenting divines, on the one hand, and the clerical majority and their supporters in the magistracy, on the other. John Norton's ecclesiastic program had been checked.

Norton's imperial program fared even worse than his church schemes. Norton and Bradstreet's embassy had received a fairly warm reception in England in the spring of 1662.[38] Puritan Lord Saye and Sele proved instrumental at court, and the king seemed pleased with the messengers' "humble addresse & petition from the Generall Court of our colony of the Massachusets in New England."[39] Assured that the colony's charter would remain inviolate, Norton and Bradstreet returned after several months. They were shortly followed by a letter dated June 28, 1662, from Charles II.

The king's letter and the partisan use to which it was put by the hard-liners among the deputies proved the undoing of both Norton and his policy of accommodation. In and of itself, the king's message was not entirely negative. The king claimed to have been satisfied with the embassy of Norton and Bradstreet. A royal pardon was graciously extended to the Bay residents "for all crimes & offences committed against us during the late troubles" of the English Revolution. The Crown's order of protection toward the Quakers was rescinded. Best of all, the colony's charter of 1629 was confirmed "that they shall freely enjoy all the priviledges & liberties granted to them in & by the same."[40]

Three royal provisions, however, severely damaged the cause of the accommodationists. The first concerned the status of Anglicans in the colony. While the king requested that the Anglican church and its adherents be tolerated, he notably declined to challenge the establishment of the congregational churches in the Bay. The second provision was somewhat more unsettling. The king demanded that "all persons of good & honest lives" be permitted to partake of the Lord's Supper and present their children for baptism.[41] This provision went beyond the half-way covenant and would have transformed the New England Way into a fully comprehensive system. The Bay congregations would retain their establishment but only on an "inclusive" basis. The third provision was the clincher. The king requested that the franchise requirements be altered to include all orthodox and upstanding "freeholders of competent estates," including those "of different persuasions concerning church government."[42] Charles II was demanding that the sectarian congregations give up their monopoly of political power. Just as the Bay churches could retain their establishment only by becoming comprehensive in scope, the king would grant the colony its political independence, but not as a Puritan one-party state.

News of the king's demands confirmed the lay hard-liners' worst suspicions. The Stuart monarch was the natural and ideological foe of the Puritan regime, and sending agents and humble apologies would only be taken as a sign of weakness precisely when a show of strength was necessary. Recently arrived James Allen claimed that the English congregationalists thought "it had beene better for the Country if they had not sent soe many adresses & Agents, which is reported to be a discovery of there pulsanimity & want of courage to stand for the cause they came hither for."[43] Understandably, the hard-liners felt that their liberties had been betrayed by Norton's embassy. The royal letter confirmed the establishment of the Bay churches but would have effected an even greater centralization of ecclesiastic authority than the clergy had sought in the assemblies of 1657 and 1662. The price of such establishment and centralization, however, was the political and religious empowerment of the godly brethren that had become a central feature of the one-party state in Massachusetts. Anger among the deputies was matched by panic among the laity. Rumors spread that a royal governor, bishop, or military force would shortly arrive from England.[44] The deputies fueled these rumors by refusing to publish the royal letter, despite the desires of the moderate magistrates and the king's explicit request.[45] While such rumors were exaggerated, they were not entirely off the mark, for the king had resolved to dispatch royal commissioners to New England. The moderates' policy of accommodation had, for the time being at least, been discredited.

Despite the unpopularity of their position, Norton and his moderate allies among the clergy and the magistracy continued to urge a nondefiant posture toward the Crown. John Higginson pointed to the example of the biblical Daniel's management of "publick affairs" under foreign domination. In Daniel's case, "the matter did so require for him to be so carefull, as that no errour nor fault might be found in him" by his foreign overlord. Such a policy, Higginson told the freemen, "is for our imitation."[46] Norton went even further. Reportedly, he warned the court that "if they complied not with the King's Letter, the Blood that should be spilt would lye at their dores, or upon their heads."[47] Such dire predictions fell on deaf ears. When the first royal commissioners arrived in 1664, the General Court had still done nothing to comply with the king's demands.

For his own part, Norton became the object of calumny. Some suspected that he and his comrades had "desperately designed to overturne Civill & Spirituall Libberties." While such an extreme view was probably not typical, Norton's own congregation seems to have considered hiring James Allen—a hard-liner and opponent of the result of 1662—to "assist" their teacher in the pulpit. "Mr. Norton hath lost himselfe much in the Esteeme of the generallity," observed Humphrey Davie from Boston, "& will doe more."[48] Vilified by his opponents, John Norton died within a year of his return from England. As Lawrence Shaw Mayo poignantly put it, "[T]here can be little doubt that a broken heart hastened his end."[49]

By 1663, then, the basic divisions within the regime that characterized half-way politics had clearly emerged. On the one side were the bulk of the laity and their representatives, roughly half the magistrates, and the dissenting divines. They opposed the clerical centralization of power contained in the half-way covenant and the consociation of churches and favored a "hard-line" stance toward the Restoration government. Opposed to them were the ministerial majority, the other half of the magistracy, and the remainder of the godly brethren, who sought accommodation with the Crown and favored the result of the Synod of 1662. The utter unwillingness of either side to give way to the other created strong feelings of ill will between the factions. This intense political tension of the 1660s was like a powder keg waiting to explode. That explosion finally came, of course, with the controversy over the third church of Boston. First, however, a fuse had to be set and lit. That fuse was the gathering of the first baptist church of Boston.[50] Like the debacle of the third church of Boston, the baptist church's case raised the issues of ecclesiastic power and imperial policy. The controversy surrounding that congregation set the stage for the larger dispute about the third church of Boston that followed on its heels.

The dispute over the half-way covenant left the clerical majority vulnerable to the incursions of antipedobaptists, or Anabaptists, as they were called. There were several causes of this vulnerability. The very fact of clerical disagreement concerning the proper subjects of baptism helped the position of the Anabaptists. Since the topic was evidently one on which learned and reasonable men could disagree, the baptists could invoke the injunction found in the preface of the "Results of the Synod of 1662": "to bear one with another."[51] This plea for toleration had a special resonance for the Particular Baptists of Boston, who shared the orthodox Puritan's Calvinist orientation and congregational church polity.[52] In the eyes of many of the laity, the Anabaptists had become, as Stephen Foster has put it, "good Christians who had gone a little far down the right road at a time when so many of the clergy were trying to force the Puritan colonies down the wrong one."[53]

There were doctrinal causes of ministerial vulnerability as well. Conceived of as a covenant seal, infant baptism had always been defended by the orthodox divines as a New Testament antitype of the circumcision of Abraham's seed. This same typological argument, in fact, was used to justify the half-way covenant. Like circumcision, infant baptism conferred "outward Membership" in the church and placed children in covenant with God.[54] As such, these children had a right to present their own children for baptism, barring censure from the church. The dissenting divines attacked the extension of baptism by undermining this typological analysis. "Though Baptism is come in place of Circumcision," acknowledged Davenport, "[y]et neither must we look at Circumcision as it was of Moses, but of the Fathers . . . nor at every subject of Circumcision, as the subject of Baptism extensively." Such a typological argument failed to take into account the progress in the "administration of the covenant . . . from less perfect, before the coming of Christ, to more perfect, after his coming."[55] The same critique of Puritan typology based on ecclesiastic progress from Old Testament to New, however, could be used to argue against infant baptism, as indeed it was by John Thrumble some years later: "The Old Testament rules are not parallel to the rule of the gospel: nor are they binding to us: and to mix law and gospel together: the apostle saith is to bring a new gospel."[56] The clerical majority was acutely aware of this danger. "Wee see evidently, that the Principles of our Dissenting Brethren give great Advantages to the Antipaedobaptists," complained John Allin, "which if we be silent, will tend much to their Encouragement and Encrease, to the Hazard of our Churches."[57]

The greatest cause of clerical vulnerability, however, was the nature of the Particular Baptists in question. Although they included a certain number of English refugees, the core of the congregation was a group of godly brethren. Thomas Goold, Thomas Osborne, and John Farnam, Sr., had all been church members and upstanding citizens before their dalliance with antipedobaptist principles. Hardly troublers of New England's Zion, these men continued to profess their loyalty to the Bay government and brotherly affection to the orthodox churches. Their peaceful dissent from the established order highlighted the issues that characterized half-way politics.

Thomas Goold, a prosperous tenant farmer on the Ten Hills farm of John Winthrop, Jr., had joined the church of Charlestown in 1640. The leader of the baptists, Goold had first developed scruples about infant baptism in the early 1650s and in 1655 refused to present his newborn daughter for that ordinance. Obstinate in his position, he was admonished by the Middlesex County Court the following year and censured by the church of Charlestown. Since such a censure disabled him from partaking of the Lord's Supper, Goold treated it as a virtual dismission and began regularly attending church services at Cambridge. Goold received a second admonition from the County Court in June 1657 and was ordered to post £20 to appear before the upcoming Court of Assistants, which warned him of the dangers of his continued dissent. Despite all of these admonitions and warnings, the court did nothing to actually punish Goold and let the matter rest. No doubt the major reason for this inaction was the fact that Goold behaved in an orderly fashion and never tried to publicly undermine the established church order. In fact, aside from his refusal to have his daughter baptized, Goold did not act on his baptist principles until the end of 1663. On February 4 of that year the church of Charlestown had formally endorsed the result of the Synod of 1662 by a three-to-one majority. In November, Goold began to hold private religious meetings with his fellow sectarians.[58]

Thomas Osborne was also a member of the church of Charlestown. In November of 1663, Osborne was admonished by the church for attending Goold's meetings instead of its own. Osborne's baptist scruples seem to have arisen from his opposition to the half-way covenant, for he justified his separation from the church on the grounds that "he did not see it to be the mind of God to continue some churches by way of natural generation." Osborne's reaction to the half-way covenant was not unique, as John Thrumble—another baptist "fellow traveler" from Charlestown—would tell the clergy some years hence: "I did as you say walk 20: years with the churches: and was as clear in my mind for infant baptism as any other: but I told some of you that you were about at the Synod to make [an] Anabaptist." There was more to Osborne's dissent, however, than a dispute over the ordinance of baptism. He also objected to the high-handed manner of the culturally dominant clergy. When the church discovered his Anabaptist principles, he complained by way of explanation that they "gave not leave to prophesy." Reportedly, he claimed the right to improve his talents through lay public oration "as being the rule of duty."[59]

John Farnam, Sr., shared Osborne's antipathy to clerical pretensions. A founder and deacon of the second church of Boston, Farnam had been a champion of Michael Powell's unsuccessful call to the ministry in the 1650s. Until his stroke in the summer of 1662, Powell had served in the anomalous position of a salaried lay preacher to the congregation. When Increase Mather was hired to replace Powell that summer, Mather tactlessly insisted on being paid the bulk of Powell's maintenance. Mather's demand, combined with his pose of superiority and disdain, succeeded in completely alienating Farnam. He not only joined the fledgling baptist group but also publicly condemned the church of Charlestown for its proceedings against Thomas Goold. When the second church of Boston finally excommunicated Farnam for these acts, he responded defiantly, "saying he cared not though others were offended at it: and that there was never an elder in [the] country that could have any read the scripture besides themselves."[60]

Under Goold's leadership, the small baptist circle was further abetted by developments on the imperial front. In the summer of 1664, two of the king's four commissioners, accompanied by 400 soldiers, arrived in Boston to a decidedly cool reception. En route to military action against the Dutch, they requested assistance from the Bay in that endeavor and announced their intention to return after its successful completion. They advised the court to use the intervening period to "further consider of his majesties letter to this colony, June twenty eight, sixteene hundred sixty & two, & give a more satisfactory answer to his majesty concerning the same than formerly."[61] Even more troubling, the king's letter of commission authorized his agents "to heare, & receive, & examine, & determine all complaints & appeales in all causes & matters."[62] Considering that one of the commissioners, Samuel Maverick, was a long-standing enemy of the Bay Puritans, the orthodox regime had little reason to expect a sympathetic judicial review or report from the royal commission.

The Bay government's reaction was swift and decisive. On August 3, the General Court passed a putative franchise reform to comply with the king's request of 1662.[63] One month later the Court of Assistants outlawed all dissent and dissaffection from the government.[64] Finally, on October 19, 1664, the court sent the king a "humble addresse" professing their loyalty, pleading their charter privileges, informing him of their franchise reform, and demanding the recall of the royal commissioners.[65] Faced with an immanent challenge to its autonomy, the Bay regime responded with an unequivocally hard-line stance. The godly brethren registered their approval in a flood of petitions "in which they testified & declared their good content & sattisfaction they tooke & had in the present government."[66]

Wisely, Goold and his comrades waited until after all four commissioners assembled in Boston at the beginning of May 1665 before taking their big step. On May 18, Goold and eight of his fellow opinionists drew up a confession of faith, rebaptized themselves, and gathered into a church of Christ.[67] Notably, they declined to seek protection from the royal commission. Nor did they publicize their action or do anything to embarrass the regime. Their hope seems to have been that in the heat of negotiation with the commission the General Court would overlook this baptist gathering. If so, their optimism was well founded in the short run, at least, for no action was taken against Goold and the others for several months.

Despite continued dispute over the rectitude of further defiance, when actually confronted by the commissioners the General Court resumed its hard-line stance. The commissioners asked that the freemen be assembled at the next Court of Elections so that they might inform them of "his majesties grace & favour to them." The magistrates refused.[68] The commissioners announced their intention to sit as a court of appeals. The court informed them that it did not recognize their jurisdiction and would not respect their decisions.[69] The royal agents were met with evasion and defiance at every turn. Stonewalled by the regime's obstinacy, the commissioners concluded that they could achieve nothing in Boston. In the early summer they departed to pursue their duties elsewhere, never to return. Armed conflict with the Dutch and French had placed the king in a weak bargaining position with Massachusetts, whose assistance he sorely needed in campaigns against the enemies' colonies. Charles II recalled his commission and confirmed the charter of 1629.[70] The hard-line stance had been vindicated.

Once the royal commissioner had been disposed of, the regime turned its attention to Goold's baptist gathering. On July 30, the church of Charlestown finally excommunicated Goold and Osborne.[71] In September they were summoned before the Court of Assistants, where Goold presented the magistrates with a signed confession of faith. Hardly an incendiary document, the confession contained an article that pledged fealty to the Bay government: "[W]ee acknowlidge magistracy to bee an ordinance of god & to submitt ourselves to them in the lord not because of wrath only but also for conscience sake."[72] The baptists did not reject the orthodox church order and refuse to support the established clergy. Loyal and peaceable brethren, they simply asked that their small gathering be tolerated. Although the magistrates could hardly allow such a "schism" from the New England Way, they were obviously reluctant to bring the brunt of their repressive power to bear. The assistants warned the baptists of their dangerous course and ordered them to cease and desist from all future meetings.[73]

Despite their claims of political loyalty, the baptists refused to obey the magistrates' injunction. On October 11, the General Court stepped up the pressure against them. The court disfranchised the freemen among them and threatened them all with imprisonment if they continued to hold meetings. Notably, the charge against the opinionists was not Anabaptism, which carried a sentence of banishment, but "a schismaticall opposition to the churches of Christ here settled."[74] Although their posture could hardly be called tolerant, the magistrates and deputies remained unwilling to invoke the full punishment the law prescribed. Against all odds, the court continued to hope that the threats and admonitions would recover these godly brethren from their error.

When it became clear that the baptists could not be reduced or intimidated in 1666, the magistrates finally began to deal with them in grim earnest. On April 17, Goold, Osborne, and a fellow congregant were fined £4 apiece and ordered to post £20 bond to appear at the Court of Assistants. The three dissidents refused to either pay their fines or post bond and were duly imprisoned, while the rest of the baptist congregation sought refuge on Henry Shrimpton's property on Noddle's Island in Boston harbor. When the dissidents were summoned before the assistants in September, their penalties were confirmed and they were threatened with banishment if they continued in their disobedience. Then the bombshell hit: the deputies refused to approve the threat of banishment. The plight of these godly victims of conscience had struck a sympathetic chord among many of the laity. The rest of the baptist congregation was left unmolested on Noddle's Island. Someone or several persons paid the dissidents' fines, and they were released within a few weeks.[75]

The reasons behind the lay sympathy for the baptists are not hard to surmise. Opponents of the half-way covenant could not help feeling that the baptists were no more erroneous in restricting the scope of baptism than the clerical majority were in expanding it. Given the ministers' efforts to centralize church power into their own hands, the baptists' practice of lay prophecy and rejection of a hireling ministry must have seemed quite attractive. The question of imperial policy may have entered here as well. If the Bay regime were to truly take a militant hard-line position, they would be best served by adopting a "popular front" strategy toward fellow Puritan anti-Royalists. In years to come, as we shall see, those who argued for a hard-line foreign policy and opposition to the half-way covenant would also urge toleration for the Particular Baptists.

The time for such tolerant attitudes, however, had not yet arrived. Although the magistrates could not banish the Particular Baptists without the concurrence of the deputies, they might still harass the baptists into exile. On April 2, 1667, Goold, Osborne, and a Mrs. Newell were fined £3 for nonattendance at church, and a levy was assessed on Goold's property when he refused to pay. When the baptists proved intransigent, however, it became clear that the magisterial intelligentsia needed a clear and public demonstration of the dangers of the baptists' dissent and the necessity of their banishment. That was precisely what the intelligentsia got on May 15, 1667, in the form of an election sermon.

By all measures, Jonathan Mitchell's *Nehemiah On the Wall in Troublesome Times* was one of the classic sermons of its genre. It was also, however, a pointed call to action against the baptists. The choice of the biblical Nehemiah was itself significant, for his glory as a ruler was that "[h]e encouraged and assisted Ezra [the high priest] in the Reformation of Religion." Nehemiah, like the Bay magistrates, understood that "[r]eligion is the chief and principal thing, wherein the welfare of a people stands."[76] Given that the congregational polity in Massachusetts was, in fact, the order of the gospel, Mitchell pleaded with the magistrates not to "wrong and marre an excellent Worke and Profession, by mixing and weaving in spurious Principles or Practices." The examples of such "spurious Principles" that Mitchell offered exactly described the Particular Baptists: "Separation, Anabaptism, Morrellian (Anarchical) Confusion, and Licentious Toleration."[77] While the unpopularity of repressing these principles might occasion "difficulties and troubles," such, in Mitchell's judgment, "do not excuse, nor should discourage Rulers from doing the work of their Places, which God calls them unto."[78] Confident that New England's Nehemiahs would harken to the call of duty, Mitchell urged the lay brethren to "prize and honour" their magistrates for fulfilling their calling.[79] Barring such approval, however, he demanded that the godly laity defer to the culturally dominant authorities: "Keep Order: keep in your places, acknowledging and attending the Order that God hath established in the place where you live. . . . [L]eave the guidance of the Ship to those who sit at the helm, and are by God and his people set there, and whom you are immediately under." The brethren's sole recourse was, according to Mitchell, to "pray for them."[80]

Despite Mitchell's oratorical offering, little headway was made against the baptists that year. The election sermon had apparently failed to convince the laymen or their representatives of the necessity of eliminating the baptist threat. Realizing that they needed more cultural sanction, the magistrates appointed six ministers to engage the dissidents in a formal public debate on March 7, 1668.[81] The debate was held on April 14–15 in the meetinghouse of the first church of Boston. In a sense, this disputation was a turning point in the religious history of Massachusetts.

Superficially, the clergy scored a stunning victory against Goold and the others. This is hardly surprising, considering that public debate and disputation were at the very heart of university education. The ministers presented a consistent line of argument that was buttressed by ample scriptural citation. They undermined the biblical grounds of their opponents and pointed out the flaws in their arguments. When Goold claimed a right to separate from the churches if they were guilty of sins "for which God may cast them off," the Reverend Thomas Cobbet sarcastically exposed his fallacy: "A dangerous inference. Because the all-seeing God may do it: therefore Goodman Goold a fallible judge and running to many errors may."[82] At almost every juncture, the spokesmen of orthodoxy bested their uneducated disputants. It was the sort of victory they could ill afford.

For all of their forensic fireworks, the clerical debators appeared to be nothing more than dialectical bullies, ganging up on an earnest and devout, if uneducated, group of laymen. When Goold asked if his side might have "liberty to choose moderators," he was testily told that "[y]ou come not on equal terms: but as a delinquent: to answer for what you have done."[83] It was not long before John Thrumble complained of the inquisitorial nature of the clerics' debating tactics: "And is this to clear the truth of God: for 6: or more persons to speak to one poor man before he hath done: not permitting him to speak. And every man [of the clergy] must have his saying before he [Goold] can give a right answer."[84] Having done more harm than good, the magistrates would never call for such an open clerical debate with religious dissenters again.

The fruits of this debate became apparent two weeks later. On May 1, the Court of Assistants entertained an appeal from Goold concerning his previous fine for absence from church services. Much to the dismay of the magistrates, the jury found for Goold and had to be sent back with more "forceful" instructions before they finally upheld the previous decision against him![85] Apparently, this show of lay support for the Anabaptist brethren finally convinced the General Court of their dangerous and corrosive influence. On May 27, 1668, Goold and two comrades were banished for endangering "the peace & order of the churches & the authority of this government."[86] After three years of admonitions and censures, the magistrates must have felt relief that the baptist episode had finally come to a close. If so, such feelings were decidedly premature.

Whatever Goold and his comrades lacked in militance they more than made up for in sheer stubbornness. Showing no intention of removing themselves from their homes, on July 20 they were duly imprisoned until they should either promise to depart or desist from their schismatic course.[87] On October 14, after twelve weeks of imprisonment, the three baptist dissidents sent a letter to the court requesting their release. Professing their loyalty to church and state, they reiterated their request for "a bearing with us" on the question of antipedobaptism and promised that "if it shall be thought meet to afford us our liberty, that we may take that care, as becomes us, of our families, we shall engage ourselves to be always in a readiness to resign up our persons to your pleasure."[88] Predictably, the court did not find this proposed course of action "meet" and instead began preparations to forcibly evict these troublers of Zion's peace. On October 23, the court ordered the publication of its previous sentence of banishment.[89]

The regime's continued pressure against the baptist schismatics produced two rather different effects. On the one hand, it seems to have impressed the dissident brethren with the perils of their continued defiance of the authorities. John Farnam agreed to cease attending the baptist meetings and return to Mather's second church of Boston and was therefore released from prison.[90] On the other hand, the continued imprisonment of Goold and William Turner prompted some orthodox brethren to work for their release. In early November, the Bay government received a petition from sixty-six freemen of Boston and Charlestown requesting the release of the baptist prisoners. Although the petitioners claimed to "neither approve of their judgment or practice," they could not help note that these godly dissenters were otherwise moral and upstanding citizens whose differences were "not in things fundamental, plain, clear, but circumstantial, more dark and doubtful, wherein the saints are wont to differ."[91] The response of the General Court was hardly sympathetic. The leading signatories were forced to retract their "many reproachfull expression against the Court" and acknowledge their error in subscribing to the petition, and, in addition, two of them were fined.[92] Having finally resolved on a course of repression and banishment toward the baptists, the General Court would brook no dissent from lay sympathizers.

The baptist episode did finally come to an end of sorts some four months later. In the spring of 1669, Goold and Turner were granted a three-day leave from prison to attend to their private business. Both shortly went into exile on Noddle's Island in Boston harbor.[93] Goold and his family remained there, unmolested by the Bay authorities. The Massachusetts government had far more pressing concerns on its hands now. A deep schism had emerged within one of the Bay's oldest and most prestigious congregations, a schism whose public manifestation divided the entire orthodox regime into two opposed camps. The debacle of the third church of Boston had begun in earnest.

The schism in the first church of Boston that resulted in the formation of the "Old South" or third church of Boston ushered in an epoch of declension politics. The controversy over this episode resulted in the emergence of two stable and public factions within the one-party regime. It did so by focusing public attention on the half-way covenant, imperial policy, and the treatment of Puritan dissenters.[94] These were precisely the issues that had divided the godly community throughout the decade. On the one side were the clerical majority, slightly more than half the assistants, and a solid cohort of lay supporters. They favored the half-way covenant, supported a conciliatory posture toward the imperial authorities, and insisted on the complete repression of heterodox opinion. Opposed to them were the bulk of the laymen, slightly fewer than half the assistants (some of whom had led the deputies in previous years), and a handful of dissenting divines. They opposed the half-way covenant, demanded a hard-line stance toward the Restoration monarch, and called for toleration of Particular Baptists and other "godly" dissenters. What lay behind these issues was the whole question of ecclesiastic power. Like an eighteenth-century "court" faction, the supporters of the half-way covenant sought to centralize power in the hands of the culturally dominant consociated clergy and "establish" the church by expanding its membership. Their "commonwealth" opponents tried to preserve the sectarian nature of the church/party cells and made common cause with Puritan dissidents in their stubborn defense of congregational autonomy and provincial independence.

The first church of Boston had been deeply divided throughout the 1660s. A majority of the congregants resented Norton's advocacy of the half-way covenant and imperial accommodation. As early as 1662, some of the congregants sought "an assistant in the ministry for preaching" to lighten Norton's "burden." Although nothing came of this request, their purported choice of recently immigrated James Allen—a noted hard-liner on foreign policy and staunch opponent of the half-way provisions—was significant.[95] It represented a desire to stem the tide of clerical "innovation" in New England's premier pulpit. Despite this challenge, Norton and Wilson were able, with the help of a determined minority of lay supporters, to secure the endorsement, if not actual implementation, of the half-way covenant in their church.[96]

John Wilson's death in the summer of 1667, four years after Norton's, left the pulpit of the first church of Boston vacant and thus ensured a struggle over his replacement. The supporters of the half-way covenant rallied behind the candidacy of forty-seven-year-old Reverend Thomas Thacher of Weymouth, a firm supporter of the synod's result who would ultimately serve as the first minister of Old South. His opponents, who included Governor Bellingham, objected that Thacher's obligations to the congregation of Weymouth precluded his installation in Boston.[97] Apparently, raiding pulpits in the hustings threatened congregational autonomy. This was a sharp critique, for Norton's tenure in Boston had been secured through just such an uninvited raid on the pulpit of Ipswich. Unfortunately, the lay majority of the first church of Boston soon discovered that this objection cut both ways. Their candidate, John Davenport of New Haven, was jealously guarded by his own congregation, who were reluctant to part with his services.

Seventy years old and irascible as ever, Davenport was the acknowledged spokesman for the antisynodic faction. The prospect of serving in Massachusetts's premier "bully" pulpit, with its reputed "Generall influences from thence through out the Country," appealed to the old spiritual warrior. Seizing the opportunity to reenter the fray with the "court" faction, Davenport informed the first church of Boston "of my strong inclination to obey this call" in early October 1667.[98] Later that month he informed them that, despite the dissent of the lay supporters of the half-way covenant, he accounted their "call as the act of the ch[urch] it being consented there to by the major by fare." Unless the judgment of the majority was decisive, he warned, "nothing Shall pass as a Ch[urch] act if the Minor part dissent, which is contrary to the Scripture and Reason." Though his own congregation at New Haven refused to actually dismiss him, they "leave that to me." Since his agreement with the church of New Haven had included the understanding that he would be at "liberty to follow the call of God," he didn't feel that its opposition precluded his removal. While nothing had been finalized, Davenport announced his intention to visit Boston next spring.[99]

When Davenport arrived in Boston on May 2, 1668, he found a bitterly divided congregation. The dissenters refused to issue an invitation to the aged divine and requested a council of churches to mediate their dispute. Unwilling to endure Davenport's ministry, the dissident minority wanted dismission so they could form a congregation of their own. The pro-Davenport majority ignored this "schismatic" request and dispatched assistant John Leverett "to goe in the Churches name to give mr. Davenport a fresh invitation." When he learned of the divided nature of his call, however, he declined to accept for the moment and waited "to see the mind of God."[100] The first church of Boston had reached an impasse, and each side waited for the other to blink first.

Finally, in midsummer the antisynodic majority of the first church of Boston agreed to call a council of neighboring churches. First, however, Davenport publicly blasted the dissenting minority during a lecture-day sermon. Whereas the first church of Boston had once been "famous for unity," Davenport lamented, "now there are risen up a company in opposition to the rest." This obstinate company refused to comply with the majority's choice of officers unless they could be dismissed to form their own church. "Such a condition," he insisted, "neither Christ himself, nor his Apostles gave any warrant for." "It is evident," Davenport fulminated, that "Satan hath a great hand in it."[101]

When the council of elders from the churches of Dorchester, Dedham, Roxbury, and Cambridge convened in Boston in early August, they promptly sided with the minority in the first church of Boston. Although the dissenters could not legitimately block the call of Davenport, the council expressed the hope that the majority "would give them up to the Lord with Love and prayers" so that they might form their own third church in Boston. On August 10, just two days later, twenty-eight members of the anti-Davenport faction of the first church of Boston formally requested dismission.[102] Their schism from the first church had received cultural sanction and ecclesiastic warrant.

That a council made up of supporters of the half-way covenant would side with their like-minded brethren in Boston is hardly surprising. Nor is it surprising that the majority of the first church of Boston chose to ignore this "brotherly counsel." What could not have been predicted, however, was that Davenport and the leadership of the first church would resort to trickery and deceit in his installation in the pulpit as well as in their dealings with their dissenting brethren. While successful in the short run, these tactics proved a great source of embarrassment to the first church and the antisynodic cause it championed when they were revealed the following summer. What made this choice of tactics particularly unfortunate was that they were probably unnecessary.

The first ruse involved Davenport's call to the pulpit from the first church of Boston. When the dissenters asked to be dismissed, the majority requested that they leave while the request was considered. Once they were gone, the majority summoned Davenport and extended to him a "unanimous" invitation to their pulpit. Davenport duly expressed his desire to accept this invitation, and messengers were dispatched to New Haven to secure his dismission from that church.[103]

Davenport could not have been pleased with the response from his old church. Writing on behalf of his congregation, teacher Nicholas Street informed the first church of Boston on August 25 that "we doe not to this day see light to give him up to you, by any voluntary act of ours." Naturally, this precluded their "sending such a dismission (which would be a voluntary act) as yourselves and our Reverend Pastor hath sent for."[104] The leaders of the majority in the first church of Boston decided to keep the news of this missive to themselves. Davenport wrote back to New Haven, informing the church that he had been called unanimously and further demanding dismission for himself and his family.[105] In late October, news spread in the church that Davenport's dismission from New Haven had finally arrived in a letter from Nicholas Street.

Dated October 12, Street's letter would prove a point of controversy in the months to come. Both Davenport's supporters and opponents exaggerated the contents of this missive. Hardly a fulsome dismission, the vast bulk of the letter was made up of objections to Boston's call and Davenport's removal. Nonetheless, interspersed throughout were brief passages that indicated that, however reluctantly, the church of New Haven would acquiesce in what it saw as a fait accompli. At the very end of the letter, Davenport's old congregation relented and dismissed "unto your holy fellowship" their aged pastor and his family.[106] To save appearances, the leaders of the first church of Boston transcribed this communiqué, reproducing the favorable passages while eliding the rest. They forged Street's signature and presented this "doctored" letter of dismission to the congregation of the first church of Boston on November 1.[107] He was admitted to the church directly and was ordained pastor in slightly more than a month.[108]

The dissenting minority did not simply acquiesce in this turn of events. Although they declined to disrupt Davenport's ordination, they repeatedly sought dismission from the first church of Boston throughout the autumn of 1668. At the end of February, they formally requested that the council either vote to dismiss them to form their own church, recall the council of the previous summer, or release them to other neighboring congregations. All of these requests were denied.[109] On March 29, the first church of Boston officially voted its denial of the dissenters' dismission. Two days later, the anti-Davenport faction of the first church of Boston wrote to several churches, requesting that a council of elders convene in Boston in two weeks.[110]

The elders' decision to convene as a council in Boston in mid-April 1669 raised several controversial issues. Not least of these was the half-way covenant. In their request for this assemblage, the dissenters of Boston explicitly stated their allegiance to the church order "sollemnly declared from the Scriptures in the Platform of discipline, and the last Synod's determination about the subjects of Baptism." The decision to meet as a council also involved the whole question of the authority of the consociated clergy. In calling for the participation of their colleagues in Salem, Ipswich, and Lynn, John Allin and John Eliot warned of the great "dishonour of God and the scandall of the way of the those churches" in Massachusetts caused by the first church of Boston's decision "to cast aside that ordinance of Communion of churches by way of Counsill." It was "high time for the Elders to Interpose" in the first church of Boston dispute and "perswad the Elders of Boston to graunt their dismission."[111] Most important, however, was the issue of congregational autonomy. The first church of Boston had not requested this council of "brotherly advisors" and did not recognize either its necessity or its legitimacy. In fact, the pro-Davenport majority had charged the dissenters with schism on April 9 and barred them from the communion table.[112] A missive from a minority of brethren under church censure was hardly a powerful ecclesiastic sanction for a council of churches. While the orthodox clergy had interposed in such intercongregational disputes before, they had always done so at the request of the magistrates. No such request was issued in this case.

As soon as the council convened in Boston on April 13, it requested a meeting with the first church of Boston. The elders of that congregation refused until the church had "come to a conclusion about our dissenting B[rethre]n." Only then would they "be willing to give them the reasons of their proceeding, which we for our owne parts judge to be most agreeable to the congregational way."[113] When the council reiterated its request, it was promptly informed by Davenport that "I doe not see that you are an orderly Councill." Since they had not been invited by the congregation,

Davenport informed his colleagues in the pulpit that, in accord with the congregational way, "we cannot meet and act with you in matters that concerne this Ch[urch]
ag[ains]t the expr[e]ssed mind of this Ch[urch]."[114] The very next day, Richard
Mather led an embassy from the council to the first church of Boston to "instantly
and importunately intreat you that you will be pleased to admit of us, into your present Church assembly." They found the doors of the town house where the first
church of Boston was meeting locked. When they knocked on the doors, they were
told by the congregation that "we desire to be in private and not disturbed." The sev-
enty-three-year-old Mather and his companions were kept waiting at the door for
hours while Davenport and his supporters debated whether they should read the letter Mather had brought from the council. Finally, they read the letter and voted to
"take no notice of it."[115] Mather's embassy had been an utter failure. Exhausted and
dispirited, eight days later he would be dead.[116] The consociated clergy would not be
allowed to meet with the first church of Boston.

On April 16, the council concluded its deliberations. Predictably, it sided with the
dissenters in the first church of Boston. The majority of that congregation was faulted
for failing to dismiss the dissenters in direct violation of the advice of the previous
council and were also criticized for refusing to meet with the present council to mediate the controversy. In fact, the dissenters were beyond the disciplinary grasp of
their opponents because "the regular sentence of a councill of churches in order and
orderly called by the Church concerned, adviseing to a dismission may (not with-
standing that Churches not hearkening to it) stand valid and regular as immunity
from censure." Having considered the evidence and circumstances, the council
judged "that the dissenting Brethren may seasonably make use of their christian liberty unto a regular coalition in an other Body."[117] The consociated clergy had authorized the schism of the supporters of the half-way covenant from the first church of
Boston.

Having secured ecclesiastic warrant for their gathering, the dissenters sought a
like sanction from the magistrates. They professed their earnest devotion to the civil
and ecclesiastic government of the colony "according to the Platt-forme of church
Government here established, and declaration of the Synod in 62, without any desire
of innovation upon either in any measure."[118] By May 10, they had procured the assent of seven of the thirteen magistrates—Daniel Gookin, Daniel Dennison, Simon
Willard, Richard Russell, Thomas Danforth, Simon Bradstreet, and John Pynchon,
all supporters of the clerical majority in their crusade for the half-way covenant.[119]
Despite an order to cease and desist from Governor Bellingham and the remaining
five magistrates, the third church of Boston was gathered on May 12, 1669, in
Charlestown. They were given the right hand of fellowship by the messengers of several neighboring congregations. Although they declined to participate in this gathering, the elders of the first church of Boston did send the assembled host a message.
"These Brethren who intend an imbodying by themselves," they stated, were, in fact,
still "members with us by covenant" and "under offences to this church which they
have not indeavored regularly to re[move]." Due to this state of affairs, the dissenters
"are not capable" of founding their own church according to the stipulations of the
congregational way and thus could not without sin be recognized as a valid church
of God.[120] An irrevocable split had occurred in Boston's oldest church. This split was
the result of deep divisions over the half-way covenant and the issues of congrega-

tional autonomy and lay/clerical power that it raised. All that remained to plunge the colony into political turmoil and upheaval was to publicize and politicize this schism. That is exactly what John Davenport did on May 19, 1669, at the Court of Elections.

Throughout the 1660s, the election sermons known as jeremiads had routinely called for lay deference toward the clerical intellectuals and magisterial intelligentsia. They also pleaded with the lay brethren to accept the result of the Synod of 1662, insisted on the necessity and legitimacy of centralized clerical power in synods and councils, and urged the assistants to root out any heterodox opinion or practice.[121] William Stoughton's jeremiad of the previous year, *New-Englands True Interest*, was typical of this genre. After noting that "God sifted a whole Nation that he might send choice Grain over into this Wilderness," Stoughton could not help but lament the declension "of later years."[122] "Thy God did expect better things from thee and thy children," Stoughton warned the brethren, "not a contempt of Superiours; not Unthankfulness and disrespect to Instruments of choice Service; not a growing weary of Government, and a drawing loose in the Yoke of God."[123] New England's great sin was the prideful will to power of the lay brethren of the outer party. The solution was obvious. First, the lay brethren must defer and submit to the judgment of their culturally dominant superiors: "Maintain Reverend and High Esteem of godly Leaders, Civil and Spiritual Guides, and be subject to them in the Lord. Account regular subjection to be an excellent thing; and that a pliableness and yieldableness in this, carries an excellency of spirit along with it." Second, they should "plead and improve the Lord's Covenant with you" by means of their baptism in accord with the stipulations of the half-way covenant.[124] Finally, Stoughton addressed the magistrates and warned them to be on the lookout for heterodox troublers of Zion's peace. "The true Christian Gospel-Liberty," he insisted, "was never unto this day a Womb big with Licentiousness."[125] In short, the jeremiad election sermon was the official vehicle for propagating the clerical majority's "party line."

Delivered at the request of the deputies, Davenport's election sermon broke from this tradition. Instead of demanding deference toward the magisterial intelligentsia, he reminded the brethren that the "Power of Rulers of the Commonwealth is derived from the Peoples free Choice."[126] As such, this power was limited by the "due Rights and Liberties of the People" as well as the word of God.[127] In fact, divine wrath was often a people's punishment for "the sins of their Rulers." This was because "bad men being in publick place, will give bad counsel to corrupt Religion."[128] While Davenport did not actually claim that the Bay magistrates were "bad men" guilty of sin, there could be no doubt that he considered the half-way covenant a corruption of true religion. Such synodic innovation ignored the fact that "[a]ll Gods Truths are Eternal and Unchangeable by men." Oblivious, the pro-synodists turned from ancient truth to pursue "a various management of matters of Religion, to the advantage of the present postures and condition of your Civil Affairs."[129] Worse than this temporizing for reasons of political expediency was the divisive effect this clerical innovation had on the Bay churches:

> Avoid carefully imposing upon the Churches any thing that Christ hath not put upon them, viz. no Mans Opinions, especially when they are such as prevailed in an hour of Temptation, though consented to by the major part of a Topical Synod, yet disliked by some of themselves, and by other godly Ministers, both in this Countrey, and in other Countries, so that they are things Controverted and under Dispute.

Obviously referring to his own congregation, Davenport charged the audience to "impose not such things upon Churches, lest Contentions arise in the Churches about Opinions, which are no part of the Faith once given to the Saints."[130]

The schism of the third church of Boston had taught Davenport more than just the dangers of the half-way covenant, however. Equally troubling was the assumption that the consociated clergy should have power to intercede without invitation into a church's affairs at the expense of the lay Christian liberties that underlay the congregational way. "Take heed and beware that you deprive not any Instituted Christian Church," he warned, "of the Power and Privilidges which Christ hath purchased for them by his precious blood." Yet this is precisely what standing clerical councils do, insisted Davenport, when, "under a pretence of helping the Church with their light," they "bereave them of their Power." Even when a council was gathered occasionally and called in an orderly fashion, there was no reason to slavishly follow the council's "Judgement" without first "considering whether it be according to the holy Mind and Will of God." This was particularly true when, as in the recent council, such judgment "suits with mens own minds, wills, and ends, above any Light for the contrary, though it be held forth from the Word of God."[131] Finally, he urged his fellow opponents of the half-way covenant to tolerate those godly dissenters who, like the Particular Baptists, "walk orderly, and peaceably, not offensively to one or other or to the Church of God."[132] Davenport's sermon demonstrated that the politics of declension could cut both ways. The real troublers of Zion's peace were the intolerant ministers and magistrates who attempted to centralize ecclesiastic power in their hands. Davenport's election sermon was a call to the lay brethren and their representatives to defend their congregational liberties from the assaults of the educated elite.

Unfortunately for Davenport and the commonwealth cause he championed, he was shortly mired in controversy and scandal. Nicholas Street's arrival in Boston in June 1669 exposed the forgery and deceit of the previous year by the elders of the first church of Boston.[133] In July, a council of seventeen ministers examined the evidence against the elders of the first church of Boston. The clergy found them guilty of "great unfaithfullness falsehood if not forgery," particularly in regard to their treatment of Street's letter of "dismission" in the previous autumn.[134] Davenport was singled out for special criticism, for his much-touted congregational principles "concerned him most to see matters carryed clearly, because he could not in conscience joine to the Church of Boston, nor take office without the consent of the Church of New Haven." The ministers found Davenport's trampling upon the church liberties of the brethren of New Haven all the more egregious because he "doth most justify the fact and himself as having no hand in the writing."[135] The first church of Boston had been found guilty of fraud, and the Bay orthodox divines had marked the renegade John Davenport persona non grata within their ranks.

Davenport remained unmoved. He refused to meet with his colleagues or recognize the legitimacy of their findings. Although some of the leaders of the first church of Boston expressed remorse for their deception—assistant John Leverett said "there was a reall injury in it to this Church to the Church of New haven and to the neighbour Churches"—Davenport refused to acknowledge that anything amiss had been done. The charge of forgery in regard to the extract of his letter of dismission "savoured of much ignorance and malice" according to the embattled divine.[136] Hardly a hypocrite, Davenport was engaged in a cultural and political struggle against the forces of presbyterial centralization and their half-way innovations. He eschewed the procedural sense of justice or "fair play" that subsequent radicals would dismiss as "bourgeois parliamentary morality." Davenport remained defiant in his insurgency right up to his death some eight months later.

The lingering controversy over the call of John Davenport and the gathering of the third church of Boston bitterly divided the orthodox regime. Supporters and opponents of the half-way covenant split into factions, each of which charged the other with schism, fraud, and disturbing the peace of the Bay churches. On May 3, 1670, the freemen of Hadley and Northampton submitted a petition to the General Court, inquiring "what it is that hath provoked the Lord (who doth not afflict willingly but if neede be) against us." The petitioners hoped that reaching a "unanimous agreeing in what our evill is" would be the first step in restoring the harmony of the churches and their "turning to the Lord."[137] The petitioners would have their answer in less than a month.

When the annual Court of Elections met on May 11, it was the magistrates' turn to choose the speaker. Their choice of Samuel Danforth reflected the pro-synodic majority within their ranks. *A Brief Recognition of New-Englands Errand Into the Wilderness* returned to the traditional themes of the jeremiad election sermon. The cause of declension in New England was a collective loss of lay ardor for "the free and clear dispensation of the Gospel and Kingdome of God."[138] This took the form of a decline in deference and reverence for the clergy. "O what a reverent esteem had you in those dayes of Christ's faithful Ambassadors," Danforth recalled of the first years of settlement. "[T]heir Persons, Names and Comforts were precious in your eyes." In those times "you counted your selves blessed in the enjoyment of a Pious, Learned and Orthodox Ministry."[139] Equally troubling was the loss of respect for the power and judgment of the consociated clergy: "[W]hat reverence was there then of the Sentence of a Council." Unlike the recent truculence of the first church of Boston, in the good old days the sentence of a clerical council had been "decisive" in "issuing the Controversie."[140] He reminded the brethren that their errand had been for "the Ministry of Gods faithfull Prophets, and the fruition of his holy ordinances."[141]

Despite this oratorical appeal and the scandal surrounding Davenport's call to the first church of Boston, the opponents of the half-way covenant among the deputies remained as committed to their cause as ever. On May 12, the assistants proposed a joint conference with the deputies and clergy to "seeke the Composing of the present differences that are of late increased among the churches."[142] The deputies refused. Instead, the following day they formed a committee to answer the question raised by the petitioners of Hadley and Northampton. Their report, issued on May 25, was so strident that it could have been written by the late John Davenport. The cause of declension, and hence God's wrath, was the high-handed behavior of the clerical majority and their half-way "innovation," which "threatened the ruin of our foundations, and the extirpation of those old principles of the congregational way."[143] Apparently, the real ecclesiastic scandal of New England was not the call of John Davenport to Boston but rather the gathering of the schismatic third church of Boston.

Naturally, the assistants could not concur with this report. They were particularly irritated by the charge that they and the local clergy were guilty of "irregularities and breach of order and law in approving the New Church of Boston." The assistants believed that their "innocency" in authorizing the gathering of the third church of Boston was "entire, and nothing hath (to our understanding) beene offered to convince of blame."[144] The deputies believed otherwise. "Our law saith no Companye of men shall Joyne in any pretended way of Church ffellowshipp," they explained, "except they have the aprobation of the magistrates and Elders of the Neibouring Churches." Surely this law didn't mean "that when some magistrates appeare and declare openlye against the proceedings of any as Irregular, That others that are absent shall abett or Incourage the same." Yet this is precisely what had happened in the case of the third church of Boston. The elders shared the magistrates' guilt, for they had given their approval to the gathering despite the disapprobation of both of Boston's churches. In so doing, they had undermined "the liberty of every Church to Exercise all the ordinances of god amongst themselves," particularly the disciplinary "liberty" of the first church of Boston. The entire imbroglio over the third church of Boston raised troubling questions about "our Civill or Ecclesiastick leaders . . . which may if not Searched out become a trouble to our Israell considering the Examples before mentioned."[145] The very existence of the third church of Boston was a sign of declension.

The pro-synodic majority among the assistants must have been stunned by the militant audacity of the deputies. On May 18, they wrote back to the deputies for clarification. Were they actually charging the ministerial intellectuals and magisterial intelligentsia with ecclesiastic crimes? The response of the deputies was unequivocal: "If we should say all was well in Churches in Elders in magistrates in other sosyeties as to publick Guilt would not the Lord reprove us and say what meanes then the Bleating of the sheepe &c: the Growing ffesteringe wounds of poore New England as to religion both in power and puritye; we Assert and Quere but what we have observed and seene as a ffretting leprosie creeping in uppon Us."[146] The deputies could not possibly have been any clearer. New England's "ffretting leprosie" was the prelatical pretensions of the clerical majority and their allies among the assistants.

The deputies had obviously overplayed their hand. Although many of the godly brethren sympathized with the cause of Davenport and the first church of Boston, they were not prepared to see calumny heaped upon their educated leaders in church and state. The deputies learned this at the next Court of Elections, where they received a solid drubbing. Fourteen of the opponents of the half-way covenant were removed from office, and six of them were replaced by members of the third church of Boston who served as nonresident representatives.[147] Stephen Foster has correctly noted the lack of any serious evidence of a ministerial electoral campaign in the winter of 1670–1671.[148] Nonetheless, given the results of the election of 1671, historians like Robert Pope and Perry Miller have not been wrong to assume that the clergy played some part in this political change; they certainly had means, motive, and opportunity.[149]

John Oxenbridge's election sermon, *New-England Freemen*, represented the high-water mark of the lay insurgency that Davenport had inaugurated some two years before. Invited by the outgoing deputies, Oxenbridge raised the same issues Davenport had raised. He warned the brethren to guard their political privileges jealously: "[Q]uit once your liberties and you must have such a Magistracy & manage[ment] of it as will please not God nor your selves, but other men will be your master."[150] He criticized the half-way covenant for admitting "a carnal party into the priviledges due here to visible Saints." The result of such a practice would "be likely to eat out the heart of liberty and religion."[151] The whole thrust of the clerical majority's program, with its synods and councils, appeared to be an attempt "to fashion your selves to the flaunting mode of England in worship or walking." "If you have a minde to turn your Churches into Parishes, and your ministers into Priests and Prelates," he declared, "I cannot think the Lord will ever endure it."[152] He also asked the brethren to defend their autonomy within the empire and stop enforcing "uniformity" of opinion—"so cruelly urged by Papists and Prelates"—on the Particular Baptists and other "sober people."[153] Yet there was also a conciliatory note in Oxenbridge's message. He recognized the disastrous effect the "appearance of disagreement among the Elders" had on "the order of Churches."[154] He therefore advised a mutual forbearance on the question of the half-way covenant. In fact, both sides really shared the same goal, namely, "to fetch in to Christ the young Generation."[155] Even the schismatic gathering of the third church of Boston need not "make any noise, heat and breach in the Land" because it was an exceptional case. "The like may not be seen in an age," he averred. "[N]either is this I hope, to be a President."[156] Although Oxenbridge charged the brethren to keep up the good fight for the congregational way, he also asked them to tone down their rhetoric.

On May 31, 1671, the General Court received a petition signed by fifteen ministers. They asked to be cleared "from the unjust charge of innovation, which, with a loud cry & clamour of apostacy, is laid upon the generality of the ministry of these churches." They utterly denied the deputies' findings of the previous year that they had perpetrated "an usurpation of a lordly & praelattical power over Gods haeritage, a subvertion of gospell order, & all this with a dangerous tendencie to the utter devastation of these churches."[157] In less than a week, the General Court fully complied with the ministers' request. Deploring the "antiministeriall spirit that too much runs through the country," the court resolved that the deputies' report of the previous year was "to be accounted uselesse."[158] As if to atone for their previous sins, the same session of the General Court "freed" the clergy "from all rates for the country, county, & church, & for the towne also."[159] Not only were their incomes among the very highest in the colony, but now they were tax-exempt as well.

The clerical majority and their allies among the magistrates had defeated the wave of "commonwealth" insurgency that Davenport had initiated in the aftermath of the schism in the first church of Boston. The reputation of the learned divines had been officially restored and vindicated. The peace this victory brought to the orthodox regime, however, was far from complete. Seventeen deputies officially registered their dissent from the order that had rescinded their charges against the clergy.[160] Moreover, the half-way covenant made very little progress in the churches until the aftermath of the tragedy of King Philip's War. In fact, the thinking class of the inner party had achieved nothing more than a return to the status quo before the controversy over the third church of Boston. The one-party regime remained divided over the half-way covenant, the treatment of baptists, and the whole question of foreign policy.

The damage had been done, however, and the Bay political and ecclesiastic scene was never to be the same again. It was not until the aftermath of the controversy over Davenport's call to the first church of Boston and the gathering of Old South that the clergy—both majority and dissenting—realized that their public disputations were seriously undermining their cultural authority. Not only had the lay opponents of the half-way covenant received some ministerial and biblical sanction, but also the very sight of learned and orthodox divines bitterly and openly fighting over the true order of the gospel demonstrated to the lay brethren that Puritan biblicism was not always a "hard science." Moreover, the ugliness of the dispute within the ministry was at best unseemly and at worst degrading. The prestige and luster of the Bay ministry had been sorely damaged by the intensification of the politics of declension.

The controversy surrounding the third church of Boston produced another effect that may have had even more profound implications for the clergy than this loss of standing. Increase Mather changed his mind about the half-way covenant. Michael Hall, Mather's most perceptive biographer, has argued that the joint impact of his father's death and the revelations of wrongdoing in the first church of Boston in the summer of 1669 triggered his about-face on this critical issue.[161] Although the scandal surrounding Davenport's call must have had an impact on him, if the third church of Boston narrative is to be credited, Mather learned about the perfidy in a letter from Nicholas Street the previous winter.[162] The death of Mather's father was undoubtedly an important factor; he later claimed that his father's dying charge to him was to "endeavour the good of the Rising Generation" so that "they might be brought under the Government of Christ in his Church."[163] Yet Richard Mather's death figured as more than a release of parental authority and, consequently, the need to rebel against that authority. Mather's death, following Norton's in 1663, Wilson's in 1667, and Jonathan Mitchell's in 1668, represented the demise of the acknowledged leadership of the clerical majority. A vacuum existed at the top of the pro-synodic movement. Although he kept his change of heart a secret for a few years, Increase Mather would then publish his new convictions and seize the leadership of the clerical majority. With a daring new rhetorical strategy, he would finally win the struggle over the half-way covenant and, for a brief moment, restore the ministerial intellectuals to a position of unrivaled influence and prestige. The Puritan thinking class of Massachusetts Bay would never fully recover from this victory.

9

INCREASE MATHER
AND THE DECLINE OF
CULTURAL DOMINATION

Between 1675 and 1686, Increase Mather exercised an unprecedented sway over the orthodox Bay regime. When King Philip's War erupted, it was Mather who first called for reform and then dictated its eventual course. Often consulted on matters of public import, Mather saw his views on imperial policy regularly accepted and implemented by the General Court. When, at his prompting, the last synod in Puritan Massachusetts's history was convened, he gave the opening address to the assembly, served as its moderator, and wrote its unanimous conclusion. He successfully led the movement on behalf of mass covenant renewal in the decade after King Philip's War. And, of course, it was Increase Mather who finally helped turn the tide in favor of the half-way covenant. To a remarkable extent, the history of Puritan Massachusetts in its final years is identical to that of the minister of the second church of Boston.

Mather's program was, in many respects, thoroughly conventional. He supported the same hard-line foreign policy that he had embraced in the early 1660s. He continued to be every bit as dogmatic and intolerant as ever, repeatedly demanding that the government suppress any and all heterodox opinion as it had in the "good old days" of his father. Even his endorsement of the synodic result of 1662 was conservative. He refused to acknowledge that the extension of baptism and church discipline was in any sense an innovation and argued that it was actually the implicit policy of the founding generation.[1] Moreover, he bitterly resisted any further extension of the obviously "parishional" thrust of the half-way covenant. While Mather's combination of a commonwealth hard-line foreign policy with a court advocacy of the half-way provisions may have been unusual, it was not his purported goals per se that enabled him to achieve such unparalleled influence.

The key to Mather's success lay in his bold new rhetorical strategy. The previous clerical chroniclers of declension had criticized current practices in light of a previous better epoch, either the period of the pure primitive churches or, in the 1660s, the "strong" time of the founding generation. Instead, Mather decried the sins of his times in terms of their prospective temporal outcome, namely, the dreadful and imminent punishment of a wrathful God. Mather's warnings were more than mere predictions based on biblical pattern and precedent, for they had that certainty and assurance that could only come from an "other worldly" source. Mather, in short, assumed the pose of God's lonely prophet in the wilderness, warning his "Israel" of the coming destruction. When that destruction actually occurred, Mather found his prophecies vindicated and his reputation unmatched among the orthodox ministry. At that point he ascended to the leadership of the clergy, and he jealously guarded that position right up to the dissolution of the Puritan government in 1686.

Like his late father-in-law, the famed John Cotton, Increase Mather supplemented his biblicist expertise with a religious charismatic appeal.[2] Just as Cotton had before him, Increase Mather was supported by a charismatic "voluntary" maintenance.[3] The youngest of six brothers and the apple of his mother's eye, Increase had always been precocious, frail, and acutely sensitive. After his father's death in 1669, Increase underwent a profound spiritual crisis, accompanied by nightmares and "hypochondriacal vapors."[4] He emerged from this crisis in 1672 with a profound sense that the Lord heard his prayers with a singular intimacy and had destined him for a position of unequaled importance. In fact, at the height of this "second conversion," Mather claimed that he "saw God before my eyes, in an inexpressible manner" while praying in his study.[5] Henceforth, Mather's public mien was constantly grim, intense, humorless, and painfully earnest.[6]

Mather's charismatic ministry proved every bit as destabilizing as Cotton's had before him. His powerful "supernatural" appeal could not help but invite invidious comparisons with the more sedate presentation of his clerical colleagues. While he regularly called for unanimity and spoke out against controversy, he felt personally free to criticize his opponents among the ministerial intellectuals and the magisterial intelligentsia. Nor was he reluctant to appeal to the lay brethren and their political representatives against those members of the inner party that dared to oppose him. Mather succeeded where Cotton had failed, however, for he was never tainted with any heretical opinion and was never forced to recant his errors. The result of Mather's charismatic course was the near-complete erosion of the cultural domination of the Puritan thinking class. The regime that Andros replaced was not so much a speaking aristocracy in the face of a silent democracy as a Puritan lay republic. Increase Mather was its clerical tribune.

Increase Mather's career as a prophet began in 1674. In that year, Mather delivered two sermons that he promptly published under the title *The Day of Trouble is Near*. In his autobiography he recalled that, "considering the sins of the Countrey, and the Symptoms of divine displeasure," he felt a strong call to offer a "Publick solemn warning of judgment near at hand."[7] The trouble Mather warned of was, in fact, "a day of Tumult," replete with scenes of "confused noise, and garments rolled in blood."[8] A devastating war was in New England's destiny, and its coming was nigh. The carnage would, of course, be divine retribution for the sins of the land. Mather's catalog of sins included a laundry list of minor carnal offenses: oppression of the poor, excesses in apparel, idle drinking, and worldliness, to name a few. One sin had a peculiar resonance, however. "I do believe, that one reason why the Lord threateneth to send upon us that Calamity of War at this day," Mather averred, "is because of wars and fightings which he hath seen, and been provoked with in the midst of us."[9] Mather's obvious reference to the recent controversy over the first and third churches of Boston was to the point. Although the insurgency that Davenport unleashed in 1669 had subsided, the churches and government remained deeply divided over the issues it had raised. Despite the fact that he had helped cause it over a decade ago, Mather informed the godly of Massachusetts that the bitter fruit of this factional strife would soon be ripe with blood.

For Increase Mather, 1675 was to be a year of personal triumph. The outbreak of King Philip's War in the summer served to vindicate his prophecy of the previous year. For roughly one year, a loose confederation of Wampanoag, Nipmuck, and Narragansett warriors successfully raided the exposed New England frontier.[10] Before they were finally subdued, they had attacked half of the towns in the region and left a dozen of them completely destroyed. The war cost New England £100,000 and one out of every sixteen men capable of bearing arms.[11] Surely Increase Mather was not alone in concluding that his previous "thoughts that God would visit with the sword for the reason mentioned" in his sermons had truly been "from God."[12]

It was in the context of this vindication of his prophetic voice that Increase Mather disclosed his change of heart concerning the half-way covenant. In 1675, he published two treatises in defense of the synodic result of 1662, *The First Principles of New-England Concerning the Subject of Baptisme & Communion of Churches* and *A Discourse Concerning the Subject of Baptisme*. Mather's theological arguments probably changed few minds—his elder brother Nathaniel characterized Increase's "notion of a catholik integrate church visible" as clear evidence of his "departing from old principles"—but he was the first to offer evidence of supernatural "providences" on behalf of the synodic result.[13] Mather recalled how, during the synod's second session, a "sore and threatening drought" had prompted the assembly to set aside a day for fasting and prayer. No sooner had they finished their prayers than the Lord sent rain to his benighted Zion, "whereby he did from Heaven own both his Servants and the work which they were about."[14] The appeal to supernatural mysteries and otherworldly providences was becoming a powerful and alluring element of Mather's rhetoric.

Increase Mather achieved more than the mere validation of his prophetic powers in 1675, however. In the autumn of that year he finally gained the importance and influence that he so desperately desired. In mid-October he delivered an occasional sermon with the General Court in attendance. Mather informed the rulers of the orthodox government that, just as he had predicted, the war had come as punishment for the sins of the land. Mather's avowed purpose was "to cause Reformation of those things which are displeasing" to the Lord. Only through a thorough "reformation of evils" could God be turned "from his displeasure" and Massachusetts spared from destruction at the hands of the "heathen."[15] Mather's sermon had an immediate and dramatic impact. A committee formed by the General Court to promote "a Reformation of those Evils which have provoked the Lord," in consultation with the elders, promptly issued a unanimous report that might have been (and probably was) cribbed from Mather's sermons.[16] This report was codified into law on November 3. In less than one month, Increase Mather had prompted the Bay government to acknowledge and reform the collective sins of New England.

The General Court's list of so-called provoking evils was almost identical to Increase Mather's litany of 1674. Strict sumptuary laws were passed, procedures were enacted to promote just prices and wages, worldly behaviors like oath swearing and tavern going were strongly discouraged, and measures were taken to ensure the pious observance of the Sabbath and all church services.[17] The very first provision, however, had been absent from *The Day of Trouble is Near*. Instead, it reflected Mather's changed public stance toward the half-way covenant. The magistrates' and deputies' first stated concern was the lack of church discipline, particularly with regard to "those that are children." The problem was the churches' failure to acknowledge their membership "according to the order of the gospell." Such presumably potential "half-way" members ought to be "brought to take hold of the covenant" so that they "may acknowledge and be acknowledged according to theire relations to God & his church, and their obligations to be the Lords." While it hadn't actually ordered the churches to incorporate the half-way provisions, the court did "solemnly recommend" that the "respective elders and brethren of the severall churches . . . take effectual course for reformation herein."[18] Here lay the key to Mather's and, as a result, the clerical majority's great rhetorical breakthrough: King Philip's War was a divine punishment for lay resistance to the elders and their synodic result! As the leading scholar of the half-way covenant, Robert Pope, has noted, King Philip's War inaugurated a period of success for the synodic result. Before the end of the century, roughly 80 percent of the churches had embraced its provisions.[19]

Another of Mather's pet peeves had been the creeping toleration of dissident Puritan sects. Just that September, he had noted with anxiety in his diary that someone in Boston had had the effrontery to, under cover of night, erect "a Pillar" on the site where several Quakers had been hung as testament to "their souls triumphing" as well as "their blood crying for Vengeance." Mather could not help but conclude that this was "an ill omen" of future judgments.[20] To prevent such Quaker "provocation of divine jealousie against" poor New England, the General Court ordered "that every person found at a Quakers meeting shall be apprehended, ex officio, by the constable, and by warrant from a magistrate or commissioner shall be committed to the house of correction" for three days or pay a fine of £5 sterling. Failure to enforce this law would result in a £4 fine against the constable for each offense proven. The court further called for the "strict execution" of the extant laws against importing such heretical idolaters.[21] Mather's program of reformation had achieved legislative fruition.

Despite his success, not everyone in the orthodox regime agreed with Mather's claim that Massachusetts was in a spiritual and moral crisis of worldliness and sin. The magisterial intelligentsia in particular had good reason to resist this diagnosis. Certainly by any comparative measure, Massachusetts was a thoroughly, if not fanatically, religious and sober colonial society. Nor were they likely to think it prudent to pass laws against mercantile "oppression" at precisely that moment when the colony's finances were most likely to be in need of private loans. Indeed, in February 1676, the General Court's insolvency forced the government to offer public lands as security "for the encouragement of such gentlemen merchants" that were willing to advance the needed funds.[22] Most disturbing of all, however, was Mather's thinly veiled charge against them. If Massachusetts were indeed in a state of spiritual and moral despair, then surely the fault lay with the assistants, whose duty it was to uphold orthodoxy and serve as "nursing fathers" to the churches. In fact, in early January 1676, Mather noted in his diary that the magistrates had been "too slow" in pushing forward the cause of reformation.[23] Understandably, the assistants chafed at the suggestion that they had failed on their watch as "Nehemiahs on the wall."

Increase Mather learned of the magistrates' displeasure on January 27, 1676. That day he delivered a weekday occasional sermon in which he lamented the lax enforcement of the laws by the Bay authorities. To illustrate his point, he repeated a report of a visitor who claimed to have "seen more drunkennes in N. E. in halfe a yeare than in E. in all their lives."[24] That evening Mather dined with Governor John Leverett and the assistants. A prominent member of the first church of Boston and a steadfast opponent of both the half-way covenant and the Cambridge Platform before it, Leverett had a long and distinguished career in the Puritan cause, including service in both chambers of the General Court and a stint as the colony's agent before the Restoration.[25] More than twenty years Mather's senior, Leverett bridled at the criticism leveled by this recent traitor to the "congregational" cause. The governor told Mather that his "visitor's report" about alcohol consumption in New England was patently absurd. Having arrived in the mid-1630s, Leverett informed the young zealot that "there was more drunkennes in N. E. many years agoe than their is now, yea at the first beginning of this Colony." Assistant William Stoughton "pleasantly" suggested that Mather recant this error in a future sermon. He naturally refused and self-righteously declared that "if men would not accept my Labors God will."[26]

The magistrates were not alone in expressing their skepticism about Mather's rhetoric. On February 1, Mather read the recently passed sumptuary legislation and "that which was recommended to churches respecting their children of the church" to his congregation. Two of the more prominent and sophisticated members of the second church of Boston told him after the meeting that "when ministers did lay a solemn charge upon people, it might take in the ignorant, but no rational man would regard what was said the more for that."[27] Earnest poses and solemn exhortations added nothing to the biblicist sanctions and rational arguments for or against any proposed course of action. Mather's congregants told him that they were not moved by his charismatic appeal and could only be convinced by the felicitous deployment of high cultural expertise. Mather's rhetoric was wearing thin with several of the better-educated laymen.

When the magistrates selected the election speaker for 1676, Mather could have been neither surprised nor pleased with their choice. A graduate of Harvard's first class in 1642, Reverend William Hubbard of Ipswich would emerge as a powerful rival to Mather's bid for ministerial leadership.[28] *The Happiness of a People In the Wisdome of their Rulers* struck a decidedly different chord than Mather had struck in his sermonic offerings of the previous years. Hubbard's analysis of New England's problems and potential solutions was decidedly this-worldly. Massachusetts's military defeat at the hands of Native Americans was not divine punishment so much as the result of "contempt of our enemies, or overweening thoughts of our own skill and courage."[29] Hubbard also disagreed with Mather about the need to root out all heterodoxy and dissent. Certainly the magistrates should uphold "all necessary and

Fundamental Truths," but when the issues were somewhat more complicated "where wise and good men have alwayes needed a latitude," Hubbard insisted that "it can be no part of wisdom to be too eager or rigorous about them."[30] Hubbard expressed his wholehearted approval of the balanced course the magistrates had followed in recent years: "I humbly conceive, you cannot doe better, then to let things be as they have been heretofore, so to countenance and encourage those that fear God and work rightiousness, but sharply to rebuke and timely to repress whatever is contrary to sound doctrine."[31]

Hubbard's sermon was less a cry for reform than a call to order. The brethren must keep in their places and defer to their high cultural superiors as God had intended, for those who advocate "a parity in any Society, will in the issue reduce things into an heap of confusion."[32] Such deference was especially due the godly magistrates, whose "natural parts Experience, Education, and Study" afforded them an advantageous familiarity "with the affairs of the world abroad, as well as with the Lawes and Customes of their own people at home."[33] He warned the brethren against replacing such men of "Humane Learning" on the grounds of mere differences in policy: "[U]nless a Countrey be very full of skilfull and expert men, by often changing their Rulers, the Government will fall into the hands of rude and ignorant Mechanicks."[34] The only crisis Massachusetts faced was military, and the best course of action was to maintain unity and discipline.

Mather's response was not long in coming. That spring, he began writing a history of the yet unfinished war and a companion piece appropriately titled *An Earnest Exhortation to the Inhabitants of New-England*. Mather's *Brief History* reiterated his claim that King Philip's War had come as divine punishment for the sins of the land. In stark contrast to Hubbard's vision, Mather saw spiritual intervention as the key to the struggle. The entire course of the war was determined by the pace and fervency of reformation within the godly regime. Surely it was no coincidence that the very same day in the autumn of 1675 that "there was a vote passed for the suppression and Reformation" of New England's sins "the Lord gave success to our Forces" against the foe at Hatfield, bringing peace to the western frontier throughout the upcoming winter.[35] On May 9, a public day of humiliation in Boston, attended by the General Court and "so many Teaching Elders as could be obtained," heralded the good news received the following day that "God had let loose the *Mohawks* upon our Enemies, and that they were sick of Fluxes and Fevers."[36] Final victory was assured in late June. On June 21, one of Boston's churches—Mather modestly demurred noting that it was his own church—"kept a day of solemn *Humiliation*." After a similar observance the following day in the Plymouth churches, the colonists received "such intelligence from diverse parts of the Countrye as doth administer ground of hope and rejoycing."[37] Indeed, Metacom, or King Philip, as he was known to the New English, was dead less than one month later.

Mather ended his history on a note of caution. Although victory seemed at hand, "there is one sad consideration which may cause humble tremblings to think of it, namely in that the *Reformation* which God Expects from us is not so hearty and so perfect as ought, to be."[38] *An Earnest Exhortation* picked up on this cautionary theme and expanded upon it. "There is yet another Storm hastening upon this Land," Mather warned, "if Repentance avert it not."[39] His program of reformation was, on the whole, familiar. He enjoined the brethren to atone for their failure to implement the half-way covenant: "[T]he body of the present Generation is guilty of *Sacramental perjury* in the sight of God, by breaking their *Baptismal vow*, and not observing all things whatsoever the Lord Jesus hath commanded them."[40] A thorough reformation would also require a "due execution of wholsome Laws which are founded upon the Word of God."[41] The magistrates' leniency in this regard jeopardized everyone's safety, for just as the Lord spared sinners from "temporal Judgements, for the sake of the Righteous amongst whom they dwell, so do the Righteous many times suffer great outward Calamity, because of the Wickedness of those they live among."[42] While Mather professed no desire to question the competence of "our faithful Magistrates"—"it shall be far from me to go about to discover the Nakedness of Fathers"—he could not help expressing the hope that they might "be more forward [in] the work of Reformation, more zealous in looking after the execution of wholsome, good and righteous Laws, more carefull to sanctifie God before the people." In short, if the magistrates would assume their role as guardians of orthodoxy and godliness, "we shall then have cause to magnify the faithfulness of that God, who hath brought such an affliction upon us and sanctifyed it to us."[43]

Mather did have one new proposal, however, that would prove extremely successful in the years ahead. He called for mass covenant renewal, whereby the members of the churches (both full and half) would publicly and solemnly reaffirm their loyalty to the Puritan tradition and its church-state in Massachusetts. Mather hoped to use this ritual to reignite the fervor and devotion that had characterized the churches when they had first been gathered out of the world. Mather feared that this procedure might "meet with insuperable obstructions in some places," no doubt due to the perverse mistrust of some of the brethren. In order to achieve mass covenant renewal in all of the churches, Mather requested that the magistrates "recommend this matter to the Churches" without quite imposing it. Each congregation could focus on "the special evils prevailing" there and publicly acknowledge, bewail, and reform them.[44]

Perhaps the most striking feature of Mather's *Exhortation* was his call for deference. In stark contrast to Hubbard, Mather asked for deference toward the ministers rather than toward the magistrates. Nor was this call based on the ministers' "humane learning" or biblicist expertise. Mather predicated clerical authority on the clergy's prophetic abilities as "*Watchmen* and *Seers*" who served as conduits of the will of God. Consequently, it was their judgment that mattered in interpreting that will in such awful providences as the recent war. "Do not say that the Ministers of God cannot tell you why this Judgment is come," he informed his audience. If they lacked this power, he asked, "how then could they give you faithfull warning thereof long enough before it came?,"[45] obviously referring to his own warnings in *The Day of Trouble*. It was precisely such supernatural performances that Mather thought set the ministry apart from other learned professions and, of course, distinguished abilities within the clergy itself.

Mather's purported prescience in foreseeing King Philip's War seems to have heightened his prophetic powers. In 1676, during the war, he warned no fewer than three times that God would soon send "some mortal disease" to punish New England for "the murmurings of the people." Although "some were troubled" by this charismatic excess, the Lord nonetheless "confirmed the word spoken, by sending mortal feavors which were epidemical, and the small pox also whereby many dyed."[46] Equally uncanny was Mather's foreknowledge of a coming conflagration within Boston itself. So strongly was he "possessed with fears that Boston would be punished with that judgment of Fire" that he felt compelled to warn his congregation in a sermon delivered on November 19, 1676. Apparently this warning went unheeded, for the following Sunday he preached from Revelation 3:3, "Remember how you hast received and heard."[47] The very next day a fire consumed roughly seventy buildings, including the meetinghouse of the second church of Boston.[48] Although Mather's house was also destroyed, the Lord "remembered mercy in this judgment," for the minister was able to save over 1,000 books and most of his manuscripts from the blaze, "which mercy was so great, as that my other Losses seemed little."[49] Mather appeared strangely attuned to the course of coming events and was not shy in advertising his unique insight into the mind of God.

Given historical hindsight, Mather's uncanny abilities are not that difficult to explain. In some cases, Mather's actual predictions were far less specific than he would subsequently claim. His sermon allegedly warning of impending fire was based on Zephaniah 3:7, "*I sayd surely you will fear me; you will receive instruction,* (so their dwellings should not be cutt off,) *howsoever I punished them.*"[50] While this text does mention the danger of the destruction of "their dwellings," it does not specify fire as the means of this destruction. Mather's prediction of epidemic disease was similar. In his autobiography, Mather recalled that these sermons were based on 1 Corinthians 10:10. This scriptural passage was, in fact, the "text" of *An Earnest Exhortation*, no doubt the published version of these speeches of warning. Now it is true that he did warn of "another Storm hastening upon this Land," yet at no point in his text did he ever mention physical disease, epidemic or otherwise. Most dubious of all of his charismatic achievements was his claim in *A Brief History* that final victory in King Philip's War was assured by a day of humiliation his second church of Boston had held on June 21. Earlier in that month, he had requested that the magistrates order a general fast throughout the colony. Governor Leverett and the assistants, in consultation with Hubbard and several other clergymen, thought that a public thanksgiving might be more appropriate. Thus, eight days after Mather's second church of Boston held its solemn ritual of humiliation, the rest of the Bay churches celebrated a day of thanksgiving.[51] On what basis Mather claimed that it was his day of humiliation rather than this day of thanksgiving that signaled final victory is never explored in his account of the war. Much of Mather's peculiar insight into future events was a result of the "spin" he put on them afterward.

Whatever its explanation, Mather's prophetic success impressed his contemporaries. When Mather had requested the court to order a general fast in June, he was supported by several clergymen, including James Allen and the aged John Eliot. An outbreak of epidemic disease in Roxbury in late November evoked a response from John Eliot that was strictly in accord with the "Mather line." "God also drew forth another rod upon our backs in epidemical sicknesse," Eliot wrote in his church records, "yet for all this it is the frequent complaint of many wise & godly that little reformation is to be seene of our chiefe wrath provoking sins." The sins were the same ones Mather had cataloged: worldliness, drunkenness, factionalism, "neglecte of gospelizing our youth," and, of course, the toleration of peaceable Quakers.[52] The most powerful evidence of Mather's growing prestige, however, was his selection by the deputies to give the next election sermon.

Delivered on May 23, 1677, *A Discourse Concerning the Danger of Apostacy* was the most important public address of Increase Mather's career. Mather diagnosed the spiritual crisis that he believed the orthodox regime faced, assessed blame for it, and offered a program of reform that would animate him until the loss of the charter in the following decade. His oration had a profound effect on the regime, for within two years the General Court would agree to his controversial proposition that Massachusetts was in "danger of apostacy" and convene a reforming synod to avert that disaster. Moreover, the cumulative effect of Mather's politics of blame and program of reformation would subtly yet profoundly transform the orthodox regime in its final days.

Mather's claim that New England was in danger of "being cast off forever" by the Lord was hardly new.[53] He had been bewailing the prevalence of "Oppression, Sensuality, Sabbath-breaking," and "sinful Toleration" since 1674.[54] What was different about *The Danger of Apostacy* was the vehemence and specificity with which he cast blame for this obvious declension. Indeed, in this regard, his election sermon was every bit as incendiary as Davenport's had been in 1669. Mather exonerated the brethren and their deputed representatives of any wrongdoing and instead pointed to the magistrates and ministers of the inner party as solely responsible for jeopardizing the foundation work of the first generation.

The assistants, Massachusetts's Nehemiahs, were charged with defending the regime from sin and protecting the interests of God and his churches. Clearly, they had failed. Pride abounded, the schools of godly learning were in desperate need of encouragement, and frontier towns were settled without a pious and orthodox ministry. "Alas," Mather lamented, "our *Nehemiahs* are gone."[55] He singled out for special criticism "the sin of Solomon," namely, the toleration of false doctrine and worship. Just as Solomon's toleration of idolatrous cults "was the reason why the Lord stirred up Adversaries against him," so the toleration exercised by the magistrates served as a provocation of divine wrath against his new Zion in the wilderness. Equally dangerous was the threat from those dissidents themselves, for although "they may plead for Toleration, and Cry up Liberty of Conscience &c. yet if once they should become numerous and get power into their hands, none would persecute more than they."[56] Given such licentious toleration, it was hardly surprising that the godly community had become increasingly worldly. "If your blessed Fathers and Predecessors were alive and in place it would not be so," Mather lamented. "[I]f *Winthrop, Dudley, and Endicot* were upon the Bench such profaness as this would soon be suppressed." Ominously, he warned the assistants that if they should "become cold and indifferent in things of God" they could expect that "God will *change* either *you* or your government *ere long*."[57] Not even Davenport had offered such a withering critique of the magisterial intelligentsia.

Mather's criticism of the clergy was no less damning. Their sacred calling conferred a duty upon them to serve as "Porters that have the Charge of his House." It was thus their task to keep out of the church sensuality and a deadness of spirit, a task they had obviously failed to perform. Particularly troubling was their pollution of the Lord's sanctuary by admitting persons to the Lord's table who were unfit. Ever since Cotton first instituted the charismatic test of saving grace, the teaching of the Fathers had been clear: "[T]here ought to be an Holding forth Faith and Repentance before Admission to the Lords Table." Though he wished it were otherwise, Mather knew there were "Teachers found in our Israel, that have espoused loose, Large Principles here, Designing to bring all Person to the Lords Supper, who have an historical Faith, and are not Scandalous in Life, altho' they never had an experience of Regeneration on their souls." Mather could not help but remark that such laxness would "corrupt Churches and ruin all in a little time."[58]

These were serious accusations against the inner-party elite, and although there was some truth to them, they were hardly as straightforward as Mather suggested. It was true, for example, that small gatherings of baptists and Quakers had been meeting in private houses in Boston since 1674.[59] The magistrates actually practiced connivance rather than toleration, however. That is to say, these conventicles were officially proscribed, but the authorities looked the other way as long as they were private, peaceable, and quiet.[60] As the religious historian George L. Smith has shown in his study of New Netherland, such connivance was the necessary price for any port of call in the world of Atlantic commerce.[61]

More important, why Mather should blame the magistrates for such connivance is not altogether clear. As the episode with the Particular Baptists in the late 1660s had demonstrated, the brethren and their representatives were none too eager to deny such "left-wing" Puritans their precious soul liberties. Mather had no reason to assume that the laity were any more likely to convict otherwise peaceable and godly dissidents than they had been a decade before. Indeed, their next choice of election speaker, James Allen, struck a decidedly tolerant tone. Himself a refugee from Restoration England, Allen urged the magistrates to "[l]et Gods out-casts dwell with you." As long as such persons "carry it without just offense," there was no reason to withhold "your Countenance and Favour."[62] In the face of such sentiment, the magistrates had little choice but to leave well enough alone.

The culpability of the clergy was equally questionable. Certainly there were ministers like John Higginson of Salem and Solomon Stoddard of Northampton who granted full church membership to those who were culturally virtuous and behaved in a godly fashion. This was no innovation, however, for the very first churches in New England had done the same. Even after Cotton's initiation of his test of saving grace in the mid-1630s, many churches and clergymen stuck with the earlier "original" requirements. Hooker had led a migration to Connecticut to do just that, and Shepard had mitigated the dangers of this charismatic excess by means of preparationist theology. Moreover, both Newbury and Hingham had been organized on a purely parishional basis from the outset. If such "liberality" in admissions to the communion table were truly as corrupting as Mather maintained, the New England Way would have dissolved long before. The clergy had been guilty not so much of innovation or apostasy as of disagreeing with Mather and his charismatic proclivities, just as their predecessors had with John Cotton.

However unjust, Mather's accusations against the inner-party elite sorely undermined its cultural authority and prestige. Particularly hard hit were the magistrates. Mather had questioned not only their judgment but their commitment to orthodoxy as well. Indeed, in his address to the brethren he encouraged them to withhold their deference for the high cultural expertise of the magisterial intelligentsia and elect men "that will be zealous for the interest of Reformation." Such men would "improve their power to suppress Transgression of the first as well as the *2nd*. Table." Should the brethren persist in choosing officers "under whose shaddow Thorns and Briars shall thrive, and those Weeds of *Pride, Contention, Heresie* shall receive Nourishment, and Encouragement," he warned them, "God will ere long deprive you of your *Liberties* until such time as you know better how to improve them."[63]

Habits of deference die hard, but tremors of change could be felt as early as 1681. In that year Reverend Simon Bradstreet, Jr., complained to Mather that he had heard the troubling rumor that his father, the current governor, "is to be layd by this election, as too great a friend to Caesar, not caring for or regarding the concerns of our R[e]publ[i]c." Even more disturbing was the selection of Peter Tilton "with others of the same complexions" as assistants in the Massachusetts General Court. Such simple farmers "have skill to guide a plow-tail" and might even be "the fittest men to stear a C[ommon] Wealth," but they sorely lacked the high cultural training and biblicist expertise necessary to serve as cultural authorities in the orthodox one-party state. "It is plain wee need no enemyes to conspire our ruine," Bradstreet pointedly informed Mather. "Our sins & follies will do it too fast."[64] Although Mather was not solely responsible for undermining the cultural domination of the magistrates—the actions of the imperial authorities played a significant role in that development, as we shall see—his criticisms had put them on the defensive and left them vulnerable to further attacks.

Mather's program of ecclesiastic reform was even more puzzling than his politics of blame. On the one hand, he seemed to embrace the agenda the clerical majority had been pursuing since the Cambridge Platform of broadening church membership and centralizing church power. His advocacy of mass covenant renewal, as well as the half-way covenant, was clearly intended to be inclusive, inviting as many people as possible to pledge fealty to the churches and the Puritan tradition they embodied. His proposal to the clergy that "our occasional meetings might be improved" was based on the rather "presbyterial" presumption that "the Care of all the Churches ought to be upon us."[65] He even urged the assistants to find "some Expedient" to limit the power of the brethren to select their own clerical officers. "That every Plantation in the Countrey should have Allowance to choose whom they please to labour in the publick Dispensation of the Word," he warned, "may be in time a great Inlet to ignorance, error & profanes."[66] On the other hand, he insisted on the extremely exclusive requirement of a profession of gracious experience, despite the opposition of many of his colleagues. Moreover, he resisted the logical implication of the clerical program of inclusion, namely, the establishment of the Bay churches on a comprehensive basis. As for his proposed centralization of ecclesiastic power, when the Reforming Synod of 1679 convened, Mather would halt its formal proceedings for a full week while lay representatives were sent for.[67] Mather's plan of reform seemed to run at cross-purposes.

The key to Mather's ecclesiastic program was not his purported goals, however contradictory they may have seemed. Rather, it was the process of reformation itself that Mather sought. He craved the excitement and tumult of mass purposeful action on behalf of some holy crusade. He also understood that such public enthusiasm could not merely be wished into existence but had to be fomented, cultivated, and nurtured. That is precisely what he had been doing ever since his first prophecies of imminent destruction in 1674. Each round of subsequent reformation only served to whet his appetite, evoking more dramatic predictions of disaster and increasingly strident calls for action. By 1677, he was preaching that "another Storm of wrath, seven times greater than the last," would shortly ravage the land unless the churches immediately performed his prescribed penance of mass covenant renewal.[68] Indeed, covenant renewal perfectly exemplified Mather's program. In addition to its obviously inclusive thrust—Mather held that half as well as full members "ought with their own mouths to ingage subjection to the Lord"—this public ritual was nothing if not enthusiastic, accompanied as it was by the public bewailing of sins and solemn promising of allegiance to the New England Way.[69] Mather sought the excitement of a public in crisis, and he was not to be disappointed. Mather got his enthusiastic thrill and in the process succeeded in enacting most of his program. The results, however, were hardly what he had anticipated.

The most daunting obstacle Mather faced, particularly in regard to his panacea of covenant renewal, was the well-earned enmity of the assistants. As early as 1676, when he first called for covenant renewal, Mather had expressed the fear that without the firm support of the General Court the ritual "will meet with insuperable obstructions in some places."[70] Mather's fears were not misplaced, for in 1678 Thomas Cobbet complained to him that "the body of our church would faine have had it [covenant renewal] put here into practise, but two leading persons in our church, startled at it, & so it sticks at present."[71] Yet as long as Mather's implacable foe, John Leverett, remained governor of the colony, the minister could expect little in the way of cooperation from the magistrates. It was only with Leverett's death in the spring of 1679 and his replacement by the far more sympathetic and pliable Simon Bradstreet that Mather was finally able to enact his program of reform.[72]

On May 28, 1679, the very day Bradstreet was elected chief executive, Mather submitted a petition signed by eighteen ministers to the General Court. The petitioners stated that despite the previous actions of the court, New England's "provoking Evils" were still "as general, as powerfull, as Incorrigible & Incurable, &, wee fear, more Judicial then they were before." In order to avert the wrath of God and arrest the apostasy of his Israel, they proposed a synod be convened to inquire "into the Causes & State of God's controversy with us."[73] The court promptly granted their request, ordering that the churches send "elder & messengers" to Boston on September 10 to enact whatever "may appeare necessary for the preventing schismes, haeresies, prophaness, & the establishment of the churches in one faith & order of the gospell."[74] The proposed questions for the synod were the very ones Mather had been addressing over the last five years:

> Question 1. What are the evills that have provoked the Lord to bring his judgments on New England?
> Question 2. What is to be donn that so those evills may be reformed?[75]

The General Court had finally acknowledged that Massachusetts was in the throes of a spiritual crisis.[76] At long last, the regime was united behind Mather and his program.

The Reforming Synod of 1679 represented the apex of Mather's clerical leadership. Its unanimous report, titled *Necessity of Reformation* and approved by the General Court on October 15, vindicated Mather's diagnosis of the Bay's spiritual malaise as well as his prescribed remedy.[77] Mather acknowledged as much in his preface to the report. "The things here insisted on," he noted, "have (at least many of them) been oftentimes mentioned and inculcated by those whom the Lord hath set as Watchmen to the house of Israel."[78] Massachusetts's provoking evils were familiar by now: pride, sumptuary excess, toleration, drunkenness, worldliness, and oppression. Notably, Mather mentioned a new sin, "opposition unto the work of reformation." Presumably referring to himself, he complained that "they that have been zealous in bearing witness against the sins of the Times, have been reproached, and other wayes discouraged." There could be no question that such intransigence "argueth an heart unwilling to Reform." The time for such obstruction had passed, however, for Massachusetts had reached a critical crossroad. "We are a perishing People," he warned, "if now we *Reform* not."[79]

The synod's proposed remedies were also thoroughly Matherian. The magistrates were urged to see to the settlement and maintenance of a pious clergy, to support "Schools of Learning," and to vigorously enforce "wholsome Laws" based on the word of God.[80] The churches must practice greater discipline, especially with respect to the rising generation, families ought to practice more devotion and prayer, and the magistrates must refrain from tolerating baptist and Quaker idolaters. Most important of all, however, was that great "scripture Expedient for Reformation," namely, the "solemn and explicit Renewal of Covenant." "We seldome read of any solemn Reformation," the report observed, "but it was accomplished in this way."[81]

Mather did face one setback, however, on the final day of the synod. In accord with his election sermon of 1677, Mather insisted that participation in the Lord's Supper and, by implication, full church membership be restricted to those who could give public testimony about their experience of saving grace. Solomon Stoddard objected and proposed instead an equivocally worded proviso demanding a profession of faith and repentance. After a brief debate between Stoddard and Mather, the assembly overwhelmingly endorsed Stoddard's wording, and the final report required "a personal and publick profession of their Faith and Repentance." Whether such faith referred to Cotton's charismatic experience of saving grace or merely the doctrinal understanding and assent known as "historical faith" was left to the discretion of each congregation. Such a profession need not be oral so long as it "shall be to the just satisfaction of the Church."[82] Like Stoddard, the bulk of the clergy recognized that the fruit of John Cotton's charismatic test had been the unchurching of the majority of Bay residents. The whole thrust of the clergy's program since the late 1640s had been to undo this damage and move the churches in a more inclusive direction. For his part, Mather had little choice but to bow to the will of his colleagues. One of the fundamental goals of the synod had been to avoid contention and controversy. In fact, in the confession of faith drafted for the second session of the synod, he specifically proscribed the airing of opinions that "either in their own nature, or in the manner of publishing or maintaining them, are destructive to the external peace and order which Christ hath established in the Church."[83] In the interests of such "external peace and order" among the clergy, Mather grudgingly granted this concession to Stoddard and his desires for comprehensive church membership.

Nonetheless, Increase Mather had good reason to be pleased with the results of his labors. His role as the leader of the Bay clergy had been acknowledged and affirmed. His view of the state of religion in Massachusetts had been officially endorsed. The General Court had even created a committee to examine whether the extant laws "were sufficiently warranted by the word of God."[84] Most important of all, his proposed program of covenant renewal had received the approbation of the synod and the court. On March 17, 1680, Mather's second church of Boston renewed its covenant.[85] In the next two years he witnessed a sharp increase in baptism and new membership.[86] Nor was this an isolated event, for in the years following the synod, many of the Bay churches renewed their covenants, igniting a spirit of evangelical outreach. Sins were acknowledged and bewailed, and fealty was pledged by an increasing percentage of the population to the cultural tradition of Puritanism as exemplified in the New England Way. Mather's program had reached fruition.

The results of Mather's program were far-reaching and complex. Covenant renewal not only drew more people into the churches but also invigorated those already under the church's discipline. It gave the orthodox community a renewed sense of collective purpose and action. This, combined with the synod's ban on controversy, promoted badly needed solidarity and unity in what had become a factionally divided one-party state. Ironically, however, the very success of Mather's program at drawing in and energizing more people in the churches tended to support Stoddardism. As churches swelled in numbers, lay participation and deliberation became increasingly devalued in the face of an ever-encroaching presbytery. Moreover, the ritual of covenant renewal itself served to undermine Cotton's charismatic test of saving grace. Mather's colleagues understood, even if he did not, that a profound and traumatic psychological rejection of the corrupt world was not to be expected from a generation that had been raised in a sober and orthodox Puritan one-party state. By giving this generation a means of registering their commitment to Puritan tradition, covenant renewal recognized that their own piety and zeal were both virtuous and sincere.[87] In one sense, this served the clergy well, for it ensured the loyalty of the bulk of the population to the Bay churches long after the charter was vacated. But Mather's public criticisms of the ministers, as well as the magistrates, had sorely undermined their cultural authority as the sole spokespersons for the orthodox state. The Bay churches would survive, but as purely religious institutions established on a largely parishional basis. They would no longer be the cells of a radical regime, and the ministers ceased to serve as the ideological leaders and political vanguard of Massachusetts.

There was one other result of Mather's program, far more local in extent but nonetheless palpable and profound. Mather had been fomenting a sense of crisis and a spirit of reformation for several years. No one had been more exposed to this spiritual whirlwind than his own congregation. Cajoled, threatened, exhorted, and pleaded with, they had been in perennial repentance and reformation. Yet Mather refused to relent. Eventually, his congregation became emotionally exhausted. When Mather continued to push and prod, this exhaustion became boredom. Thus, in 1682, Mather could not help noticing Satan's latest "Artifice which he useth, to deprive men of that good, which they might receive by hearing the Word." That artifice was both simple and increasingly obvious: "[H]e causeth them to sleep at Sermons."[88] Although most people considered such lapses from consciousness a mere "peccadillo," they were sorely mistaken, because "danger and death is in it."[89] Not only were they forgoing the means of conversion, but they were also guilty of slighting God's "ambassadors."[90] The ultimate offense was against the Lord himself, however, for those "that shew no more respect unto his Word, then to sleep at it, are guilty of despising his Name."[91] Mather reminded his auditors that during sermonic addresses "God himself is speaking to you, in the way of his Ordinance, though by mortal men like unto your selves."[92] Nonetheless, Mather could not help observing that "men are most sleepy at Sermon-time." Nor was this merely a general exhaustion, for "before the Sermon began, they were not drowsie, and after the sermon is ended, they are not so." There was no avoiding the conclusion that in Mather's church, "just at that season when they are called to attend unto the word of God, they are apt to drowse and sleep."[93] Ultimately, Increase Mather's program of exhortation and reformation proved soporific.

Increase Mather's influence was not restricted to ecclesiastic matters. Mather also played an important role in formulating Bay policy toward the imperial authorities. He had adopted a hard-line commonwealth posture on this issue in the 1660s, and he remained loyal to this position. Indeed, part of Mather's popularity among the laity may have been a result of his status as the foremost clerical hard-liner. Yet Mather's impact went far beyond merely advocating complete colonial autonomy. He politicized the dispute over this issue, just as he had the issues of ecclesiastic and spiritual reformation, inviting the brethren to withhold their deference toward those members of the inner party who favored conciliation. In so doing, he undermined what was left of the cultural domination of the magisterial intelligentsia. Mather's leadership and success often proved costly for his educated peers.

Mather was first consulted on imperial matters in the summer of 1676. Governor Leverett had received a letter from the king in June informing him of several outstanding complaints against the colony. Several London merchants had complained of the colony's complete disregard of the extant Navigation Acts. Robert Mason and Ferdinando Gorges had protested the illegal extension of Massachusetts's jurisdiction over the patents they held in Maine and New Hampshire. There were also the other unresolved and by now perennial issues: the orthodox regime's refusal to tolerate peaceable Protestants despite previous instructions from the king, the incompatibility of the Bay's scriptural laws with those of England, and the restriction of the franchise to members of the churches. This last issue proved the most troubling of all. The king would allow the Bay government its autonomy and charter privileges, but not as a Puritan one-party state. Graciously Charles II promised to withhold judgment until such time as the General Court could dispatch agents to represent its side of these disputes.[94]

Leverett summoned a special session of the General Court on August 9. The court decided to ask the advice of those elders in Boston at the time.[95] The perceived stakes were enormous. Samuel Nowell feared "a Generall Governour" would be imposed for all of New England.[96] With the notable exception of William Hubbard, the ministers prescribed a dilatory policy that the regime would follow for the next ten years.[97] The court should dispatch agents, but only after "they be with utmost care &

caution, qualified as to their instructions."[98] The two chosen representatives, William Stoughton and Peter Bulkeley, were ordered to deal exclusively with the claims of Mason and Gorges. "To all other clamours & accusations," the court declared, "yow shall answer, you have no order nor instruction."[99] Presumably, Stoughton and Bulkeley's embassy was to be as brief as possible.

Despite a stay of roughly two years in England, little came of Bulkeley and Stoughton's representation. Although they purchased Gorges's patent for £1,200, Massachusetts was nonetheless denied jurisdiction over Maine and New Hampshire. The Lords of Trade requested that the agents help revise the colony's code of laws, something their instructions strictly forbade. The only recourse left to the Bay delegation was to declare the good intentions of the General Court, attempt to mitigate the charges against them, and promise that the regime would amend their errors in the future.[100] Their task was made more difficult by the intransigence of the authorities in Boston. While the court did order all merchants to obey the Navigation Acts in the summer of 1677 and instituted an oath of loyalty to Charles II in October 1678, it refused to yield on any of the major issues.[101] Although it had acceded to the king's request regarding the Navigation Acts, it told the attorney general that "the lawes of England are bounded within the fower seas, and doe not reach America."[102] The court specifically informed its agents that since the charter was "our only security against the malice of our adversaries," Stoughton and Bulkeley should not grant any concessions regarding the laws and form of the Puritan regime.[103]

Stoughton and Bulkeley returned to Massachusetts in the winter of 1679–1680 with instructions from the royal authorities. The colonial government was requested to dispatch fully authorized agents within six months to answer the outstanding charges against the regime and negotiate an acceptable agreement. Complete toleration was to be exercised toward all peaceable Protestant dissenters.[104] The king also demanded that the government scrupulously obey the rules of its charter by increasing the number of assistants from ten to the prescribed number of eighteen.[105] The results could hardly have been what the imperial authorities desired since five of the newly elected assistants were staunch hard-liners. The call for toleration was, of course, officially out of the question. Increase Mather's program of reformation had made it an unbroachable subject.

For roughly one year, the Puritan Bay regime ignored the king's request until a second letter arrived warning that failure to promptly dispatch agents fully accredited to resolve all outstanding issues would result in legal proceedings against the colony's charter.[106] In consultation with the clergy, the court resolved on January 21, 1681, to send two agents to represent the interests of Massachusetts. The court wisely chose men who favored conciliation with the imperial authorities and could therefore expect a more sympathetic reception. Joseph Dudley, son of the late governor, was a graduate of Harvard and had served as an assistant in the General Court since 1676.[107] Captain John Richards, a prosperous merchant in Boston and a prominent member of Mather's second church of Boston, was chosen to replace William Stoughton, who refused to go on what he understandably thought was a fool's errand.[108]

Selected in March 1681, the agents did not actually depart for England until May 1682.[109] Their agency was extremely limited by their instructions. Like the previous embassy of Bulkeley and Stoughton, they were not to agree to any alteration of the form of the Puritan regime. They were to inform the imperial authorities that there was no discrimination against "such as are of the perswasion of the church of England" and deny that there was any persecution of baptists and Quakers.[110] Although it deceptively claimed that freemanship "hath not binn restrayned to Congregational men," the court insisted that it had the right according to the charter to confer freemanship upon whomever it should choose. The agents were further instructed to inform the king that legal appeals to his courts concerning Massachusetts's violations of the Navigation Acts "may proove extreamly burdensome, and, as it may be improoved, intollerable."[111] Most important of all, they must not "doe nor consent to any thing that may violate or infringe the liberties & privileges granted to us by his majesties royall charter, or the government established thereby." When asked about such issues, they were to stall for time by informing the authorities that "yow have received no instruction in that matter."[112]

When Dudley and Richards submitted the General Court's replies to the king's missives, they received a rather frosty reception. The attorney general insisted that the Bay government had done nothing to narrow the gulf between the laws of Massachusetts and England and had continued to allow violations of the Navigation Acts. On August 21, John Richards wrote to Increase Mather to inform him that the colony's affairs were "under great disadvantages." "What ever is objected or reported against us findes great creditt, & is difficultly taken off," Richards complained, and as such the Bay Puritans were considered "a people as need great regulations." Certainly the intransigence of the Bay regime had hardly helped the situation. Nor were the intolerance and scriptural laws demanded by Mather's program of reformation likely to win favor with the Committee for Plantation Affairs. Ominously, Richards warned that "I feare, if mercy prevent not, the dissolution of our Government is intended."[113]

In less than a month, Dudley and Richards were informed by the imperial authorities that, as their instructions revealed, they lacked sufficient authority to negotiate the necessary changes in Massachusetts's governance.[114] Richards reported to Mather that they were faced with an ultimatum "either to empower persons here fully instructed & commissionated, to accept of such Regulations of our Government as shall be propounded, &c., or else a Quo Warranto will within 4 moneths proceed against our Charter."[115] Still, the General Court remained unmoved. When January 1683 arrived and the four months had come to an end, the colony's agents had little choice but to offer their most profuse apologies and beg for more time. Finally, the receipt of a letter in January from the king informing them of his intention to proceed against the charter evoked a response. Bradstreet summoned a special session of the General Court in early February. On February 9, the court finally passed legislation to implement the various enforcement provisions of the Navigation Acts.[116] The deputies and magistrates called for a day of humiliation on February 13 and requested the consultation of the clergy in drafting a letter to the king and instructions to their agents.[117]

On March 30, the General Court issued its reply to the king and its instructions to its agents. The magistrates and deputies expressed their deepest affection and loyalty to their "most gracious & dread soveraigne." They were truly sorry about their past indiscretions and had rectified their errors with regard to the Navigation Acts, as they would in the future in similar cases. Nevertheless, they warily offered to accept only "such regulations as may more fully adapt the administrations of your majesties government here unto the rules of our charter."[118] This inflexible posture precluded the large-scale political reconstruction or "regulation" that the imperial authorities demanded. Indeed, in complying with the king's request for an additional empowerment of the colony's agents, the court specifically authorized them to act "on our behalfe for the regulation of anything wherein we have ignorantly or through mistake deviated from our charter" or "such proposalls & demands as may consist with the maine end of our predecessors in their removall hither."[119] The court explained to the agents that this "maine end" had been the ecclesiastic arrangements of the New England Way, "which yow are therefore in nowise to consent to any infringement of." If the matter of legal appeals to the king's courts should arise, they should "plead what ever may be argued from the patent to the contrary" and, in the event of failure, refuse to agree to anything until the General Court had been consulted. Most critical of all, however, was the form of the Puritan one-party state. "It being of the essentialls in our charter to use our owne liberty with respect to freemen," the court strictly forbade them from agreeing to "any alteration of the qualliffications that are required by law." The franchise must be open to all full members of the churches, and the General Court must be located in Boston and organized into its two chambers of assistants and deputies.[120] Like the previous embassy of Bulkeley and Stoughton, Dudley and Richards were to make excuses for the past and promises for the future. Above all, they should buy the regime as much time as possible without actually granting any significant concessions.

If the commonwealthmen among the regime thought this overture would mollify the Crown, they were sorely mistaken. As early as May 1683, Nathaniel Mather wrote to his brother in Boston to warn him that quo warranto proceedings were likely to begin soon.[121] The writ was issued in late June, and Edward Randolph arrived at the end of October with official notification of the suit and a message from the king.[122] The king demanded that the inhabitants of Massachusetts be informed that, notwithstanding the quo warranto proceedings, "the privat interests and properties of all persons within that our colony shall be continued and preserved to them, so that no man shall receive any prejudice in his ffreehold or estate." He also graciously offered to make minimal changes in the frame of the Bay government if they would not contest the suit and "make a full submission and entire resignation to our pleasure." If they should challenge the writ, however, they must then accept the consequences.[123] The question of imperial policy had reached a point of no return for the orthodox regime.

The assistants summoned a special session of the General Court in early November to formulate a response to the latest developments from England. The magistrates were deeply divided as to the most prudent course of action, and the debate raged for almost a month. It was at this juncture that Mather re-injected himself into the dispute. He had received several papers from his fellow hard-liners arguing against complying with the king's request. Mather compiled these arguments and added some of his own in a manuscript that he submitted to his fellow hard-liners among the assistants. With their approbation, copies were disseminated among the brethren, and, according to Mather, "were a meanes to keep the Countrey from complying" with the king's conditions. Mather had politicized the issues, reaching over the heads of the magistrates in the General Court and appealing directly to the judgment of the lay brethren of the outer party. Not surprisingly, those assistants who favored conciliation were "not a little displeased" at Mather for undermining their authority.[124] On December 5, the court appointed Robert Humphreys to represent them as their attorney in the quo warranto proceedings.[125]

Despite this decision, the regime remained deeply divided over the government's stance toward the imperial authorities. Many members of the inner-party elite, including Governor Bradstreet, were convinced that the time for resistance had come to an end. With the threat of the loss of the charter, they felt that the wisest course of action was to capitulate to the king's requests and make the best accommodation possible. On January 23, 1684, Boston held a town meeting to debate the issue. At the request of the town's deputies, Mather addressed the assembled freemen. He sternly told his auditors that "wee shall sin against God if wee vote" to comply with the demands of the Crown. "If wee make a full submission and entire Resignation to the pleasure, we fall into the hands of men immediately," he explained, "but if wee do it not, we keep ourselves still in the hands of God." The best policy was to put their trust in the providence of the Lord, for "who knoweth what God may do for us?" Sternly, Mather enjoined the brethren to fight for their liberties and the cause of God: "I hope there is not one Freeman in Boston that will dare to be guilty of so great a sin." Mather later reported that his speech brought tears to the eyes of the freemen, "and they said generally, we thank you Sir for this instruction and encouragement."[126] The brethren unanimously resolved to stand their ground against the encroachments of the Restoration monarchy. As news of this speech spread, other towns held meetings to register their support for the hard-line commonwealth position that Mather had championed.[127]

Mather had, of course, done more than merely advocate a policy of intransigent resistance. He had politicized the dispute, and he continued to do so right up to the Court of Elections that May. By accusing the opponents of his hard-line policy among the assistants of sin and betrayal of the brethren's political liberties, he had violated the most basic requirement of the whole system of cultural domination. Mather had done the unthinkable act of prompting the lay brethren of the outer party to withhold their deference from the magisterial intelligentsia and instead choose assistants who represented their views of the imperial situation. From the unthinkable came the unimaginable. On May 7, 1684, three so-called moderate assistants—Joseph Dudley, William Browne, and Bartholomew Gedney—failed to be reelected. With the sole exception of John Endecott's and the Antinomians' censures in the early 1630s, no assistants had ever been removed from office. Unlike the deputies, the assistants did not represent the interests and views of the lay brethren and therefore did not serve at their pleasure. Rather, their biblicist and high cultural expertise had previously been the source of a cultural authority such that their election authorized them to serve as the bearers of Puritan wisdom and culture. The laity might question their orthodoxy and rectitude but lacked the requisite training and education to legitimately question the magisterial intelligentsia's political judgment. Such magisterial cultural domination had been an essential aspect of the orthodox one-party regime, serving as a critical brake on the "democratic" impulses of the freemen.

Mather's divisive action, in conjunction with the growing crisis with the imperial authorities, had finally eroded this lay deference toward the assistants. The distinction between the inner and outer party within the General Court had broken down, and both assistants and deputies would henceforth represent the views and interests of the lay brethren. The system of cultural domination had at last been undermined from within, and what emerged was a Puritan lay republic. Two of the most prominent advocates of conciliation, William Stoughton and Peter Bulkeley, recognized the critical turn the orthodox Bay regime had taken and refused to accept their reelection to the Board of Assistants. Disgusted and angered, they simply seceded from the regime, along with Dudley, Gedney, and Browne. With others like Richard Wharton and the sons of John Winthrop, Jr., many of this disaffected rump of the magisterial "court" faction would serve in the regime of the royally appointed successor to the orthodox Puritan government.

Having been purged of its "accommodationist" elements, the General Court promptly resolved to continue its legal battle against the writ and urged its attorney to "use your endeavour to spinn out the case to the uttermost."[128] In June the English judiciary found in favor of the king, and the patent of the Massachusetts Bay Company was vacated on October 23, 1684.[129] The king had resolved to unite the New England provinces under the rule of Colonel Percy Kirke, a professional soldier with a reputation for ruthlessness. Yet the Puritan republic remained defiant and optimistic. Increase Mather continued to fight the good fight for the independence of the wilderness Zion. On February 6, 1685, he sought divine assistance through prayer, fasting, and meditation in his study. At long last he was "much moved and melted before the Lord, not being able to speake for some time." When his powers of speech returned, he could not help proclaiming, *"God will deliver New England! God will deliver New England! God will deliver New England!"* Sure enough, Mather's prayers were answered. That very day Charles II died, "by whose death Kirk's coming as Governor to New England was prevented, and New England was that day delivered."[130] Once again, Mather's supernatural powers had come to the rescue of the orthodox community.

Mather's victory was, of course, pyrrhic. James II proved no friendlier to the Puritan government of Massachusetts than his brother had been. The final meeting of the General Court was held on May 20, 1686, after it was informed that it was no longer a legal government and was to be replaced by an interim council headed by Joseph Dudley.[131] While Kirke never did rule New England, Edmund Andros did, and his tenure proved every bit as bellicose and high-handed as anything Kirke could have dished out. The court faction had ultimately been proven correct. Massachusetts would have been better off striking a bargain with the Restoration empire than undergoing the dictatorial Dominion of New England. Indeed, had the regime followed Norton's advice instead of Mather's and reached an accommodation in the early 1660s, it, like Rhode Island and Connecticut, might have had that government restored in the aftermath of the Glorious Revolution. It had not, however, and it ultimately was forced to accept a far less generous charter than its New England neighbors enjoyed. It was both ironic and poetically just that Increase Mather would negotiate this charter and would finally himself be charged with betraying the precious liberties of the colony and its culturally virtuous laymen. The calumnies heaped upon Mather perfectly symbolized the breakdown of cultural domination for which he had been largely responsible.

APPENDIX A

Key Terms

Power Social power is the ability of agents to affect their social or human environment. Political power, the primary focus of my analysis, is the ability to affect public policy or the institutions and practices of the state. One of the central themes of my narrative is the pursuit and acquisition of political power by the thinking class in Puritan Massachusetts. Much of the analysis embedded within this narrative is based on the following four assumptions about power.

1. Power is convertible. Power can be transferred or transformed from one form to another. One of the primary functions of the institutional structure of any society is to mediate such transformations and routinize the distribution of power among the various agents within that community. The thinking class of Massachusetts arranged the institutions of church and state to facilitate the transformation of their religious and intellectual prestige (i.e., high cultural power) into mass cultural and political power. The means for so doing was the construction of a Puritan one-party state.

2. Social power is a zero-sum game. Within a given institution or society, the growth of power of one party means the relative loss of power of another. The rise of the bourgeoisie entails the relative decline of the aristocracy, and similarly an increase of executive power within a government must result in a relative loss of power for the legislature or judiciary. The gain of power, as with all fixed mediums of exchange, thus follows the ancient dictum "nihil ex nihilo": nothing comes from nothing. The rise of the Massachusetts thinking class to political ascendancy resulted in a relative loss of power by the nascent bourgeoisie of the port towns.

3. Power requires legitimation. In order for power relations to become stable and enduring, they must acquire cultural sanction and justification. Such legitimation can take many forms, varying from loosely accepted folkways to fully articulated moral and ideological doctrines. The amount of physical coercion required to maintain any given distribution of power or power relations is inversely proportional to the extent to which the belief in the legitimacy or rectitude of such a distribution is shared by the various parties within a society. The fact that Puritan Massachusetts was not a police state and functioned with nothing more than a militia shows that in the eyes

of the vast bulk of the residents the Bay government was afforded a high degree of legitimacy.

Although power requires legitimation, this does not mean that such justification is ideological "window dressing," added as a callous afterthought. The legitimating principle of power within a society or institution has a profound effect on the way such power is actually used. In Puritan Massachusetts, the purpose for which such power was exercised was the salvation of souls and the currying of divine favor for the community as a whole. Such singularly imposing and sincerely felt purposes served to "raise the stakes" of power and led the Bay regime to be far more repressive than it might otherwise have been.

4. Power is an end in itself. The cause of the human pursuit of power is power itself. It is in the nature of humans, and all animals for that matter, to pursue power whenever possible and to acquire increasing amounts of it until checked by some obstacle. I do not conceive of the will to power as a conscious motive. Rather, I think it is operative at a more instinctual, possibly biological level. The desire of an agent to increase its effect on its environment is essential to its survival. At its most primitive level, this will to power is a will to life.

I do not wish to give the impression that I monomaniacally believe that all human interactions are merely moves in some grand power game. The pursuit of power is but one cause of human behavior, and it is rarely the dominant one in "consciousness." Rather, I would urge that it is an operable drive at the subconscious or organic level and thus often stands in sharp contradistinction to the avowed, and perhaps sincerely maintained, convictions of a particular agent. Power may tell us what caused (efficiently) a particular action but rarely informs us *why* or for what purpose (final cause) an agent acted the way he or she did.

Although I have focused primarily on political power, it is not necessarily the most important form of power in a given society. The ranking of powers within a community is the result of a particular configuration of institutions. In the case of Puritan Massachusetts, the institutions of church and state favored political and cultural power over wealth and birth. Nor need agents exclusively pursue one form of power. The Massachusetts thinking class may have been primarily interested in political and cultural power, but they also had a healthy regard for their social prestige and pecuniary compensation.

Class   The collective agencies of classes, like estates, castes, and strata, are all species of the genus interest. My most basic intuitions about classes stem from the ascription of rational self-interest to various agents on the basis of their position within the social division of labor and reward. The class analysis that I offer may seem unconventional in that there is a popular belief that classes, at least according to Marx, are defined by their relations to the means of production. Although Marx did characterize classes in such terms for advanced capitalist societies, he was certainly aware that such a characterization fell far short of definition. His discussion of the great "oriental despotisms" of India and China (the so-called Asiatic Mode of Production) revealed that those civilizations lacked proprietary classes characterized by multiple productive relations but nonetheless contained distinct social and political interests as well as pronounced disparities in income. This, I believe, is the reason Marx never actually defined "class" despite a lifetime of abortive efforts. On the issue of class, then, I adopt a more-Marxist-than-thou posture and insist that the term remain an undefined primitive that gestures at divergent interests arising from the social division of labor and reward.

There is, however, one regard in which I differ from Marx, though not from Weber. Marx conceived of social reward and class interest exclusively in terms of wealth or income (he was, to that extent at least, a "bourgeois thinker"!). Although such a view may go a long way toward revealing the relations of the bourgeoisie and proletariat in the modern West, it obscures the interests of other classes in the present epoch and even some ruling classes in earlier periods. Thus, with Weber, I conceive of wealth or control of the means of production as one particular form of the basic currency of social interaction and reward, namely, power.

Thinking class Let me offer a disclaimer at the very outset. I am aware that the phrase "thinking class" will jar on the ears of some readers, suggesting a snobbish or elitist tone. Although such a tone is the furthest thing from intention, I am convinced that the problem is unavoidable. The reason is that, as intellectuals, we imbue all of the terms used to describe our status or vocation with profoundly honorific connotations. Thus any term that I might substitute—"knowledge class," "educated class," and so forth—would render me guilty of using the same elitist tone. All I can do in my defense is state that I do not have such honorific connotations in mind when I use "thinking class" or any other term to describe the social group or any of its activities that I have studied. I am convinced that almost every member of our species thinks, and I do not mean to imply that those who belong to other classes are thoughtless any more than a labor historian would claim that investment bankers or lawyers don't work because they are not members of the working class.

Like "working class," "thinking class" is an attempt at colloquial characterization of an interest on the basis of its most intuitively salient social function. Just as one would define "working class" as the sum of several strata or classes (artisans, proletarians, reserve army of the unemployed, etc.), I define "thinking class" in terms of its two constituent strata, the intellectuals and the intelligentsia. I define "intellectuals" as those whose vocation requires the assimilation and production of high culture, *not* those who think deep and profound thoughts. The principal intellectuals of my study are the Puritan ministers, the university-educated soul doctors who had learned the mysteries of orthodox divinity as well as the ancient tongues and hermeneutical techniques essential to interpreting Scripture. I define "intelligentsia" as those whose vocation requires the assimilation and application of high culture. The significant intelligentsia for my study are the Bay magistrates, who were largely trained in the law and additionally might have some university training or a self-taught equivalent. By "high culture" I mean the relatively abstract (in terms of extension) and formal use of symbols within a given culture. The term is not meant in an honorific sense but is rather intended to be historicist and contextual in nature. Finally, by "symbols" I mean physical inscriptions and marks of various kinds, like characters on a page.

APPENDIX B

Toward a Postrevisionist Interpretation of Puritanism:
Religion, Society, and Politics

S tudents of Puritan New England may feel bemused by my interpretation of seventeenth-century Massachusetts. Certainly my Walzerian conception of Puritan divines as the ideological leaders of a radical movement is out of step with our present understanding of New England Puritanism. Whereas the current historiography has focused on a quest for doctrinal rectitude and consensus, I have found a struggle for political power and cultural authority. Since I have avoided historiographic disputation in the body of the text, readers may wonder how I square my analysis with the extant lines of interpretation. Is my argument meant to replace or supplement such views, and to what extent do I depend on and differ from that literature? In short, where does this book fit in the contemporary historiography of Puritan New England?

The answer to this question is rather complicated because my relation to the current literature is complex. In one sense, my work fills an obvious lacuna, one that David Hall first noted almost a decade ago. In the conclusion of an article chronicling the "coherence of American Puritan studies," Hall called on the next generation of historians to investigate the "politics of culture" and integrate this "struggle for power" in the reigning doctrinal "frame of reference."[1] In another sense, my book is not about Puritanism at all. Rather, it is an examination of a particular educated elite whose ideology happened to be "precise" Protestantism. Thus my analysis of Puritan cultural politics has taken doctrinal and pietistic concerns as given and has focused on the centrality of the "struggle for power." But while my work is not intended as a traditional Puritan doctrinal study, it has, I think, important implications for our understanding of early Massachusetts and its role in the larger trans-Atlantic Puritan movement. The purpose of this essay is to explore some of these implications. To that end, I will briefly sketch the outlines of the current doctrinal interpretation. Then I will discuss several problems that have emerged with that interpretation. Finally, I will offer some remarks on how we might reconfigure our understanding of the Puritan movement that settled the rocky shores of New England.

A ny discussion of modern American Puritan studies must begin with Perry Miller. It was Miller who first stressed the centrality of Calvinist theology in the structuring of Puritan experience in the New World. His insistence that such doctrinal considerations be taken seriously and at face value has become the reigning assumption behind almost every major subsequent study of New England Puritanism. Although Miller's interpretive strategy has held court, much of the substance of that interpretation has been dramatically revised, if not refuted.[2] Central to Miller's vision was the notion that the arbitrary nature of Calvinist predestinarian theology induced a profound sense of spiritual anxiety on the part of the purportedly godly, an anxiety that could only be sustained through a sort of existential heroism. The New England clergy tried to relieve this spiritual anxiety with a "federal" or covenant theology that mitigated the absolute decree of election with a conditional and contractual description of the divine promises of grace. Even this dilution of the spirit of Calvinist divinity could not be sustained beyond the first generation of settlement. The second and third generations lacked the existential toughness of their parents; unable to face the terrifying decrees of an inscrutable deity, the majority of them failed to join the churches and became increasingly "worldly." Symbolic of this spiritual declension was the half-way covenant, a shabby compromise with the Calvinist heritage that extended baptism and a mitigated membership in the community of the godly on a hereditary basis. Miller's story of New England Puritanism was thus a tragic narrative of a heroic but failed effort to sustain a purely Calvinist divinity that ultimately resulted in a largely parishional and pietistic religious establishment.

In his aforementioned essay, David Hall chronicled the revision and refutation of Miller's vision from the late 1960s to the mid-1980s.[3] Covenant theology did not compromise the predestinarian spirit of Calvinism; despite its ambiguous and "ambidextrous" language, it offered no real conditionality at all.[4] To the contrary, covenant theology was designed to protect the arbitrary nature of the divine decrees, not circumscribe them in a scheme of works righteousness.[5] E. Brooks Holifield has shown that the half-way covenant was not a rejection of orthodox Calvinism but rather a thoroughly reformed sacramental renaissance.[6] Ross Beals, Jr., and Robert Pope have questioned whether there really was any spiritual decline in the second generation to be symbolized in these half-way measures.[7] Finally, Charles Cohen has applied the coup de grâce by demonstrating that the spiritual anxiety of Puritan conversion was itself a means of inducing the desired state of divine agape.[8] Hall has aptly summarized this emergent revisionist consensus with the maxim, "[N]o shabby compromises, no repudiation of Calvinism."[9]

One of Miller's substantive claims, however, has survived this revisionist assault. Behind Miller's posit of a collective New England Mind lay an argument for a fundamental unity of clerical thought in the seventeenth-century American "zion." Despite a salutary awareness that this unity was far from monolithic, Puritan scholars continue to detect a broad and deep clerical consensus issuing from a religious tradition rooted in Calvinist doctrine, reformed practical divinity, nonseparating congregationalism, and a bibliocentric worldview.[10] This underlying consensus became a critical issue in the doctrinal understanding of Puritan New England as a result of Philip Gura's landmark study of radical Puritan thought. Gura asked why anyone,

given the rich variety of radical Puritan thought "and its spiritual and social libera-
tion," would willingly "accept the ideological limitation of New England congregationalism"?[11]

The most plausible answer to Gura's question has come from two scholars, Francis Bremer and Stephen Foster. Over the last decades, both Bremer and Foster have
stressed the necessity of analyzing New England Puritanism in a trans-Atlantic context, arguing that the roots of American Puritan development lay in the soil of English ecclesiastic and doctrinal history.[12] Thus the self-imposed "ideological limitations" of the New England Puritans can be seen as the result of their participation
and experience in the irenic Jacobean establishment that cherished doctrinal consensus and peace as a bulwark of order. By insisting on the uniquely profound rele-
vance of the English context, Foster and Bremer have not only broadened the framework of interpretation but also forced students to grapple with the vast and hoary
literature on English Puritanism and society.

Even the most cursory sketch of English doctrinal studies must begin with the
work of Patrick Collinson. More than any other author, Collinson has been responsible for revising our understanding of Puritanism as a movement and as a form of
religious life. In a series of magisterial books, he has promulgated the view that, despite a multiplicity of voices, from the Elizabethan settlement to the onset of Civil
War, Puritan divinity cohered around a shared evangelical Calvinist worldview and
a genuine horror of the excesses of popery on the one hand and separatism on the
other.[13] Collinson has shown that Elizabethan Puritan divines were "conscious of
their membership in a select brotherhood."[14] Nor was this a radical or proto-revolu-
tionary cabal but rather the moderate advance guard of the Reformation in England.
Even the renowned radicalism of the presbyterian movement of the 1580s is seen as
a reaction to Whitgiftian repression rather than the unfolding of some inherent tendency within the Puritan movement.[15] Indeed, Peter Lake has shown that John Whitgift's repressive tactics utterly failed to achieve their purported goal of detaching the
moderate, mainstream Puritanism of the universities from the radical presbyterian
"London underground."[16] If anything, "the conformist campaign against Puritanism"
drove moderate academics like William Whitaker "further into the puritan camp."[17]
Not only have English doctrinal scholars undermined the distinction between radicals and moderates, but they have also narrowed the gap between Puritans and their
more conformable clerical brethren. Collinson has argued that the ideological disagreements that did exist among the clergy were differences of degree, and he questions whether the terms "Anglican" and "Puritan" might not be anachronistic.[18]

What unified the clergy of the Church of England, particularly after the defeat of
the presbyterian movement made the abolition of episcopacy a dead issue, was a
broad and inclusive Calvinist consensus that "all but submerged the old differences
between conformity and non-conformity."[19] Nicholas Tyacke has found that this consensus centered "on a belief in divine predestination, both double and absolute."[20]
This Calvinist consensus has been traced from the outset of the Elizabethan settlement right up to the ascendancy of William Laud in the reign of Charles I.[21] Elizabeth's first episcopal bench, filled largely by Marian exiles, was thoroughly Calvinist, and her promotion of Edmund Grindal to the see of Canterbury placed a divine
of Puritan sympathies at the head of the church.[22] Even the repressive conformist

Archbishop Whitgift was a Calvinist, as evidenced by his promulgation of the thoroughly predestinarian Lambeth Articles in the 1590s.[23] James Stuart, Elizabeth's successor, was widely renowned for his orthodox Calvinism, as was the chief primate for the bulk of his reign, the moderate George Abbot.[24] This theological consensus found expression in the church's willing participation in the Calvinist crusade against Arminian heresy in the Synod of Dort.[25] It is the ubiquity and depth of this Calvinist consensus that underlies Collinson's conviction that Puritans were merely the "hotter" element in the English "religion of Protestants."

The Jacobean establishment was certainly the most important for American Puritans, for it was during James I's reign that they came of theological age. English doctrinal studies have characterized that establishment as fundamentally irenic and inclusive. Kenneth Fincham and Peter Lake have shown that James's basic strategy from the outset of his reign was to isolate the handful of presbyterian radicals—and Catholic recusants—from their moderate brethren, a policy that had largely succeeded by 1611.[26] Derek Hirst has argued that James's promotion of solid Calvinists to his episcopal bench "explains why puritanism in any ecclesiastical sense figures so small as a grievance in the Jacobean parliaments."[27] Despite a harsh, if brief, response to clerical petitions on behalf of nonconformity in 1604, the operation of the High Commission and episcopal courts through most of James's reign was remarkably lenient toward peaceable Puritans.[28] Moreover, Collinson has claimed that such Puritan institutions as combination lectures—whose roots lay in the prophesyings and clerical consociation of the Elizabethan classis movement—and gadding and conventicling were actually characteristic of the religious establishment of Jacobean England.[29] Indeed, it was in the aftermath of the presbyterian failure to achieve further reformation that the godly preachers turned "with vigour to the reformation of towns, parishes, families and individuals."[30] The resulting campaigns for Sabbatarian reform, reformation of manners, voluntary religion, and personal piety were part of a veritable flowering of Puritan practical divinity.[31] In many ways, the period between the failure of the presbyterian movement and the ascendancy of Laud was the cultural and evangelical high-water mark of English Puritanism.[32]

This doctrinal account of Elizabethan and early Stuart church history has fundamentally revised our understanding of the English Puritan movement. No longer is Puritanism seen as the religion of Christopher Hill's rising "industrious sort" or as the radical ideology of Walzerian alienated clerical intellectuals.[33] To the contrary, Collinson has insisted that the Puritan movement was neither radical nor oppositional and was fundamentally "consistent with an intensely conservative world view."[34] Indeed, both Collinson and Lake have argued that for most of the Elizabethan period and beyond, moderate Puritans constituted the normative mainstream of the Church of England, buttressing its Calvinist orthodoxy and supplying antipapal rhetoric whenever required.[35] Occasional nonconformity was met with the "connivance" of an indulgent Jacobean establishment that, through such lenient measures, succeeded in gradually bringing around the bulk of moderate Puritan clergymen.[36] Aside from issues of foreign policy, Puritanism was politically unengaged and conventional and ecclesiastically quiescent.[37] Margo Todd has shown that the purported goals of Puritan social theory—reformation of manners, godly civic magistracy, "rational" charity, and so forth—were, in fact, conventional desiderata of an

Erasmian Renaissance humanism that was ubiquitous among educated Englishmen.[38] Those few moments of genuine Puritan opposition, such as the Vestment controversy of the 1560s and the presbyterian movement of the 1580s, have been seen as reactive to prior drives for conformity rather than authentic radicalism.[39] In short, the early Stuart church, like the provincial society in which it was embedded, is now seen as fundamentally settled and stable.[40] Not surprisingly, many of the New England town studies have focused on the establishment of just such stable and harmonious socioreligious communities in the New World.[41]

This sense of the basic stability of early Stuart England has been greatly enhanced by a "revisionist" account of English politics and society. This revisionist literature has attacked the conventional view of the early seventeenth century as a time of rising opposition.[42] Conrad Russell has argued that Parliament hardly constituted an opposition to the Crown and was merely "one more among the manifold pressures the king reacted to when choosing his course of action."[43] Indeed, perhaps the greatest testimony to the stability of early Stuart political society was the fact that from the accession of James I to the onset of the personal rule of Charles I, Parliament only sat for slightly more than four years.[44] J. S. Morrill has shown that the political culture of the times was local and provincial in outlook and was predicated on consensus rather than conflict. As Derek Hirst has reminded us, those few occasions when the Commons successfully pursued an activist agenda, such as in 1624, were largely the result of Namierian manipulation by the lords and court (Buckingham and the prince in the case in question).[45] The result of this account has been a newfound appreciation of the contingency of the English Revolution.[46]

Although this doctrinal and sociopolitical revisionism has greatly broadened our understanding of early Stuart England, it has also generated its own anomalies. Most obviously, given all of this consensus and stability, how do we explain the ensuing "Puritan" revolution? What about the obvious religious and sociopolitical radicalism of the 1640s?[47] Similar questions emerge on the New England side as well. If English society was so stable and peaceful, why was there any Great Migration at all? Moreover, how do we account for the clear evidence of radical innovation in Massachusetts's political and religious institutions? As Karen Ordahl Kupperman has shown, the Puritan peers were acutely aware that the newly established Bay churchstate was dangerously theocratic and threatened to become a clerically dominated intolerant regime.[48] Finally, what are we to make of the emergence and subsequent careers of such indubitable New English radicals as Roger Williams, Anne Hutchinson, and Samuel Gorton?

Much to their credit, revisionist scholars have produced compelling answers to these questions. On the religious side, the critical figure has been Nicholas Tyacke. Tyacke has argued that it was the rise of Arminianism under the ecclesiastic leadership of William Laud that produced a potentially revolutionary situation.[49] Laud's innovations undermined the Calvinist consensus that had characterized the church in the previous reign.[50] This Arminian campaign, coming as it did on the heels of the Crown's failure to meaningfully support the protestant cause in the Thirty Years' War and the subsequent proposed Spanish Match, raised the paranoid fear of a popish plot in the minds of stolid English Calvinists.[51] Laud's repressive campaign against voluntary religion and moderate nonconformity created a radical Puritan opposition where none had previously existed.[52] On the political side, Conrad Russell has suggested that the eruption of the Civil War ought not to be seen through the lens of revolutionary politics but was rather the result of the inherent instability associated with a seventeenth-century "multiple monarchy."[53] Such instability was only enhanced by the Laudians' vocal support of the "arbitrary" and absolutist features of Charles's personal rule.[54] The result has been an almost complete reversal of the traditional interpretation. Now Laud and his Arminian allies are seen as the true revolutionaries and his Puritan opponents as conservatives attempting to preserve the remnants of the Calvinist Jacobean establishment.[55]

The implications for New England are obvious. The seemingly radical features of the initial establishment of the New England Way were simply a reaction to the Laudian/Arminian repression of the 1620s and 1630s. Stephen Foster has shown that the later immigrants arrived in the 1630s, the more likely they were to be radical.[56] It was only the eruption of radical lay dissent in the figures of Anne Hutchinson and Samuel Gorton that convinced the clergy of the dangers of "enthusiasm" and initiated a return to moderation and order.[57] The social peace and cohesion that Stephen Foster has chronicled were simply the reenactment of the normative pattern of Jacobean local society.[58] In short, after a radical start, New England quickly returned to its stable early Stuart roots.

Despite its virtues, this doctrinal and revisionist interpretation of Puritanism and early Stuart England has come under fire in recent years. Scholars have not only noted evidentiary problems with the revisionist case but also called into question some of the interpretive strategies and assumptions that underlay the entire doctrinal view. By examining both the weaknesses and strengths of the revisionist account, we can begin to draw the outlines of what a postrevisionist picture of Puritanism, one with the politics and society put back in, might look like.

The most apparent problem with the doctrinal account has been its handling of Arminianism and its purported role in destroying the church's Calvinist consensus. Recent work by Julian Davies and Peter White on the Caroline church has disputed some of Tyacke's most crucial claims.[59] Davies has questioned just how repressive the Laudian regime really was, given that the roughly twenty clerical deprivations between 1625 and 1640 pale in comparison to the purge of nonconformists at the beginning of James's reign.[60] Susan Holland has noted that the thoroughly Calvinist Archbishop Abbott had little patience for factious "separatists" like William Ames and suspended and deprived nonconformists far more often than did Laud.[61] Moreover, Laud and his allies in the push for conformity in the 1630s were only enforcing the canons of the church, some of which had never been vigorously enforced before.[62] Davies has also insisted that Arminianism was not the sum and substance of the Laudian program and that Laud's vision was not identical to his monarch's. Neither Calvinist nor Arminian, Charles's prohibition of predestinarian preaching reflected "his lack of interest in academic theology."[63] Carolinism was essentially antidoctrinal and focused on a ceremonial conception of the church that was meant to buttress hierarchy and obedience.[64] Laudianism, on the other hand, was a patristic renaissance whereby ceremonies were seen as a means of grace and the church was seen as both sacerdotal and inclusive.[65] Furthermore, Sheila Lambert has raised questions about how draconian the Arminian operation of press censorship really was in the 1630s, as well as just how pro-Calvinist censorship had been in the previous decade.[66] "While some Arminian doctrine spread during the 1630s," Julian Davies has acknowledged, "the Arminianization of the decade is a myth."[67] Finally, several scholars have claimed that the views of Laud and Neile were really not that innovative after all and that their roots can be found in the thought of Whitgift, Barro, Hooker, Bancroft, and others.[68]

If these scholars have doubted the extent of the Arminian onslaught on the Calvinist consensus of the church in the 1630s, that is because many of them doubt whether such a consensus ever existed. Peter White has insisted that there had always been a spectrum of views concerning predestination since the Elizabethan era, and even Tyacke has acknowledged that "the Elizabethan Prayer Book needed careful exposition in order not to contradict predestinarian theology."[69] While much has been made of Whitgift's promulgation of the Lambeth Articles and the hierarchy's participation in the Calvinist campaign at the Synod of Dort, it is significant that neither result achieved confessional status in the Church of England.[70] Certainly not all of the monarchs were part of a Calvinist consensus; neither Charles nor Elizabeth was attracted to the predestinarian position, and even the avowedly Calvinist James seems to have endorsed Richard Montague's Arminian views by the end of his reign.[71] In fact, all of Charles's Arminian bishops were first appointed by his father and fared better under his rule than his successor's.[72] Peter White has even challenged the hyper-Calvinism of the Lambeth Articles, arguing that Whitgift's goal was simply to silence a university debate between infralapsarian and supralapsarian interpretations of predestination.[73] Most important, Peter Lake distinguishes between experimental Calvinists, like Perkins and Preston, who defined the godly community as those who internalize and act on the doctrine of predestination, and credal Calvinists, like Whitgift and Abbott, who neither preached the doctrine nor derived their sense of the Christian community from it. This distinction raises questions about just how significant a merely doctrinal assent to Calvinist teachings really was.[74] Finally, it is worth recalling that any Calvinist consensus in the Church of England must exclude the bottom half of the social order, whose Protestantism was tenuous at best.[75]

Another criticism of the revisionists has been their tendency to draw a sharp line between religion and politics.[76] Certainly James I did not draw this distinction, as evidenced by the famous dictum, "no bishop, no king," attributed to him at the Hampton Court conference. What James and his fellow monarchs recognized, as Christopher Hill has reminded us over the decades, was that the legitimating principle of the ecclesiastic polity was identical to that of the state/society in a nation with an established church.[77] Thus a presbyterian "parity" in the church would support political rule by the gentry and middling sort, since in both cases governance would be in the hands of the "natural rulers."[78] Nor was it a coincidence, as Tyacke has claimed, that the same Arminian churchmen who asserted *juro divino* episcopacy were also the principal spokesmen and champions of *juro divino* monarchy. Surely it is revealing of the sociopolitical implications of early Stuart religion that these high-flying Arminians were among the first Englishmen in the seventeenth century to reject the Renaissance humanist social/civic ideal in favor of the scholastic doctrine of the great chain of being.[79] If anything, the Reformation in England collapsed the religious and political into each other; by eliminating iconic and ritual modes of communication and instruction, it greatly enhanced the political importance of preaching.[80] Finally, of course, the confessional wars of the seventeenth century furthered the interpenetration of the political and religious spheres, as evidenced by the saliency of antipopery as a political issue during the Thirty Years' War and the Spanish Match.[81]

Problems have also emerged in the revisionist treatment of early Stuart politics. Several scholars have insisted that Parliament, and the Commons in particular, was far more politically important than Russell has allowed and that its operation was far more ideological than Namierian.[82] As David Underdown has noted, the Parliaments of the 1620s "articulated the grievances of a wide spectrum of 'Country' opinion."[83] Derek Hirst has shown that the early seventeenth century was an era when the electorate was expanding and contested elections were on the rise.[84] Richard Cust and Christopher Hill have noted the increasing publicity of parliamentary politics and the growing tendency of the Commons to publish its opinions and thus appeal to popular opinion (a tactic that Charles was ultimately forced to engage in).[85] The early seventeenth century was thus a time of profound politicization, when middling-sort voters were not only politically active but also highly attuned to political developments at the "center" or national level.[86] In fact, on closer examination the "country ideology" appears more of an anticourt rhetoric, replete with popish conspiracies and titanic struggles between power and liberty as well as corruption and virtue, rather than the sort of localism described by Morrill.[87] Derek Hirst has concluded that "for all their exaggerations, older accounts of the crown and Commons as adversaries were thus not *wholly* wide of the mark."[88]

Doctrinal scholars have also failed to incorporate the findings of researches on the social basis of Puritanism. J. T. Cliffe has shown that godly gentry patrons sought and received from their clerical clients a healthy dose of preaching on behalf of due order, the reformation of manners, and other Weberian themes.[89] Two studies of Puritan Essex County suggest that the Puritan campaign for godly reformation and the suppression of sin represented a "culture of discipline" imposed by middling-sort parish elites on the growing and menacing tribe of propertyless and masterless men.[90] Both Christopher Hill and Lawrence Stone have long held that Puritanism had a marginal appeal for the peerage, whose aristocratic ethos was antithetical to the self-discipline of the Protestant worldview.[91] As David Zaret has noted, Puritanism appealed to people whose social position required economic autonomy and rewarded a heightened market rationality, and that was why, in his view at least, the contractual idiom loomed so large in "federal" theology.[92] In a study of the regional basis (or ecology) of partisan loyalties in several counties during the English Civil War, David Underdown has found that the bastion of Parliament and Puritanism was in the thinly settled, relatively industrial, and demographically mobile woodland/pasture regions where middling-sort parish elites rallied around the Puritan culture of discipline in their struggle against the older, traditional culture of revelry and ritual.[93] As Kevin Sharpe has noted, the godly "clearly divided the parishes, and nowhere was the division more visible than their trek to hear a sermon while others played on the village green."[94] Part of what distinguished this region from the nucleated arable "corn" country was its heightened orientation to commerce and the market, which seems to be the common thread in all of these accounts.[95]

Taken together, these problems suggest that the significance of doctrine has been overblown. Undoubtedly, theological convictions were a primary concern of godly persons, particularly churchmen. Nonetheless, Peter Lake's aforementioned distinction between experimental and credal Calvinists demonstrates that mere doctrinal assent is not all that critical in differentiating Protestants. Thus he has proposed a more fruitful polarity based on whether one perceived popery or separatism as the greatest threat to the church.[96] G. W. Bernard and Kevin Sharpe have reminded us that for most Englishmen, the religious life of their parish was likely to be largely ceremonial and liturgical, with an occasional evangelical sermon in the plain style—hardly the "word and doctrine" image conveyed by most doctrinal studies.[97] In fact, Puritan doctrinal complaints against the church were only expressed at the very end of James's and Charles' reigns. Most previous complaints had been about church discipline, where Presbyterianism was sought as a means to reforming the Christian community.[98] Moreover, we must assume that much doctrinal exposition was strained at best and disingenuous at worst, given the fact of an established church that practiced censorship and repression toward "stiff-necked" dissent.[99] After all, both monarchs and elite patrons sought preaching that would buttress order and obedience, and while doctrinal considerations may have been significant, they were by no means the only desiderata in the religious compromises that constituted the church establishment at any given time.[100]

The lesson to be drawn here is not that doctrinal concerns were unimportant but rather that they must be seen in the context of the social, political, and institutional structures of pre–Civil War England. These structures constituted the parameters or constraining forces within which clergy and laity alike had to operate in pursuit of their various projects and agendas, whether doctrinally motivated or otherwise. Any assessment of the overall impact of these projects must take into account this context of constraining forces. Only then can we begin to see the lineaments of a postrevisionist view of the trans-Atlantic Puritan movement and the peculiar significance of New England in that view.

Certainly the most obvious factor constraining any religious agenda was the monarchy itself. G. W. Bernard has warned against "any view of the Church of England that fails to give due weight to its 'monarchical' element."[101] He is also right to remind us that Henry's break with Rome was dictated by purely dynastic considerations. The central issue in the Henrician Reformation was the political supremacy of the monarchy within the English church—and therefore nation—vis-à-vis the pope.[102] A Renaissance prince with absolutist ambitions, Henry realized that the only way to defeat the pope was to mobilize the political nation and clergy and to empower the former in Parliament to authorize Henry's bid for ecclesiastic supremacy while directing the latter to preach obedience as well as the rectitude of his course. The central problem facing Henry (and all of his Tudor and Stuart successors) was how to demobilize the political nation and "reforming clergy" once they had served their purpose.[103] Had the monarchy defeated its ecclesiastic foe at the expense of its political supremacy? Was the Crown now constrained in its church policy by the very parliamentary power it had helped to create? Elizabeth shared her father's doctrinal conservatism and preferred both a celibate clergy and ceremonial trappings of a distinctly "Romish" character. Yet such was her need of the legitimating sanction of Parliament that she was forced to accept a far more Protestant settlement than she would otherwise have desired.[104] Nonetheless, it is important to recognize that for both her and her successors that settlement was final and would admit of no further reformation.[105] Like her successors, Elizabeth sought from the church doctrinal peace, ceremonial conformity, and an acknowledgment of her supremacy.[106] Above all, the monarchs did not want the church to be a source of controversy that might hinder their quest for centralized absolute power.

For the monarchy, the danger of Puritanism lay in its potential "popularity"—that is, its ability to galvanize the political nation, particularly on issues of foreign policy, on behalf of the cause of true religion.[107] This fear of Puritanism as a threat to the Crown's political prerogatives, a fear shared by all monarchs, underlay the drift toward an Arminian church policy that began at the end of James's reign and was confirmed and expanded by his son. Convinced of a Puritan plot against him "orchestrated by elements within the Commons, judiciary, and the populace at large," Charles not only repressed nonconformist dissent but also mobilized the least Protestant elements of the nation, the peerage and "bottom half," against their middling-sort Puritan/parliamentary opponents.[108] What the court masque did for the aristocracy, Sunday sports and ceremonial religion did for the lower classes, appealing to their basic cultural assumptions and desires.[109] As Christopher Hill has insisted, the central issue in the rise of Arminianism was the politics of absolutism, for Laud's regime represented "the culmination of long-standing government policies aimed at reducing the hard won authority of the new ruling elites."[110]

The social context of Puritanism can be uncovered by deepening Collinson's conception of Puritanism as a movement. If Puritanism was a cultural movement, then it was supported by a coalition of members from distinct social groups. The nature of that movement at any given time depended, in part at least, on the configuration of elements and power within that coalition. Puritanism was not merely a theological creed that bound discrete individuals; its practical tactics and reforms expressed a carefully negotiated, if ever-shifting, balance of interests.

The most important element in the Puritan coalition was undoubtedly the clergy itself. In addition to a pure and reformed doctrine, "painful" preachers sought an increased social prestige and public authority for their increasingly professional calling, and their attempts to gain this status depended on the movement for further reformation.[111] Within that movement, godly learning and biblicist expertise gave precise clergymen tremendous power as the political spokesmen for the will of God as revealed in his word.[112] As William Hunt has noted, the Puritan biblicists' "exaltation of preaching constituted an audacious bid for social prestige, and implicitly for power, by the preachers themselves."[113] John Morgan has shown that Puritan preaching both required and privileged higher education and that godly sermonizing was meant to command deference and respect from auditors of all classes.[114] And as Patrick Collinson has noted, the clergy did rise in prestige from the yeomanlike "Sir John" status of the pre-Reformation priesthood to the honorary gentry status they enjoyed in the early seventeenth century.[115] This boost in status was reflected, from the mid-Elizabethan period, in a rise in ministerial incomes and educational standards, as well as the prior status of clerical aspirants.[116]

Puritan gentry and peers also had extradoctrinal interests in the movement for further reformation. Any "prelatical" or "high church" policy might threaten their control of church lands and livings, a fear that "Charles I did nothing to allay."[117] More important, their political role and self-conception as "godly magistrates" were based on their function as public defenders of the campaign for further reformation.[118] Like any sensible elite, these precise aristocrats shared the king's fear of "popularity" and preferred to avoid further confrontation and mobilization whenever possible. Thus their invaluable services as patrons and protectors of painful preachers came at the price of muting the radical implications of Puritanism. "Although the clergy may have aimed to change the world," Derek Hirst has concluded, "their close involvement with the lay elite ensured that they directed themselves only towards the elimination of sin and the erection of a godly discipline."[119]

Middling-sort precisians—lesser gentry, professionals, merchants, yeomen, and substantial artisans—sought in Puritanism a culture of discipline and a legitimation of their market rationality and mores. Hill has claimed that "one element of the Puritan appeal" was "the view that a parochial discipline, supervised by lay elders and backed up by excommunication, would be effective in solving England's unemployment problem. It would provide relief for the impotent poor, work for the sturdy, and punishment for the idle."[120] They, too, had been mobilized by the politics of the Reformation. Unlike their elite brethren, however, middling-sort Puritans tended to push the clergy toward greater radicalism and nonconformity, through either the patronage of lectures or more direct measures like gadding and conventicling.[121] Indeed, as Patrick Collinson has shown, it was lay opposition to the "popish rag" that pushed many painful preachers to first oppose the hierarchy in the Vestment Controversy of the 1560s.[122]

One of the implications of this coalitional conception is that rather than a quiescent retreat from ecclesiastic opposition, the flowering of Puritan practical divinity may have been a far more radical religious strategy than the failed presbyterian program it replaced. Presbyterianism was a largely clerical initiative that sought to impose further reformation "from above" by seizing control of the ecclesiastic hierarchy. What followed the defeat of that movement was, as Christopher Hill has noted, "a broader, looser brand of Puritanism, which appealed to the laity no less than to the clergy."[123] By appealing to the middling sort to internalize the Puritan message on an individual and gathered basis, precise preachers sought to generate further reformation "from below."[124] Such common folk were thus mobilized in the Puritan crusade, and one result was a heightened accent on the shared middle-class experience of thinking-class and entrepreneurial Englishmen that underlay the "culture of discipline." The Puritan divines themselves occupied at best a quasimembership within the official church, scrupling to conform as little as possible or, in the case of borough and parish lecturers, hardly at all.[125]

The flowering of Puritan divinity was then, in part at least, the religious mobilization of the "popular" elements of the political nation by a semiunderground ministry.[126] The growth of sermon gadding, conventicling, congregational "gatherings" within parishes, and the other features of voluntary religion were thus all part of the mobilization and organization of local ideological groups or "party cells."[127] Like the congregations of Massachusetts, these cells gave power to the laity but restricted authority to the clergy.[128] Puritan antipapal sermons on behalf of the Protestant cause in the Thirty Years' War and against the Spanish Match and Arminian heresy were meant to mobilize what Peter Lake has called "the 'fused group' of the godly" to serve as the political vanguard "of the 'serial group' of the non-popish, whose unity derived only from a common opposition to popery."[129] While such middling-sort mobilization was undoubtedly facilitated by the fear that Laudianism represented a challenge to their newfound status as parish elites and their culture of discipline, its fundamental radicalism is nonetheless striking.

Even biblicism, for all its vaunted "primitivism," had decidedly radical implications.[130] Avihu Zakai has shown that the Puritan eschatological view of history was, in William Hunt's phrase, "a revolutionary creed" in that "it prophesied the most radical subversion of the established order of things."[131] Christopher Hill has recently shown that the Geneva Bible was rife with antimonarchical translations, commentaries, and marginalia.[132] What made Puritan bibliocentricity radical was that it sought solutions for sociopolitical problems from a high cultural tradition of textual analysis and casuistry, thus completely ignoring the traditional authorities associated with the great chain of being. The Bible, then, was the ultimate authority, binding discrete and autonomous individuals and households in a bond of loyalty and solidarity above and beyond king and country.[133] The fact that the sense of the Scriptures could often seem like putty in the precise preacher's hands can hardly have been reassuring for the Crown and its ecclesiastic hierarchy.[134]

Puritan biblicism also bore many of the marks of a modern ideology. In addition to creating a shared universe of discourse with social and political implications, biblicism's promotion of literacy and the relative rationality of textual exegesis and criticism, as well as the development of the "lay logic" of plain style sermonizing, all suggest that it participated in an early variant of the "culture of critical discourse" that the late Alvin Gouldner held was the sine qua non of modern ideological formations.[135] Here lay the key to Puritan iconoclasm. The vaguely related notions and worldviews transmitted by ritual and imagery were part of a distinctly pre-ideological mode of discourse that violated the culture of critical discourse by grounding their claims to rectitude on tradition and authority rather than the intersubjective rationality of scriptural criticism.[136] As Gouldner claimed, modern ideological thinking "premises the deritualization of public communication so characteristic of the Puritan revolution."[137] Puritanism was thus fighting for a new mode of thinking as well as a religious vision, and the mode was at least proto-ideological. Not surprisingly, this culture of critical discourse first arose in the guild halls of the high cultural initiates, universities like Oxford and Cambridge. The very existence of that mode of discourse outside of the schools, and particularly among godly "middling sorts," has profoundly radical, indeed revolutionary, implications.

Like all modern ideologies, Puritan biblicism reserved a peculiarly exalted role for the ideologue. Although the Bible was the source of relevant political and ecclesiastic knowledge, only those trained in the ancient tongues (Greek, Hebrew, and Aramaic) and the dominant biblical hermeneutic of the day (typology) could fathom its deepest meaning and import. While anyone could—and everyone should—read the Bible, actually "opening Scripture" or interpreting text required the high cultural expertise acquired at the universities. The importance placed on such expertise had profound implications for the structure of authority in church and state. Tracing those implications in the New England context has been the focus of this book and requires no further comment.

Such a postrevisionist view has profound ramifications for the significance of New England within the trans-Atlantic Puritan movement. If Puritanism was a coalition movement, organized around the clergy, whose radicalism was inhibited by a hostile environment, then New England should be the perfect laboratory for finding the inner dynamics of that coalitional movement. This is because New England lacked the three great hostile forces that inhibited Puritan aspirations on the other side of the Atlantic. The absence of any ecclesiastic hierarchy completely changed the context of action and opened unlimited vistas to the first founders. New England also lacked any significant number of propertyless and masterless men, the ungodly multitude whose taste for ritual, revelry, and ceremony offended godly sensibilities, for the Great Migration largely excluded the lowest strata of English society. The absence of the peerage, most of whom were anti-Puritan anyway, meant that New England, though hardly faithful to local English society, was a precise replica of the English society of the Puritan "middling sort."

The most profound political result of the truncation of the English social order was a dramatic increase in the power of the educated gentry, professionals, and clergy who crossed the Atlantic. The absence of the peerage made the Puritan divines and godly magistrates the upper class, and the system of cultural domination they imposed made them the ruling class. This novel form of cultural authority, predicated on Puritan biblicism, effectively unified the church and state in a polity structure.

The absence of any large number of anti-Puritan elements in New England allowed for the development of fault lines within the Puritan coalition of the middling sort. Within the thinking class there was a struggle, early and often, between the godly magisterial intelligentsia and clerical intellectuals over prerogatives and power, on issues as diverse as just wage/just price regulations, the propriety of a magisterial legislative veto, and the relation of taxation to representation. As Emery Battis has shown, the most market-oriented segment of the "urban bourgeoisie" valiantly struggled against the cultural domination of the clergy during the Antinomian controversy.[138] Humbler dissidents opted for the quietistic dissent of baptism, while the lowest strata of society expressed their heterodoxy in such radical sectarian movements as Gortonism and Quakerism.

New England is thus the key to unfolding the radical nature of Puritan dissent in Jacobean and Caroline England and understanding some of the inner dynamics of that movement. A postrevisionist interpretation puts New England back at the center of Miller's Calvinist internationale, with Hill's middling sort led by Walzer's clerical intellectuals. English Puritanism could never really flower because it rarely extended beyond the political nation. Its minority status within English society almost ensured the Protectorate's failure to produce "further reformation." The truly radical potentiality of Puritan governance can only be found in the American Zion. There we find every variety and every possible sociopolitical-ecclesiastic combination. At the one extreme of one-party fanaticism was New Haven, with the tolerant proto-republican society of Rhode Island at the other. Massachusetts was closer to New Haven in form than Rhode Island, and Connecticut and Plymouth were pretty much at the center. Each of these colonial societies was a variation on a theme that had been developing for generations. Inhibited in its fruition by a hostile English environment, New England would unleash the potentialities of Puritanism in, as Samuel Eliot Morison put it, "the 'free aire of a new world' liberating repressed desires and energies, rendering explicit in America what was implicit in England."[139]

NOTES

PROLOGUE

1. Samuel Eliot Morison, *Builders of the Bay Colony* (Boston, 1930; reprint, Boston, 1981), pp. 26–27. This claim has recently been supported in Anne Natalie Hansen, *The Dorchester Group: Puritanism and Revolution* (Columbus, Ohio, 1987), pp. 16–17.

2. Hansen, *Dorchester Group*, pp. 18–20.

3. On White's role in "radicalizing" Dorchester and its environs, see ibid., p. 5, and David Underdown, *Fire from Heaven: Life in an English Town in the Seventeenth Century* (London, 1993). For a discussion of White's role in promoting immigration to New England, see ibid., pp. 131–138.

4. For Humfrey's educational background, see Joseph G. Bartlett, "University Alumni Founders of New England," in *Publications of the Colonial Society of Massachusetts* (Boston, 1924) 25:16. On his relation to the earl of Lincoln, see Thomas Hutchinson, *The History of the Colony and Province of Massachusetts Bay,* ed. Lawrence Shaw Mayo (Cambridge, Mass., 1936; reprint, Millwood, N.Y., 1970), 1:15.

5. See Hansen, *Dorchester Group,* pp. 22–25.

6. "Their land patent not only cut the heart out of New England; it overlapped several grants by the Council of New England to Mason, Gorges, and others. Sir Ferdinando Gorges declared that the patent had been obtained surreptitiously from this Council during his absence in the war with France, through the influence of the Puritan Earl of Warwick; and he was probably right." Morison, *Builders,* p. 33.

7. "It was our indefatigable clerical promoter who 'managed a treaty' or in modern parlance, arranged a deal, with an important group of London merchants." Ibid.

8. Ibid., pp. 33–34.

9. Hansen, *Dorchester Group,* pp. 24–25. Morison ascribes responsibility for the procurement of the royal charter specifically to the London merchants. Morison, *Builders,* p. 34.

10. "It is probable that the charter of the Massachusetts Bay Company was procured under his advice; he may actually have drafted it." *The Winthrop Papers* (Boston, 1931), 2:82, n. 5. Hansen, however, noting the similarity between some of the language in the charter and the Dorchester constitutions, has argued that Reverend John White "had a hand in drawing up the charter." Hansen, *Dorchester Group,* p. 26.

11. So, at least, Dudley later claimed in a letter to the countess of Lincoln. See Alexander Young, ed., *Chronicles of the First Planters of the Colony of Massachusetts From 1623–1636* (Boston, 1846), pp. 303–340.

12. Cotton Mather, *Magnalia Christi Americana; or, the Ecclesiastical History of New England, From its First Planting in the Year 1620, Unto the Year of Our Lord, 1698* (Hartford, 1820), 1:102. On the education of Pynchon and others, see Bartlett, "University Alumni," pp. 15–18. Morison refers to Pynchon as "the squire of Springfield in Suffolk." Morison, *Builders*, p. 35. Hutchinson estimates that Johnson "had much the largest estate of any of the undertakers." Hutchinson, *History*, p. 15.

13. Young, *Chronicles*, pp. 309–310.

14. Hansen has characterized this transplantation as a "bold stroke" whose legality "has always been in question. . . . At any rate, the action was in direct opposition to the intentions of the charter which had created a trading company." Hansen, *Dorchester Group*, p. 29.

15. *Winthrop Papers*, 2:91.

16. Quoted from Edmund Morgan, ed., *The Founding of Massachusetts: Historians and the Sources* (New York, 1964), p. 176. No doubt this corruption was a large part of the reason that John Winthrop, Jr., was sent to Dublin to study.

17. Young, *Chronicles*, pp. 303–340.

18. Thomas Hutchinson, ed., *A Collection of Original Papers Relative to the History of the Colony of Massachusetts-Bay* (Boston, 1769; reprint, Albany, N.Y., 1865), 1:27–28 (hereafter referred to as *Hutchinson Papers*).

19. "By the end of June 1628 the Abigail sailed from Weymouth with about fifty colonists, and a generous stock of supplies. . . . Captain John Endecott, a stout soldier of Devon, accompanied the fleet as governor of the plantation." Morison, *Builders*, p. 35.

20. "First General Letter of the Governor and Deputy of the New England Company for a Plantation in Massachusetts Bay, to the Governor and Council for London's Plantation in the Massachusetts Bay in New England," in Morgan, *Founding of Massachusetts*, pp. 453–457.

21. Nathaniel B. Shurtleff, ed., *The Records of the Governor and Company of the Massachusetts Bay in New England* (Boston, 1853), 1:37. A *ruling elder* was a lay church officer who helped preside over matters of church government. Unlike a *teaching elder*, i.e., a minister, he could not dispense the word or the sacraments.

22. On July 8 he wrote Downing, "It had been an excellent tyme for Mr. Winthrop to have beene this Commencement att Cambridge, where I heare are many reverend Divines, to consider of Mr. White's Call." *Winthrop Papers*, 2:103.

23. Shurtleff, *Records*, 1:49.

24. Ibid.

25. Ibid., p. 55.

26. Ibid., p. 58.

27. Ibid., p. 59.

28. Ibid.

29. Ibid.

30. *Winthrop Papers*, 2:155.

31. Shurtleff, *Records*, 1:62.

32. Ibid., p. 63.

33. Ibid., pp. 63–64.

34. This and the immediately following quotes are from the "Address of John Winthrop to the Company of the Massachusetts Bay," in *Winthrop Papers*, 2:175–177.

35. Shurtleff, *Records*, 1:64–65.

36. Ibid., p. 67.

37. Ibid.

CHAPTER ONE

1. Ronald D. Cohen, "Church and State in Seventeenth-Century Massachusetts: Another Look at the Antinomian Controversy," in *Puritan New England: Essays on Religion, Society, and Culture,* ed. Alden T. Vaughan and Francis J. Bremer (New York, 1977), p. 174; John Cotton, *A Discourse About Civil Government in a New Plantation Whose Design is Religion* (Cambridge, Mass., 1663), Evans Early American Imprints #79, p. 14; Thomas Jefferson Wertenbaker, *The Puritan Oligarchy: The Founding of American Civilization* (New York, 1947).

2. Michael Walzer, *The Revolution of the Saints: A Study in the Origins of Radical Politics* (New York, 1976). Also see Stephen Foster, *The Long Argument: English Puritanism and the Shaping of New England Culture, 1570–1700* (Chapel Hill, N.C., 1991), pp. 1–32.

3. Stephen Foster has argued that Massachusetts "anticipated" revolutionary England: "[C]ongregational polity, the communitarianism of the New England towns, the fixed codes of law and the church-based franchise all foreshadowed similar developments in Cromwell's England." Stephen Foster, *Their Solitary Way: The Puritan Social Ethic in the First Century of Settlement in New England* (New Haven, 1971), p. xvi. In his most recent work he claims that the New England Way "was neither uniquely American nor a simple English transplant but a further and continuing development in America of an ongoing and long-running English process of adjustments." Foster, *Long Argument,* p. 153.

4. Max Weber, *Economy and Society: An Outline of Interpretive Sociology,* ed. Guenther Roth and Claus Wittich (Los Angeles, 1978), 2:1204–1211.

5. Nathaniel Morton, *New-Englands Memoriall* (Cambridge, Mass., 1669; reprint, Boston, 1903), p. 75.

6. Samuel Eliot Morison, *Builders of the Bay Colony* (Boston, 1930; reprint, Boston, 1981), p. 40.

7. Morton, *New-Englands Memoriall,* p. 75.

8. "First General Letter of the Governor and Deputy of the New England Company for a Plantation in Massachusetts Bay, to the Governor and Council for London's Plantation in the Massachusetts Bay in New England," in *The Founding of Massachusetts: Historians and the Sources,* ed. Edmund Morgan (New York, 1964), pp. 453–457.

9. See the "Agreement of the New-England Company with the Ministers," in *Chronicles of the First Planters of the Colony of Massachusetts From 1623–1636,* ed. Alexander Young (Boston, 1846), pp. 207–212.

10. Morgan, *Founding of Massachusetts,* pp. 453–457.

11. Ibid.

12. Morton, *New-Englands Memoriall,* p. 77.

13. Morgan, *Founding of Massachusetts,* p. 462.

14. While they do not specifically address the cultural authority of early Massachusetts as such, both recognize and demonstrate the disproportionate amount of cultural influence exercised by the ministers. See George Selement, "The Meeting of Elite and Popular Minds at Cambridge, New England, 1638–1645," *William and Mary Quarterly,* 3rd ser., 41 (1984): 32–48, and Harry Stout, *The New England Soul: Preaching and Religious Culture in Colonial New England* (New York, 1986).

15. On Puritan biblicism, see Theodore Dwight Bozeman, *To Live Ancient Lives: The Primitivist Dimension in Puritanism* (Chapel Hill, N.C., 1988), and John S. Coolidge, *The Pauline Renaissance: Puritanism and the Bible* (London, 1970).

16. Larzer Ziff, *Puritanism in America: New Culture in a New World* (New York, 1973), p. 112. Harry Stout has claimed that "the ministers enjoyed awesome powers in New England society" as a result of "their specialized knowledge of the Scriptures and their ordination." Stout, *New England Soul,* p. 19.

17. William Hunt claims that the Puritan divines were "structuralists avant la lettre. They believed that they could uncover, through the interpretation of the revealed Word, the deep structure of God's will, which is to say of ultimate reality." William Hunt, *The Puritan Moment: The Coming of Revolution in an English County* (Cambridge, Mass., 1983), p. 117. The most popular hermeneutic device of the time, typology, was a technique of deep interpretation in which Old Testament personages, events, and practices were said to prefigure those of the New Testament. See Sacvan Bercovitch, *Typology and Early American Literature* (Amherst, 1972). On deep interpretation, see Arthur C. Danto, "Deep Interpretation," *Journal of Philosophy* 78 (1981): 691–706.

18. As in the case of Salem, these elections do not require more than one candidate per office to be effective. Their primary function is to register the consent and obligation of the governed. This is not to say such elections are shams, for the voters always have the option of voting no or denying the cultural authority of the aspirant.

19. Alvin Gouldner called this sociocultural phenomenon "crediting": "To have 'credit' is to be believed in advance of demonstration; without demonstration; or with only loose demonstration. Intellectuals and intellectual products have 'credit' when they are associated with prestigious and powerful social forces. . . . [P]rofessors from great universities are taken more seriously (and take themselves more seriously) than those who are not. Theorists associated with successful revolutions—for example, Lenin and Mao—are read more widely and more carefully than those whose revolutions failed." Alvin Gouldner, *The Dialectic of Ideology and Technology: The Origins, Grammar, and Future of Ideology* (New York, 1976), p. 6. It was because of such credit that "the godly laity still recognized the elucidation of intellectual responses and broad social attitudes as one of the aspects of the prerogative and specific vocation of ministers." John Morgan, *Godly Learning: Puritan Attitudes towards Reason, Learning, and Education, 1560–1640* (Cambridge, England, 1986), p. 19.

20. "Not truth, but men's apprehension of it was subject to a measure of progression, to be accomplished exclusively by a deeper penetration of the sacred writings through which truth was conveyed." Bozeman, *To Live Ancient Lives,* p. 126. The contrasting instrumental view of biblicism, reason, or other intellectually legitimating principles conceives of them as tools used to achieve specific ends.

21. Thomas Hooker, *A Survey of the Summe of Church-Discipline* (London, 1648; reprint, New York, 1972), preface to part 1, p. 1 (unpaginated).

22. For a vivid demonstration of the essential "plasticity" of clerical biblicist interpretation, see Charles L. Cohen, "Two Biblical Models of Conversion: An Example of Puritan Hermeneutics," *Church History* 58 (1989): 182–196.

23. Cotton Mather, *Magnalia Christi Americana; or, the Ecclesiastical History of New England, From its First Planting in the Year 1620, Unto the Year of Our Lord, 1698* (Hartford, 1820), 1:68. Mather claims that this is the original covenant, but it is uncertain whether the original form was altered when the covenant was "renewed" in the aftermath of the Roger Williams debacle.

24. Morgan, *Founding of Massachusetts,* p. 462.

25. Ibid., p. 457.

26. Morton, *New-Englands Memoriall,* p. 74.

27. John Cotton, *The Keys of the Kingdom of Heaven* (1644), in *John Cotton on the Churches of New England,* ed. Larzer Ziff (Cambridge, Mass., 1968), p. 136.

28. John Fiske, *The Watering of the Olive Plant in Christs Garden* (Cambridge, Mass., 1657), Evans Early American Imprints #45, p. 73.

29. Mather, *Magnalia,* 1:68.

30. Hooker, *Survey,* part 1, p. 192.

31. Morton, *New-Englands Memoriall,* p. 75.

32. Mather, *Magnalia*, 1:67.

33. See his account of a typical church gathering in Thomas Lechford, *New-Englands Advice to Old-England* (London, 1644), UMI microfilms, p. 2.

34. "The virtues that identified the Saint were religious, in the narow sense of the word, rather than ethical. Godly behavior consisted primarily of prayer, attendance at sermons, and association with other putative Saints." Hunt, *Puritan Moment*, p. 118.

35. Ibid., p. 123.

36. John Cotton, *The Keyes to the Kingdom of Heaven* (London, 1644), in *John Cotton on the Churches of New England*, ed. Larzer Ziff (Cambridge, Mass., 1968), pp. 101–102.

37. John Allin and Thomas Shepard, *A Defense of the Answer made unto the Nine Questions or Positions sent from New-England, Against the Reply Thereto By the Reverend Servant of Christ, Mr. John Ball* (London, 1648), UMI microfilm, p. 13.

38. Hooker, *A Survey of the Summe of Church Discipline,* part 1, p. 190.

39. Richard Mather, *Church-Government and Church-Covenant Discussed* (London, 1643), reprinted in Richard Mather, *Church Covenant: Two Tracts* (New York, 1972), p. 51.

40. The English historian Patrick Collinson has styled these measures "popular protestantism" and has claimed that "an investigation of the tendencies and pressures contained within the popular protestantism of the later sixteenth century . . . suggests that its habits and embryonic forms were those of 'the congregational way', as this would be defined in the third quarter of the seventeenth century." Patrick Collinson, *Godly People: Essays on English Puritanism and Protestantism* (London, 1983), pp. 13–14.

41. This is for the simple reason that, although people are always willing to fight and suffer for an ideal, the actual number of people doing so in any given case is largely a function of the risks posed by the current regime and the rewards offered by the dissident movement. Larzer Ziff has noted that the quasicongregationalism of early seventeenth-century England—Collinson's "popular protestantism"—"was a system admirably suited for revolutionary as well as reform purposes because it provided those who were forced into such a position by the opposition of authority with an organization that mixed clerical and lay participation, giving all a stake in its vitality, an organization that was local and therefore enjoyed the advantage of the cell." Ziff, *Puritanism in America,* p. 31. Also see Christopher Hill, *The English Bible and the Seventeenth-Century Revolution* (New York, 1993), and Lawrence Stone, *The Causes of the English Revolution, 1529–1642* (New York, 1972), p. 103.

42. Thomas Morton, *New England Canaan, or New Canaan* (Amsterdam, 1637), Sabin Microcard series, pp. 158–159.

43. Bozeman, *Ancient Lives,* p. 171.

44. Morton, *New Canaan,* p. 159.

45. "An intellectual class became an inevitable component of the new Christian commonwealth, just as a strong strain of anti-intellectualism was developed by those who in the name of liberty and toleration opposed it." Ziff, *Puritanism in America,* p. 137.

46. It is well worth noting at this early juncture an interesting phenomenon that would affect the subsequent history of the thinking class for the next thirty years, namely, that many Puritan professionals, lawyers and others who largely generated their incomes as intelligentsia, on occasion demonstrated an ability and propensity to create works of high culture on their own. This dual strata membership, both as intellectuals and as intelligentsia, was somewhat rare but led to no small amount of friction and anger from the ministers. The most pronounced examples of this propensity and ability and the hostile reaction of the ministers to it were Winthrop's occasional sallies into theological disputation, most notably over the Antinomian affair. The response of Thomas Shepard to Winthrop's musings on the subject was remarkably uncharitable and betrays a strong sense of anxiety and defensiveness over protected

cultural "turf." This territorial defensiveness was reciprocated by Winthrop when Hobart, Ward, and others tried their hands at the political application of high culture.

47. "It had been an excellent tyme for mr. Winthrop to have beene this Commencement att Cambridge, where I heare are many reverend Divines, to Consider of Mr. White's call." "Isaac Johnson to Emmanuel Downing," in *The Winthrop Papers* (Boston, 1931), 2:103.

48. Ibid., pp. 163–164.

49. "Good sir, . . . I have adventured to presente unto your view, some few lines, upon occation of your intended voyage into the plantation, in the behalfe of our minister, Mr. Phillips, who is fully resolved, to undertake thee same with you, if God will. . . . His exelency in matters of divinity is such (as I make noe question but experience will make good,) as that hee is inferiour to very few, if to any." "John Maidstone to John Winthrop," in ibid., pp. 164–165.

50. "Arthur Tyndal to John Winthrop, Nov. 10, 1629," in ibid., p. 166. Tyndal went on to promise, "I shall be an example, and true light to continue manie refractaries in flexibilitie, and obedience."

51. Nathaniel B. Shurtleff, ed., *The Records of the Governor and Company of the Massachusetts Bay in New England* (Boston, 1853), 1:73.

52. James Savage, ed., *The History of New England From 1630 to 1649. By John Winthrop, Esq. First Governour of the Colony of the Massachusetts Bay, From Original Manuscripts* (Boston, 1825), 1:31–33 (hereafter referred to as *Winthrop Journal*). The church seems to have been gathered on July 30 of that year, which is the same date offered for the gathering of the Watertown congregation and the ordination of Mr. Phillips. Frederick Lewis Weis, *The Colonial Clergy and the Colonial Churches of New England* (Lancaster, Mass., 1936), pp. 241, 164, 276.

53. One of the first churches of Massachusetts did avoid several of the rituals of cultural domination, particularly lay ordination and the formal subscription to a covenant. The original church of Dorchester was gathered in the West Country of England by Reverends John Warham and John Maverick just prior to their embarkation, with the Reverend John White of Dorchester officiating. It is perhaps not coincidental that this congregation chose to remove en masse to Windsor, Connecticut, in early 1636. For information on the gathering of this church, see Roger Clap, "Captain Roger Clap's Memoirs," in Young, *Chronicles,* pp. 347–348. Also see Weis, *Colonial Clergy,* pp. 137, 215, 247.

54. This is, of course, based on the Morgan interpretation that the assistants had "thrown open the first meeting of the General Court to the whole body of settlers assembled at Charlestown." Edmund S. Morgan, *The Puritan Dilemma: The Story of John Winthrop* (Boston, 1958), pp. 90–91.

55. Shurtleff, *Records,* 1:79. It should be noted that this was a direct violation of the charter, which vested legislative and appointive powers in the General Court, of which the Court of Assistants was an executive or administrative agency.

56. James Truslow Adams, *The Founding of New England* (Boston, 1921), p. 142.

57. In fact, this early government would not have been, strictly speaking, an oligarchy, for freemanship was a corporate privilege based on stock holding, not wealth.

58. Shurtleff, *Records,* 1:79.

59. *Winthrop Journal,* 1:55. As for the exact order of business of the day, the entry in the *Records* begins with the election of Winthrop and others by the court "according to the meaneing of the pattent." I take this clause to mean that the court, for the purposes of this election, was constituted of the stockholders. Once elected, this new (although identical) court administered the oaths to the new freemen and entertained new motions. Shurtleff, *Records,* 1:87.

60. Morgan, *Founding of Massachusetts,* pp. 443–445.

61. By an act of August 23, 1630, the assistants had empowered themselves to act as jus-

tices of the peace. This act was never rescinded, making the office of assistant that of magistrate as well. Shurtleff, *Records,* 1:74.

62. Stout, *New England Soul,* p. 21.

63. Shurtleff, *Records,* 1:87. It goes without saying that this was a direct violation of the terms of the charter, which placed legislative authority in the General Court, or "commons."

64. These persons were John Winthrop, governor; Thomas Dudley, deputy governor; and Increase Nowell, Simon Bradstreet, William Pynchon, John Endecott, William Coddington, Roger Ludlow, and Sir Richard Saltonstall (who returned to England in 1632), all assistants. William H. Whitmore, ed., *The Massachusetts Civil List for the Colonial and Provincial Periods, 1630–1774* (Albany, 1870), p. 21. Even a cursory look at these civil lists gives one food for thought. In the period between this General Court and the year 1660, 304 office terms for assistants were held by a mere thirty-five men, averaging well over eight years of office per incumbent! Ibid., pp. 21–23.

65. William Hubbard, *The Happiness of a People In the Wisdome of the Rulers Directing and in the obedience of their Brethren Attending Unto what Israel ought to do:* . . . (Cambridge, Mass., 1676), Evans Early American Imprints #214, p. 28.

66. Though largely biblicist in orientation, natural law also figured as part of the fundamental law of the Bay Colony. Like biblicism, natural law "provided a good part of the one unalterable way that the votes of the freemen could only assent to, never shape, and that could be interpreted only by the learned few versed in the esoteric skills essential to statecraft." Stephen Foster, *Their solitary Way: The Puritan Social Ethic in the First Century of Settlement in New England* (New Haven, 1971), p. 170.

67. Thomas Cobbet, *The Civil Magistrates Power in Matters of Religion Modestly Debated,* . . . (London, 1653; reprint, New York, 1972), p. 47.

68. Shurtleff, *Records,* 1:87.

69. Edmund S. Morgan, *Visible Saints: The History of a Puritan Idea* (Ithaca, N.Y., 1963), pp. 80–88.

70. Upon close examination, many of the Differences between this early Puritan regime and contemporary one-party states prove to be rather insubstantial. Although the Puritans' cultural interests were theological and contemporaries urge "secular" theories, both constitute "ideologies" in the technical sense of the term (see Edward Shils, *The Intellectuals and the Powers and Other Essays* [Chicago, 1972], pp. 23–25). As William Hunt has observed, the "Protestant eschatology, which Foxe, so to speak, Anglicized, was a revolutionary creed in the strictest sense of the word; it prophesied the most radical subversion of the order of things. . . . The downfall of Rome would be the culminating and concluding event in secular history, to be followed by the Second Coming and the Last Judgement." Hunt, *Puritan Moment,* p. 88. Nor does secularization affect any great change in the structure of belief, since the immanent teleological forces of history neatly fill the metaphysical vacuum left by the "death of God."

There are, however, two fundamental differences, which were to have profound import for the Puritan regime. Whereas the "inner party" of contemporary regimes is generally divided between civilian and military elements, the inner party of the Puritans was constituted of magistrates and ministers. Thus, during power struggles within the inner party, the Massachusetts clerics used cultural sanctions instead of military force against their erstwhile colleagues. The other difference was the proscription, instituted in 1632, against dual-office holding in church and state. This ban of clerical office holding is the reason why Massachusetts was decidedly not a theocracy as is, for example, contemporary Iran.

71. For present purposes, I have adopted Orwell's taxonomy of one-party structures. In Eastern European and socialist one-party states, the Central Committee usually functions as the inner party, giving direction and leadership to the card-carrying elements of the outer party of ideologically committed (and virtuous) cadres.

72. While the Winthrop clique had not, in fact, been ritually elected, all future magistrates were. The danger was, of course, that at any time the freemen could simply pack the court by electing their own "representative" assistants. Within a year this became even more likely as the assistants were thenceforth required to annually stand for reelection. "After dinner, the governour told them [the assistants], that he had heard, that the people intended, at the next general court, to desire, that the assistants might be chosen anew every year." *Winthrop Journal,* 1:74.

73. Gouldner comments as follows on the "strict party discipline" of the early Bolshevik Party: "The party's centralized organizational character aimed, in part, to protect the theoretical germ plasm of its leaders, placing the party under the control of the most theoretically informed, ensuring their influence on those less theoretically trained." Alvin Gouldner, *The Two Marxisms: Contradictions and Anomalies in the Development of Theory* (New York, 1980), p. 6.

74. Williams's counterpart in the tradition of ideological politics is Mikhail Bakunin, the irrepressible and magnetic anarcho-syndicalist. Fervently committed to socialist emancipation, Bakunin was adamantly opposed to the construction of any regime led by socialist theoreticians. To those outside of the ideological tradition in question, Williams and Bakunin inevitably appear to be courageous and sincere men. Those who share in the tradition, however, recognize in them the dizzying heights of fanaticism.

75. Morgan, *Puritan Dilemma,* p. 117. Philip Gura has claimed Williams had "espoused the extreme separatism advocated by Browne and Smyth" during the 1620s. Philip F. Gura, *A Glimpse of Sion's Glory: Puritan Radicalism in New England, 1620–1660* (Middletown, Conn., 1984), p. 35.

76. *Winthrop Journal,* 1:50–51. Not only were Winthrop and his colleagues obliged to disavow such separatist sentiments by their subscription to the "Humble Request" (see *Winthrop Papers,* 2:231–233), in which they "call the Church of England, from whence wee rise, our deare Mother," but they were also obliged by their own pretensions to eschew such a position. It was their ecclesiological interpretation that they were the true reformed Church of England and that in suppressing dissident factions they were upholding the laws of the English nation. If such a church were to prove illegitimate, then the inference could be drawn that any attempt to make other congregations conform to that church was in turn illegitimate and a violation of conscience. This was precisely the inference that Williams ultimately drew.

77. *Winthrop Journal,* 1:53.

78. Ibid.

79. Shurtleff, *Records,* 1:75.

80. Ibid., p. 88. It is likely that Ratcliffe was referring to Salem's retraction of its offer to Williams.

81. Ibid., p. 91.

82. Ibid., p. 103.

83. Cotton Mather, *Magnalia,* 1:111.

84. *Winthrop Journal,* 1:58–59.

85. Ibid.

86. Ibid., p. 67.

87. Ibid.

88. Ibid., pp. 67–68.

89. Ibid.

90. Ibid. This is not to suggest that the strife in Watertown had ended but that after the authority of the magistrates was acknowledged this strife ceased to pose a dangerous challenge to the cultural domination of the thinking class. Indeed, it was not until October 31, 1632, that Winthrop could record in his journal that "[t]he congregation of Watertown dis-

charged their elder, Richard Brown, of his office, for his unfitness in regard passion and distemper in speech, having been oft admonished and declared his repentance for it." Ibid., pp. 93–94. Nor was this the end of Browne's public career, for having been purged from the inner party, he quickly became a leading figure in the outer party, serving as a deputy for most of the next two decades.

91. *Winthrop Journal,* vol. 1, quoted in Adams, *The Founding of New England,* p. 155.

92. Quoted in Morgan, *Puritan Dilemma,* p. 108. That an agreement was made whereby the elders would back down and Winthrop would incorporate their suggestions at the next General Court is suggested by Winthrop's canny foreknowledge of popular agitation: "After dinner, the governour told them [the assistants], that he had heard, that the people intended, at the next general court, to desire . . ." *Winthrop Journal,* 1:74.

93. Shurtleff, *Records,* 1:95.

94. Timothy Breen, *The Character of the Good Ruler: A Study of Puritan Political Ideas in New England, 1630–1730* (New York, 1970), p. 73.

95. This commitment to the value of prudence has been the characteristic metaphysical posture of Anglo-American "empiricist" high culture ever since William of Occam. Continental "rationalist" high culture, on the other hand, has generally found confident optimism a more amenable stance. Miller was certainly correct in holding that the Puritans were the spiritual children of Augustine, for he was the spokesman of prudence par excellence among the Church Fathers.

96. *Winthrop Journal,* 1:81. The elder in question was Increase Nowell, who promptly gave up his church office in favor of his position as an assistant.

97. Bozeman, *Ancient Lives,* p. 51.

98. For a relatively disinterested account of this controversy, see Roger Clap, "Captain Roger Clap's Memoirs," in Young, *Chronicles,* pp. 350–351.

99. *Winthrop Journal,* 1:74. Dudley had apparently cornered the local corn market and proceeded to reap a handsome profit in the trade of this vital necessary. No doubt it was these sharp business practices that had recommended him to the earls of Warwick and Lincoln in the old country.

100. *Winthrop Journal,* 1:83. Winthrop was also required to help procure and maintain a minister for the town for a brief period.

101. Lechford, *New-Englands Advice,* p. 25.

CHAPTER TWO

1. "They got out of England with much difficulty, all places being belaid to have taken Mr. Cotton and Mr. Hooker, who had been long sought for to have been brought into the high commision." James Savage, ed., *The History of New England From 1630 to 1649. By John Winthrop, Esq. First Governour of the Colony of the Massachusetts Bay. From Original Manuscripts* (Boston, 1825), 1:108–109 (hereafter referred to as *Winthrop Journal*). On the spiritual brotherhood, Hall states: "By the turn of the century, some thirty years after Puritanism emerged in England, certain preachers in the church were joined together in a 'spiritual brotherhood' of like–minded men." Among other things, "members of the brotherhood took control of certain common rooms: Christ's college, Cambridge, while Perkins was alive, and Emmanuel, which Lawrence Chaderton directed from its founding in 1584." David D. Hall, *The Faithful Shepherd: A History of the New England Ministry in the Seventeenth Century* (New York, 1972), pp. 49–50.

2. Thompas Shepard, "Thomas Shepard's Memoir of Himself," in *Chronicles of the First Planters of the Colony of Massachusetts From 1623–1636,* ed. Alexander Young (Boston, 1846), pp. 529–530.

3. Frederick Lewis Weis, *The Colonial Clergy and the Colonial Churches of New England* (Lancaster, Mass., 1936), p. 110. As a fellow of the college, "he acquitted himself . . . with such ability and fidelity as to secure universal respect and admiration." William B. Sprague, *Annals of the American Pulpit,* vol. 1, *Trinitarian Congregational* (New York, 1857; reprint, New York, 1969), p. 30.

4. Weis, *Colonial Clergy,* p. 110. Sprague relates that Hooker's ministry at this time was "abundantly blessed, and an extensive reformation followed not only in the town but in the adjacent country." Sprague, *Annals,* 1:31.

5. Sprague, *Annals,* 1:31. The Winthrop clique had extended an invitation to Hooker in 1629. See "Isaac Johnson to John Winthrop," in *The Winthrop Papers* (Boston, 1931), 2:177–179.

6. Hooker "was at first employed as an assistant of Mr. Paget at Amsterdam. . . . Mr. Paget exerted an influence in the Classis against him, from having taken up a suspicion that he favoured the Brownists. . . . As Mr. Hooker found it impossible to disabuse of this unfounded suspicion, and as he found, too, that the congregation sympathized strongly in the jealousies of their pastor . . . he removed to Delft, and became associated with the Rev. Mr. Forbes. . . . Mr. Hooker, after continuing with Mr. Forbes two years, accepted a call to Rotterdam, to assist the Rev. Dr. William Ames." Sprague, *Annals,* 1:32. Holland seems to have also served in the "seasoning" of the wild young Hugh Peter, who left the low countries for early Massachusetts an eminently serviceable young man.

7. Samuel Whiting, "Concerning the Life of the Famous Mr. Cotton, Teacher to the Church of Christ at Boston, in New England," in Young, *Chronicles,* pp. 420–422.

8. Weis, *Colonial Clergy,* p. 67.

9. Whiting, "Life of Mr. Cotton," pp. 422–423.

10. Larzer Ziff, ed., *John Cotton on the Churches of New England* (Cambridge, Mass., 1968), pp. 9–10. Ziff goes on to state that "as a result of such efficient political practices, Cotton held his Puritan course under Bishops Barlow, Monteigne, and Williams while one after another Puritan minister, in the years 1613–1632, was silenced, imprisoned, or forced to flee." On Thomas Leverett's role in the initial prosecution, see Sprague, *Annals,* 1:242.

11. Cotton Mather, *Magnalia Christi Americana; or, the Ecclesiastical History of New England, From its First Planting in the Year 1620, Unto the Year of Our Lord, 1698* (Hartford, 1820), 1:242. Ziff relates that Cotton had intended to remove to Holland when "Thomas Hooker, who had tried residence in Delft and Rotterdam, now secretly appeared in London to tell Cotton that he had found this an impossible experience and was going to go to New England. . . . Migrating Boston parishioners also pressed Cotton to join them in New England." Ziff, *John Cotton,* p. 13.

12. *Winthrop Journal,* 1:53.

13. Hall, *Faithful Shepherd,* p. 78. While Hall is probably correct in assigning responsibility for this "new charisma" to the repressive policies of the Laudian regime, Cotton seems to have found warrant for his innovative practices in the accounts of the primitive apostolic church, a religious organization that was the paradigm case of the charismatic community. Weber defined charisma as "a certain quality of an individual personality by virtue of which he is considered extraordinary and treated as endowed with supernatural, superhuman, or at least specifically exceptional powers or qualities." Max Weber, *Economy and Society: An Outline of Interpretive Sociology,* ed. Guenther Roth and Claus Wittich (Los Angeles, 1978), 1:241.

14. Weber, *Economy and Society,* 1:247. It was just such a rule requiring unanimity that Winthrop used to save John Wilson's office in the church of Boston and ward off the early challenges of the Antinomians.

15. Ibid., 2:1113.

16. John Cotton, *The True Constitution of a Particular Visible Church, Proved by Scripture* (London, 1642), reprinted in John Cotton, *Two Sermons* (New York, 1972), pp. 7–8.

17. *Winthrop Journal,* 1:112.

18. Ibid., p. 118. Again, Weber states, "What is despised, so long as the genuinely charismatic type is adhered to, is traditional or rational everyday economizing, the attainment of a regular income by continuous economic activity devoted to this end. Support by gifts, either on a grand scale involving donation, endowment, bribery and honoraria, or by begging, constitute the voluntary type of support." Weber, *Economy and Society,* 1:244–245.

19. *Winthrop Journal,* 1:118. Cotton was ordained teacher of the church of Boston on October 10, 1633.

20. Ibid., p. 121.

21. Thomas Lechford, *New-Englands Advice to Old-England* (London, 1644), UMI microfilm, p. 19.

22. John Fiske, *The Watering of the Olive Plant in Christs Garden* (Cambridge, Mass., 1657), Evans Early American Imprints #45, p. 74.

23. Richard Mather, *Church-Government and Church-Covenant Discussed, . . .* (London, 1643), reprinted in Richard Mather, *Church Covenant: Two Tracts* (New York, 1972), pp. 76–77. Such "set stipends" were not to be confused with biblical tithes, Thomas Hooker pointed out, for "those Tithes in the Old Testament were out of the seed of the land, the fruit of the trees, or of the herd of the flocks," whereas the Bay minister's maintenance "is raised out of all good things, the person that is taught hath." Thomas Hooker, *A Survey of the Summe of Church Discipline* (London, 1648), part 2, p. 31.

24. Hooker, *Survey,* part 2, p. 28.

25. "An organized group subject to charismatic authority will be called a charismatic community. . . . The prophet has his disciples; the warlord his bodyguard; the leader, generally, his agents. There is no such thing as appointment or dismissal, no career, no promotion. . . . There is no such thing as a salary or benefice." Weber, *Economy and Society,* 1:121. As David Hall has noted, this "communitarian ethic inspired the Boston church to require that its members resolve disputes by arbitration instead of turning to the civil courts. And more broadly, the ethic encouraged a loosening of traditional restraints, as love took the place of more coercive forms of power." Hall, *Faithful Shepherd,* p. 87.

26. John Cotton, "A Sermon Delivered at Salem, 1636," in Ziff, *John Cotton,* p. 56. The most striking feature of this passage is its remarkably anticlerical tone. Such statements raise important questions about John Cotton's role in the antiministerial activities that underlay the Antinomian movement in the two years following this sermon, for here he is clearly implying that in proffering covenants that institutionalized their cultural domination his colleagues had, in fact, been preaching a covenant of works.

27. Ibid., pp. 48, 55. Cotton goes on to state, "Build a church upon any other foundation but faith, and the profession of faith, and it will break into manifold distempers." Ibid., p. 57. So much for Cotton's keen political insight: no church was more fraught with manifold distempers than his own, which was built exclusively on a covenant of grace.

28. The best discussion of Cotton's initiatory role in the spread of tests for saving grace is still Edmund S. Morgan, *Visible Saints: The History of a Puritan Idea* (Ithaca, N.Y., 1963), pp. 95–100. For a recent challenge to Morgan's claim, see Michael G. Ditmore, "Preparation and Confession: Reconsidering Edmund S. Morgan's *Visible Saints,*" *New England Quarterly* 67 (1994): 298–319.

29. Weber, *Economy and Society,* 1:243. As Ziff has noted, "His emphasis on the exclusive importance of grace is what made Cotton so popular a preacher in New England as well as England." Ziff, *John Cotton,* p. 20.

30. Mather, *Magnalia Christi Americana,* 1:243.

31. Quoted in Morgan, *Visible Saints,* p. 100.

32. *Winthrop Journal,* 1:183–184. By August 23 the residents of Dorchester, no doubt through a dispensation of providence, had achieved a sufficient "closing with Christ" to constitute themselves as a church "with approbation of the magistrates and elders." Ibid., p. 189.

33. Lechford, *New-Englands Advice,* p. 16.

34. It is well worth noting that when the congregants of Dorchester were found "not meet" to form a church, an exception was made of the Reverend Richard Mather, who was accorded full charismatic qualifications by the ministers and magistrates in attendance. *Winthrop Journal,* 1:183–184.

35. Weber held that the recognition "freely given and guaranteed by what is held to be a proof, originally always a miracle" is always "decisive for the validity of charisma." He went on to state, rather portentously, "If proof and success elude the leader for long, if he appears deserted by his god or his magical or heroic powers, above all, if his leadership fails to benefit his followers, it is likely that his charismatic authority will disappear." Weber, *Economy and Society,* 1:242.

36. For a discussion of this revival and Cotton's role in initiating it, see David D. Hall, ed., *The Antinomian Controversy, 1636–1638: A Documentary History* (Middletown, Conn., 1968), pp. 13–16.

37. Young, *Chronicles,* pp. 354–355.

38. *Winthrop Journal,* 1:121.

39. Collated from "The Records of the First Church in Boston, 1630–1868," ed. Richard D. Pierce, in *Publications of the Colonial Society of Massachusetts* (Boston, 1961), 39:13–22.

40. "When such an authority comes into conflict with the competing authority of another who also claims charismatic sanction, the only recourse is to some kind of contest. . . . In principle, only one side can be right in such a conflict; the other must be guilty of a wrong which has to be expiated." Weber, *Economy and Society,* 1:244.

41. Mather, *Magnalia Christi Americana,* 2:496.

42. The best discussion of Williams's charismatic conception of the ministry is still Edmund S. Morgan, *Roger Williams: The Church and the State* (New York, 1967), pp. 50–56.

43. Richard P. Gildrie, *Salem, Massachusetts, 1626–1683: A Covenant Community* (Charlottesville, Va., 1975), p. 33.

44. Perry Miller, *Roger Williams: His Contribution to the American Tradition* (New York, 1970), p. 75. Also, see Philip F. Gura, *A Glimpse of Sion's Glory: Puritan Radicalism in New England, 1620–1660* (Middletown, Conn., 1984), p. 35.

45. *Winthrop Journal,* 1:116–117. Winthrop adds, apparently without intentional irony, that "this fear was without cause." Winthrop's reference in this passage to clerical consociation is the first of its kind in the early history of Massachusetts. There is no evidence of any regular clerical consociation in the Bay Colony prior to this reference despite Increase Mather's claim that "in the beginning of the country" the clergy held "frequent meetings, which were most usually after their publick and weekly or monthly lectures." Mather, *Magnalia Christi Americana,* 1:220. There is plenty of evidence, however, of prior clerical consociation in England by the leading ministers of Massachusetts that arrived with or in the few years after Cotton: "Quite probably John Cotton and Richard Mather met in one or another of these [Lincoln diocese] conferences with neighborhood colleagues, while Thomas Hooker himself established a Chelmsford conference attended by Thomas Weld and Thomas Shepard. Yet another future Bay divine, Ezekiel Rogers, son of a member of the old Daventry Classis, participated in an East Riding conference." Robert F. Scholz, "Clerical Consociation in Massachusetts Bay: Reassessing the New England Way and Its Origins," *William and Mary Quarterly,* 3rd ser., 29 (1972): 401. Also see Stephen Foster, *The Long Argument: English Puritanism and the Shaping of New England Culture, 1570–1700* (Chapel Hill, N.C., 1991), p. 152.

46. *Winthrop Journal,* 1:122. That this meeting was private is suggested by several facts. Winthrop refers to it and the next such meeting as between the governor and assistants, whereas when the magistrates met as the Court of Assistants or the upper half of the General Court, Winthrop refers to it as the court or general court. More significant is the absence of any entry or evidence of any court meeting in these months in Nathaniel B. Shurtleff, ed., *The Records of the Governor and Company of the Massachusetts Bay in New England* (Boston, 1853). Even more suspect is a crossed-out entry of a Court of Assistants in Boston, January 17, 1634. John Noble, ed., *Records of the Court of Assistants of the Colony of the Massachusetts Bay, 1630–1692* (Boston, 1904), 2:38. The reason for such secrecy may have been to avoid publicizing any rift within the ministry, particularly as the imperial situation continued to deteriorate.

47. "Williams declared that the King's authority to grant such control rested on 'a solemn public lie.' He also charged the King with blasphemy for referring to Europe as Christendom and applied to the King certain uncomplimentary passages from the Book of Revelation." Edmund S. Morgan, *The Puritan Dilemma: The Story of John Winthrop* (Boston, 1958), p. 121.

48. *Winthrop Journal,* 1:122.

49. Morgan, *Puritan Dilemma,* p. 122.

50. *Winthrop Journal,* 1:122.

51. Ibid., p. 123.

52. Ibid., p. 125.

53. "Shortly after he returned to that town [Salem] in the fall of 1633, Williams supported Skelton's view that women should be veiled in church meetings." Gura, *Sion's Glory,* p. 41.

54. *Winthrop Journal,* 1:125.

55. *Winthrop Journal,* 1:128–129.

56. Ibid.

57. In brief, Laud had risen to a position of great power in matters concerning the Crown's colonial possessions and was eager to institute quo warranto proceedings to vacate Massachusetts's charter.

58. "It was further ordered, that every man of or above the age of twenty yeares, whoe hath bene or shall hereafter be resident within this jurisdiction by the space of six monethes, as an householder or sojourner, and not infranchised, shall take the oath hereunto written . . . and upon his refuseall the second tyme, hee shalbe banished, except the Court shall see cause to give him further respite." Shurtleff, *Records,* 1:115.

59. *Winthrop Journal,* 1:128–129.

60. Ibid., p. 132.

61. Shurtleff, *Records,* 1:117.

62. Ibid., pp. 117–121.

63. Thomas Cobbet, *The Civil Magistrates Power in Matters of Religion Modestly Debated,* . . . (London, 1653; reprint, New York, 1972), p. 68.

64. In the aftermath of the Williams debacle, when a commission of elders and magistrates attempted to resolve the conflict between Dudley and Winthrop, Dudley cited Winthrop's leniency as the sole issue separating them.

65. Morgan, *Puritan Dilemma,* p. 113. It is likely that Dudley, who had been Cotton's parishioner in England, informed his former pastor of his machinations, prompting Cotton's election sermon.

66. Shurtleff, *Records,* 1:117–121.

67. The account, delivered at the General Court, was one of Winthrop's great public performances. The gist of the address was that "I have spent by occasion, of my late office above £1200; towards this I have receaved by way of benevolence from some townes about £50, & by the last yeares allowance £150, & by some provision sent by Mr. Humfrey . . . aboute £50, or it may be somewhat more." Ibid., p. 131.

68. *Winthrop Journal,* 1:140–142.

69. Ibid.

70. On the expectation of military conflict, the following order was enacted on the first day of the court: "It is ordered, that the present Governour, John Winthrop, Senior, John Haynes, John Humfrey, & John Endicott, Esq., shall have power to consulte, direct, & give command for the manageing & ordering of any warr that may befall us for the space of a yeare nexte ensueing, & till further order be taken herein." Shurtleff, *Records,* 1:125.

71. "The Spirituall Kingdome of Christ, is most opposed by a generation of Enthusiasts; and Familists, who having refined the loathsome follies of their former predecessours, do adventure to set open their conceits, with greater insolency, to the view of the world, and under the pretence of free-grace, they destroy the grace of God in the power and operations of it." Hooker, *Survey,* p. a-2.

72. Ibid., part 2, p. 27.

73. Ibid., pp. 31, 37.

74. "R. Stansby to John Wilson," in *Winthrop Papers* (Boston, 1943), 3:389–390.

75. Lechford, *New-Englands Advice,* p. 7.

76. John Cotton, *A Discourse About Civil Government in a New Plantation Whose Design is Religion* (Cambridge, Mass., 1663), Evans Early American Imprints #79, p. 21.

77. Hooker, *Survey,* part 3, p. 5.

78. Ibid., part 2, p. 3.

79. Ibid., part 1, pp. 14–15.

80. Ibid., p. 24.

81. Ibid., p. 15.

82. *Winthrop Journal,* 1:140–142.

83. On domination by honoratiores, see Weber, *Economy and Society,* 2:1009–1010.

84. *Winthrop Journal,* 1:140–142. The only features that the bicameral representative government of the Puritan party in Massachusetts lacked were separate meetings and records for the two legislative bodies. These were added in the aftermath of the Goody Sherman–Robert Keayne case.

85. *Winthrop Journal,* 1:151.

86. Ibid.

87. Ibid.

88. Shurtleff, *Records,* 1:132–133.

89. Ibid., p. 137.

90. *Winthrop Journal,* 1:152–153.

91. Shurtleff, *Records,* 1:140.

92. Ibid., pp. 142–143.

93. John Cotton, *The Keyes to the Kingdom of Heaven* (London, 1644), in Ziff, *John Cotton,* p. 153.

94. Hooker, *Survey,* part 2, pp. 79–80. For a cogent analysis of the remarkably gendered language of this and other religious writings of the Bay divines, see Amanda Porterfield, *Female Piety in Puritan New England: The Emergence of Religious Humanism* (New York, 1992).

95. Cobbet, *Civil Magistrates Power,* pp. 1 (from unpaginated preface), 88.

96. Winthrop records that Williams was "very clearly confuted." *Winthrop Journal,* 1:152–153. Mather claims that Hooker was able to silence Williams by proving from Williams's own premises that it was "unlawful for a father to call upon his child to eat his meat." Mather, *Magnalia Christi Americana,* 2:498. Williams, apparently, was reluctant to acknowledge the validity of reductio ad absurdum.

97. *Winthrop Journal,* 1:152–153.

98. William H. Whitmore, ed., *The Massachusetts Civil List for the Colonial and Provincial Periods, 1630–1774* (Albany, 1870), p. 21.

99. Shurtleff, *Records*, 1:146.

100. Mather, *Magnalia Christi Americana*, 2:496.

101. *Winthrop Journal*, 1:162–163.

102. Ibid.

103. Mather, *Magnalia Christi Americana*, 2:496.

104. Ibid.

105. While Winthrop claims that the "whole church was grieved with the letter," the subsequent actions of some who continued to support their teacher suggest that this assessment was somewhat hyperbolic. *Winthrop Journal*, 1:166.

106. Shurtleff, *Records*, 1:156–157.

107. Ibid.

108. Ibid., p. 158.

109. Ibid., pp. 160–161; Morgan, *Puritan Dilemma*, p. 128.

110. *Winthrop Journal*, 1:170–171. Following Winthrop, Morgan records this sentence as occurring in early October. The Colony Records, however, state that it occurred in September. I have chosen to follow the latter, as it was recorded as it occurred, rather than recollected. Shurtleff, *Records*, 1:157–161.

111. Shurtleff, *Records*, 1:160–161.

112. *Winthrop Journal*, 1:175–176.

113. Ibid.

114. This is, of course, based on Morgan's account in *Puritan Dilemma*, p. 129. Morgan quotes a letter written by Williams in 1670 that states, "When I was unkindly and unchristianly, as I believe, driven from my house and land and wife and children, (in the midst of a New England winter, now about thirty-five years past,) at Salem, that ever honored Governor, Mr. Winthrop, privately wrote to me to steer my course to Narragansett Bay."

115. *Winthrop Journal*, 1:178.

116. Ibid.

CHAPTER THREE

1. Larzer Ziff, ed., *John Cotton on the Churches of New England* (Cambridge, Mass., 1968), p. 22.

2. "Virtually all of the Boston authorities, in short, sympathized with Hutchinson, and it is precisely the implications of this near unanimous support that historians have failed to recognize." James F. Cooper, Jr., "Anne Hutchinson and the 'Lay Rebellion' against the Clergy," *New England Quarterly* 61 (1988):382.

3. James Savage, ed., *The History of New England From 1630 to 1649. By John Winthrop, Esq. First Governour of the Colony of the Massachusetts Bay. From Original Manuscripts* (Boston, 1825), 1:253 (hereafter referred to as *Winthrop Journal*).

4. Bernard Bailyn, *The New England Merchants in the Seventeenth Century* (Cambridge, Mass., 1955). Bailyn goes on to note that Anne Hutchinson's husband, son, and brother-in-law "were among the most prominent early merchants. . . . The 'Antinomian schism' uprooted some of the most flourishing merchants of Boston and prepared the soil of Rhode Island for the growth of a commercial community." Ibid., pp. 40–41. While Bailyn is undoubtedly right in suggesting the predominant role played by the merchants in the controversy, Emery Battis has shown that a significant portion of the urban petit bourgeoisie, such as urban artisans and tradesmen, also made up an important constituency of the Antinomian

movement. Hence my reference to the urban bourgeoisie rather than the merchants of Boston. See Emery Battis, *Saints and Sectaries: Anne Hutchinson and the Antinomian Controversy in the Massachusetts Bay Colony* (Chapel Hill, N.C., 1962), table 5, p. 268.

5. Natural economies are characterized by the liturgical satisfaction of wants, household production, and exchange in kind between "commensurable" use values. Such economies are relatively natural to the extent that they minimize the role of money and the cash nexus in the economy. Max Weber, *Economy and Society: An Outline of Intrepretive Sociology,* ed. Guenther Roth and Claus Wittich (Los Angeles, 1978), 1:100.

6. Bailyn characterizes a just charge (either price or wage) as "one willingly paid by a person experienced in such matters and in need of the article but under no undue compulsion to buy it." Bailyn, *New England Merchants,* p. 21. One of the most articulate spokesmen of this medieval economic theory was Saint Thomas Aquinas, who wrote that "if either the price exceed the quantity of the thing's worth, or conversely, the thing exceed the price, there is no longer the equality of justice; and consequently, to sell a thing for more than its worth, or to buy it for less than its worth, is in itself unjust and unlawful." Thomas Aquinas, *The Political Ideas of St. Thomas Aquinas,* ed. Dino Bigongiari (New York, 1953), p. 144.

7. Bailyn, *New England Merchants,* pp. 22, 20.

8. Battis, *Saints and Sectaries,* p. 103.

9. "Initially their regulatory measures were calculated to limit the profits of construction workers whose skills were at a premium during this period of rapid population growth." Ibid., p. 98.

10. Nathaniel B. Shurtleff, ed., *The Records of the Governor and Company of the Massachusetts Bay in New England* (Boston, 1853), 1:141–142.

11. Bailyn, *New England Merchants,* p. 34. Bailyn adds that "the group of importers which the Puritan magistrates failed to create by franchise grew independently. The key to its formation was credit, for it was by credit alone that the necessary goods were brought from Europe to America." Ibid.

12. Shurtleff, *Records,* 1:160. Indeed, six months later provisions for licensing and restricting mercantile activity were reenacted only to be repealed once again upon Vane's election as governor. Ibid., pp. 166, 174–175.

13. Larzer Ziff, *Puritanism in America: New Culture in a New World* (New York, 1973), p. 75.

14. As Bailyn points out, "Despite their strategic economic position and their rapid assumption of authority in the port towns, they did not attain control of the colonies' governments." Bailyn, *New England Merchants,* p. 38.

15. Philip F. Gura, *A Glimpse of Sion's Glory: Puritan Radicalism in New England, 1620–1660* (Middletown, Conn., 1984), pp. 69–70.

16. *Good News from New-England* (London, 1648), in *Massachusetts Historical Society Collections,* 4th ser., (Boston, 1852), 1:213–214.

17. Edward Johnson, *Wonder Working Providence of Sions's Saviour in New England* (London, 1654; reprint, New York, 1974), p. 95.

18. John Winthrop, *"A Short Story of the Rise, reign, and ruine of the Antinomians, Familists & Libertines"* (London, 1644), in *Antinomian Controversy, 1636–1638: A Documentary History,* ed. David D. Hall (Middletown, Conn., 1968), p. 209.

19. Ibid.

20. Ziff, *John Cotton,* p. 23. Ziff, following Cotton, dates Cotton's realization of the Antinomian danger to the Synod of 1637. Ibid., p. 21. Cotton recounts that at the opening of the synod "I perceived that some of the members and messengers of our church, were ready to rise up, and plead in defense of sundry corrupt opinions, which I verily thought had been far from them." John Cotton, "The Way of the Congregational Churches Cleared, 1648," in ibid., p. 234.

21. At this point, Shepard was particularly anxious to warn Cotton not to be deceived by his flock's apparent doctrinal rectitude, "as if that the Familists doe not care for woord or ordinances but only the spirits motion; for I have bin with many of them and hence have met with many of there bookes; and I doe know thus much of them that scarce any people honour woord and ordinances more, for they will professe that there they meet with the Spirit and there superlative raptures. . . . [T]his I speake from the enforcement of my conscience, *lest under this colour of advancing woord together with the Spirit, you may meet in time with some such members (though I know none nor judge any) as may doe your people and ministry hurt, before you know it"* (italics mine). "Letters between Thomas Shepard and John Cotton," in Hall, *Antinomian Controversy,* pp. 28–29.

22. Norman Petit has argued that as late as the Synod of 1637 Cotton "identified himself with the Bostonians to such an extent that he fully believed their cause to be his own." Norman Petit, *The Heart Prepared: Grace and Conversion in Puritan Spiritual Life* (New Haven, 1966), p. 151.

23. Vane arrived with Shepard and others on October 6, 1635, settled in Boston, and was admitted to Cotton's congregation on November 1, less than a month later. *Winthrop Journal,* 1:170, and "The Records of the First Church in Boston, 1630–1868," ed. Richard D. Pierce, in *Publications of the Colonial Society of Massachusetts* (Boston, 1961), 39:19.

24. The cadres, culled from Battis's core group and the colony records, were, with the sole exception of John Spencer, all merchants and members of Cotton's congregation: Mr. Brenton, William Coddington, John Coggeshall, and William Hutchinson (the husband of Anne Hutchinson). See Battis, *Saints and Sectaries,* appendix 2, pp. 304–307, and appendix 3, pp. 312–316, as well as Shurtleff, *Records,* 1:178, 184–185, 191–192, 194.

25. *Winthrop Journal,* 1:187. It was probably in the interim between the failed gathering at Dorchester and the removal to Connecticut roughly two months later that Hooker preached against these polity arrangements, reportedly stating, "I knowe all must not be admytted, yet this may do more hurt, yf one come amongst you of another minde, & they should joyne with hym." "R. Stansby to John Wilson," in *The Winthrop Papers,* (Boston, 1943), 3:389–390.

26. Shurtleff, *Records,* 1:174–175. The text of "Moses His Judicialls" is reprinted in Thomas Hutchinson, ed., *A Collection of Original Papers Relative to the History of the Colony of Massachusetts-Bay* (Boston, 1769; reprint, Albany, N.Y., 1865), 1:181–204 (hereafter referred to as *Hutchinson Papers*).

27. Shurtleff, *Records,* 1:174–175.

28. Ibid., p. 183.

29. Thomas Shepard, "Thomas Shepard's Memoir of Himself," in *Chronicles of the First Planters of the Colony of Massachusetts From 1623–1636,* ed. Alexander Young (Boston, 1846), pp. 546–548.

30. Cotton, "Way of the Congregational Churches Cleared," p. 227.

31. Richard Mather, *The Summe of Certain Sermons Upon Genesis* (Cambridge, Mass., 1652), Evans Early American Imprints #35, p. ii.

32. Peter Bulkeley, *The Gospel Covenant,* 2nd ed. (London, 1651), UMI microfilm, pp. 360, 313. Norman Petit has claimed that Bulkeley's works represent the "full flowering" of covenant theology in Massachusetts. Petit, *Heart Prepared,* p. 114.

33. Battis has argued that the Antinomian doctrine held that free grace "was essentially a mystical experience preceding and precluding any moral effort on the part of the believer." Battis, *Saints and Sectaries,* p. 105. On the doctrine of preparation, see Petit, *Heart Prepared.*

34. Thomas Shepard, *Wine for Gospel Wantons: or, Cautions Against Spirituall Drunkenness* (Cambridge, Mass., 1668), Evans Early American Imprints #130, p. 9.

35. "Mrs. Hutchinson's views, in divorcing questions of conduct from evaluations of one's spiritual state, were of the sort that would have offered spiritual and psychological solace to

those mercantile elements in Boston who were troubled and doubt-ridden by the community's criticism of their business practices." Francis J. Bremer, *The Puritan Experiment: New England Society from Bradford to Edwards* (New York, 1976), p. 69.

36. Winthrop, "A Short Story," p. 224. Philip Gura has remarked that "many New England spiritists were convinced that, once a person was justified, the Son of God dictated his every action. Thus assured of their salvation, such radical Puritans acknowledged no law but Christ within them." Gura, *Sion's Glory,* p. 60.

37. "In Puritan covenant theology, the terms and form of God's dealing with mankind for salvation are established in the covenant of works at the foundation of the world, and the covenant of grace functions as a means of applying to the elect the righteousness obtained by Christ, who satisfies the conditions of the first covenant." William K. B. Stoever, *"A Faire and Easie Way to Heaven": Covenant Theology and Antinomianism in Early Massachusetts* (Middletown, Conn., 1978), p. 96.

38. Bulkeley, *Gospel Covenant,* p. 384. What made this view at least marginally Calvinist was his conception of faith as a sort of action that he enjoined to his readers: "[P]lead the promise of his grace, touch the top of his scepter, and take hold of the Covenant, and then certainly the Lord will enter into Covenant with thee." Ibid., p. 51.

39. Thomas Shepard, *Theses Sabbaticae, or The Doctrine of the Sabbath,* in *The Works of Thomas Shepard, First Pastor of the First Church Cambridge, Massachusetts* (Boston, 1853; reprint, New York, 1967), 3:92.

40. Gura, *Sion's Glory,* p. 53. Much the same point can be found in Stoever, *Faire and Easie,* p. 14. Stoever also notes that the oft-made "suggestion that Cotton's colleagues were departing from normative Reformed doctrine and that Cotton and Hutchinson were not is scarcely correct." Ibid., p. 175.

41. No doubt this theology is what made Cotton so attractive to the mercantile community of Boston, Lincolnshire.

42. Roger Clap, "Roger Clap's Memoirs," in Young, *Chronicles,* pp. 359–361.

43. Johnson, *Wonder Working,* p. 95

44. Winthrop, "A Short Story," pp. 221–235.

45. John Norton expressed the doctrine of means as follows: "Waiting for the Lord Jesus in the use of means, with preparatory hope, is our seeking after him in the wayes which he hath instituted in his Word for that end; until we find him such as are hearing of the Word, Reading, Meditation, Conferring, Praying, & C." John Norton, *The Orthodox Evangelist* (London, 1657), UMI microfilm, p. 159. William Stoever has put the point somewhat more clearly: "If justification is by faith, and if faith comes by hearing the preached word, then it is only by going to meeting and attending on the minister's words that a person may be saved." Stoever, *Faire and Easie,* p. 113.

46. "At issue was the manner of the Spirit's witnessing. In the case of justification, the ministers insisted, it is by the call of Christ in the biblical word." Stoever, *Faire and Easie,* p. 78. Religious culture is in this particular context construed as the system of wisdom contained in the Scriptures and espoused by the orthodox ministry in their "legalistic preaching."

47. "It was not that great a conceptual leap for those who felt threatened by 'legal' preaching to extend their condemnation to any preaching by a regular ministry, under the assumption that he who was saved by God's free grace had within him a testimony more valid than anyone else could provide." Gura, *Sion's Glory,* p. 69. Even John Norton, who is generally thought to be the closest to Cotton theologically among the orthodox divines of the first generation, insisted that "though the means cannot work without the Spirit, the Spirit (ordinarily) will not work (upon subjects of discretion) without the means" and thus "we are with dilligence to atttend upon God in the use of means." Norton, *Orthodox Evangelist,* p. 213.

48. Hall dates the correspondence between Cotton and both Shepard and Bulkeley from

early to mid-1636, "when the ministers were sounding Cotton out on his theological views." Hall, *Antinomian Controversy,* p. 34.

49. "Letters between Thomas Shepard and John Cotton," p. 26.

50. Ibid., p. 30.

51. "Peter Bulkeley and John Cotton: On Union with Christ," in Hall, *Antinomian Controversy,* p. 39. The other three Aristotelian causes—material, formal, and final—were uncontroversially assigned.

52. This was not only because such an "instrument" would stand in a position of temporal precedence to its causal consequent but also because the other causal relations had already been supplied with the required values.

53. Cotton, "Way of the Congregational Churches Cleared," pp. 224–225.

54. Ibid.

55. "The Elders Reply" in Hall, *Antinomian Controversy,* p. 62. Hall dates this "Reply" in January 1637. Cotton claimed that after he had publicly rejected the objectionable doctrines, his Antinomian parishioners continued to "falsely father" or attribute their views on him: "No matter (say the other [i.e., the Antinomian]) what you hear him say in public: we know what he saith to us in private. This answer bred in some of my brethren and friends, a jealousy that myself was a secret fomenter of this spirit of familism." Cotton, "Way of the Congregational Churches Cleared," pp. 224–225. Although his ministerial colleagues were polite enough not to contradict this account publicly, it is entirely unsupported by the available evidence. Indeed, in his memoir Shepard confessed that "the opinions of familists" were "begun by Mrs. Hutchinson, raised up to a great height by Mr. Vane, too suddenly chosen Governor, and maintained too obscurely by Mr. Cotton." Shepard, "Thomas Shepard's Memoir of Himself," p. 546.

56. *Winthrop Journal,* 1:201.

57. Ibid. Stoever has argued that aside from this legal context, when he thought he was under scrutiny Cotton "tended to shift the discussion from an evidential connection between sanctification and justification to a causal connection, which permitted him to sound very Protestant while making the other elders sound less so." Stoever, *Faire and Easie,* p. 47.

58. "The Examination of Mrs. Anne Hutchinson at the Court at Newtown," in Hall, *Antinomian Controversy,* p. 320. None of the ministers contradicted Peter's account in this regard. Gura claims that Hutchinson channeled the "religious fervor" of her fellow congregants in Boston "into open criticism of all the colony's ministers." Gura, *Sion's Glory,* p. 244. For a similar observation, see Ziff, *Puritanism in America,* p. 64.

59. "The Examination of Mrs. Hutchinson," p. 320.

60. Ibid., pp. 325–326. This stands, of course, in stark contrast to the "preparationist view" of the passage in question: "For the apostle doth not call them ministers of the letter and of the Old Testament because they did preach the law to the humble and lead unto Christ, but because they preached the law for righteousness without Christ, whom he calls the spirit." Shepard, *Theses Sabbaticae,* p. 114.

61. "The Examination of Mrs. Hutchinson," p. 334. Stoever has argued that, contrary to Cotton's recollection at the Hutchinson trial, Cotton had "indirectly" accused the other ministers of professing a doctrine of works. Stoever, *Faire and Easie,* p. 14.

62. Hall, *Antinomian Controversy,* p. 6. Apparently, John Wilson had sided with the bulk of the clergy in their conference with the Antinomian leaders of Boston.

63. In July 1632 a questionnaire had been circulated by the church of Boston asking "[w]hether there might be diverse pastors in the same church," which was answered as "doubtful," though not outright "negative." *Winthrop Journal,* 1:81. The quotation is from Winthrop's account of the proceedings. Ibid., p. 202.

64. Felt notes that Winthrop specifically objected to Wheelwright's teaching on the rela-

tion of the believer and the Holy Ghost. "Upon this Governor Vane expresses his surprise, because *Mr. Cotton had lately approved of Mr. Wheelwright's doctrine* [italics mine]. . . . There being an endeavor to explain away the difference of use between him and Winthrop, the latter remarks, that though this is likely to be done, and he highly esteems the ability and piety of Wheelwright still he is indisposed to sit under his ministry." Joseph Felt, *The Ecclesiastical History of New England; Comprising Not Only Religious, But Also Moral, and Other Relations* (Boston, 1855), 1:263–264.

65. Ibid.

66. Shurtleff, *Records,* 1:185.

67. *Winthrop Journal,* 1:207.

68. Hall, *Antinomian Controversy,* p. 7. Some three weeks before this court, on November 17, Winthrop recorded that "[t]he governour, Mr. Vane, a wise and godly gentlemen held, with Mr. Cotton and many others, the indwelling of the person of the Holy Ghost in a believer, and went so far beyond the rest, as to maintain a personal union with the Holy Ghost." *Winthrop Journal,* 1:206–207.

69. *Winthrop Journal,* 1:207–208.

70. Ibid.

71. Ibid., p. 208.

72. Ibid.

73. "John Cotton's response to Sixteene Questions of Serious and Necessary Consequence," in Hall, *Antinomian Controversy,* p. 46.

74. "The Elders Reply," p. 61.

75. "Mr. Cottons Rejoynder," in Hall, *Antinomian Controversy,* p. 85.

76. Bulkeley, *Gospel Covenant,* pp. 253, 252.

77. *Winthrop Journal,* 1:208–209.

78. Ibid.

79. Ibid.

80. Ibid. Winthrop notes that Vane and two others, presumably Coddington and Dummer, dissented from Wilson's speech, as well as two of the ministers, undoubtedly Cotton and Wheelwright.

81. Ibid., pp. 210–211.

82. Ibid.

83. "John Wheelwright, a Fast-Day Sermon," in Hall, *Antinomian Controversy,* p. 157.

84. Ibid., p. 163. Wheelwright warned the congregation not to be fooled by the holiness of some of their orthodox foes: "Brethren, those under a covenant of works, [the] more holy they are, the greater enimyes they are to Christ." Ibid., p. 164.

85. Ibid., p. 165.

86. *Winthrop Journal,* 1:213–214. Ziff has noted that as "tempers ran higher and higher," the "oral clashes that followed sermons were becoming slanderous." Ziff, *Puritanism in America,* p. 65.

87. The records of the court state that on March 9 "[t]he Courte did approve of Mr. Wilsons speach, in their judgements." Shurtleff, *Records,* 1:189.

88. *Winthrop Journal,* 1:214.

89. Ibid., pp. 214–216.

90. Thomas Cobbet, *The Civil Magistrates Power in Matters of Religion Modestly Debated,* . . . (London, 1653; reprint, New York, 1972), p. 17.

91. Shurtleff, *Records,* 1:189. On Stephen Greensmith's occupational status, see Battis, *Saints and Sectaries,* appendix 3, p. 313.

92. Specifically, he was "enjoyned to make acknowledgement to the satisfaction of every congregation, & was fined 40 pounds, & standeth bound in 100 pounds till this bee done; both

the satisfaction bee given to the ministers & the churches, & the Courte satisfied for the fine."
Shurtleff, *Records,* 1:189.

93. Winthrop, "A Short Story," p. 284.

94. Cobbet, *Civil Magistrates Power,* p. 39.

95. Winthrop, "A Short Story," p. 186.

96. Felt, *Ecclesiastical History of New England,* pp. 273–274.

97. Winthrop, "A Short Story," pp. 288–289.

98. Ibid., p. 289.

99. Shurtleff, *Records,* 1:189.

100. *Winthrop Journal,* 1:216.

101. "Remonstrance or Petition by members of Boston Church, in favour of Wheelwright, March, 1637," appendix in *Winthrop Journal,* 1:401–403.

102. Shurtleff, *Records,* 1:191.

103. *Winthrop Journal,* 1:218.

104. Ibid., pp. 219–220.

105. Ibid. Thomas Hutchinson, who was well acquainted with provincial electoral procedures, offered a trenchant explanation of Vane's tactic: "[T]his being the day, by charter for elections, and the inhabitants all convened for that purpose, if other business was allowed to take up the time the elections would be prevented." Thomas Hutchinson, *The History of the Colony and Province of Massachusetts Bay,* ed. Lawrence Shaw Mayo (Cambridge, Mass.; reprint, Millwood, N.Y., 1970), 1:54.

106. *Winthrop Journal,* 1:219–220.

107. See note in Hutchinson, *History,* 1:54.

108. *Winthrop Journal,* 1:219–220.

109. Ibid.

110. Ibid.

111. Ibid.

112. Although in many cases, no doubt, both of these moments were collapsed into a single barter exchange.

113. Shurtleff, *Records,* 1:200.

114. *Winthrop Journal,* 1:222.

115. Ibid.

116. Shurtleff, *Records,* 1:196.

117. *Winthrop Journal,* 1:224.

118. Winthrop's account of this faux pas is as follows: "The differences grew so much here, as tended fast to a separation; so as Mr. Vane, being, among others, invited by the governour to accompany the Lord Ley at dinner, not only refused to come, (alleging by letter that his conscience withheld him,) but also, at the same hour, he went over to Nottle's Island with Mr. Maverick, and carried the Lord Ley with him." *Winthrop Journal,* 1:232.

CHAPTER FOUR

1. The significance of Davenport's presence was that, in direct contradiction of his putative strict congregationalist principles, he could both exercise in the pulpit of Boston on August 17 and attend the synod without having been called to any office.

2. David D. Hall, ed., *The Antinomian Controversy, 1636–1638: A Documentary History* (Middletown, Conn., 1968), p. 173.

3. Ibid.

4. James Savage, ed., *The History of New England From 1630 to 1649. By John Winthrop,*

Esq. First Governour of the Colony of the Massachusetts Bay. From Original Manuscripts (Boston, 1825), 1:221 (hereafter referred to as *Winthrop Journal*).

5. Ibid., p. 236.

6. Thomas Shepard, "Thomas Shepard's Memoir of Himself," in *Chronicles of the First Planters of the Colony of Massachusetts From 1620–1636,* ed. Alexander Young (Boston, 1846), pp. 547–548.

7. *Winthrop Journal*, 1:237–238.

8. Ibid., pp. 237–239. Winthrop played a pivotal role in the synod not only as an authority figure but, more important, as a force of conciliation between Cotton and the other ministers. Hutchinson quotes an anonymous letter's glowing report of Winthrop's actions: "[T]herein was the wisdom and excellent spirit of the governor seen, silencing passionate and impertinent speeches . . . adjourning the assembly when he saw heat and passion, so that, through the blessing of God, the assembly is dissolved, and jarring and dissonant opinions, if not reconciled, yet are covered; and they who came together with minds exasperated, by this means depart in peace." Thomas Hutchinson, *The History of the Colony and Province of Massachusetts Bay,* ed. Lawrence Shaw Mayo (Cambridge, Mass., 1936; reprint, Millwood, N.Y., 1970), 1:61. On the justification for civil intrusion into religious disputes, see Thomas Cobbet, *The Civil Magistrates Power in Matters of Religion Modestly Debated, . . .* (London, 1653; reprint, New York, 1972), p. 24: "Who seeth not, that Corruption in matters of Religion, . . . themselves occasion breaches upon mens natural, and civil good; even their lives, safety, estates, civil peace and liberty, and the like. Witnesse the sad fruits of Popery, too oft in England; of Anabaptisme in Germany, in John of Leyden and Cnipper Doolings dayes; of Levelisme not long since in England."

9. John Winthrop, "A Short Story of the Rise, Reign, and Ruine of the Antinomians, Familists & Libertines," in Hall, *Antinomian Controversy,* p. 248.

10. Larner Ziff, ed., *John Cotton on the Churches of New England* (Cambridge, Mass., 1968), p. 234.

11. From John Cotton, "The Way of the Congregational Churches Cleared, 1648," in ibid., p. 235.

12. See Perry Miller, "Preparation for Salvation in Seventeenth-Century Massachusetts," in *Nature's Nation* (Cambridge, Mass., 1967); "The Marrow of Puritan Divinity," in *Errand into the Wilderness* (Cambridge, Mass., 1956); and especially *The New England Mind: The Seventeenth Century* (Cambridge, Mass., 1939), pp. 365–397. The latter work and its sequel, *The New England Mind: From Colony to Province* (Cambridge, Mass., 1953), were his most important contributions and possibly the greatest work in all of American historiography.

13. "God demands of him [man] now not a deed but a belief, a simple faith in Christ the mediator. And on His own side, God voluntarily undertakes, not only to save those who believe, but to supply the power of belief. . . . Man has only to pledge that, when it is given him, he will avail himself of the assistance which makes belief possible. If he can believe, he has fulfilled the compact; God then must redeem him and glorify him." Miller, "Marrow," p. 62.

14. John Norton, *The Orthodox Evangelist* (London, 1657), UMI microfilm, p. 85.

15. Miller, "Marrow," p. 83.

16. Cotton Mather, *Magnalia Christi Americana; or, The Ecclesiastical History of New England, From Its First Planting in the Year 1620, Unto the Year of Our Lord, 1698* (Hartford, 1820), 2:514.

17. The actual formulation, as Winthrop recorded it, was "that there was no marriage union with Christ before actual faith, which is more than habitual." Winthrop also recorded two other theological compromises: "that some saving sanctification (as faith &c.) were coexistent, concurrent and coapparent (or at least might be) [again, note the lack of temporal and causal

precedence] with the witness of the Spirit always" and "[t]hat the new creature is not the person of a believer, but a body of saving graces in such a one; and that Christ as a head, doth enliven or quicken, preserve and act the same, but Christ himself is not part of this new creature." *Winthrop Journal,* 1:237–239.

18. Hutchinson, *History,* 1:60.

19. *Winthrop Journal,* 1:239.

20. Ibid., 239–240.

21. Ibid.

22. Ibid.

23. Ibid.

24. Ibid., pp. 240–241.

25. Ibid., pp. 244–249.

25. Joseph Felt, *The Ecclesiastical History of New England; Comprising Not Only Religious But Also Moral, and Other Relations* (Boston, 1855), 1:319–320.

27. *Winthrop Journal,* 1:244–249. Felt records that in the aftermath of the synod, "Mr. Wheelwright continued in his usual strain of preaching, and Mrs. Hutchinson her meetings and exercises." Felt, *Ecclesiastical History of New England,* 1:319–320.

28. *Winthrop Journal,* 1:244–249.

29. Nathaniel B. Shurtleff, ed., *The Records of the Governor and Company of the Massachusetts Bay in New England* (Boston, 1853), 1:205. Actually, Coggeshall had not signed the petition, but "though his hand were not to the petition, yet professing himself to approve of it, &c. [he] was also dismissed, and after disfranchised." *Winthrop Journal,* 1:244–249.

30. *Winthrop Journal,* 1:244–249.

31. Shurtleff, *Records,* 1:206.

32. There are, of course, notable exceptions, such as Edmund Morgan, "The Case against Anne Hutchinson," *New England Quarterly* 10 (1937): 635–649, and *The Puritan Dilemma: The Story of John Winthrop* (Boston, 1958), as well as Ronald D. Cohen, "Church and State in Seventeenth-Century Massachusetts: Another Look at the Antinomian Controversy," in *Puritan New England: Essays on Religion, Society, and Culture,* ed. Alden T. Vaughn and Francis J. Bremer (New York, 1977), pp. 174–186. Both see the threat as substantial and the response as in many ways measured. A more interesting case is James F. Cooper, Jr., "Anne Hutchinson and the 'Lay Rebellion' against the Clergy," *New England Quarterly* 61 (1988): 381–397, wherein the author argues both that the Antinomians were not a significant threat and that the government response reflected this fact in its unusual mildness.

33. Specifically, they assaulted the third formal requirement of cultural domination, i.e., that all public expressions of the culturally dominant must be socially privileged.

34. Shurtleff, *Records,* 1:207.

35. Ibid., pp. 205, 207.

36. Ibid. Aspinwall was also required to post bond of £100 for his good behavior until his departure.

37. In the best piece on the Hutchinson trial in the historiography, Ann Withington and Jack Schwartz argue that the purpose of the political trial of Anne Hutchinson was to buttress "the moral equilibrium of political authority" by "providing a ritual for obscuring the crude application of power." Ann Withington and Jack Schwartz, "The Political Trial of Anne Hutchinson," *New England Quarterly* 51 (1978): 231.

38. The trial of Anne Hutchinson, and those of most Bay "heretics" for that matter, differed from twentieth-century show trials in that, while the guilt of the accused in Massachusetts was never really in question, their performance during the trial could profoundly influence the outcome. Confession, followed by recantation and repentance, generally was rewarded with clemency and reintegration within the community of the godly. Even a carefully worded pitch

to the concerns of the deputies by a dangerous heretic could result in a more lenient sentence, as Samuel Gorton demonstrated in the following decade.

39. "The Examination of Mrs. Anne Hutchinson at the Court of Newtown," in Hall, *Antinomian Controversy,* p. 312. Winthrop is even more direct in his account of the examination in "A Short Story." He recounts the following opening statement on his part: "Now the end of your sending for, is, that upon sight of your errors, and other offences, you may bee brought to acknowledge, and reforme the same, or otherwise that wee may take such course with you as you may trouble us no further." Winthrop, "A Short Story," p. 266.

40. Most historians have seen Hutchinson as the victor in most of her disputational exchanges during her trial. As Edmund Morgan has put it, "[I]n nearly every exchange of words she defeated him [Winthrop], and the other members of the General Court with him." Morgan, *Puritan Dilemma,* pp. 147–148. Also see Withington and Schwartz, "Political Trial," pp. 232–234. Not only is this outcome highly unlikely, given the superior training and numbers of her opponents, but it also is hardly justified by the record of the trial. While Hutchinson's defense was doggedly determined and she certainly had her innings, on the whole she was the loser in most exchanges, particularly with Winthrop.

41. "The Examination of Mrs. Hutchinson," p. 312.

42. Ibid.

43. Ibid., p. 316.

44. Ibid., p. 312. While Edmund Morgan has found this argument convincing—"Winthrop was unable to find his way around this logical impasse and took refuge in blind dogmatism"—it apparently proved unconvincing to the courts that convicted Ethel Rosenberg and Anne Pollard of abetting their treasonous husbands. Morgan, *Puritan Dilemma,* p. 149.

45. *Winthrop Journal,* 1:244–249.

46. Morgan, *Puritan Dilemma,* p. 149. It is perhaps worth noting that the reference to and discussion of the text from Acts are not in the transcript of the examination but appear only in Winthrop's account in the "Short Story." I follow Morgan in assuming that this discussion preceded the discussion of the "customary" practices in Boston and the citation from Titus.

47. Winthrop, "A Short Story," p. 269. The citation in question reads as follows: "And he [Apollo] began to speak boldly in the synagogue: whom when Aquila and Priscilla had heard, they took him unto them, and expounded unto him the way of God more perfectly." This and all other citations are from the King James Version of *The Holy Bible* (New York, 1974).

48. "The Examination of Mrs. Hutchinson," p. 314.

49. Ibid., p. 315.

50. Ibid., p. 316.

51. The King James Version is as follows: "The aged women likewise, that they be in behaviour as becometh holiness, not false accusers, not given too much wine, teachers of good things: That they may teach the young women to be sober, to love their husbands, to love their children, To be discreet, chaste, keepers at home, good, obedient to their own husbands, that the word of God be not blasphemed."

52. "The Examination of Mrs. Hutchinson," p. 316.

53. Ibid.

54. In his opening remarks, Winthrop had charged, "[Y]ou have spoken divers things as we have been informed very prejudicial to the honour of the churches and ministers thereof." Ibid., p. 312.

55. Ibid., pp. 317–318.

56. Hutchinson unsuccessfully attempted to transform Dudley's charge into an absurdity: "I pray Sir prove that I said they preached *nothing but a covenant of works* [italics mine]." Dudley, who was fully aware of the "quantificational implications" of his charge, was having

none of this gambit. "Nothing but a covenant of works," he sardonically quipped, "why a Jesuit may preach truth sometimes." Ibid., p. 318.

57. Ibid., p. 319.

58. Ibid.

59. Ibid., pp. 320–321.

60. Ibid., pp. 321–324. George Phillips recalled a damaging example of Hutchinson's dogmatic pugnacity: "I asked her of myself (being she spoke rashly of them all [the other divines]) because she never heard me at all. She likewise said that we were not able ministers of the new testament and her reason was because we were not sealed." Ibid., p. 322.

61. Ibid., p. 324.

62. Ibid., p. 325.

63. Ibid.

64. The testimony Dudley alluded to was that of Nathaniel Ward, sometime minister of Ipswich. Ibid. Dudley worded the position as follows: "that the scriptures in the letter of them held forth nothing but a covenant of works." Ibid., p. 324.

65. Ibid., pp. 325–326. It is worth noting that Hutchinson had the better side of this argument and was able to cite an appropriate text, 2 Corinthians 3:6: "Who also hath made us able ministers of the new testament; not of the letter, but of the spirit: for the letter killeth, but the spirit giveth life."

66. Ibid.

67. Morgan, *Puritan Dilemma,* p. 150.

68. "The Examination of Mrs. Hutchinson," p. 327.

69. "By employing a procedural device of great religious import, Hutchinson threw her accusers into confusion and shifted the focus away from the content of their testimony to the form of it." Withington and Schwartz, "Political Trial," p. 233.

70. "The Examination of Mrs. Hutchinson," p. 330. While all of the ministers professed a decided reluctance to submit to an oath, Shepard was the most outspoken on the issue. When Dudley informed the ministers that "[i]f the country will not be satisfied you must swear," Shepard tersely replied, "I conceive the country doth not require it." Ibid., p. 332. Hugh Peter, on the other hand, understood the necessity of removing all doubts: "We cannot tell what was first or last [in Hutchinson's statements], we suppose that an oath is the end of all strife and we are tender of it, yet *this is the main thing against her that she charged us to be unable ministers of the gospel and to preach a covenant of works* [italics mine]." Winthrop wisely seconded Peter's sentiments. "You do understand the thing," he replied, "that the court is clear for *we are all satisfied that it is the truth but because we would take away all scruples, we desire that you would satisfy the spectators by your oath* [italics mine]." Ibid., p. 331.

71. Ibid.

72. Ibid., p. 332.

73. Ibid., p. 333.

74. Ibid.

75. Ibid., p. 334.

76. Morgan, *Puritan Dilemma,* p. 151.

77. Hall, *Antinomian Controversy,* pp. 334–335.

78. Ibid., pp. 335–336.

79. Ibid.

80. Ibid., pp. 341–342.

81. Ibid., p. 338.

82. Ibid. It was Stoughton who led the charge on behalf of the ministerial oath.

83. Ibid., p. 340.

84. Ibid. Apparently, Cotton had already forgotten that Hutchinson had claimed an imme-

diate revelation. Indeed, it was this immediate revelation, according to her, that revealed the meaning of the Scriptures, rather than the Scriptures revealing the will of God.

85. Ibid. Cotton's attempts to interpret Hutchinson's locutions as moderate and inoffensive are patently absurd and mendacious in light of some of her more outlandish ejaculations, including: "But now having seen him which is invisible I fear not what man can do unto me." Ibid., p. 338.

86. Ibid., p. 341.

87. Following her teacher's cue, Hutchinson obligingly answered, "By a providence of God I expect to be delivered from some calamity that shall come to me." Ibid.

88. Ibid., p. 342.

89. Ibid.

90. Ibid.

91. Ibid.

92. Ibid., p. 343.

93. Ibid. This similarity with the case of Münster was the court's justification for subsequently disarming all those who had signed the remonstrance on behalf of John Wheelwright.

94. Ibid.

95. Ibid., pp. 347–348.

96. Ibid., p. 348.

97. *Winthrop Journal,* 1:244–249. Those summoned, aside from Underhill, were Edward Hutchinson, William Balston, Richard Gridley, Thomas Marshall, William Dyre, and William Dinely. Shurtleff, *Records,* 1:207–208. On their residence, see Emery Battis, *Saints and Sectaries: Anne Hutchinson and the Antinomian Controversy in the Massachusetts Bay Colony* (Chapel Hill, N.C., 1962), appendixes 2 and 3.

98. *Winthrop Journal,* 1:244–249. In addition, William Balston was fined £20 and Edward Hutchinson was fined £40. Shurtleff, *Records,* 1:207–208.

99. Ibid., p. 208.

100. Ibid., p. 209; Battis, *Saints and Sectaries,* appendixes 2 and 3.

101. Shurtleff, *Records,* 1:211.

102. Cooper, "Anne Hutchinson and the 'Lay Rebellion,'" p. 391.

103. Shurtleff, *Records,* 1:212.

104. Winthrop placed the number of such recantations at "near twenty" in *Winthrop Journal,* 1:244–249. Cooper, on the other hand, claims that "thirty-five immediately acknowledged their error," in "Anne Hutchinson and the 'Lay Rebellion,'" p. 391. Battis records thirty-seven recantations, six of which occurred prior to the disarmament order, leaving thirty-one subsequent confessions, in *Saints and Sectaries,* appendixes 2 and 3.

105. Shurtleff, *Records,* 1:213.

106. *Winthrop Journal,* 1:250.

107. Ibid., p. 249. Also see Battis, *Saints and Sectaries,* p. 223.

108. *Winthrop Journal,* 1:249.

109. Battis, *Saints and Sectaries,* p. 223.

110. Winthrop Journal, 1:253.

111. Winthrop lists the following six propositions: "That there is no inherent righteousness in a child of God. That neither absolute nor conditional promises belong to a Christian. That we are not bound to the law, not as a rule, & c. That the Sabbath is but as other days. That the soul is mortal, till it be united to Christ, and then it is annihilated, and the body also, and a new given by Christ. That there is no resurrection of the body." Ibid.

112. Ibid.

113. On December 13, 1638, during a public fast, "Mr. Cotton, in his exercise that day at Boston, did confess and bewail, as the churches', so his own security, sloth and credulity,

whereupon so many and dangerous errours had gotten up and spread in the church; and went over all the particulars, and showed how he came to be deceived." Ibid., pp. 280–281.

114. "The Records of the First Church in Boston, 1630–1868," ed. Richard D. Pierce, in *Publications of the Colonial Society of Massachusetts* (Boston, 1961), 39:22.

115. Ibid.

116. Ibid.

117. The only evidence of excommunication in the church of Boston prior to Anne Hutchinson is the following entry in the church records from July 24, 1636: "Robert Parker our brother whoe was excommunicate the 6th of the 10th Moneth 1635 for scandalous oppression of his wives children in selling away their inheritance from them, and other hard usage both of her and them, was this day upon profession of his repentance received againe to the fellowship of the Church." Ibid., p. 20.

118. Cooper, "Anne Hutchinson and the 'Lay Rebellion,'" p. 391.

CHAPTER FIVE

1. David D. Hall, *The Faithful Shepherd: A History of the New England Ministry in the Seventeenth Century* (New York, 1972), p. 130.

2. The first formal arrangement of this circuit was recorded by Winthrop on October 5, 1634: "It being found that the four lectures [per week!] did spend too much time, and proved over burdensome to the ministers and people, the ministers, with the advice of the magistrates, and with the consent of their congregations, did agree to reduce them to two days, viz. Mr. Cotton at Boston one Thursday, or the 5th day of the week, and Mr. Hooker at Newtown the next 5th day, and Mr. Warham at Dorchester one 4th day of the week, and Mr. Welde at Roxbury the next 4th day." James Savage, ed., *The History of New England From 1630 to 1649. By John Winthrop, Esq. First Governour of the Colony of the Massachusetts Bay. From Original Manuscripts* (Boston, 1825), 1:144 (hereafter referred to as *Winthrop Journal*).

3. Harry S. Stout, *The New England Soul: Preaching and Religious Culture in Colonial New England* (New York, 1986), p. 27. The numbers Stout marshals on behalf of ministerial influence are staggering. He estimates that in the course of a lifetime the average resident (not necessarily freeman) heard a whopping 7,000 sermons, "totaling somewhere around fifteen thousand hours of concentrated listening." Ibid., p. 4.

4. "Assuming, then, that the records mean what they say, I have found only four jury trials for noncapital crimes in Massachusetts before 1660." John Murrin, "Magistrates, Sinners, and a Precarious Liberty: Trial by Jury in Seventeenth-Century New England," in *Saints and Revolutionaries: Essays on Early American History,* ed. David Hall, John Murrin, and Thad Tate (New York, 1984), p. 163.

5. Ibid., p. 164.

6. "In order to discover the role of Mosaic law in this historic setting, it is essential to see it in relation to an already-established tradition of advocacy for the Judicials understood 'according to equity' and sagely 'proportioned' to current circumstances." Theodore Dwight Bozeman, *To Live Ancient Lives: The Primitivist Dimension in Puritanism* (Chapel Hill, N.C., 1988), p. 169.

7. Thomas Cobbet, *The Civil Magistrates Power in Matters of Religion Modestly Debated,* . . . (London, 1653; reprint, New York, 1972), p. 75.

8. The famed "Standing Council," created by the court at the behest of John Cotton on March 3, 1636, quickly came to naught. Instead, the assistants filled the role of interim governors and drew on the counsel of those elders in close proximity to the court. Nathaniel B.

Shurtleff, ed., *The Records of the Governor and Company of the Massachusetts Bay in New England* (Boston, 1853), 1:167.

9. The committee was comprised of the magistrates, Richard Bellingham, William Spencer, William Hawthorne (the leader of the deputies), and five ministers: Peter Bulkeley, George Phillips, Hugh Peter, Thomas Shepard, and the retired Nathaniel Ward of Ipswich. Ibid., p. 222.

10. Ironically, the document that issued from this second committee, Nathaniel Ward's "Body of Liberties," was also a code of fundamental law, delimiting the power of magistrates, deputies, and ministers, and was woefully lacking in specific laws and sentences. It was not until 1645 that Ward finally accommodated the deputies and drafted a set of statutes that were subsequently adopted.

11. *Winthrop Journal*, 1:275.

12. Ibid.

13. Ibid., p. 299. Winthrop, who seems to have been more than willing to serve as governor for life, adds approvingly that some of the ministers, presumably Cotton among others, thought such a life tenure "as most agreeable to God's institution and the practice of all well-ordered states." Ibid.

14. Shurtleff, *Records*, 1:256.

15. Ibid., p. 271.

16. "Ezekiel Rogers to John Winthrop," in *The Winthrop Papers* (Boston, 1944), 4:151.

17. *Winthrop Journal*, 1:313.

18. Ibid.

19. Shurtleff, *Records*, 1:281.

20. Ibid., p. 279.

21. "Nathaniel Ward to John Winthrop," in *Winthrop Papers*, 4:162. Ward was generally distrustful of the symbolic "populism" of the New England Way. When he returned to England in 1646 he sided with the presbyterian party against the independents. Francis J. Bremer, *Puritan Crisis: New England and the English Civil Wars, 1630–1670* (New York, 1989), p. 241.

22. *Winthrop Journal*, 1:324–325.

23. Ibid. There is some uncertainty as to the exact date of this order and whether it was made by the General Court or the Court of Assistants. Winthrop's entry in his *Journal* is dated December 3, 1639, at which time only the Court of Assistants has recorded business. On the other hand, Winthrop specifically ascribes the action to the General Court twice and mentions the participation of the deputies. Moreover, although there is no record in Shurtleff, *Records,* of this order, in the following year the *Records* do record its repeal. See Shurtleff, *Records,* 1:290. Since the acts of the Court of Assistants were not considered legislative edicts, I conclude that the General Court passed the order and the secretary failed to enter it.

24. *Winthrop Journal*, 1:324–325.

25. Ibid.

26. Ibid.

27. John Norton, *A Brief Catechisme Containing the Doctrine of Godlines, or Living Unto God* (Cambridge, Mass., 1660), Evans Early American Imprints #63, p. 20.

28. John Fiske, *The Watering of the Olive Plant in Christs Garden* (Cambridge, Mass., 1657), Evans Early American Imprints #45, p. 70.

29. *Winthrop Journal*, 1:324–325.

30. Shurtleff, *Records,* 1:288.

31. *Winthrop Journal*, 2:3–4.

32. Shurtleff, *Records,* 1:290, 292–293.

33. *Winthrop Journal*, 2:3–4.

34. "Ezekiel Rogers to John Winthrop," in *Winthrop Papers*, 4:277–278.

35. Ibid.

36. Ibid., pp. 281–282.

37. *Winthrop Journal*, 2:16.

38. Winthrop records that this "further consideration" revealed that "divers of the elders did not agree in these points." Ibid. David Hall has noted that "the principal of congregational independence left the state as the only vehicle for keeping order" and that "as threats to order appeared in other towns, the ministers as a whole came to look with greater favor on state action." Hall, *Faithful Shepherd*, p. 125.

39. *Winthrop Journal*, 2:16–18.

40. Ibid. Also see Shurtleff, *Records*, 1:305.

41. Shurtleff, *Records*, 1:319.

42. Winthrop records that "some of the freemen [presumably the deputies] . . . had chosen Mr. Nathaniel Ward to preach the election sermon," this notwithstanding the facts that it was the governor's right to issue such an invitation and that Ward was no longer a minister, having retired from his office in the church of Ipswich a few years before. Ward, for his part, made the unconscionable error of "grounding his propositions much upon the old Roman and Grecian governments." He argued that the voters ought to "keep all their magistrates in an equal rank, and not give more honour or power to one than to another," presumably by rotating the highest offices among each of them. As for the mechanics of the election count, Winthrop records that "when the votes were numbered he [Bellingham] had six votes more than the others; but there were divers who had not given their votes, who now came into the court and desired their liberty, which was denied by some of the magistrates [presumably Bellingham, Saltonstall, and perhaps Stoughton], because they had not given them in at the doors. But others thought it was an injury, yet were silent, because it concerned themselves [no doubt Winthrop, Dudley, and Endecott]." *Winthrop Journal*, 2:35–37. On Nathaniel Ward, see William B. Sprague, *Annals of the American Pulpit*, vol. 1, *Trinitarian Congregational* (New York, 1857; reprint, New York, 1969), pp. 39–40.

43. Bellingham seems to have been the only governor to have been singly endowed with this authority. Shurtleff, *Records*, 1:320.

44. Ibid., p. 346.

45. Hall, *Faithful Shepherd*, p. 123.

46. Edmund S. Morgan, ed., *Puritan Political Ideas, 1558–1794* (New York, 1965), p. 201.

47. *Winthrop Journal*, 2:43.

48. Ibid.

49. Ibid., pp. 50–51.

50. The civil case in question was between Mr. Howe and Thomas Dudley over the title of a mill. While the evidence on behalf of Dudley convinced the ministers, magistrates, and deputies, Bellingham "still laboured to have the cause carried against Mr. Dudley, reproved some of the elders for their faithfull advice, . . . refusing to put things to the vote that made against his purpose." Ibid.

51. Ibid., pp. 52–56.

52. Ibid.

53. Ibid.

54. Hall, *Faithful Shepherd*, p. 136.

55. As historian Robert Wall has put it, "They were the obvious issues, since one involved the power of the magistrates to exclusive rule when the General Court was not in session, and the other involved their ability to dominate even when the Court was sitting." Robert Wall, *Massachusetts Bay: The Crucial Decade, 1640–1650* (New Haven, 1972), p. 41.

56. *Winthrop Journal*, 2:64–65.

57. The freeman in turn received it from Hawthorne, the speaker of the deputies, who had procured it from the author, Richard Saltonstall. Ibid.

58. Ibid.

59. Shurtleff, *Records,* 2:5.

60. These orders were made on June 14, 1642. Ibid., pp. 20, 21.

61. *Winthrop Journal,* 2:89–91.

62. Ibid.

63. Wall, *Massachusetts Bay,* pp. 51–52.

64. Ibid., p. 52.

65. Ibid., p. 57.

66. "John Winthrop's Summary of the Case Between Richard Sherman and Robert Keayne," in *Winthrop Papers,* 4:349–350.

67. "John Winthrop to the Elders of Massachusetts Churches," in *Winthrop Papers,* 4:359.

68. Shurtleff, *Records,* 2:12.

69. *Winthrop Journal,* 2:71–72.

70. "John Winthrop to the Elders," pp. 359–360.

71. Wall, *Massachusetts Bay,* p. 57.

72. *Winthrop Journal,* 2:115–116.

73. Wall, *Massachusetts Bay,* p. 58.

74. This line of defense, Winthrop sarcastically commented, "shows plainly the democratical spirit which acts our deputies." Yet this was a perfectly legitimate explanation, for Winthrop himself acknowledged that the deputies were the representatives of the freemen. Indeed, Winthrop understood precisely why this was such a controversial case and a perfect device for the deputies in their campaign against the negative voice: "Now that which made the people so unsatisfied, and unwilling the cause should rest as it stood, was the £20 which the defendant had recovered against the plaintiff in an action of slander. . . . But he being accounted a rich man, and she a poor woman, this so wrought with the people, as being blinded with unreasonable compassion, they could not see, or not allow justice her course." Prudently, Winthrop convinced Keayne to remit the entire fine to Goody Sherman. *Winthrop Journal,* 2:116–119.

75. Ibid.

76. Winthrop states that this second treatise was written by an assistant, and the only assistants to oppose the negative voice were Bellingham, Stoughton, and Saltonstall, and Saltonstall had been "recovered" from that error at the previous meeting with the elders over the sow case. Ibid.

77. Ibid.

78. Shurtleff, *Records,* 2:40.

79. "They had received support from the ministers before on the question of reelection of governors and had received their endorsement for participation in the Standing Council the previous October." Wall, *Massachusetts Bay,* p. 60.

80. Wall has argued that "[h]ad the decision of the elders supported the deputies and called for the abolition of the negative voice, there is good evidence that the magistrates still would have resisted." Ibid., p. 63. Unfortunately, he does not supply any of this evidence. Rather, as Wall himself states, the magistrates had promised that if the elders "agreed that the negative voice was 'inconvenient, or not warranted by the patent and the said order, etc.,' then the magistrates would consent to abolish it." In the absence of any contradictory evidence, there is no reason to doubt the veracity of the magistrates' pledge. Ibid., p. 60.

81. "John Winthrop's Defense of the Negative Vote," in *Winthrop Papers,* 4:382. Foster specifically credits Winthrop with ensuring that "the government of Massachusetts was a mixed aristocracy, not a mixed or pure democracy. The bulk of political power, executive, legislative, and judicial, resided in that branch of government not responsible to the people."

Stephen Foster, *Their Solitary Way: The Puritan Social Ethic in the First Century of Settlement in New England* (New Haven, 1971), pp. 89–90.

82. "John Winthrop's Defense," p. 386.

83. Ibid., p. 388.

84. "The Negative Vote," in *Proceedings of the Massachusetts Historical Society* (Boston, 1913), 3rd ser., 46:279.

85. Ibid., pp. 284–285. While somewhat more reluctant to celebrate his own "natural" aristocratic pretensions, Winthrop had also had harsh words for democratic government: "Democratie is, among most Civill nations, accounted the meanest and worst of all formes of Government. . . . Historyes doe recorde, that it hath been allwayes of least continuance and fullest of troubles." "John Winthrop's Defense," p. 383.

86. "Negative Vote," p. 282. Winthrop was here appealing to the Puritan belief that "there was a sphere in which natural reason was fully competent—'the knowledge of civill and humane things', as Richard Greenham put it." John Morgan, *Godly Learning: Puritan Attitudes towards Reason, Learning, and Education, 1560–1640* (Cambridge, England, 1986), p. 48.

87. Shurtleff, *Records,* 2:46.

88. Cotton's advocacy of a ministerial veto within each church was undoubtedly one of the differences that prompted Hooker to remove to Connecticut.

89. "John Winthrop's Defense," p. 386.

90. Ibid., p. 387. Revealingly, Winthrop reached for a mechanical metaphor to illustrate his consequentialist political theory. Such mechanical metaphors would come to replace the organic imagery of the Aristotelian teleological theory in the political philosophy of the Anglo-American Enlightenment.

91. "Negative Vote," p. 282.

92. Ibid., p. 283.

93. This sense of unity was undoubtedly reinforced by the deputies' use of the negative voice to thwart the elders' and magistrates' attempt to inflict the death penalty on the Gortonists.

94. Shurtleff, *Records,* 2:58.

95. Wall, *Massachusetts Bay,* p. 64.

96. *Winthrop Journal,* 2:168–169.

97. Ibid.

98. Ibid., p. 169.

99. "The Governour Dep: Gov. and [Assis]tants doe hereby declare for the full satisfaction of all men, That as by the patent, and election of the people, they are sett aparte to be the councell of this Common wealth to governe the people in the vacancy of the Generall Courte, and that none can be added unto them of equall power, but by like election." "Declaration of the Governor, Deputy Governor, and Assistants of Massachusetts," in *Winthrop Papers,* 4:467.

100. *Winthrop Journal,* 2:169–171.

101. Ibid., pp. 185–186. The date of Endecott's speech is uncertain, for it is entered in the *Winthrop Journal* shortly after the reportage on the emergency meeting but dated May 3.

102. Ibid., p. 204.

103. Ibid., pp. 204–206.

104. Shurtleff, *Records,* 2:95.

CHAPTER SIX

1. The four committees, with their ministerial representatives, are the College Committee (November 20, 1637): Cotton, Wilson, Davenport, Welde, Shepard, and Peter; Legal Code Committee (March 12, 1638): Bulkeley, Phillips, Peter, and Shepard; Wage and Price Com-

mittee (March 12, 1638): Peter, Noyes, Rogers, Norton, Cobbet, Symmes, Shepard, Phillips, Bulkeley, Wilson, Mather, Eliot, Hubbard, and Hull; and Harvard Governance Committee (September 27, 1642): Mather, Cotton, Wilson, Phillips, Knowles, Eliot, Symmes, Allen, and Shepard. See Nathaniel B. Shurtleff, ed., *The Records of the Governor and Company of the Massachusetts Bay in New England* (Boston, 1853), 1:217, 222–223, 2:30.

2. For a list of the first churches in the Bay Colony, replete with dates, see James Savage, ed., *The History of New England From 1630 to 1649. By John Winthrop, Esq. First Governour of the Colony of the Massachusetts Bay. From Original Manuscripts* (Boston, 1825), 1:95–96 (hereafter referred to as *Winthrop Journal*). The total of thirty-four ministers was collated from Frederick Lewis Weis, *The Colonial Clergy and the Colonial Churches of New England* (Lancaster, Mass., 1936), pp. 241–280.

3. George Selement, "Publication and the Puritan Minister," *William and Mary Quarterly,* 3rd ser., 37 (1980):224.

4. The four Massachusetts "prolific ministers" were Cotton, Eliot, Shepard, and Mather. See ibid., table 2, p. 226.

5. Ibid., p. 230.

6. Shurtleff, *Records,* 2:30.

7. Ibid., 1:208.

8. Quoted from Thomas Shepard, "Thomas Shepard's Memoir of Himself," in *Chronicles of the First Planters of the Colony of Massachusetts From 1623–1636,* ed. Alexander Young (Boston, 1846), pp. 550–552. The selectmen of Salem had, on May 2, 1636, set aside a tract of land on Marble Head Neck for a colonial college. Five months later the General Court authorized the first subsidy for what became, after the ensuing Antinomian affair, Harvard College. Both Morison and Stearns suggest that Hugh Peter of Salem was the principal agent behind this first venture in higher education. "Peter's hand is evident in the attempt to secure the College for Salem," states Morison, adding that "he may well have coached the Salem deputies, or John Humfrey, so that the matter of founding the College came to a head at the autumn session." Samuel Eliot Morison, *The Founding of Harvard College* (Cambridge, Mass., 1935), p. 169. Also see Raymond Phineas Stearns, *The Strenuous Puritan: Hugh Peter, 1598–1660* (Urbana, Ill., 1954), pp. 140–141. For the first subsidy by the court, see Shurtleff, *Records,* 1:183.

9. Davenport had earlier contradicted the principle of congregational independence and autonomy by participating in the Synod of 1637.

10. David D. Hall, *The Faithful Shepherd: A History of the New England Ministry in the Seventeenth Century* (New York, 1972), p. 89.

11. Ibid., p. 180.

12. Harry Stout, *The New England Soul: Preaching and Religious Culture in Colonial New England* (New York, 1986), p. 57.

13. "New England's First Fruits," reprinted in Arthur O. Norton, "Harvard College (1636–1660)," in *Commonwealth History of Massachusetts: Colony, Province, and State,* ed. Albert Bushnell Hart (New York, 1927), 1:351.

14. The act ordered "that every towneship in this jurisdiction, after the Lord hath increased them to the number of 50 householders, shall then forthwith appoint one within their towne to teach all such children as shall resort to him to write & reade, whose wages shall be paid either by the parents or masters of such children, or by the inhabitants in generall . . . & it is further ordered, that where any towne shall increase to the number of 100 families or householders, they shall set up a grammar schoole, the master therof being able to instruct youth so far as they may be fitted for the university." Shurtleff, *Records,* 2:203.

15. The following list is culled from John Langdon Sibley, *Biographical Sketches of Graduates of Harvard University in Cambridge, Massachusetts,* vol. 2, (Cambridge, Mass.,

1873; reprint, New York, 1967): Samuel Mather (class of '60), Samuel Carter ('60), Daniel Weld ('61), Caleb Watson ('61), Benjamin Tompson ('62), Samuel Cobbett ('63), John Foster ('67), Daniel Epps ('69), Samuel Phipps ('71), Joseph Hawley ('74), and James Minot ('75).

16. This was the first piece of primary educational legislation in Massachusetts, requiring the selectmen in the various towns to provide for basic literacy. Shurtleff, *Records,* 2:6.

17. Jonathan Mitchell, "A Modell for the Maintaining of students & fellows of choise Abilities at the Colledge in Cambridge," in *Publications of the Colonial Society of Massachusetts* (Boston, 1925), 15:317–321. Mitchell's desire for an educated magistracy also led him to propose a teaching position at Harvard for "the Law & especially in the Laws of the English nation." Ibid., p. 318.

18. The list is, as follows, culled from Sibley, *Biographical Sketches,* vols. 1–2: William Stoughton ('50), Samuell Nowell, ('53), Richard Hubbard ('53), Samuel Bradstreet ('53), Phillip Nelson ('54), Thomas Graves ('56), Elisha Cooke ('57), Nathaniell Saltonstall ('59), Peter Bulkeley ('60), John Holyoke ('62), Joseph Pynchon ('64), Joseph Dudley ('65), Adam Winthrop ('68), Samuel Phipps ('71), Samuel Sewall ('71), Thomas Bowles ('71), and Joseph Hawley ('74).

19. Thomas Shepard, Jr., *Eye-Salve, Or A Watchword from Our Lord Jesus Christ unto his Church* . . . (Cambridge, Mass., 1673), Evans Early American Imprints #182, p. 11. Shepard urged his auditors to "pray that the Lord will please to maintain and uphold the same, even a godly and learned Magistracy and Ministry among us, that the Lord will make our Leaders in both orders instrumental to keep the people chast and loyall to Christ Jesus." Ibid., p. 26.

20. Shurtleff, *Records,* 1:183.

21. Morison, *Founding of Harvard,* p. 169.

22. Shurtleff, *Records,* 1:208.

23. Norton, "Harvard College," p. 347. Morison reports that according to treasurer Thomas Danforth, the actual value of the John Harvard bequest was £779, 17s., 2d. Morison, *Founding of Harvard,* p. 222.

24. Collated from "Harvard College Book III," in *Publications of the Colonial Society of Massachusetts* (Boston, 1925), 15:174–175.

25. Winthrop reports that many in the General Court disliked the mission, "supposing that it would be [correctly] conceived we had sent them on begging." *Winthrop Journal,* 2:31–32.

26. Morison, *Founding of Harvard,* p. 309; "Harvard College Book III," p. 175.

27. *Winthrop Journal,* 2:31–32.

28. Morison, *Founding of Harvard,* p. 292.

29. *Winthrop Journal,* 2:214–215.

30. "Harvard College Book III," pp. 179–180.

31. Lawrence A. Cremin, *American Education: The Colonial Experience, 1607–1783* (New York, 1970), p. 222.

32. Shurtleff, *Records,* 2:30.

33. Mark H. Curtis, *Oxford and Cambridge in Transition, 1558–1642: An Essay on Changing Relations between the English Universities and English Society* (Oxford, 1959), p. 18. It is worth noting, however, that subsequent colonial colleges would share Harvard's governing structure, with trustees in the place of overseers.

34. "The Harvard College Charter of 1650," in *Publications of the Colonial Society of Massachusetts* (Boston, 1935), 31:3.

35. Thirty pounds of the fine was to be paid to Mr. Briscoe for "satisfaction for the wrong done him." Shurtleff, *Records,* 1:275. Briscoe was held down while Eaton delivered some 200 blows over two hours with a yard-long walnut tree plant. Eaton's undoing was to lay charges on Briscoe for pulling a knife (in self–defense) and swearing to God (for help) before the Gen-

eral Court. The subsequent inquiry by the magistrates revealed the tyrannical nature of Eaton's presidency. Morison, *Founding of Harvard*, p. 234.

36. Morison reports that Winthrop estimated Eaton's malfeasance at a whopping £1,000! Morison, *Founding of Harvard*, p. 223.

37. Ibid., p. 292.

38. *Winthrop Journal*, 2:87–88.

39. Norton, "Harvard College," pp. 349–350.

40. Morison, *Founding of Harvard*, p. 293.

41. Gura claims that Dunster's refusal to present his child for baptism "shocked the colony." He also notes that Dunster "had the rite administered to his three older children," suggesting that his scruple was newly formed. Philip F. Gura, *A Glimpse of Sion's Glory: Puritan Radicalism in New England, 1620–1660* (Middletown, Conn., 1984), p. 121.

42. William G. McLoughlin, *New England Dissent, 1630–1833: The Baptists and the Separation of Church and State* (Cambridge, Mass., 1971), 1:21. The baptist position was that the "ordinance" was "a sign with which the faithful believer publicly demonstrated his obedience to the command of Christ, as a symbol of inward spirituality," and ought to therefore be reserved for adults. E. Brooks Holifield, *The Covenant Sealed: The Development of Puritan Sacramental Theology in Old and New England, 1570–1720* (New Haven, 1970), p. 77. Also see Gura, *Sion's Glory*, p. 94.

43. Shurtleff, *Records*, 3:343–344.

44. Samuel Eliot Morison, *Builders of the Bay Colony* (Boston, 1930; reprint, Boston, 1981), p. 215.

45. McLoughlin, *New England Dissent*, p. 22. Also see Gura, *Sion's Glory*, pp. 121–122.

46. Shurtleff, *Records*, 2:85.

47. Morison, *Builders of the Bay Colony*, p. 215.

48. McLoughlin, *New England Dissent*, p. 22.

49. For example, see the cases of Thomas Painter, Christopher Goodwine, Benaual Bowers, and William Witter in ibid., pp. 16–20.

50. Ibid., p. 22.

51. Joseph Felt, *The Ecclesiastical History of New England; Comprising Not Only Religious, But Also Moral, and Other Relations* (Boston, 1855), 1:342.

52. Morison, *Founding of Harvard*, p. 386.

53. Ibid.

54. On September 6, 1639, Peter offered to travel to Boston "when hee [Knollys] speakes with the ministers." Apparently, Knollys had already offended or alarmed the authorities, for Peter states that "the business will bee to satisfye the State, which how it will bee before the Generall Court I cannot tell." Even so, Peter made a small plea for clemency with Winthrop: "I need not cast my drop into your ocean, who knowe how to deale in these matters, only I tender the man etc." *The Winthrop Papers* (Boston, 1944), 4:140.

55. Ibid., p. 177.

56. *Winthrop Journal* 1:326.

57. Morison, *Founding of Harvard*, p. 386.

58. Ibid.

59. *Winthrop Journal*, 1:250–251.

60. "Conference of the Elders of Massachusetts with the Rev. Robert Lenthall, of Weymouth, Held at Dorchester, Feb. 10, 1639," *Congregational Quarterly* 19 (1877): 248. "Conference" is based on the sketchy notes taken by Robert Keayne, who was in attendance. Israel Stoughton also noted the financial failings of the congregants: "It is a sad thing that here in N.E. there should be any that should desire to enter into a church covenant as members of Jesus Christ, [and should] suffer a godly faithful man to take pains amongst you, and yet not

to give him recompense according to his labor; but that he should be forced to complain to the magistrate, in point of maintenance." Ibid.

61. *Winthrop Journal*, 1:287–288.

62. Ibid.

63. Ibid. At the conference, Jenner claimed that Lenthall had previously told him "that a man was actually justified before God without faith" and that his argument for this doctrine was that "how else could Infants be saved?" "Conference," p. 247.

64. *Winthrop Journal*, 1:287–288.

65. "Conference," p. 237.

66. Reverend Symmes quickly brought Lenthall to his senses by asking, "Dare you lay down your life upon that?" It was not long after that Lenthall saw the error of his ways. Ibid., p. 238.

67. Shurtleff, *Records*, 1:252.

68. *Winthrop Journal*, 1:287–289.

69. Ibid.

70. Shurtleff, *Records*, 1:254.

71. Ibid., p. 14. When Smith recanted of his error to the General Court on May 22, 1639, the court "had ten pounds [of his fine] remitted him." Ibid., p. 258.

72. Ibid., p. 252; *Winthrop Journal*, 1:288–289.

73. "Propositions Concerning Evidence of God's Love," in *Winthrop Papers*, 4:286.

74. Ibid., pp. 286–287.

75. Ibid.

76. Weis, *Colonial Clergy*, p. 47.

77. *Winthrop Journal*, 2:22–23.

78. Ibid.

79. Ibid.

80. Ibid.

81. Weis, *Colonial Clergy*, p. 47.

82. The traditional "left-right" dichotomy is used here in an extremely impressionistic and informal sense. For a more precise analysis of these positions and their relations to each other, see Chapter 9.

83. *Winthrop Papers*, 4:151.

84. At the time of Rogers's letter, the only confirmed practicing presbyterian ministers in the colony were James Noyes and Thomas Parker of Newbury and Peter Hobart and Robert Peck of Hingham.

85. *Winthrop Journal*, 1:241.

86. Shurtleff, *Records*, 1:216. The suggestion took the form of a circular letter signed by Increase Nowell and sent to the various churches calling for the ministers to convene or submit their preferred form of maintenance.

87. Ibid., pp. 240–241.

88. *Winthrop Journal*, 1:295.

89. Ibid., 2:24–25.

90. Ibid., pp. 73–74.

91. William Hubbard, *The Happiness of a People in the Wisdome of their Rulers Directing and in the Obedience of the Brethren Attending Unto what Israel ought to do:* . . . (Cambridge, Mass., 1676), Evans Early American Imprints #214, p. 36.

92. Thomas Lechford, *New-Englands Advice to Old-England*, (London, 1644), UMI microfilms, p. 14.

93. *Winthrop Journal*, 2:91.

94. Ibid., pp. 93–94.

95. Thomas Parker, *The True Copy of a Letter: Written By Mr. Thomas Parker, a learned and godly Minister in New England, unto a Member of the Assembly of Divines now at Westminster* (London, 1644), UMI microfilm, p. 4.

96. *Winthrop Journal*, 2:136–137.

97. According to Francis Bremer, Parker spent his first year in the colony as an assistant to the presbyterian sympathizer Nathaniel Ward, who was then the pastor of Ipswich. Francis J. Bremer, *Puritan Crisis: New England and the English Civil Wars, 1630–1670* (New York, 1989), p. 288.

98. Parker, *True Copy*, p. 4.

99. Lechford, *New-Englands Advice*, pp. 21–22.

100. David Hall has seen this drift toward presbyterianism by the ministers as an attempt to foster stability: "The renewed emphasis upon the synods in the 1640s, the strengthening of the ministers' power in church government, their alliance with the magistrates in defence of 'mixed' government, the requiring of maintenance and the laws against 'contempt'—all these steps they had welcomed as means of stabilizing order." Hall, *Faithful Shepherd*, p. 154.

101. Edward Winslow, *Hypocrisie Unmasked: A True Relation of the Proceedings of the Governor and Company of the Massachusetts Against Samuel Gorton of Rhode Island* (London, 1646; reprint, Providence, R.I., 1916), p. 1.

102. Wall, *Massachusetts Bay*, p. 122.

103. Winslow, *Hypocrisie Unmasked*, p. 55.

104 Ibid.

105. The Gortonists' inability to live peacefully with their neighbors may have been in part the result of their belief that "heaven was a condition of the soul *on earth,* and the divine spark of regeneration implied the immediate and eternal destruction of evil as well as the salvation of good." Gura, *Sion's Glory*, p. 89.

106. Wall, *Massachusetts Bay*, pp. 123–124.

107. *Winthrop Journal*, 2:84.

108. Ibid.

109. Ibid., p. 121.

110. Samuel Gorton, "Simplicity's Defense Against Seven Headed Policy" (London, 1647), in *Collections of the Rhode Island Historical Society* (Providence, R.I., 1835), 2:63. As Larzer Ziff has put it, "Gorton saw the allegiance between the Puritan reliance on learning and Puritan social control. He raised the voice of anti-intellectualism in defence of the disinherited because of intellectualism's alliance with suppression." Larzer Ziff, *Puritanism in America: New Culture in a New World* (New York, 1973), p. 95.

111. Gorton, "Simplicity's Defense," pp. 74–75.

112. Ibid., pp. 84–85.

113. Wall, *Massachusetts Bay*, pp. 129–130.

114. Shurtleff, *Records*, 2:41.

115. Winslow, *Hypocrisie Unmasked*, p. 28.

116. Ibid., pp. 30–31.

117. Ibid., p. 34.

118. Shurtleff, *Records*, 2:44; *Winthrop Journal*, 2:137–138; Winslow, *Hypocrisie Unmasked*, pp. 4–5.

119. Gorton, "Simplicity's Defense," p. 119.

120. *Winthrop Journal*, 2:142.

121. Ibid., pp. 142–144.

122. Shurtleff, *Records*, 2:51.

123. Gorton, "Simplicity's Defense," p. 123.

124. *Winthrop Journal*, 2:146.

125. Ibid.

126. "On every major subject that concerned the church and ministry, the course of their opinion had first run in one direction, the same direction that so many radicals in the history of Puritanism had travelled before them. But events and circumstances accumulating in the late 1630s set a counter trend in motion, and by 1643, with most of the spiritistically minded ministers and laymen silenced or in exile, the immigrants were turning back toward the mainstream of tradition." Hall, *Faithful Shepherd,* p. 115.

127. Shurtleff, *Records,* 2:52.

128. *The Winthrop Papers* (Boston, 1944), 4:456.

129. *Winthrop Journal,* 2:156.

130. Although Gorton would later return to Massachusetts with some vindication from the English authorities, Ziff notes that it was "of special importance" for the Bay Colony "that the short range appeal of Gorton's class-consciousness and anti-intellectualism had been effectively squelched." Ziff, *Puritanism in America,* p. 97.

CHAPTER SEVEN

1. David D. Hall, *The Faithful Shepherd: A History of the New England Ministry in the Seventeenth Century* (New York, 1972), p. 145.

2. Richard Mather, *A Farewell Exhortation* (Cambridge, Mass., 1657), Evans Early American Imprints #47, p. 7.

3. Quoted in Joseph Felt, *The Ecclesiastical History of New England; Comprising Not Only Religious, But Also Moral, and Other Relations* (Boston, 1855), 2:17–18.

4. Nathaniel B. Shurtleff, ed., *The Records of the Governor and Company of the Massachusetts Bay in New England* (Boston, 1853), 2:197.

5. In one respect, the circumstances of this second synod could not have been more ironic. A gathering made up of congregational ministers denounced parts of the presbyterian "way" while their opponents successfully rested on their "congregational" church liberties.

6. Edmund Morgan, *Visible Saints: The History of a Puritan Idea* (Ithaca, N.Y., 1963), p. 143.

7. "A Remonstrance and Petition of Robert Child, and Others," in Thomas Hutchinson, ed., *A Collection of Original Papers Relative to the History of the Colony of Massachusetts-Bay* (Boston, 1769; reprint, Albany, N.Y., 1865), 1:220 (hereafter referred to as *Hutchinson Papers*).

8. Ibid., p. 221.

9. Ibid., p. 220.

10. Shurtleff, *Records,* 2:149, 3:64. On the mercantile petition see ibid., 2:141, 3:51. Winthrop claimed that a portion of the General Court had initially favored the suspension of the laws "for a season" as requested by the merchants. Before the church members could even respond with their own counterpetition, "the elders, hearing of it, went first to the magistrates, and laying before them what advantage it would give to the anabaptists . . . entreated that the law might continue still in force, and the execution of it not suspended." James Savage, ed., *The History of New England From 1630 to 1649. By John Winthrop, Esq. First Governour of the Colony of the Massachusetts Bay. From Original Manuscripts* (Boston, 1825), 2:250–251 (hereafter referred to as *Winthrop Journal*).

11. John Norton, "Sion the Out–cast healed of her Wounds," in *Three Choice and Profitable Sermons* (Cambridge, Mass., 1664), Evans Early American Imprints #90, p. 12.

12. *Winthrop Journal,* 2:264.

13. Ibid., pp. 264–265.

14. John Eliot, *Communion of Churches: or the Divine Management of Gospel-Churches by the Ordinances of Councils, Constituted in Order according to the Scriptures* (Cambridge, Mass., 1665), Evans Early American Imprints #101, p. 4.

15. John Cotton, *A Discourse About Civil Government in a New Plantation Whose Design is Religion* (Cambridge, Mass., 1663), Evans Early American Imprints #79, p. 7. Cotton wrote the document in 1638 for John Davenport, who was then fashioning the church and state of New Haven. See "Notes and Suggestions," *American Historical Review* 37, no. 2 (January 1932): 267–269.

16. *Winthrop Journal,* 2:264–265.

17. Ibid.

18. Shurtleff, *Records,* 3:72–73.

19. Ibid., 2:155–156.

20. Ibid., pp. 154–155, 3:70–72.

21. Richard Mather, *Church-Government and Church-Covenant Discussed* (London, 1643), reprinted in Richard Mather, *Church Covenant: Two Tracts* (New York, 1972), p. 64.

22. *Winthrop Journal,* 2:269–279.

23. Ibid.

24. Ibid., pp. 270–271.

25. Ibid.

26. Ibid.

27. Ibid.

28. Eliot, *Communion of Churches,* pp. 4–5.

29. *Winthrop Journal,* 2:271.

30. Robert Wall, *Massachusetts Bay: The Crucial Decade, 1640–1650* (New Haven, 1972), p. 176.

31. "The Tentative Conclusions of 1646," in *The Creeds and Platforms of Congregationalism,* ed. Williston Walker (New York, 1893; reprint, Boston, 1960), p. 190.

32. Ibid., p. 192.

33. Ibid., p. 193.

34. *Winthrop Journal,* 2:277. For some reason, Felt reports exactly the same story, except that it is situated in Hobart's congregation at Hingham. Felt, *Ecclesiastical History,* 1:579.

35. *Winthrop Journal,* 2:277.

36. Ibid.

37. Shurtleff, *Records,* 2:177.

38. Ibid., 3:98.

39. Ibid., pp. 101–102.

40. Ibid., 2:177–178.

41. Ibid., p. 179.

42. *Winthrop Journal,* 2:308.

43. The court did not actually ban lay "prophesying" or preaching until a few years later. When it did so, it was quickly forced to rescind the order by the storm of protest unleashed by the lay members of the churches.

44. Shurtleff, *Records,* 2:217.

45. "A decade after Cotton called for voluntary maintenance, the ministers were asking the state to intervene on their behalf. The history of maintenance, like the larger history of the ministers' changing social role, reveals that theory was soon tempered by conditions in New England." Hall, *Faithful Shepherd,* p. 122.

46. "The Cambridge Platform," in Walker, *Creeds and Platforms,* p. 205.

47. Ibid., p. 207.

48. Ibid., p. 208.

49. John Cotton, "A Sermon Delivered at Salem, 1636," in *John Cotton on the Churches of New England,* ed. Larzer Ziff (Cambridge, Mass., 1968), p. 57.

50. "The Cambridge Platform," pp. 217–218.

51. Ibid., p. 214.

52. Ibid., p. 219.

53. The platform stated that the withholding of consent without a valid and serious justification was "manifestly contrary unto order, & government, & in-lets of disturbance, & tend to confusion." Ibid.

54. Ibid., p. 221.

55. John Allin, *Animadversions Upon the Antisynodalia Americana* (Cambridge, Mass., 1664), Evans Early American Imprints #83, p. 5.

56. "The Cambridge Platform," p. 224.

57. Shurtleff, *Records,* 2:285.

58. Ibid., 4, part 1, p. 22.

59. Ibid., p. 55.

60. Ibid., pp. 57–58.

61. The dissenters were listed as "Mr. Browne, Capt. Hawthorne, John Johnson, Mr. Henry Bartholomew, Edras Reade, William Cowdry, Walter Haynes, Roger Shaw, Stephen Kinsley, John Holbrooke, Mr. Thomas Clarke, Capt. Leveritt, Mr. Howchean, and Capt. Tynge." Ibid., 3:240.

62. For the case of Mathewes and Malden, see Felt, *Ecclesiastical History,* 2:18, 42–43, 53–54, 60, 62, 69, as well as Shurtleff, *Records,* 3:158–159, 203, 237–238, 250, 276, 294, 4, part 1:21, 42–43, 71, 90, 113. On the baptists in Lynn, see John Clark, *Ill Newes From New-England: or A Narrative of New-Englands Persecution* (London, 1652), reprinted in *Massachusetts Historical Society Collections,* 4th ser. (Boston, 1854), 2:1–118, and Thomas Cobbet, *A Brief Answer to a Scandalous Pamphlet called, Ill News from New-England, written by John Clark of Rhode Island, Physitian,* in Cobbet, *The Civil Magistrates Power in Matters of Religion Modestly Debated, . . .* (London, 1653; reprint, New York, 1972). Also see William G. McLoughlin, *New England Dissent, 1630–1833: The Baptists and the Separation of Church and State* (Cambridge, Mass., 1971), 1:18–21, and Philip F. Gura, *Sion's Glory: Puritan Radicalism in New England, 1620–1660* (Middletown, Conn., 1984), pp. 118–124.

63. Felt, *Ecclesiastical History,* 2:69–70. On the gathering of the second church of Boston, see Frederick Lewis Weis, *The Colonial Clergy and the Colonial Churches of New England* (Lancaster, Mass., 1936), p. 241.

64. Shurtleff, *Records,* 4, part 1, pp. 113–114.

65. Thomas Shepard, *Wine for Gospel Wantons: or, Cautions Against Spiritual Drunkenness* (Cambridge, Mass., 1668), Evans Early American Imprints #130, p. 10. Shepard first preached the sermon at Cambridge on June 25, 1645, during a public fast.

66. Shurtleff, *Records,* 4, part 1, p. 122.

67. Quoted in Felt, *Ecclesiastical History,* 2:96.

68. Ibid., p. 98.

69. Shurtleff, *Records,* 4, part 1, p. 151.

70. Ibid., pp. 156–157.

71. Ibid., 3:334.

72. Ibid., 4, part 1, p. 177.

73. John Mayo was ordained on November 9, 1655. He had been a minister at Barnstable, Plymouth, from 1640 to 1646. Weis, *Colonial Clergy,* p. 241.

74. Shurtleff, *Records,* 4, part 1, p. 199.

75. Peter Bulkeley, *The Gospel Covenant*, 2nd ed. (London, 1651), UMI microfilm, pp. 301–302.

76. Shurtleff, *Records*, 4, part 1, pp. 286–287.

77. These numbers are based on the following list of towns and clergymen: Hingham (100 families) and Hobart (£90), Weymouth (60 families) and Thatcher (£100), Braintree (80 families) and Flint and Thompson (£55 each), Dorchester (120 families) and Mather (£100), Roxbury (80 families) and Eliot and Danforth (£60 each), Dedham (66 families) and Allin (£60), Meadfield (40 families) and Wilson (£50), second church of Boston (no number) and Mayo and Powell (£55 each), and Hull (20 families) and their unnamed minister (£40). Felt, *Ecclesiastical History*, 2:160–161. An earlier and larger list in *Good News from New-England* yields a somewhat smaller average of £54 per year. See *Good News from New-England* (London, 1648), in *Massachusetts Historical Society Collections*, 4th ser. (Boston, 1852), 1:212.

78. Hall, *Faithful Shepherd*, p. 183.

79. Shurtleff, *Records*, 4, part 1, pp. 314–315.

80. Carla Gardina Pestana, "The City upon a Hill under Siege: The Puritan Perception of the Quaker Threat to Massachusetts Bay, 1656–1661," in *New England Quarterly* 56, no. 3 (1983): 323.

81. Felt, *Ecclesiastical History*, 2:143.

82. "From the first visit in 1656 to the first hangings in 1659, thirty-three Quakers entered the Bay Colony, a figure unmatched by any other colony except New Plymouth over which many of them traveled." Jonathan M. Chu, *Neighbors, Friends, or Madmen: The Puritan Adjustment to Quakerism in Seventeenth-Century Massachusetts Bay* (Westport, Conn., 1985), p. 39.

83. Chu notes that the magistrates never punished Quakers for mere heresy, but as with other dissenters, "they punished the Quakers because their heterodoxy led to the disturbance of public tranquility." Ibid., p. 13.

84. Richard P. Gildrie, *Salem, Massachusetts, 1626–1683: A Covenant Community* (Charlottesville, Va., 1975), p. 133. Jonathan Chu claims that the two visiting Quakers, Christopher Holder and John Copeland, had come expressly to "disturb the services of the orthodox Salem congregation" rather than "preach to the embryonic Quaker meeting." Chu, *Neighbors*, p. 62.

85. Shurtleff, *Records*, 3:415–416.

86. Ibid., 4, part 1, pp. 314–315.

87. Chu, *Neighbors*, p. 75.

88. Kai Erikson offers a vivid and dramatic account of the public "festivities" surrounding the execution of William Robinson and Marmaduke Stevenson. It is a particularly compelling and well-written example of the morbid fascination that absorbed both the historical agents and their chroniclers. Kai T. Erikson, *Wayward Puritans: A Study in the Sociology of Deviance* (New York, 1966), pp. 120–121.

89. For Quaker tactics toward the churches, see Pestana, "The City upon a Hill under Siege," pp. 330–336.

90. Ibid., p. 347. Also see Gildrie, *Salem*, p. 130.

91. John Norton, *The Heart of New England Rent* (Cambridge, Mass., 1659), Evans Early American Imprints #56, p. 39.

92. Ibid., p. 40. Norton had been commissioned to draft this treatise by the General Court in December 1658. Chu, *Neighbors*, p. 22.

93. Norton, *Heart Rent*, p. 39.

94. John Cotton, *A Discourse About Civil Government in a New Plantation*, p. 21.

95. "In effect, the synod's majority was arguing for a broad view of the Church as an institution that not only nourished the regenerate but also dispensed grace to the unsaved."

E. Brooks Holifield, *The Covenant Sealed: The Development of Puritan Sacramental Theology in Old and New England, 1570–1720* (New Haven, 1974), p. 171.

96. Increase Mather, *A Discourse Concerning the Subject of Baptisme* (Cambridge, Mass., 1675), Evans Early American Imprints #207, p. 30.

97. Allin, *Animadversions,* p. 7.

98. Robert G. Pope, *The Half-Way Covenant: Church Membership in Puritan New England* (Princeton, 1969), pp. 266–269.

99. See "Result of the Synod of 1662," in Walker, *Creeds and Platforms,* p. 303.

100. Young, *Good Order,* pp. 110–111.

101. "Result of the Synod of 1662," p. 337.

102. Ibid., p. 339.

103. John Davenport, *Another Essay for the Investigation of the Truth* (Cambridge, Mass., 1663), Evans Early American Imprints #78, p. 1.

104. It is important to note that this "innovation" was not the result of a "declining" second generation of ministers, as some have supposed. Rather, as Hall has noted, first-generation ministers were still a majority of the participants at the Synod of 1662. Hall, *Faithful Shepherd,* p. 199.

105. Thomas Hooker, *A Survey of the Summe of Church Discipline* (London, 1648), part 3, pp. 13–14.

106. Mather, *Church-Government,* p. 22.

107. Quoted in Increase Mather, *The First Principles of New-England, Concerning the Subject of Baptisme & Communion of Churches* (Cambridge, Mass., 1675), Evans Early American Imprints #208, pp. 15–16.

108. Mather, *Church-Government,* p. 20.

109. Quoted in Mather, *First Principles,* pp. 2–3.

110. For the orthodox view of the half-way covenant that baptism or descent from a full member in communion itself confers membership, there is Norton's comment: "Children of Parents in Church Covenant are Church members, and ought to be baptized." Quoted in ibid., p. 15. Thomas Shepard argued to the same effect on the basis of a distinction between the "outward" and "inward" covenants. "Hence therefore it is," he wrote, "that when we say that Children are in Covenant, and so Church–Members the meaning is, not that they are alwaies in inward Covenant, and inward Church–Members, who enjoy the inward, and saveing benefits of the Covenant, but that they are in external, and outward Covenant, and therefore outwardly Church Members, to whom belongs some outward priviledges of the Covenant for their inward and eternall good." Thomas Shepard, *The Church Membership of Children and their Right to Baptisme* (Cambridge, Mass., 1663), Evans Early American Imprints #82, p. 2.

111. John Davenport, *An Answer of the Elders of the Severall Churches in New-England Unto Nine Positions, Sent Over to them (By Divers Reverend and Godly Ministers in England) to Declare Their Judgements Therein* (London, 1643), reprinted in Richard Mather, *Church Covenant: Two Tracts* (New York, 1972).

112. Allin, *Animadversions,* p. 5.

113. On this disjunction Allin was particularly ruthless toward the clerical and lay opponents: "We see evidently, that the Principles of our Dissenting Brethren give great Advantages to the Antipoedobaptists, which if we be silent, will tend much to their Encouragement and Encrease, to the Hazard of our Churches." Ibid., p. ii.

114. Mather, *First Principles,* p. iv.

115. "That the Infant-seed are in their own persons actually Members of the Church, being actually in this Covenant with God as his People, and he Their God, and having the Covenant in their flesh, the Seal of it [baptism] applied to their persons. And hence they cannot be cutt off from their interest in God, and his Covenant-Priviledges, but in such a

way as he hath ordained, which in Gospel times is by Church-censures." Allin, *Animadversions,* p. 18.

116. "Result of the Assembly of 1657," in Walker, *Creeds and Platforms,* pp. 294–295.

117. Shurtleff, *Records,* 4, part 1, p. 420.

118. Wall, *Massachusetts Bay,* p. 150.

119. Norton, "Sion the Outcast," p. 8.

120. Ibid., p. 13.

121. Shurtleff, *Records,* 4, part 2, p. 38.

122. Ibid., p. 60.

123. Emory Elliott, *Power and the Pulpit in Puritan New England* (Princeton, 1975).

CHAPTER EIGHT

1. James Allen was ejected from his fellowship at New College, Oxford, for nonconformity in 1662. He arrived in Boston on June 10 of that year. Oxenbridge had been a lecturer at Berwicke-on-Tweed and was also silenced in 1662. He moved to Suriname in that year and settled in Barbados some five years later. He arrived in Boston in 1670 and became a minister in the first church of Boston, filling the position that Davenport had held. Frederick Lewis Weis, *The Colonial Clergy and the Colonial Churches of New England* (Lancaster, Mass., 1936), pp. 19, 155.

2. John Mayo came to Plymouth Colony in 1638, was ordained pastor at Barnstable in 1640, and moved to the pulpit of Eastham in 1646. He moved to Boston in 1655 and became the first minister of the second church of Boston. Ibid., p. 139. Chauncy arrived in Plymouth in the same year as Mayo and served as minister at Scituate from 1641 to 1654, when he became president of Harvard. Samuel Eliot Morison, *The Founding of Harvard College* (Cambridge, Mass., 1935), appendix B, p. 371.

3. Notably, Eleazar Mather switched sides and became a vigorous proponent of the half-way covenant in the aftermath of the conflict over the third church of Boston and his father's death. See Eleazar Mather, *A Serious Exhortation to the Present and Succeeding Generation in New England* (Cambridge, Mass., 1671), Evans Early American Imprints #162, esp. pp. 18–19, 24.

4. On Increase Mather's pre-Restoration career, see Michael G. Hall's excellent biography, *The Last American Puritan: The Life of Increase Mather, 1639–1723* (Middletown, Conn., 1988), pp. 29–49.

5. "Nathaniel Mather to John Rogers, March 23, 1651," in *Mather Papers, Massachusetts History Society Collections* (Boston, 1868), 4th ser., 8:3.

6. Mather reported receiving two ministerial offers after being in the city for less than three hours. One of the offers he calculated as worth £104 per year: "Tis incredible what an advantage to preferment it is to have been a New English man." "Nathaniel Mather to John Rogers, December 23, 1651," in *Mather Papers,* pp. 4–5.

7. John Norton, "Sion the Outcast healed of her Wounds," in *Three Choice and Profitable Sermons* (Cambridge, Mass., 1664), Evans Early American Imprints #90, p. 3.

8. Ibid.

9. Ibid., p. 6.

10. Ibid., p. 7.

11. Ibid., p. 12. Norton made the same claim about the Cambridge Platform in a lecture he delivered on April 2, 1663, three days before his death: "That our polity may be a Gospel polity, and may be compleat according to the Scriptures answering fuly the Word of God: this the work of our generation, and the very end of it, that which is written upon the forehead of

New England, viz *The compleat walking in the Faith of the Gospel according to the Order of the Gospel.* And for your direction; . . . you have the *Platform of Church-Discipline* given to you in way of Council." John Norton, "The Evangelical Worshipper, Subjecting to the Prescription and Sovereignty of Scripture Pattern," in *Three Choice and Profitable Sermons,* p. 37.

12. Norton, "Sion the Outcast," p. 8.

13. Ibid., pp. 9–10.

14. Ibid., p. 13.

15. Ibid., p. 10.

16. Urian Oakes, *New England Pleaded With* (Cambridge, Mass., 1673), Evans Early American Imprints #180, p. 50.

17. Nathaniel B. Shurtleff, ed., *The Records of the Governor and Company of the Massachusetts Bay in New England,* (Boston, 1853), 4, part 2, pp. 24–26. The best discussion of the disputes over imperial policy in these years is Paul R. Lucas, "Colony or Commonwealth: Massachusetts Bay, 1661–1666," *William and Mary Quarterly,* 3rd ser., 24 (1967): 88–107.

18. Shurtleff, *Records,* 4, part 2, p. 34.

19. Ibid., p. 37. On the political wrangling behind the agency of Norton and Bradstreet, see Lucas, "Colony or Commonwealth," pp. 93–94.

20. Shurtleff, *Records,* 4, part 2, p. 38.

21. On the opposition of Bartholomew and Hawthorne, see Richard P. Gildrie, *Salem, Massachusetts, 1626–1683: A Covenant Community* (Charlottesville, Va., 1975), p. 144. On lay support for the half-way covenant at the synod, see Robert G. Pope, *The Half-Way Covenant: Church Membership in Puritan New England* (Princeton, 1969), p. 48.

22. This proposition described the adult noncommunicating seed of the brethren as "Church-members who were admitted in minority" and stated that if they had historical faith and godly conversation they could voluntarily "own the covenant" and present their children for baptism. See "Result of the Synod of 1662," in *The Creeds and Platforms of Congregationalism,* ed. Williston Walker (New York, 1893; reprint, Boston, 1960), p. 314. Since baptism had confirmed their own "half-way" membership, the obvious implication was that having their children baptized would confer the same membership and discipline on them.

23. Shurtleff, *Records,* 4, part 2, p. 60.

24. "Eleazar Mather to John Davenport, July 4, 1662," in *Mather Papers,* pp. 192–193.

25. "Result of 1662," p. 304.

26. "Eleazar Mather to John Davenport, July 4, 1662," pp. 192–193.

27. John Allin, *Animadversions Upon the Antisynodalia Americana* (Cambridge, Mass., 1664), Evans Early American Imprints #83, p. 5.

28. "Increase Mather to J. Davenport, October 21, 1662," in *Mather Papers,* p. 205.

29. The printing of Davenport's essay was made possible by an act of the General Court lifting the censorship of the press on May 27, 1663. Shurtleff, *Records,* 4, part 2, p. 73.

30. Hall, *Last American Puritan,* p. 60.

31. John Davenport, *Another Essay for the Investigation of the Truth* (Cambridge, Mass., 1663), Evans Early American Imprints #78, p. 1.

32. Ibid., unpaginated preface.

33. Allin, *Animadversions,* preface, p. 11.

34. Richard Mather and Jonathan Mitchell, *A Defense of the Answer and Arguments of the Synod Met at Boston in the Year 1662* (Cambridge, Mass., 1664), Evans Early American Imprints #89, p. 3.

35. Ibid., p. 1.

36. John Higginson, *The Cause of God and His People in New-England* (Cambridge, Mass., 1663), Evans Early American Imprints #80, p. 4.

37. Ibid., p. 14. On the subject of the consociation of churches, Higginson urged that "there should be a frequent use of Councils amongst us to enquire after the mind of God and his word." Ibid., p. 16.

38. Lawrence Shaw Mayo, *John Endecott: A Biography* (Cambridge, Mass., 1936), p. 270.

39. "A Copy of the King's Letter to the General Court of Massachusetts, June 28, 1662," in Shurtleff, *Records,* 4, part 2, p. 164.

40. Ibid., p. 165.

41. Ibid.

42. Ibid., p. 166.

43. "Eleazar Mather to John Davenport, July 4, 1662," in *Mather Papers,* p. 193.

44. Lucas, "Colony or Commonwealth," p. 96.

45. The king had specifically stated that "at the next Generall Court of that our colony, this our letter & declaration be communicated & published, that all our loving subjects within that our plantation may know our grace & favour to them." "Copy of the King's Letter to the General Court," p. 166.

46. Higginson, *Cause of God,* pp. 20–21.

47. "Mr. Humphrey Davie to J. Davenport," in *Mather Papers,* p. 204.

48. Ibid.

49. Mayo, *John Endecott,* p. 272.

50. The church was actually gathered in Charlestown but shortly thereafter moved to Noddle's Island and finally settled in Boston in 1674. William G. McLoughlin, *New England Dissent, 1630–1833: The Baptists and the Separation of Church and State* (Cambridge, Mass., 1971), 1:49.

51. Walker, *Creeds and Platforms,* p. 304.

52. On the distinction between Particular and General Baptists, see Philip F. Gura, *A Glimpse of Sion's Glory: Puritan Radicalism in New England, 1620–1660* (Middletown, Conn., 1984), p. 107.

53. Stephen Foster, *The Long Argument: English Puritanism and the Shaping of New England Culture, 1570–1700* (Chapel Hill, N.C., 1991), pp. 176–177.

54. See, for example, Thomas Shepard, *The Church Membership of Children and their Right to Baptisme* (Cambridge, Mass., 1663), Evans Early American Imprints #82, pp. 1–6, and Allin, *Animadversions,* pp. 14–18.

55. Davenport, *Another Essay,* pp. 3–4.

56. "The Baptist Debate of April 14–15, 1668," ed. William G. McLoughlin and Martha Whiting Davidson, in *Proceedings of the Massachusetts Historical Society* (Boston, 1964), 3rd ser., 76:127.

57. Allin, *Animadversions,* p. ii.

58. McLoughlin, *New England Dissent,* 1:51–57. For a more detailed account of Goold's case, see the transcript from the records of the Church of Charlestown and Goold's own narrative in Nathan E. Wood, *The History of the First Baptist Church of Boston (1665–1899)* (Philadelphia, 1899; reprint, New York, 1980), pp. 39–51.

59. The account of Osborne's dealings with the church of Charlestown is from the written account presented by Thomas Shepard during the baptist debate of 1668. See McLoughlin and Davidson, "Baptist Debate," p. 120. The quote is from ibid., p. 117.

60. On Farnam's dealings with the second church of Boston, and Increase Mather in particular, see Hall, *Last American Puritan,* pp. 66–71. The quote is from the narrative of the church of Boston read at the baptist debate in McLoughlin and Davidson, "Baptist Debate," p. 125.

61. Shurtleff, *Records,* 4, part 2, p. 164.

62. Ibid., p. 162.

63. The act enfranchised all twenty-four-year-old freeholders ratable at 10 shillings per year in taxes who could obtain a letter from the local minister certifying "that they are orthodox in religion, & not vitious in theire lives." Shurtleff, *Records,* 4, part 2, pp. 117–118. As J. M. Sosin has noted, very few householders could meet this property qualification. J. M. Sosin, *English America and the Restoration Monarchy of Charles II: Transatlantic Politics, Commerce, and Kinship* (Lincoln, Nebr., 1980), p. 112. Moreover, it is highly unlikely that any clergyman would certify that any Anglican, baptist, or Quaker was "orthodox in religion."

64. Sosin, *English America,* p. 112; Lucas, "Colony or Commonwealth," p. 101.

65. The letter is in Shurtleff, *Records,* 4, part 2, pp. 129–133.

66. These petitions came from Cambridge, Woburn, Dorchester, Redding, Chelmsford, Concord, Billerica, Boston, Dedham, Medfield, and Roxbury. Ibid., pp. 136–137.

67. McLoughlin, *New England Dissent,* 1:57.

68. Shurtleff, *Records,* 4, part 2, p. 173.

69. Ibid., pp. 195–199.

70. Sosin, *English America,* p. 119.

71. Wood, *First Baptist Church,* p. 42.

72. Ibid., p. 66.

73. McLoughlin, *New England Dissent,* 1:58.

74. Shurtleff, *Records,* 4, part 2, pp. 290–291.

75. McLoughlin, *New England Dissent,* 1:60.

76. Jonathan Mitchell, *Nehemiah On the Wall in Troublesome Times* (Cambridge, Mass., 1671), Evans Early American Imprints #163, p. 3.

77. Ibid., p. 27.

78. Ibid., p. 13.

79. Ibid., p. 23.

80. Ibid., p. 26.

81. McLoughlin, *New England Dissent,* 1:61.

82. McLoughlin and Davidson, "Baptist Debate," p. 112.

83. Ibid., p. 110.

84. Ibid., p. 115.

85. McLoughlin, *New England Dissent,* 1:61.

86. Shurtleff, *Records,* 4, part 2, p. 374.

87. McLoughlin, *New England Dissent,* 1:71; Wood, *First Baptist Church,* p. 81.

88. Wood, *First Baptist Church,* p. 82.

89. Shurtleff, *Records,* 4, part 2, p. 404.

90. McLoughlin, *New England Dissent,* 1:72; Wood, *First Baptist Church,* p. 88.

91. Wood, *First Baptist Church,* p. 86.

92. Shurtleff, *Records,* 4, part 2, p. 413; Wood, *First Baptist Church,* p. 86; McLoughlin, *New England Dissent,* 1:71–72.

93. McLoughlin, *New England Dissent,* 1:72; Wood, *First Baptist Church,* p. 89.

94. On the role of the imperial question in the schism in the first church of Boston, see Richard C. Simmons, "The Founding of the Third Church in Boston," *William and Mary Quarterly,* 3rd ser., 26 (1969):241–252.

95. "Mr. Humphrie Davie to J. Davenport, 1662," in *Mather Papers,* p. 204.

96. The dissenting minority in the first church of Boston who would form the Old South specifically listed the church's prior endorsement of the synodic result as an objection to the proposed ministry of John Davenport. See their letter to the majority of the first church of Boston, dated September 30, 1677, in the "Third Church Narrative," which is reproduced in Hamilton A. Hill, *History of the Old South (Third Church) Boston, 1669–1884* (New York, 1890), 1:17.

97. On the candidacy of Thacher in the first church of Boston, see ibid., p. 17. On Thacher, see Weis, *Colonial Clergy,* p. 202.

98. "John Davenport to the First Church, Boston," in *Letters of John Davenport,* ed. Isabel MacBeath Calder (New Haven, 1937), pp. 269–270.

99. Ibid., pp. 271–273.

100. Hill, *Old South,* p. 23.

101. The sermon was delivered on July 16. Ibid., p. 24.

102. Ibid., pp. 25–27.

103. Ibid., p. 29.

104. See the copy of this letter in ibid., pp. 30–31.

105. The "Third Church Narrative" claims that this letter was read to some twenty–two members of the first church majority, "which managed the whole." Ibid., p. 29.

106. Ibid., p. 36.

107. Copies of the two versions of the letter of dismission from New Haven are reproduced in ibid., pp. 33–36.

108. On the same day, December 9, James Allen was ordained as the teacher of the first church of Boston. In his ordination sermon, Davenport cheekily claimed, "Thou Lord knowest I did not make hast to be a Past[o]r over this people, but waited on these to know thy mind." "John Davenport to the First Church, Boston," in Calder, *Letters of John Davenport,* p. 279.

109. Hill, *Old South,* p. 49. In fact, this council had reconvened on November 23 at the behest of the dissenters. The fruit of their labors was minimal, however, for all they could extract from Davenport and his fellow elders was an acknowledgment that the dissenters' silence at his ordination would not "conclude them, as Coactors with the Church there in." Ibid., p. 37.

110. Ibid., pp. 52–53.

111. The dissenters' and Eliot and Allin's requests for this council of churches are reproduced in ibid., pp. 53–55.

112. Ibid., pp. 55–57.

113. "Elders of the First Church, Boston, to a Council of the Neighboring Churches," in Calder, *Letters of John Davenport,* p. 279.

114. "John Davenport and James Penn to a Council of the Neighboring Churches," in ibid., p. 280.

115. The third letter from the council and the proceedings of the first church of Boston are in Hill, *Old South,* pp. 60–63.

116. Weis, *Colonial Clergy,* p. 136.

117. The report of the council is reproduced in Hill, *Old South,* pp. 63–67.

118. This letter is reproduced in ibid., pp. 50–51.

119. These letters of approbation are reproduced in ibid., p. 27.

120. "John Davenport, James Allen, and James Penn to the Elders and Messengers of the Churches Assembled at Charlestown for the Gathering of the Third Church, Boston," in Calder, *Letters of John Davenport,* pp. 280–281.

121. Examples include Norton, "Sion the Outcast"; Higginson, *The Cause of God and His People in New-England;* and Mitchell, *Nehemiah On the Wall in Troublesome Times.* These election sermons were delivered in 1661, 1663, and 1667, respectively.

122. William Stoughton, *New-Englands True Interest* (Cambridge, Mass., 1670), Evans Early American Imprints #156, p. 19.

123. Ibid., p. 20.

124. Ibid., p. 31.

125. Ibid., p. 35.

126. John Davenport, *A Sermon Preach'd at the Election of the Governour, at Boston in New-England, May 19th 1669* (1670), in *Publications of the Colonial Society of Massachusetts* (Boston, 1907), 10:5.

127. Ibid., p. 6.

128. Ibid., p. 11.

129. Ibid., p. 12.

130. Ibid., p. 13.

131. Ibid.

132. Ibid., p. 12.

133. The two versions of Davenport's letter of dismission were read in the first church of Boston on June 17, 1669, by the entire congregation. Teacher Allen and ruling elder Penn attempted to take the blame for this forgery upon themselves. Hill, *Old South,* p. 82.

134. The report is reproduced in ibid., pp. 84–87. The quote is on p. 86.

135. Ibid., p. 87.

136. Ibid., p. 82.

137. This petition is reproduced in ibid., p. 96.

138. Samuel Danforth, *A Brief Recognition of New-Englands Errand Into the Wilderness* (Cambridge, Mass., 1671), Evans Early American Imprints #160, p. 3.

139. Ibid., p. 11.

140. Ibid., p. 12.

141. Ibid., p. 18.

142. The magistrates' letter to the deputies is reproduced in Hill, *Old South,* p. 95.

143. This charge is reproduced in ibid., p. 98.

144. The letter to the deputies is reproduced in ibid., p. 99.

145. The letter to the magistrates is reproduced in ibid., p. 101.

146. This letter to the magistrates is reproduced in ibid., p. 103.

147. Hill, *Old South,* p. 107; Perry Miller, *The New England Mind: From Colony to Province* (Cambridge, Mass., 1953), p. 108; Foster, *The Long Argument,* p. 207.

148. Foster, *Long Argument,* p. 207.

149. Miller, *The New England Mind,* p. 18; Pope, *The Half-Way Covenant,* p. 174.

150. John Oxenbridge, *New-England Freemen* (Cambridge, Mass., 1673), Evans Early American Imprints #181, p. 22.

151. Ibid., p. 26.

152. Ibid., p. 19.

153. Ibid., p. 37. On foreign policy, he claimed that the charter was "the true and proper ligament to the Crown" and insisted that "the Graunt is paid and cannot be re-landed." Ibid., p. 29.

154. Ibid., p. 44.

155. Ibid., pp. 43–44.

156. Ibid., p. 43.

157. This petition is reproduced in Shurtleff, *Records,* 4, part 2, pp. 489–493. The quote is from p. 490.

158. Ibid., p. 493.

159. Ibid., pp. 485–486.

160. This letter of dissent is reproduced in Hill, *Old South,* p. 111.

161. Hall, *Last American Puritan,* p. 81.

162. This letter is reproduced in Hill, *Old South,* pp. 44–45.

163. Increase Mather, *The First Principles of New-England, Concerning the Subject of Baptisme & Communion of Churches* (Cambridge, Mass., 1675), Evans Early American Imprints #208, p. v.

CHAPTER NINE

1. See Increase Mather, *The First Principles of New-England, Concerning the Subject of Baptisme & Communion of Churches* (Cambridge, Mass., 1675), Evans Early American Imprints # 208.

2. On March 6, 1662, Increase married Maria, the only surviving daughter of the late John Cotton. She was his stepsister since his father, Richard, had already married Cotton's widow. Increase Mather, "The Autobiography of Increase Mather," in *Proceedings of the American Antiquarian Society,* ed. M. G. Hall, new ser. (Worcester, Mass., 1961), 71:286.

3. Michael G. Hall, *The Last American Puritan: The Life of Increase Mather, 1639–1723* (Middletown, Conn., 1988), p. 66.

4. Mather, "Autobiography," p. 291. Despite constant complaints of his ill health, this "delicate flower" lived well into his eighties.

5. Ibid., p. 297.

6. Hall, *Last American Puritan,* p. 92.

7. Mather, "Autobiography," p. 301.

8. Increase Mather, *The Day of Trouble is Near* (Cambridge, Mass., 1674), Evans Early American Imprints #192, p. 6.

9. Ibid., p. 23.

10. For a brief account of the causes and course of this conflict, see Ian K. Steele, *Warpaths: Invasions of North America* (New York, 1994), pp. 96–109.

11. Larzer Ziff, *Puritanism in America: New Culture in a New World* (New York, 1973), p. 176; Richard Slotkin and James K. Folsom, eds., *So Dreadfull a Judgment: Puritan Responses to King Philip's War, 1676–1677* (Middletown, Conn., 1978), pp. 3–4.

12. Mather, "Autobiography," p. 302.

13. "Nathaniel Mather to Increase Mather, Feb. 26, 1676," in *Mather Papers, Massachusetts Historical Society Collections,* 4th ser. (Boston, 1868), 8:7–8.

14. Mather, *First Principles,* p. ii.

15. Increase Mather, "Diary of Increase Mather," in *Proceedings of the Massachusetts Historical Society,* 2nd ser. (Boston, 1900), 13:353.

16. Increase Mather, *A Brief History of the Warr With the Indians in New-England* (Boston, 1676), in Slotkin and Folsom, *Dreadfull Judgment,* p. 105; Hall, *Last American Puritan,* p. 107.

17. Nathaniel B. Shurtleff, ed., *The Records of the Governor and Company of the Massachusetts Bay in New England* (Boston, 1853), 5:59–63.

18. Ibid., p. 59.

19. Robert G. Pope, *The Half-Way Covenant: Church Membership in Puritan New England* (Princeton, 1969), p. 185.

20. Mather, "Diary," p. 401.

21. Shurtleff, *Records,* 5:60.

22. Ibid., p. 71.

23. Mather, "Diary," p. 357.

24. Ibid., p. 358.

25. Hall, *Last American Puritan,* p. 113; *Dictionary of American Biography* (New York, 1933), 11:196–197.

26. Mather, "Diary," p. 358.

27. Ibid., pp. 359–360. The two members were Captain Thomas Lake and John Richards, the latter of whom would later serve as an agent for the regime to the king of England.

28. Frederick Lewis Weis, *The Colonial Clergy and the Colonial Churches of New England* (Lancaster, Mass., 1936), pp. 112–113; John Langdon Sibley, *Biographical Sketches of*

Graduates of Harvard University, in Cambridge, Massachusetts (Cambridge, Mass., 1873; reprint, New York, 1967), 1:19. For Hubbard's rivalry with Mather, see Anne Kuesner Nelsen, "King Philip's War and the Hubbard-Mather Rivalry," *William and Mary Quarterly,* 3rd ser., 27 (1970): 615–629.

29. William Hubbard, *The Happiness of a People In the Wisdome of their Rulers Directing and in the Obedience of their Brethren Attending Unto what Israel ought to do . . .* (Cambridge, Mass., 1676), Evans Early American Imprints #214, pp. 46–47.

30. Ibid., p. 31.

31. Ibid., dedicatory epistle to Governor Leverett and the assistants, unpaginated.

32. Ibid., p. 8.

33. Ibid., p. 28.

34. Ibid., p. 26.

35. Mather, *Brief History,* p. 106.

36. Ibid., p. 118.

37. Ibid., p. 126.

38. Ibid., p. 142.

39. Increase Mather, *An Earnest Exhortation to the Inhabitants of New-England, . . .* (Boston, 1676), in Slotkin and Folsom, *Dreadfull Judgment,* p. 167.

40. Ibid., pp. 180–181.

41. Ibid., p. 182.

42. Ibid., p. 167.

43. Ibid., pp. 183–184.

44. Ibid., pp. 182–183.

45. Ibid., p. 174.

46. Mather, "Autobiography," pp. 301–302.

47. Ibid., pp. 302–303.

48. Mather, "Diary," p. 373; Hall, *Last American Puritan,* pp. 127–128.

49. Mather, "Autobiography," p. 303.

50. Ibid.

51. The details of this dispute over whether to hold a day of thanksgiving or fasting are given in "Reverend John Eliot's Records of the First Church in Roxbury, Mass.," in *The New England Historical and Genealogical Register* (Boston, 1879), 33:298–299.

52. Ibid., p. 415.

53. Increase Mather, *A Discourse Concerning the Danger of Apostacy,* published with *A Call from Heaven, To the Present and Succeeding Generations* (Boston, 1685), Evans Early American Imprints #393, p. 76.

54. Ibid., pp. 90, 104.

55. Ibid., p. 90.

56. Ibid., pp. 104–105.

57. Ibid., p. 109.

58. Ibid., pp. 116–117.

59. Hall, *Last American Puritan,* p. 130.

60. Thus, for example, when a group of baptists began to meet in a "publick meetinghouse in Boston" in 1680, the parties were promptly summoned before the General Court. A humble petition by the principal baptists resulted in a mere admonition and order to cease and desist "to meet in that publick place they have built, or any other publick house." Note that the court said nothing about conventicles held in private residences, which was the standard practice of connivance. Shurtleff, *Records,* 5:271–272.

61. George L. Smith, *Religion and Trade in New Netherland: Dutch Origins and American Development* (Ithaca, N.Y., 1978).

62. James Allen, *New-Englands Choicest Blessing* (Boston, 1679), Evans Early American Imprints #260, p. 9.

63. Mather, *Danger of Apostacy,* pp. 130–131.

64. "Simon Bradstreet, Jr., to Increase Mather, April 20, 1681," in *Mather Papers,* p. 31.

65. Mather, *Danger of Apostacy,* p. 121.

66. Ibid., p. 103.

67. Hall, *Last American Puritan,* p. 149.

68. Increase Mather, *Renewal of Covenant* (Boston, 1677), Evans Early American Imprints #239, p. 16.

69. Ibid., p. 19.

70. Mather, *An Earnest Exhortation,* p. 183.

71. "Thomas Cobbet to Increase Mather, November 12, 1678," in *Mather Papers,* p. 290.

72. Hall, *Last American Puritan,* p. 147.

73. The extract of this petition in Williston Walker, ed., *The Creeds and Platforms of Congregationalism,* (New York, 1893; reprint, Boston, 1960), p. 414.

74. Shurtleff, *Records,* 5:215.

75. Ibid., p. 216.

76. Stephen Foster, *The Long Argument: English Puritanism and the Shaping of New England Culture, 1570–1700* (Chapel Hill, N.C., 1991), p. 229.

77. Shurtleff, *Records,* 5:244.

78. "Result of 1679," in Walker, *Creeds and Platforms,* p. 425.

79. Ibid., pp. 432, 426.

80. Ibid., pp. 434–437.

81. Ibid., p. 435.

82. Ibid., p. 433. An account of this debate can be found in the extract from Peter Thacher's journal in ibid., p. 419. For a brief and sympathetic account of Stoddard's role in the synod and his long-standing rivalry with Mather, see Perry Miller, "Solomon Stoddard, 1643–1729," *Harvard Theological Review* 34 (1941): 277–320.

83. *Confession of Faith Owned and Consented unto by the Elders and Messengers of the Churches Assembled at Boston in New-England, May 12, 1680* (Boston, 1680), Evans Early American Imprints #280, p. 51.

84. Shurtleff, *Records,* 5:244.

85. Samuel Willard of the third church of Boston preached at this event. See Samuel Willard, *Duty of a People that have Renewed their Covenant with God* (Boston, 1680), Evans Early American Imprints #296.

86. Hall, *Last American Puritan,* p. 181.

87. Foster, *Long Argument,* p. 227.

88. Increase Mather, *Practical Truths, Tending to Promote the Power of Godliness* (Boston, 1682), Evans Early American Imprints #322, p. 198.

89. Ibid., p. 210.

90. Ibid,. p. 201.

91. Ibid., p. 196.

92. Ibid., p. 219.

93. Ibid., p. 198.

94. J. M. Sosin, *English America and the Restoration Monarchy of Charles II: Transatlantic Politics, Commerce, and Kinship* (Lincoln, Nebr., 1980), pp. 276–277.

95. Shurtleff, *Records,* 5:99.

96. "Samuel Nowell to Jonathan Bull, Sep. 25, 1676," in *Mather Papers,* p. 573.

97. According to Mather, John Eliot also "scrupled" at the wisdom of this intransigent position, "yet at last Hee consented." Mather, "Diary," p. 369.

98. Shurtleff, *Records,* 5:99.

99. Ibid., pp. 113–114.

100. Sosin, *English America,* pp. 279–282.

101. Shurtleff, *Records,* 5:155, 191–193.

102. Ibid., p. 200.

103. Ibid., p. 202.

104. Sosin, *English America,* p. 286.

105. The court complied with this order in a special session on February 4, 1680. Shurt-leff, *Records,* 5:262.

106. Sosin, *English America,* p. 289.

107. Sibley, *Biographical Sketches,* 2:166.

108. Hall, *Last American Puritan,* p. 189.

109. Shurtleff, *Records,* 5:307; Sosin, *English America,* p. 290.

110. Shurtleff, *Records,* 5:347.

111. Ibid.

112. Ibid., p. 349.

113. "John Richards to Increase Mather, London, Aug. 21, 1682," in *Mather Papers,* p. 495.

114. Sosin, *English America,* p. 291.

115. "John Richards to I. Mather, London, Sept. 25, 1682," in *Mather Papers,* p. 496.

116. Shurtleff, *Records,* 5:383–384.

117. Ibid., p. 385.

118. Ibid., pp. 385–386.

119. Ibid., p. 386.

120. Ibid., p. 390.

121. "Nathaniel Mather to Increase Mather, May 19, 1683," in *Mather Papers,* p. 51.

122. Sosin, *English America,* pp. 292–293.

123. Shurtleff, *Records,* 5:423.

124. Mather, "Autobiography," pp. 307–308.

125. Shurtleff, *Records,* 5:423–425.

126. Mather, "Autobiography," p. 308.

127. Ibid.

128. Shurtleff, *Records,* 5:439.

129. Sosin, *English America,* pp. 296–297.

130. Mather, "Autobiography," p. 313.

131. Shurtleff, *Records,* 5:516–517.

APPENDIX B

1. David Hall, "On Common Ground: The Coherence of American Puritan Studies," *William and Mary Quarterly,* 3rd ser., 44 (1987): 229.

2. The following synopsis of Miller is culled from my reading of *The New England Mind: The Seventeenth Century* (Cambridge, Mass., 1939), *Orthodoxy in Massachusetts, 1630–1650* (Boston, 1933), *The New England Mind: From Colony to Province* (Cambridge, Mass., 1953), and *Errand into the Wilderness* (Cambridge, Mass., 1956).

3. Readers are advised to read that article for a fine and detailed review of the literature. What is offered here is merely a thumbnail sketch of issues that are critical to my own interpretation.

4. William K. B. Stoever, *"A Faire and Easie Way to Heaven": Covenant Theology and Antinomianism in Early Massachusetts* (Middletown, Conn., 1978).

5. Michael McGiffert, "From Moses to Adam: The Making of the Covenant of Works," un-

published manuscript. I am grateful to the author for allowing me to read this valuable and eagerly anticipated manuscript.

6. E. Brooks Holifield, *The Covenant Sealed: The Development of Puritan Sacramental Theology in Old and New England, 1570–1720* (New Haven, 1974).

7. Ross W. Beales, Jr., "The Half-Way Covenant and Religious Scrupulosity: The First Church of Dorchester, Massachusetts, as a Test Case," *William and Mary Quarterly,* 3rd ser., 31 (1974): 465–480; Robert G. Pope, *The Half-Way Covenant: Church Membership in Puritan New England* (Princeton, 1969).

8. Charles Cohen, *God's Caress: The Psychology of Puritan Religious Experience* (New York, 1986).

9. Hall, "Common Ground," p. 211.

10. Ibid., p. 199. On biblicism, see John Coolidge, *The Pauline Renaissance in England: Puritanism and the Bible* (New York, 1970), and Theodore Dwight Bozeman, *To Live Ancient Lives: The Primitivist Dimension in Puritanism* (Chapel Hill, N.C., 1988). Two recent "literary" scholars have dissented from this view and argued for fundamental schisms in clerical thought. See Andrew Delbanco, *The Puritan Ordeal* (Cambridge, Mass., 1989), and Janice Knight, *Orthodoxies in Massachusetts: Rereading American Puritanism* (Cambridge, Mass., 1994).

11. Philip F. Gura, *A Glimpse of Sion's Glory: Puritan Radicalism in New England, 1620–1660* (Middletown, Conn., 1984), p. 9.

12. Francis J. Bremer, *Shaping New Englands: Puritan Clergymen in Seventeenth-Century England and New England* (New York, 1994) and *Congregational Communion: Clerical Friendship in the Anglo-American Puritan Community, 1610–1692* (Boston, 1994); Stephen Foster, *The Long Argument: English Puritanism and the Shaping of New England Culture, 1570–1700* (Chapel Hill, N.C., 1991), "New England and the Challenge of Heresy, 1630 to 1660: The Puritan Crisis in Transatlantic Perspective," *William and Mary Quarterly,* 3rd ser., 38 (1981): 624–660; "English Puritanism and the Progress of New England Institutions, 1630–1660," in *Saints and Revolutionaries: Essays on Early American History,* ed. David Hall, John Murrin, and Thad Tate (New York, 1984), pp. 3–37, and "The Godly in Transit: English Popular Protestantism and the Creation of a Puritan Establishment in America," *Publications of the Colonial Society of Massachusetts* (Boston, 1984), 63:183–238.

13. Patrick Collinson, *The Elizabethan Puritan Movement* (London, 1967), *The Religion of Protestants: The Church in English Society, 1559–1625* (Oxford, 1982), and *Godly People: Essays on English Protestantism and Puritanism* (London, 1983).

14. Collinson, *Elizabethan Puritan Movement,* p. 26. In his study of Puritanism at Cambridge, Peter Lake has argued that "the links of thought and feeling which bound moderate scholars to presbyterian activists and which were rooted in their common evangelical protestant world–view, were more important than mere academic differences over the details of church polity." Peter Lake, *Moderate Puritans and the Elizabethan Church* (New York, 1982), p. 75.

15. Collinson, *Elizabethan Puritan Movement,* pp. 115–119, 232.

16. Lake, *Moderate Puritans,* pp. 73–75.

17. Ibid., p. 113.

18. On Anglicanism, see Collinson, *Elizabethan Puritan Movement,* pp. 26–27, and on Puritanism, see Collinson, "A Comment: Concerning the Name Puritan," *Journal of Ecclesiastical History* 31 (1980): 483–488.

19. Patrick Collinson, "The Jacobean Religious Settlement: The Hampton Court Conference," in *Before the Civil War: Essays on Early Stuart Politics and Government,* ed. Howard Tomlinson (New York, 1983), p. 50.

20. Nicholas Tyacke, *Anti-Calvinists: The Rise of English Arminians, c. 1590–1640* (New York, 1987).

21. For a critical review of this Calvinist consensus, see Richard Cust and Ann Hughes, "Introduction: After Revisionism," in *Conflict in Early Stuart England: Studies in Religion and Politics, 1603–1642,* ed. Richard Cust and Ann Hughes (New York, 1989), esp. pp. 4–6. Peter Lake, noting the occasional promotion of anti-Calvinists, has argued that "consensus" is too strong a term. Instead, he has argued for a Calvinist "hegemony." Peter Lake, "Calvinism and the English Church, 1570–1635," *Past and Present* 114 (1987): 34–35.

22. Collinson has noted that these bishops imposed on the church "a character which was more protestant than the queen had evidently intended." Collinson, *Religion of Protestants,* p. 37. On the Puritan leanings of Grindal, see Collinson, *Elizabethan Puritan Movement,* p. 159, and *Godly People,* pp. 371–397. Tyacke has argued that Calvinist dominance in the church can be found in the composition of the episcopal bench, the operation of press censorship, and the official doctrine of Oxford and Cambridge. See his exchange with Peter White in Nicholas Tyacke, "The Rise of Arminianism Reconsidered," *Past and Present* 115 (1987): 202–203.

23. Lake, *Moderate Puritans,* pp. 225–226. Also see Tyacke, *Anti-Calvinists,* p. 5, and Tyacke, "Arminianism Reconsidered," pp. 204–205.

24. On James's Calvinist credentials, see Nicholas Tyacke, "Puritanism, Arminianism, and Counter-Revolution," in *The Origins of the English Civil War,* ed. Conrad Russell (New York, 1973), p. 123. Susan Holland has recently argued that the stolid Calvinism and conciliatory moderation toward tender Puritan consciences exhibited by Abbot exemplified the church during his tenure in the second decade of the seventeenth century. Susan Holland, "Archbishop Abbot and the Problem of 'Puritanism,'" *Historical Journal* 37 (1994): 24–25.

25. Tyacke has seen the Church of England's participation at Dort as exemplifying its predestinarian heritage, a heritage that was only overthrown in the following decade. Tyacke, "Puritanism, Arminianism, and Counter-Revolution," pp. 128–129.

26. Fincham and Lake argue that the religious peace of the Jacobean establishment was destroyed by the confessional politics of the Thirty Years' War. Kenneth Fincham and Peter Lake, "The Ecclesiastic Policy of King James I," *Journal of British Studies* 24 (1985): 170–182. Bremer also places the end of the Calvinist consensus in the 1610s. Bremer, *Shaping New Englands,* pp. 6–7.

27. Derek Hirst, *Authority and Conflict: England, 1603–1658* (Cambridge, Mass., 1986), p. 100.

28. In his study of the Puritan East Anglian county of Essex, William Hunt has found that only sixteen clerics were deprived of their livings for nonconformity between 1603 and 1610, "hardly a reign of terror." William Hunt, *The Puritan Moment: The Coming of Revolution in an English County* (Cambridge, Mass., 1983), pp. 108–109. Julian Davies has recently argued that this leniency, at least until 1622, was due to the nonenforcement of the terms of the Elizabeth Settlement and the Canons of 1604. Julian Davies, *The Caroline Captivity of the Church: Charles I and the Remoulding of Anglicanism, 1625–1641* (Oxford, 1992), p. 8.

29. Collinson, *Religion of Protestants,* pp. 136–139.

30. Collinson, *Elizabethan Puritan Movement,* p. 443.

31. For a fine recapitulation of this "flowering," see Foster, *Long Argument,* pp. 65–93.

32. Collinson, *Elizabethan Puritan Movement,* p. 444. Collinson has noted that this "steady progress in the country" was accompanied by an erosion of Puritan influence in the court. Ibid., p. 443.

33. Collinson, *Religion of Protestants,* p. 241.

34. Ibid., pp. 149–150. For an extended critique of Michael Walzer, Christopher Hill, and Lawrence Stone, see ibid., pp. 179–187.

35. Collinson, *Elizabethan Puritan Movement,* pp. viii, 60; Lake, *Moderate Puritans,* p. 57. Lake differs from Collinson in that, although he does see moderate Puritan divinity as "the

predominant style current in the Elizabethan Church," he is careful to add that "this is not to replace a crude view of an ideologically monolithic 'oppositionist' puritan movement by an equally distorting consensus and political orthodoxy." Ibid., p. 280.

36. Collinson, *Religion of Protestants,* p. 89. On the distinction between connivance and toleration, see George L. Smith, *Religion and Trade in New Netherland: Dutch Origins and American Development* (Ithaca, N.Y., 1973), pp. 242–244.

37. Ian Green has noted that the bulk of the clergy were, by and large, conformable and even accepted some of the Laudian innovations of the 1630s. Ian Green, "Clerical Prospects and Clerical Conformity in the Early Stuart Church," *Past and Present* 90 (1981): 109–115.

38. Margo Todd, *Christian Humanism and the Puritan Social Order* (New York, 1987). Collinson has also insisted that Puritans pursued social goals that were "common to their class." Collinson, *Religion of Protestants,* p. 187.

39. Collinson, *Elizabethan Puritan Movement,* pp. 27, 71–83. Tyacke has argued that the Puritan opposition to the Laudian regime was actually a conservative counterrevolution against Arminian innovation. Tyacke, "Puritanism, Arminianism, and Counter-Revolution."

40. Cust and Hughes, "Introduction," p. 5.

41. See Kenneth Lockridge, *A New England Town, the First Hundred Years: Dedham, Massachusetts, 1636–1736* (New York, 1970); Philip J. Greven, Jr., *Four Generations: Population, Land, and Family in Colonial Andover, Massachusetts* (Ithaca, N.Y., 1970); and David Grayson Allen, *In English Ways: The Movement of Societies and the Transferal of English Local Law and Custom to Massachusetts Bay in the Seventeenth Century* (New York, 1982). The harmonious nature of New England society has been contested by Darrett B. Rutman, *Winthrop's Boston: A Portrait of a Puritan Town, 1630–1649* (Chapel Hill, N.C., 1965); Stephen Innes, *Labor in a New Land: Economy and Society in Seventeenth-Century Springfield* (Princeton, 1983); and John Frederick Martin, *Profits in the Wilderness: Entrepreneurship and the Founding of the New England Towns in the Seventeenth Century* (Chapel Hill, N.C., 1991).

42. Conrad Russell, *The Crisis of Parliaments: English History, 1509–1660* (New York, 1971); J. S. Morrill, *The Revolt of the Provinces* (London, 1976).

43. Conrad Russell, "The Nature of a Parliament in Early Stuart England," in Tomlinson, *Before the Civil War,* p. 130.

44. Hirst, *Authority and Conflict,* p. 36.

45. Ibid.

46. Tyacke has claimed that "there was an element of accident in the Arminian and royalist partnership." Tyacke, "Puritanism, Arminianism, and Counter-Revolution," p. 139.

47. Over a generation ago, Paul S. Seaver warned against trying to explain the "excesses" of the 1640s "solely in terms of a natural reaction to grievances and oppression." Paul S. Seaver, *The Puritan Lectureships: The Politics of Religious Dissent, 1560–1662* (Stanford, Calif., 1970), p. 69. More recently, Margo Todd has remarked that "until it becomes clear how the conservative, godly magistrates and ministers of Stuart England managed so radically to re-channel English politics and society in the 1640s, historians are not rid of the puritan problem." Todd, *Christian Humanism,* p. 3.

48. Karen Ordahl Kupperman, "Definitions of Liberty on the Eve of Civil War: Lord Saye and Sele, Lord Brooke, and the American Puritan Colonies," *Historical Journal* 32 (1989): 17–33.

49. Tyacke, "Puritanism, Arminianism, and Counter-Revolution."

50. Tyacke, "Arminianism Reconsidered," pp. 211–215, and *Anti-Calvinists,* pp. 166–167. Fincham and Lake have agreed with Lake in finding the real turning point in the rise of Arminianism in the reign of Charles I. Fincham and Lake, "Ecclesiastic Policy," p. 206. Collinson concurs with Tyacke that Laud was "the greatest calamity ever visited upon the English Church." Collinson, *Religion of Protestants,* p. 90.

51. On the combination of Arminian churchmanship and the Crown's support of the Spanish Match and neutrality in the Thirty Years' War, see Tyacke, *Anti-Calvinists,* pp. 46–47, 102–103.

52. Tyacke has claimed that it was in the 1630s that "the earlier Jacobean policy of occasional conformity was abandoned. Nonconformists were now harried with a new intensity and those suspected of such inclinations were assumed to be guilty until they proved their innocence." Ibid., p. 224. He has also argued that the principal evidence of the end of the Calvinist consensus can be found in the operation of print censorship and the theological controversies in the universities. Ibid., pp. 184–186. For the Arminian assault on lectures and such Puritan initiatives as the Feoffees for Impropriations, see Tyacke, "Puritanism, Arminianism, and Counter-Revolution," pp. 138–139.

53. Conrad Russell, "The British Problem and the English Civil War," *History* 72 (1987): 395–415.

54. Tyacke, *Anti-Calvinists,* p. 167.

55. Tyacke, "Puritanism, Arminianism, and Counter-Revolution," pp. 120–121, 143, and "Arminianism Reconsidered," p. 209. Tyacke has found concurrence in his view of the Arminians as revolutionaries and the Puritans as conservative opponents in Lake, "Calvinism and the English Church," p. 33, and J. S. Morrill, "The Ecology of Allegiance in the English Revolution," *Journal of British Studies* 26 (1987): 453.

56. Foster, *Long Argument,* pp. 138–174.

57. David D. Hall, *The Faithful Shepherd: A History of the New England Ministry in the Seventeenth Century* (New York, 1972), pp. 110–111.

58. Stephen Foster, *Their Solitary Way: The Puritan Social Ethic in the First Century of Settlement in New England* (New Haven, 1971); T. H. Breen and Stephen Foster, "The Puritans' Greatest Achievement: A Study of Social Cohesion in Seventeenth-Century Massachusetts," *Journal of American History* 60 (1973–1974): 5–22.

59. Davies, *Caroline Captivity;* Peter White, *Predestination, Policy, and Polemic: Conflict and Consensus in the English Church from the Reformation to the Civil War* (Cambridge, 1992).

60. Davies, *Caroline Captivity,* p. 73.

61. Holland, "Archbishop Abbott," pp. 36–40.

62. Davies, *Caroline Captivity,* pp. 62–63. Also see G. W. Bernard, "The Church of England c. 1529–c. 1642," *History* 75 (1990): 201. Bernard also disputes Tyacke's claim that the Calvinist works were censored by an Arminian plot in the 1630s. Ibid., pp. 197–198.

63. Davies, *Caroline Captivity,* p. 12.

64. Hirst has noted that this policy was reflected in Charles's attempt to "reform" the court's culture/image and prop up the prestige of the peerage. Hirst, *Authority and Conflict,* pp. 162–165. Kevin Sharpe has claimed that "an obsessive concern with order" was central to Charles's directives. Kevin Sharpe, "The Personal Rule of Charles I," in Tomlinson, *Before the Civil War,* p. 59.

65. Davies, *Caroline Captivity,* pp. 46–86. Lake has argued that Arminianism can be seen as fundamentally about sacramental grace and a vision of the Christian community centered around the rites and observances of the holy Church of England rather than antipredestination. Lake, "Calvinism and the English Church," p. 75.

66. Sheila Lambert, "Richard Montague, Arminianism, and Censorship," *Past and Present* 124 (1989): 61–63.

67. Davies, *Caroline Captivity,* p. 122.

68. Ibid., pp. 89–93; Cust and Hughes, "Introduction," p. 24. Peter White has noted that not everyone thought the Elizabethan church was Calvinist and that between 1610 and 1619 Bishop Overall articulated an Anglican view of the church as a via media based on the Thirty-

nine Articles and the Book of Common Prayer, an irenic and patristic view that was not necessarily Calvinist. Peter White, "The Rise of Arminianism Reconsidered," *Past and Present* 101 (1983): 35, 44–45. Peter Lake has argued that Hooker was "close to" the origins of Arminianism. Lake, "Calvinism and the English Church," pp. 41–42. Bernard argues that Hooker's was the view of the church from the perspective of the monarchy and was an apt articulation of Elizabeth's policy. Bernard, "Church of England," pp. 190–191.

69. White, "Rise of Arminianism," p. 5; Tyacke, *Anti-Calvinists*, p. 3. Lake has noted that Bancroft's assault on the antinomian implications of predestinarian preaching at the Hampton Court conference expressed a "very different view of the relations between religion and the social order from that outlined by Cartwright and Chaderton." Lake, *Moderate Puritans*, p. 289.

70. Lake has stated that James's refusal to grant the Lambeth Articles such a confessional status at the Hampton Court conference refuted the "Calvinist claim to represent the sole fount of orthodoxy in the Church of England." Lake, *Moderate Puritans*, p. 236. White has noted that although James tried to play both sides at Hampton Court, his refusal to incorporate the Lambeth Articles or admit any Calvinist buttressing of the Thirty-nine Articles indicated his resolve to deny any further doctrinal reformation. White, "Rise of Arminianism," pp. 38–39.

71. On Elizabeth's lack of Calvinist sympathies, see Collinson, *Religion of Protestants*, p. 31, and Bernard, "Church of England," pp. 186–187. Fincham and Lake argue that James's Calvinism was always mitigated by his view of predestination as a "secondary doctrine." Moreover, they have shown that it was the popular antipapal crusade on behalf of the Protestant cause in the Thirty Years' War and against the proposed Spanish Match for Prince Charles that led James to rethink his indulgent policy toward moderate Puritans and ultimately prompted him to embrace Arminian views. Fincham and Lake, "Ecclesiastic Policy," pp. 191, 199–205. Also see Lake, "Calvinism and the English Church," pp. 70–72, and Davies, *Caroline Captivity*, pp. 104, 130–131. Bernard sees James's doctrinal trimming in the face of foreign policy imperatives as evidence that he was not a partisan Calvinist. Moreover, Bernard argues that the reason for James's attraction to Arminianism was because it expressed a monarchical view of the church as inclusive, ceremonial, and, above all, absolutist in nature. Bernard, "Church of England," pp. 193–195, 201–202.

72. Davies, *Caroline Captivity*, pp. 98–99; Lambert, "Montague," pp. 36–40; White, "Rise of Arminianism," pp. 39–42. In his recent study of Charles's reign, Kevin Sharpe has insisted that "the division in the church, always latent, came to the surface in the last years of James's reign and were a problem bequeathed *to* his son." Kevin Sharpe, *The Personal Rule of Charles I* (New Haven, 1992), p. xvii.

73. White, "Rise of Arminianism," p. 37. Bernard faults Tyacke for ignoring the distinction between single and double predestination in the debates leading to the Lambeth Articles. Bernard, "Church of England," p. 192. Davies argues similarly that "it was less predestination *per se* which was attacked than predestination to reprobation (which was not necessarily synonymous with Calvinist doctrine and certainly alien to Augustinian doctrine)." Davies, *Caroline Captivity*, pp. 92–93. Lake notes that Whitgift stumbled over the issue of final and total assurance in his formulation of the Lambeth Articles, and it was precisely this doctrine/experience that justified the Puritans' reliance on godly conversation as a qualification for membership in the godly community. Lake, "Calvinism and the English Church," pp. 46–47.

74. Lake, "Calvinism and the English Church," pp. 39–41. Cust and Hughes agree that "Whitgift's Calvinism was a matter of belief" that had "few implications for religious practice." Cust and Hughes, "Introduction," p. 25.

75. Two recent studies of the failure of Puritan reformation during the interregnum have both shown how limited the previous Puritan campaign had been among the lower strata of society: Derek Hirst, "The Failure of Godly Rule in the English Republic," *Past and Present*

132 (1991): 33–36, and Christopher Durston, "Puritan Rule and the Failure of Cultural Revolution, 1645–1660," in *The Culture of English Puritanism, 1560–1700,* ed. Christopher Durston and Jacqueline Eales (London, 1996), pp. 210–233.

76. See, for example, Davies, *Caroline Captivity,* p. 2, and Cust and Hughes, "Introduction," p. 12.

77. Christopher Hill, *The English Bible and the Seventeenth-Century Revolution* (New York, 1993), p. 171; Hirst, *Authority and Conflict,* p. 61. Lake argues that it was the Puritan campaign against the Spanish Match that led James to accept the conformist charge that Puritanism was "a populist threat to monarchy." Peter Lake, "Anti-Popery: The Structure of a Prejudice," in Cust and Hughes, *Conflict in Early Stuart England,* pp. 84–85.

78. This argument can be found in Hill, *English Bible,* p. 174. Lake has agreed with Stone that Puritan "claims to a status based on 'grace' undercut existing hierarchies of political office, birth or property." Lake, "Anti-Popery," p. 85.

79. Todd, *Christian Humanism,* pp. 223–224; Hill, *English Bible,* p. 187.

80. This argument is developed in David Zaret, *The Heavenly Contract: Ideology and Organization in Pre-Revolutionary Puritanism* (Chicago, 1985), p. 70. Lawrence Stone has compared the political role of the pulpit with that of "the radio and television networks of the twentieth century." Lawrence Stone, *The Crisis of the Aristocracy, 1558–1641* (Oxford, Eng., 1965), p. 27.

81. Lake has seen this antipopery as "a real limitation on the Crown's autonomy. No monarch, who was not a Calvinist zealot, could be expected to welcome this intrusion on his or her traditional prerogatives." Lake, "Anti-Popery," p. 87 For a careful examination of antipopery as a political ideology that focuses on foreign policy but has broader "parliamentary" implications for government, see P. G. Lake, "Constitutional Consensus and Puritan Opposition in the 1620s: Thomas Scott and the Spanish Match," *Historical Journal* 25 (1982): 805–825. Nicholas Tyacke has acknowledged Calvinist politics emerging from the dispute over the Thirty Years' War, and White has argued that the crisis over Montague's books and the context for the York House conference was not really the rise of Arminianism so much as the political pressures attendant on the French marriage treaty for the prince. Tyacke, "Arminianism Reconsidered," p. 211; White, "Rise of Arminianism," pp. 48–50.

82. See, for example, S. P. Salt, "The Origins of Sir Edward Dering's Attack on the Ecclesiastical Hierarchy, c. 1625–1640," *Historical Journal* 30 (1987): 21–52; and Linda S. Popofsky, "The Crisis over Tonnage and Poundage in Parliament in 1629," *Past and Present* 126 (1990): 44–75. The best brief statement of this critique can be found in Theodore Rabb and Derek Hirst, "Revisionism Revised: Two Perspectives on Early Stuart Parliamentary History," *Past and Present* 92 (1981): 55–99, and Christopher Hill, "Parliament and People in Seventeenth-Century England," *Past and Present* 92 (1981): 100–124. For a critique of the Namerian method in the seventeenth century, see Hill, *English Bible,* pp. 47–49.

83. David Underdown, *Revel, Riot, and Rebellion: Popular Politics and Culture in England, 1603–1660* (Oxford, 1985), p. 120.

84. Hirst, *Authority and Conflict,* pp. 38, 136. Also see Richard Cust, "Politics and the Electorate in the 1620s," in Cust and Hughes, *Conflict in Early Stuart England,* pp. 134–135, and Christopher Hill, *The Century of Revolution, 1603–1714,* 2nd ed. (New York, 1980), p. 37.

85. "Speeches at the hustings and circular letters which resembled manifestoes became a regular feature of elections; and there was a growing expectation that once MPs reached Westminster they would keep constituents informed about their actions." Cust, "Politics and the Electorate," p. 134. Also see Hill, *English Bible,* pp. 18–19; Hirst, *Authority and Conflict,* p. 42; and Rabb and Hirst, "Revisionism Revised," pp. 92–93. David Underdown has found "the crucial period of politicization" in the beginning of Charles's rule: "By 1627 the circulation of subversive writings had become ominously common." Underdown, *Revel, Riot, and Rebellion,* p. 121.

86. Rabb and Hirst, "Revisionism Revised," pp. 91–92. Richard Cust has shown that electors expected Parliament to defend Protestantism and liberty against the corruptions of the court. Moreover, while "county leaders might select the candidates," if they failed to accommodate the wishes of the middling electorate the result could be a divisive political contest "of the sort which occurred in Norfolk in 1624." Cust, "Politics and the Electorate," pp. 140–142, 150–151, 156. Ann Hughes has noted that the political career of Lord Brooke, "like that of the Earl of Lincoln in Lincolnshire during the Forced Loan or the Earl of Warwick's position in Essex from the 1620s to the 1640s, reveals how effective an appeal based on ideology could be." She thus concludes that the conservative localism of the revisionist account of political culture is "greatly overestimated" and that "in a European context the English Civil War is remarkable for its ideological sophistication, for the existence of widespread divisions over abstract principles." Ann Hughes, "Local History and the Origins of the Civil War," in Cust and Hughes, *Conflict in Early Stuart England,* pp. 228, 246–249. Also see Underdown, *Revel, Riot, and Rebellion,* p. 123.

87. Ann Hughes and Derek Hirst agree that contemporaries saw "the political process as characterized by conflict and divisions rather than as the harmonious and consensual system depicted in recent studies." Hughes, "Local History," p. 235; Hirst, *Authority and Conflict,* p. 42. Also see Rabb and Hirst, "Revisionism Revised," pp. 65–69, 78. For the common perception of Parliament as the bastion of liberty and Protestantism, see Cust, "Politics and the Electorate," p. 142. For an analysis of the divergent royalist and parliamentarian conceptions of the English constitution, see Johann Sommerville, "Ideology, Property, and the Constitution," in Cust and Hughes, *Conflict in Early Stuart England,* pp. 47–71. Lake has noted the "basic structural similarity between the Protestant view of the effects of popery on the Church and, say, Sir Edward Coke's view of the effects of corruption on the commonwealth. In both cases, a sinister force, based on the corruption of human nature, spread gradually through what had started out as a perfectly stable and sound institutional structure, until it was utterly subverted and undermined." Lake, "Anti-Popery," p. 89.

88. Hirst, *Authority and Conflict,* p. 42.

89. J. T. Cliffe, *The Puritan Gentry: The Great Puritan Families of Early Stuart England* (Boston, 1984), pp. 104–105. Also see Hirst, *Authority and Conflict,* p. 68. Seaver has claimed that the governing elite's control of patronage in the prerevolutionary era left "the preacher with at best a junior partnership in the efforts to reform the life and manners of the local community." Seaver, *Puritan Lectureships,* pp. 292–293.

90. Hunt, *The Puritan Moment;* K. Wrightson and D. Levine, *Poverty and Piety in an English Village* (New York, 1979). This argument has been briefly summarized in Hill, "Parliament and People," pp. 118–120; Hirst, *Authority and Conflict,* pp. 14–15; and Hughes, "Local History," p. 241. For a critique of this view, see Margaret Spufford, "Puritanism and Social Control?," in *Order and Disorder in Early Modern England,* ed. Anthony Fletcher and John Stevens (New York, 1985), pp. 41–57.

91. Christopher Hill, *Society and Puritanism in Pre-Revolutionary England* (London, 1964); Stone, *Crisis of Aristocracy,* pp. 8–9, 42, 185–188. Stone notes that in the post-Elizabethan era the Puritan peerage was distinguished by its rent-racking "severity." Ibid., p. 330. Hunt notes that Puritan conviction "tempered, though it did not efface, the class consciousness of the godly aristocrats." Hunt, *Puritan Moment,* p. 232.

92. Zaret, *The Heavenly Contract.*

93. Underdown, *Revel, Riot, and Rebellion.* This argument has been summarized in Hughes, "Local History," pp. 241–243. Hirst has also seen in Puritanism "a deliberate assault on the old patterns of communal culture." Hirst, *Authority and Culture,* p. 76.

94. Sharpe, *Personal Rule of Charles I,* p. 749.

95. Underdown, *Revel, Riot, and Rebellion,* pp. 5, 40–47; Hunt, *Puritan Moment,*

pp. 26–41, 63–83; Zaret, *Heavenly Contract,* p. 12. Using the same geographic taxonomy as Underdown, Richard Cust has noted that "electoral transformation was often a feature of those areas experiencing rapid economic change." Cust, "Politics and the Electorate," p. 160.

96. Lake, *Moderate Puritans,* p. 77. Elsewhere, Lake has argued that the crucial divide between Puritans and the conformist colleagues was over the "visible godliness of the visible church" or the "extent and nature of the Christian community." Lake, "Calvinism and the English Church," p. 39. White has also pointed out other issues in lieu of predestination to characterize the divisions within the church and proposes that the critical splits are whether "Anglicans" should discursively engage with the extant Counter-Reformation apologetics or whether the Church of Rome ought simply be denounced and dismissed as anti-Christian. White, "Rise of Arminianism," p. 54.

97. Bernard, "Church of England," pp. 195–196; Sharpe, *Personal Rule of Charles I,* pp. 277, 383–392.

98. Underdown sees the critical difference between the Laudians and Puritans over whether the "revived" Christian community should include the entire parish or just the godly. David Underdown, "A Reply to John Morrill," *Journal of British Studies* 26 (1987): 473. While both Collinson and Lake acknowledge this fact, only the latter seems to realize that this implies one can't "conflate puritan divinity with a formal doctrinal consensus." Indeed, Lake seems to be alone among the doctrinal scholars in recognizing that the Puritan "insistence on the transformative effect on the attitudes and behaviour of all true believers" gives rise to the very culture of discipline that Hunt and the social historians have chronicled. Lake, *Moderate Puritans,* p. 282.

99. For a discussion of "Aesopian" language in Puritan and subsequent "underground" movements, see Hill, *English Bible,* pp. 49, 78. Cust and Hughes have warned that "insufficient account is taken of what particular sources would be likely to include, or of people's caution in a censored and authoritarian society." Cust and Hughes, "Introduction," p. 13. Bernard, for example, has argued that the Calvinism of Whitgift's Lambeth Articles and the general implication of doctrinal consensus was simply "a debating device" against Puritanism. Bernard, "Church of England," p. 191.

100. Zaret has noted that the repressive, "Walzerian" features of Puritanism "were an essential part of clerical efforts to gather official support and aristocratic patronage." Zaret, *Heavenly Contract,* p. 64.

101. Bernard, "Church of England," p. 191.

102. Ibid., pp. 184–185. Davies reports that Charles shared this conception of "the Reformation as little more than a state act, inaugurated by authority, without any impulse from below." Davies, *Caroline Captivity,* p. 17.

103. This proved impossible because, as Hughes has noted, "England was an integrated but not bureaucratized polity; consequently the Crown was dependent on the involvement and consent of some at least amongst local elites." Hughes, "Local History," pp. 233–234.

104. Collinson, *Religion of Protestants,* p. 31; Sharpe, *Personal Rule of Charles I,* pp. 276–277.

105. Bernard, "Church of England," pp. 186–187.

106. This argument is developed in ibid., pp. 188–193.

107. Davies argues that "the royal fear of Puritanism was at its heart a dread of disorder, disunity, and the contamination of 'popularity.'" Davies, *Caroline Captivity,* p. 13. For James's anti-Puritan reaction to the outcry over the Spanish Match, see Holland, "Archbishop Abbott," p. 30. Lake claims that the transference of personal religious zeal to politics in the ideal of active citizenship may have been the "most important effect of puritan ideology on the political attitudes of the period." Lake, "Constitutional Consensus and Puritan Opposition in the 1620s," p. 824.

108. Davies, *Caroline Captivity,* p. 300. Sharpe has claimed that the Personal Rule "saw a return to the careful maintenance of aristocratic privilege. It was one characteristic of the old society of degree and deference for which Charles increasingly yearned." Sharpe, "Personal Rule of Charles I," p. 61.

109. Underdown, *Revel, Riot, and Rebellion,* pp. 63–65; Sharpe, *Personal Rule of Charles I,* p. 355. Also see Morrill, "Ecology," pp. 456–457. Tyacke claims that "the Arminian Sunday, which reversed a long-standing trend towards the imposition of strict sabbatarianism, was undoubtedly popular." Tyacke, *Anti-Calvinists,* p. 223. Hirst has observed "how much support, often semi-pagan and superstitious, there was in the countryside for a ritualist and ceremonialist church. To the godly elites it must have appeared that Laud and his allies were gratifying the baser instincts of the meaner sort." Hirst, *Authority and Conflict,* p. 168. Christopher Hill has noted that while the parliaments of the 1620s passed legislation facilitating enclosures, "from 1633 onwards when the government was ruling without Parliament, depopulators were prosecuted. . . . Laud's activities on the Enclosure Commission were attacked as a breach of the common law, and contributed not a little to his unpopularity." Hill, *Century of Revolution,* p. 13.

110. Hill, "Parliament and People," pp. 122–123.

111. William Hunt has claimed that "the social group whose interests were most directly advanced by the spread of Protestant doctrine was the rising new class of intellectuals who expounded it: the preachers themselves. The immediate beneficiaries of the Reformation were men to whom Protestantism opened the novel prospect of an intellectual career, attended with considerable prestige and reasonable economic security, without the need to practice (or feign) celibacy." Hunt, *Puritan Moment,* p. 113. Rosemary O'Day has argued in her study of the professionalization of the ministry that "clerical marriage was probably more important than has usually been thought," especially among "the less conservative" clergy. Rosemary O'Day, *The English Clergy: The Emergence and Consolidation of a Profession* (London, 1979), p. 29. She also finds "overwhelming evidence for the view that it was increased status" that attracted educated aspirants to the clerical profession. Ibid., p. 244.

112. Collinson has noted the "autocratic tendencies" exhibited by those Elizabethan divines associated with the presbyterian movement. Collinson, *Elizabethan Puritan Movement,* p. 326. Hill has noted a similar tendency within congregationalist thought. Hill, *English Bible,* p. 174.

113. Hunt, *Puritan Moment,* p. 114.

114. John Morgan, *Godly Learning: Puritan Attitudes towards Reason, Learning, and Education, 1560–1640* (Cambridge, England, 1986).

115. Collinson, *Religion of Protestants,* p. 96.

116. O'Day, *English Clergy,* pp. 188–189; Hirst, *Authority and Conflict,* p. 63; Green, "Career Prospects and Clerical Conformity in the Early Stuart Church," p. 73.

117. Davies, *Caroline Captivity,* p. 291.

118. See, for example, Hughes's discussion of the ideological basis of Warwick's, Lincoln's, and Brooke's political power. Hughes, "Local History," p. 246. Cust and Hughes have noted how Puritanism "combined with Renaissance humanist ideals which drew on classical exemplars to produce a new model for elements in the ruling elite: the well-informed, conscientious, morally upright governor—the 'godly magistrate.'" Cust and Hughes, "Introduction," p. 22.

119. Hirst, *Authority and Conflict,* p. 67. Christopher Hill has agreed that elite patronage "produced a majority of ministers whose political outlook, if they had one of their own, was conservative. . . . Puritan patrons might appoint Puritan ministers; but their Puritanism would be moderate." Hill, *Century of Revolution,* p. 65.

120. Hill, *Century of Revolution,* pp. 70–71. More recently, Hill has argued that "the Puri-

tan and separatist congregations perhaps played a more important part in humanizing and cherishing the work ethic than has been appreciated. . . . The congregation established trading connections in time of prosperity, and provided social assurance in bad times. Vagabonds 'commonly are of no civil society or corporation, nor of any particular church.' They were outside church and commonwealth unless and until they could be restored by labour discipline and hard work. Just like the Irish, or the American Indians." Hill, *English Bible*, pp. 160–161.

121. Zaret, *Heavenly Contract*. Zaret's central claim is that "popular dissent continuously pushed Puritan clerics in the direction of radical reforms that generally undermined ministerial authority and specifically threatened to force clerics out of the Church of England." Ibid., p. 6.

122. Collinson, *Elizabethan Puritan Movement*, p. 94.

123. Hill, *Century of Revolution*, p. 68. Ironically, the most vehement argument for the radical, even revolutionary, nature of early Stuart Puritanism has been made by a leading revisionist, Kevin Sharpe. See Sharpe, *Personal Rule of Charles I*, pp. 731–751.

124. Zaret, *Heavenly Contract*, p. 16.

125. O'Day, *English Clergy*, p. 103.

126. Christopher Hill has recently drawn the analogy with Eastern European democratic centralism: "The congregations in the early seventeenth century, like the Soviet C. P. in the 1920s, formed a minority in an unfriendly world, whose strength lay in its agreement and its solidarity." Hill, *English Bible*, pp. 174–175.

127. Lawrence Stone has noted that "the congregations clustering around the Puritan lecturers in the urban churches of the 1620s and 1630s were the models for ideological party organization. Like Communist Party cells in the twentieth century, they were organized in exclusive units of dedicated enthusiasts under the leadership of an elite." Lawrence Stone, *The Causes of the English Revolution, 1529–1642* (New York, 1972), p. 103. Also see Larzer Ziff, *Puritanism in America: New Culture in a New World* (New York, 1973), pp. 31–33.

128. This argument can be found in Zaret, *Heavenly Contract*, p. 129, and Hill, *English Bible*, p. 172.

129. Lake, "Anti-Popery," p. 96.

130. On the primitivism of Puritan biblicism, see Theodore Dwight Bozeman, *To Live Ancient Lives*, and Coolidge, *The Pauline Renaissance*.

131. Hunt, *Puritan Moment*, p. 88; Avihu Zakai, *Exile and Kingdom: History and Apocalypse in the Puritan Migration to America* (New York, 1992). Also see Sharpe, *Personal Rule of Charles I*, p. 738.

132. Hill, *English Bible*, pp. 60, 72. Also see Hirst, *Authority and Conflict*, p. 78.

133. Seaver, *Puritan Lectureships*, p. 49.

134. As Charles Cohen has observed, "exegetes imposed themselves on Scripture as much as they followed it." Charles L. Cohen, "Two Biblical Models of Conversion: An Example of Puritan Hermeneutics," *Church History* 58 (1989): 183–185. Also see Hill, *English Bible*, p. 188, and Todd, *Christian Humanism*, p. 17.

135. Gouldner defined the culture of critical discourse as an elaborated speech variant: "The culture of critical discourse (CCD) is an historically evolved set of rules, a grammar of discourse, which (1) is concerned to *justify* its assertions, but (2) whose *mode* of justification does not proceed by invoking authorities, and (3) prefers to elicit the *voluntary* consent of those addressed solely on the basis of arguments adduced." Alvin W. Gouldner, *The Future of Intellectuals and the Rise of the New Class: A Frame of Reference, Theses, Conjectures, Arguments, and an Historical Perspective on the Role of Intellectuals and Intelligentsia in the International Class Contest* (New York, 1979), p 28. On the significance of CCD for modern ideology, see Alvin W. Gouldner, *The Dialectic of Ideology and Technology: The Origins, Grammar, and Future of Ideology* (New York, 1976).

136. Peter Lake has noted that "for Protestants, the Reformation was a gradual process of enlightenment" whose illumination by "the clear light of the gospel" led them to regard "their faith as more rational, more internally coherent than popery." Lake, "Anti-Popery," p. 76.

137. Gouldner, *Dialectic of Ideology,* p. 28. Also see Lake, "Anti-Popery," p. 80, and Hunt, *Puritan Moment,* p. 93. David Zaret's interpretation of covenant theology as an early expression of possessive individualism suggests that the culture of critical discourse bears at least some relationship to the practical rationality of market-oriented economically autonomous middling sorts, of which clergy are a part. This may, in part, explain the ease and avidity with which they were assimilated to Puritan doctrine. Zaret, *Heavenly Contract,* pp. 183–198, 208.

138. Emery Battis, *Saints and Sectaries; Anne Hutchinson and the Antinomian Controversy in Massachusetts Bay Colony* (Chapel Hill, N.C., 1962). Also see Zaret, *Heavenly Contract,* p. 104.

139. Samuel Eliot Morison, *Builders of the Bay Colony* (Boston, 1930; reprint, Boston, 1981), p. 40.

INDEX